Sex, Drugs, and Body Counts

Sex, Drugs, and Body Counts

The Politics of Numbers
in Global Crime
and Conflict

EDITED BY

Peter Andreas

AND

Kelly M. Greenhill

Cornell University Press

Ithaca and London

First published 2010 by Cornell University Press
First printing, Cornell Paperbacks, 2010

Printed in the United States of America

Library of Congress Cataloging-in-Publication Data

Sex, drugs, and body counts : the politics of numbers in global crime and conflict / edited by Peter Andreas and Kelly M. Greenhill.
    p. cm.
  Includes bibliographical references and index.
  ISBN 978-0-8014-4861-4 (cloth : alk. paper) —
  ISBN 978-0-8014-7618-1 (pbk. : alk. paper)
  1. Statistics—Political aspects—Case studies. 2. Statistical methods—Political aspects—Case studies. 3. Transnational crime—Statistics—Political aspects—Case studies.
4. International relations—Statistics—Political aspects—Case studies. 5. Policy sciences—Statistical methods—Case studies. I. Andreas, Peter, 1965– II. Greenhill, Kelly M., 1970–
  HA29.S558 2010
  363.32072'7—dc22   2009046277

Cloth printing   10 9 8 7 6 5 4 3 2 1

Paperback printing   10 9 8 7 6 5 4 3 2 1

Contents

Contributors

PETER ANDREAS is associate professor of political science and international studies at Brown University.

THOMAS J. BIERSTEKER is the Curt Gasteyger Chair in International Security and Conflict Studies at the Graduate Institute of International and Development Studies—Geneva.

SUE E. ECKERT is a senior fellow at the Watson Institute for International Studies, Brown University.

DAVID A. FEINGOLD is director of the Ophidian Research Institute and International Coordinator for HIV/AIDS and Trafficking for the United Nations Educational Scientific and Cultural Organization (UNESCO), Bangkok.

H. RICHARD FRIMAN is Eliot Fitch Professor for International Studies, professor of political science and Director of the Center for Transnational Justice at Marquette University.

KELLY M. GREENHILL is assistant professor of political science and international relations at Tufts University and a research fellow at the Belfer Center for Science and International Affairs at Harvard University's Kennedy School of Government.

JOHN HAGAN is the John D. MacArthur Professor of Sociology and Law at Northwestern University.

LARA J. NETTELFIELD is postdoctoral fellow at the Institut Barcelona d'Estudis Internacionals and assistant professor at Simon Fraser University's School for International Studies.

WENONA RYMOND-RICHMOND is assistant professor of sociology at the University of Massachusetts—Amherst.

WINIFRED TATE is assistant professor of anthropology at Colby College.

KAY B. WARREN is the Charles B. Tillinghast Jr. '32 Professor of International Studies and professor of anthropology at Brown University.

Acknowledgments

This book is the product of a multi-year collaboration involving authors who cross disciplinary boundaries as well as the boundaries between academia and the policy world. The contributors include political scientists, anthropologists, sociologists, policy analysts, and practitioners. Despite widely varying backgrounds, training, and professional experience, all share a core interest in the politics of numbers and the use of numbers in politics.

We thank the World Peace Foundation and the Belfer Center at the Kennedy School of Government at Harvard University (and especially Robert Rotberg) for funding and hosting the conference in December 2006 that inspired the idea for this volume. We also thank the Watson Institute for International Studies at Brown University (the Global Security Program, the Politics, Culture and Identity Program, and especially Thomas Biersteker) for funding and hosting the December 2007 authors' conference where early drafts of many of the chapters were first presented. Some of the draft chapters were subsequently presented on a panel at the 2008 Annual Convention of the International Studies Association in Chicago. We are grateful to Roger Haydon at Cornell University Press, who was sufficiently intrigued by the topic of this book to overcome his initial allergic reaction to taking on another edited volume. Two external reviewers for the press provided thoughtful and constructive comments. We also thank Solomon Eppel for his research assistance and Elizabeth Bennett for her help in getting this book ready for publication.

Finally, we would like to thank our co-authors without whose contributions this volume would have remained little more than an inchoate set of ideas and concerns that we shared and believed warranted greater attention, both by the academy and in the policy world. We believe that taken together the chapters herein represent far more than the sum of their parts, and we appreciate the substantial effort each of the contributors devoted to producing this volume.

Peter Andreas and Kelly M. Greenhill

1

Introduction

THE POLITICS OF NUMBERS

Peter Andreas and Kelly M. Greenhill

Not everything that counts can be counted, and not everything
that can be counted counts.

Albert Einstein

We live in a hyper-numeric world preoccupied with quantification. In
practical political terms, if something is not measured it does not
exist, if it is not counted it does not count. If there are no "data," an issue
or problem will not be recognized, defined, prioritized, put on the agenda,
and debated. Therefore, to measure something—or at least claim to do
so—is to announce its existence and signal its importance and policy relevance. As Deborah Stone observes, "Measures imply a need for action,
because we do not measure things except when we want to change them
or change our behavior in response to them."[1] How exactly we go about
measuring things and what we decide to measure are similarly important.

The political use of numbers is readily apparent across a broad range
of domestic and international policy issue areas.[2] Indeed, some numbers

---

1. Deborah Stone, *Policy Paradox: The Art of Political Decision Making* (New York:
Norton, 1997), 167–68.
2. For a useful introduction to "the politics of numbers," see Joel Best, *Damned Lies and
Statistics: Untangling Numbers from the Media, Politicians, and Activists* (Berkeley: Univer-
sity of California Press, 2001); Joel Best, *More Damned Lies and Statistics: How Numbers
Confuse Public Issues* (Berkeley: University of California Press, 2004); and Deborah Stone,
Policy Paradox: The Art of Political Decision Making (New York: Norton, 1997), ch. 7. For a
broader examination of the role of quantification in modern society, see Theodore M. Porter,
Trust in Numbers: The Pursuit of Objectivity in Science and Public Life (Princeton: Princeton
University Press, 1995), and Martha Lampland and Susan Leigh Star, eds., *Standards and
Their Stories: How Quantifying, Classifying, and Formalizing Practices Shape Everyday Life*
(Ithaca: Cornell University Press, 2009). For brief, and eminently accessible, recent primers
on identifying questionable statistics, see Joel Best, *Stat-Spotting: A Field Guide to Identifying*

are so politically sensitive and divisive that their release to the public can provoke charges of political motivation. This was recently dramatized in the British immigration minister's accusation that the office of national statistics was "playing politics" with population figures when it released data on the size of the foreign born population. The Tories, in turn, accused the government of "bullying" the statistics office and attempting to "suppress" embarrassing numbers.[3] The political importance of numbers is equally evident in the U.S.-led global "war on terror." Alan Krueger and David Laitin argue that not only is the counting of terrorist attacks "becoming as important as the unemployment rate or the GDP," but is now also highly politicized, with yearly State Department reports becoming "glossy advertisements of Washington's achievements in combating terrorism" that are nevertheless marred by dubious statistical claims, glaring methodological inconsistencies, and opaque measurement procedures.[4]

The creation, selection, promotion, and proliferation of numbers are thus the stuff of politics. Because quantification is politically consequential, it can also be highly contentious. Both proponents and opponents of any given policy will marshal reams of data to bolster their position and to weaken support for rival positions. For instance, if those formulating the numbers think the issue at hand is a big problem "they want a big number, and if they want to minimize it, they want a small number."[5] If consumers trust or favor the numbers they are given, they call them "estimates" or "best guesses"; if they do not, they call them "cooked" or "fudged." Some statistics are, as Joel Best puts it, simply "born bad"—they are based on made up or dubious data. Others become distorted, accidentally or intentionally, through carelessness or mutation during replication.[6] Still others "go bad" when causality is ascribed to mere correlation, suggesting the existence of important, potentially manipulable, cause-effect relationships where no such relationships exist.[7]

Statistics—both good and bad—are often uncritically accepted and reproduced because they are assumed to have been generated by experts who

Dubious Data (Berkeley: University of California Press, 2008); and Michael Blastland and Andrew Dilnot, *The Numbers Game: The Commonsense Guide to Understanding Numbers in the News, in Politics, and in Life* (New York: Gotham Books, 2009).

3. "Minister 'Appalled' by Stats Body," BBC News, March 4, 2009.

4. Alan B. Krueger and David D. Laitin, "'Misunderestimating' Terrorism," *Foreign Affairs* 83 (September/October 2004).

5. Lynn Smith, "Putting a Spin on the Truth with Statistics and Studies; Not Only Are Figures Being Molded More and More to Promote Causes, the Research Itself Can Be Manipulated," *Los Angeles Times,* June 6, 2001.

6. Best, *Damned Lies and Statistics,* 5.

7. Nicholas Eberstadt, *The Tyranny of Numbers: Mismeasure and Misrule* (Washington, DC: American Enterprise Institute, 1995); and Blastland and Dilnot, *The Numbers Game,* 182–93.

possess specialized knowledge and who know what they are doing. As one journalist—in defending the controversial 2006 study, published in the *Lancet,* that suggested that well over 600,000 Iraqis had died as a direct result of the U.S.-led invasion—put it: "This was, after all, not a group of high school students handing out questionnaires at a Baghdad bazaar. These are scientists from a respected public health school—Johns Hopkins—conducting a study funded by another respected school—MIT."[8]

Moreover, once produced, numbers are not dependent on their creators to be perpetuated and legitimated. The public announcement of an impressively large sounding number, regardless of its origins or validity, can generate prominent press coverage, which in turn legitimates and perpetuates the use of the number. As George Orwell once quipped: "I heard it on the BBC is almost the equivalent of saying 'I know it to be true.'"[9] Conversely, skeptical treatments of statistics tend to receive significantly less media attention. This is due in part to the fact that many people are relatively innumerate. They have trouble thinking critically about statistics and overly rely on the presumed expertise of their producers. As Marc E. Garlasco, a senior military analyst for Human Rights Watch, conceded after admitting he had publicly weighed in on the results of the *Lancet* study without having actually read the report: "I'm not a statistician. I don't really understand statistics. I try to stay away from numbers as much as possible."[10] And as Blastland and Dilnot have lamented, "Too many find it easier to distrust numbers wholesale, affecting disdain, than to get to grips with them.... [Indeed], a well-known writer explained to us that he had heard quite enough numbers, thank you—he didn't understand them and didn't see why he should."[11]

Yet, given the chronic and pervasive nature of political use and abuse of numbers, it behooves consumers of numbers to assess them with a critical eye and ask hard questions about their origins, even if doing so requires consumers to step outside their numeracy comfort zones. It likewise behooves producers of numbers to think harder about their sources of data, the conclusions they draw from these data, and the assumptions on which they are predicated. At a minimum, as Sarah Sewall, former director of

8. Gal Beckerman, "Debating the Body Count in Iraq," *Columbia Journalism Review,* October 12, 2006, http://www.cjr.org/politics/debating_the_body_count_in_ira.php. For the study itself, please see Gilbert Burnham, Riyadh Lafta, Shannon Doocy, and Les Roberts, "Mortality after the 2003 Invasion of Iraq: a Cross-sectional Cluster Sample Survey," *Lancet* 368, no. 9545 (October 21, 2006).

9. Miles Hudson and John Stanier, *War and the Media: A Random Searchlight* (Bodmin, UK: Sutton, 1997), 68.

10. Quoted in Carl Bialik, "Counting the Civilian Dead in Iraq," *Wall Street Journal,* August 5, 2005.

11. Blastland and Dilnot, *The Numbers Game,* xii.

Harvard University's Carr Center for Human Rights put it: greater and more systematic interrogation of politically relevant statistics could introduce "some accuracy and some temperance to the [most] far-flung allegations, both from the left and the right."[12] The alternative—namely, turning up one's nose "at evidence in case it proves inconvenient"—results in "bad policy, bad government, gobbledygook news, and it ends in lost chances and screwed-up lives."[13]

The Politics of Numbers in Global Crime and Conflict

Some of the most heated and high profile political battles are over phenomena that are exceptionally difficult to measure and quantify, whatever the bona fides of those doing the measuring. One such realm is that of armed conflict, where competing estimates of combatant and noncombatant death tolls, war-related atrocities and the size of refugee and internally displaced populations can bring parties to blows, as well as imperil the governments deemed responsible for them. In the context of ongoing struggles not only on the battlefield, but also for influence over the hearts and minds of friends, foes, and fence-sitters alike, the incentives to politicize, and to systematically inflate or deflate, what data does exist are myriad. In the case of war-related refugee flows, for example, governments that find themselves hosting refugees may face powerful incentives to inflate or deflate the numbers of displaced in order to attract international aid or, conversely, to forestall potential anxiety within their own populations.

Contemporary armed conflicts by their very nature often occur in dangerous and difficult to access terrain, among hostile parties, making acquisition of accurate conflict-related statistics especially arduous. Consider, for example, the fact that most of the coverage of the 1994 Rwandan genocide focused on the humanitarian disaster that beset those Hutu who fled to Zaire in its aftermath rather than on the horror show that was the bloodbath itself. Consequently, estimates of the total number killed during the genocide still vary by as much as half a million people, from under 500,000 to well over one million.[14] To make matters worse, in many parts of the world the relevant data gathering apparatuses may be internally

---

12. Bialik, "Counting the Civilian Dead in Iraq."
13. Blastland and Dilnot, *The Numbers Game*, xii.
14. Such a gap is particularly striking given that Rwanda's total prewar population was under eight million. "Rwanda: 'Genocidal Slaughter' Claims as Many as One Million; UN Authorizes 'Operation Turquoise' to Protect Displaced Persons," *UN Chronicle On-Line Edition*, http://www.un.org/Pubs/chronicle/1994/issue4/0494p4.asp.

inept, externally obstructed, or simply corrupt—and thus engaged in politicizing population data (e.g., through skewed census taking)—even before the outbreak of hostilities; the situation can hardly be expected to improve under fire.[15] Among other problems, hospital and morgue reporting systems are often disrupted, while separating combatants from noncombatants can be problematic even under the best of conditions.

Another realm in which the acquisition of good data is particularly problematic is that of illicit transnational activities, such as the smuggling of drugs and people. Given the type of activity being measured, the quality of statistics is inherently suspect.[16] After all, the success of clandestine border crossings depends on not being detected and thus they are designed to be as invisible as possible; getting good data is correspondingly difficult, to say the least. Moreover, "organized crime" and illicit activities have long possessed a particular quality that inspires both fear and awe in the public and in governments and engenders a peculiar willingness to accept mythical claims about the size and magnitude of lurking dangers. In the late nineteenth and early twentieth centuries, for example, lurid media exposés of the alleged "white slave trade," dominated by Chinese opium traffickers and warlords, threw the authorities in England, the United States, and Australia into a moral panic—despite the fact that little evidence ever surfaced to confirm the existence of such a vast transnational trade.[17]

Statistics also come into play in the politics of measuring efforts to combat illicit cross-border activities, such as numbers of arrests, seizures, asset forfeitures and confiscations. These numbers often have more to do with political imperatives and bureaucratic incentives than actual deterrence. For instance, a long history of high apprehension numbers (often repeat arrests) of unauthorized migrants attempting to cross the U.S.-Mexico border has not necessarily reduced entry attempts. But it has made it possible

15. See, for instance, Tim Judah, "Serb Returns to Kosovo Not Impossible, Says Report," *ISN Security Watch,* July 6, 2004, http://www.esiweb.org/pdf/esi_lausanne_reactions_id_1. pdf; and Megan McArdle, "Iraq Body Count: Why Is It so Hard to Count, Anyway?" *Atlantic Monthly On-Line,* March 27, 2008, http://meganmcardle.theatlantic.com/archives/2008/03/iraq_body_count_why_is_it_so_h.php.

16. In the case of illegal immigration data, for example, see the discussion in Kamal Sadiq, "Lost in Translation: The Challenges of State-Generated Data in Developing Countries," in *Perestroika! The Raucous Rebellion in Political Science,* ed. Kristen Renwick Monroe (New Haven: Yale University Press, 2005).

17. See, for instance, Fiona David, "New Threats or Old Stereotypes? The Revival Of 'Trafficking' as a Discourse," paper presented at the History of Crime, Policing and Punishment Conference convened by the Australian Institute of Criminology in conjunction with Charles Stuart University, 1999. Moreover, there is reason to believe that such assertions had as much, or more, to do with rising fears of Chinese migration than with concerns about kidnapping and prostitution. "White Slavery on Film; Audience Sees Various Alleged Methods of the Traffickers," *New York Times,* December 9, 1913.

for border patrol agents to boast that they make more arrests than any other federal law enforcement agency—and plead for more resources in annual budget requests.[18] Similarly, increased eradication of drug crops may simply prompt more planting elsewhere (often in more difficult to detect and reach terrain), but pointing to record numbers of hectares destroyed provides a politically appealing indicator of "doing something" about drug production at the source—while at the same time keeping funds flowing to anti-drug agencies.

What the diverse phenomena of armed conflict and illicit transnational activities have in common is that they typically involve low visibility behavior that is the subject of highly visible and morally charged policy debates—debates that tend to be framed by "truth claims" and causal stories that rely on often-questionable numbers and problematic quantitative indicators. Nevertheless, these difficult to observe phenomena are not perceived to be "real" until they are quantified and given a number. Consequently, death tolls, refugee flows, trafficking numbers, and smuggling estimates are commonly inflated, deflated, or simply fabricated, all in the service of political goals. Identifying the sources of such numbers—as well as recognizing the agendas of their producers and proliferators—can be critically important in helping to mitigate some of their more pernicious effects.

This volume evaluates the politics and process of knowledge production in two international issue areas where quantification is particularly treacherous terrain: transnational crime and armed conflict. Both have similar informational shortcomings and difficulties. This lack of transparency coupled with strong incentives to cite and deploy highly politicized numbers can, under certain conditions, result in a virtual surfeit of policy pathologies. The volume covers topics ranging from sex trafficking and the illicit drug trade to counterinsurgency, ethnic conflict, refugee flows, and genocide. The volume examines the diverse methodologies (and lack thereof) employed in estimating the magnitude and nature of these often hidden activities and policy effectiveness in addressing them. Two of the chapters (focusing on paramilitaries and drug trafficking, and the campaign to counter terrorist financing, respectively) combine the themes of transnational crime and conflict.

In recent years, a raft of articles and books has been published that examine the issue of the politicization of numbers, measures, and metrics. This volume draws from and contributes to this interdisciplinary

---

18. See Peter Andreas, *Border Games: Policing the U.S.-Mexico Divide*, 2nd ed. (Ithaca: Cornell University Press, 2009), 36–37.

policy-oriented literature. However, most of the research to date has focused principally, albeit not exclusively, on domestic issues, such as violent crime and other social problems. In contrast, far less has been written about the politics of quantification in the international realm. This volume helps to bring the politics of numbers more centrally into the study of international politics, and likewise helps to bring international politics more centrally into the study of the politics of numbers. Drawing on the expertise of a diverse group of scholars, practitioners, and policy analysts, this is the first book that critically evaluates the politics of numbers across a range of policy-making levels, international issue areas, disciplinary perspectives, and geographical contexts.

This volume is unusual, if not unique, in another way as well. Most of the previously published literature has focused principally on some combination of three, nonmutually exclusive, issues. The first is how problematic statistics come to be generated (e.g., through statistical fallacy, sample bias, false causality) and/or how they become manipulated—that is, sources of bad science and bad behavior.[19] A second cluster surrounds the issue of why consumers are so prone to be duped by such numbers,[20] while a third highlights danger signs of which consumers of potentially bad statistics should be aware.[21] In contrast, far less analysis has been devoted to identifying the material fallout, the concrete policy consequences, and the human costs of the adoption of—and debates over—politicized numbers.[22] As the authors of *Misused Statistics* acknowledge: they, like many others, focus on the question of how one can know whether the statistics one encounters are sound, while self-consciously ignoring the question of "what of it."[23]

This volume explicitly addresses the "what of it" question. Indeed, it is one of the first to explore the concrete policy consequences and implications of

---

19. See, for instance, Herbert F. Spirer, Louise Spirer, and A.J. Jaffe, *Misused Statistics,* 2nd ed. (New York: Marcel Dekker, 1998); William Fairley and Frederick Mosteller, eds., *Statistics and Public Policy* (Reading, MA: Addison-Wesley, 1977); and the classic, Darrell Huff, *How to Lie with Statistics* (New York: W.W. Norton, 1993). Also see Carl Bialik, "The Numbers Guy" blog for the *Wall Street Journal,* http://blogs.wsj.com/numbersguy/.

20. See John Allen Paulos, *Innumeracy: Mathematical Illiteracy and Its Consequences* (New York: Hill and Wang, 2001); Best, *Damned Lies and Statistics* and *More Damned Lies and Statistics;* Rob Estaway, *How Long Is a Piece of String? More Hidden Mathematics of Everyday Life* (London: Robson Books, 2002), esp. ch. 2; and Blastland and Dilnot, *The Numbers Game.*

21. See Blastland and Dilnot, *The Numbers Game;* Best, *Stat-Spotting;* and Spirer, Spirer, and Jaffe, *Misused Statistics.*

22. It is worth noting that the aforementioned *Numbers Guy* blog (fn 19) does tackle this issue on occasion.

23. Spirer, Spirer, and Jaffe, *Misused Statistics,* 243.

the politics of numbers, particularly in the international realm.[24] As such, its findings complement recent work on the politics behind, the origins of, and the policy implications of the adoption of international standards. Just as is the case with standards, we find that statistics in the realm of international crime and conflict tend to be nested inside one another; unevenly distributed across the socio-cultural landscape; increasingly linked to and integrated with one another across organizations, nations, and systems; and even used to codify, embody, or prescribe ethics and values, often with great consequences.[25] Many of the crucic illustrate in some detail *how* the politics of numbers can play a crucial role in policy debates and in policy outcomes. In other words, herein we demonstrate that although politicized numbers are not autonomous, independent variables, through instrumental adoption, promulgation, and dissemination by interested actors, they may function as intervening variables, which exercise concrete effects and can affect political outcomes. In short, this volume may usefully be conceived of as a collection of foreign and public policy-related case studies, in which cross-cutting cleavages, interest group competition, organizational and bureaucratic imperatives, and the intrigues of international politics and diplomacy are all prominently on display.

We hope that the volume will be of interest not only to those hoping to make better sense of how the politics of numbers plays out in various international policy realms, but will also contribute to much broader cross-disciplinary discussions about the centrality of quantification and measurement in modern society.[26] As Jacqueline Urla has pointed out, "There are probably few features more characteristic of modernity than the notion that we can know ourselves through numbers."[27] And it is precisely this trust and faith in counting that makes quantification so politically potent and consequential.

At the same time, we should say at the outset what this volume is not. First, it is far from being comprehensive. The focus is restricted to cases of global crime and conflict, given that these are two areas where numbers are most difficult to find and are most desired, and where the resulting numerical uncertainty provides the greatest opportunities for manipulation

---

24. See Eberstadt, *The Tyranny of Numbers,* which offers a very interesting, if somewhat less broadly accessible, demographer's evaluation of the virtues and vices of government counting.

25. Lampland and Star, *Standards and Their Stories,* 4–5.

26. See, ibid. See also David Hand, *Information Generation: How Data Rule Our World* (Oxford: Oneworld, 2007); and Michael Power, *The Audit Society* (New York: Oxford University Press, 1997).

27. Jacqueline Urla, "Cultural Politics in an Age of Statistics: Numbers, Nations and the Making of Basque Identity," *American Ethnologist* 20 (1993): 818.

and distortion. Second, we make no claim to cover all cases of global crime and conflict in which the politicization of numbers occurs. Rather, the case studies in this volume are illustrative of what we believe to be a larger pattern across issue areas—one that invites further and more systematic scrutiny. Third, the purpose here is not to come up with more sophisticated and rigorous quantitative techniques and design better metrics of policy effectiveness. Instead, the objective is to critically assess the politics of numbers—what is (and is not) counted across a range of often hidden and extremely difficult to measure phenomena—and to encourage greater scrutiny as well as a measure of diffidence among number producers and consumers alike.

The authors in this volume interrogate the following set of questions: Where do the estimates come from, who produces them, what legitimating function do they serve, and how (if at all) are they explained in official reporting? What are the implications and consequences (intended and unintended) of choosing one set of numbers over another? To what degree are the numbers accepted or challenged, and why? What purposes do they serve? Why do many statistics, even particularly dubious ones, become so difficult to debunk and displace once they have been adopted? We set out to do far more than simply reiterate the unfortunate fact that statistics are frequently used and abused for political ends. We also seek to explain where these numbers originate and why they can be so critically important, in no small part because numbers—even, and maybe especially, bad ones—tend to be sticky and to take on lives of their own.[28]

Some of the volume's contributors explore related questions regarding the measurement of policy "progress" and "success." Specifically, what metrics do government agencies, international institutions, and nongovernmental organizations use to determine the effectiveness in curbing illicit activities such as drug smuggling, human trafficking, and terrorist financing? How are these metrics created, why are some metrics chosen and prioritized over others, and what purpose do they serve in policy debates, media reporting, and diplomacy? How are countries rated and ranked in terms of their efforts to combat these activities, where do the rating and ranking mechanisms come from, and what are their functions and consequences (such as shaming and legitimation)?

The answers to these inherently political and contentious questions not only provide interesting and important analytical insights but also have broad and significant implications for the formulation, funding, and implementation of public policy. The volume's findings reveal that the favored

---

28. Best, *Damned Lies and Statistics*.

numbers tend to be highly problematic yet are often embraced and promoted because they serve multiple functions that inhibit critical scrutiny. Demonstrating this does not require engaging in a protracted debate over the most appropriate statistical methods and tools. Indeed, as some of the case studies in this volume show, there is often not even an attempt to justify and explain the official numbers—which raises interesting questions about why they are so often unquestioningly embraced and accepted as "facts."

Historical Antecedents, Contemporary Resonance

The politicization of numbers is certainly not new and has a long historical lineage. As long ago as 1840, the social critic Thomas Carlyle commented that, "A witty statesman said you might prove anything with figures."[29] The nineteenth century was marked by a burgeoning respect for science, and statistics were viewed as a way to "bring the authority of science to debates about social policy."[30] In England, for example, Patricia Cline Cohen argues that the new faith in "numeracy" fueled the growth of quantitative materials in the 1820s and 1830s, and that measuring things gave people "satisfaction" through "certainty."[31] But, as Best tells us, from the beginning, statistics have had two purposes, "one public, the other often hidden." The public purpose "is to give an accurate, true description of society. But people also use statistics to support particular views about social problems...[although] this political purpose is often hidden behind assertions that numbers, simply because they are numbers, must be correct."[32]

More broadly, the emergence and spread of quantification in earlier centuries was inherently political in that it was an integral component of state building.[33] The field of statistics emerged in the service of the state,[34] as

29. Quoted in Best, *Damned Lies and Statistics,* 5.
30. The term statistics acquired its current meaning of "numeric statements about social life" in the 1830s—as a successor of what had been known since the previous century as "political arithmetic." Best, *Damned Lies and Statistics,* 11–13. Also see Theodore M. Porter, "Statistics and the Politics of Objectivity," *Revue de Synthese* 114 (1993): 86–103, and Theodore M. Porter, *The Rise of Statistical Thinking 1820–1900* (Princeton: Princeton University Press, 1986).
31. Patricia Cline Cohen, *A Calculating People: The Spread of Numeracy in Early America* (Chicago: University of Chicago Press, 1982), 4, 18.
32. Best, *Damned Lies and Statistics,* 13.
33. Paul Starr, "The Sociology of Official Statistics," in *The Politics of Numbers,* ed. William Alonso and Paul Starr (New York: Russell Sage Foundation, 1987), 15–17.
34. See especially Alain Desrosieres, *The Politics of Large Numbers: A History of Statistical Reasoning* (Cambridge: Harvard University Press, 1998).

part of state attempts to make society "legible."[35] The politics of numbers, in other words, has long been about the politics of statecraft. As Theodore Porter emphasizes, the quantification of social phenomenon for political ends was essential to centralization, bureaucratization, and ultimately the "consolidation of state power."[36] "Calculative practices"[37]—counting and categorizing things—ranging from trade flows to crime incidents to population numbers (including the development of the national census), became increasingly important to statecraft, even if the numbers were not always as reliable as its creators proclaimed.[38]

For example, one of Alexander Hamilton's advisers apparently wrote economic reports to Congress filled with "guesswork beneath the superficial glitter of definite numbers."[39] In his review of the rise and proliferation of government statistics, Paul Starr points to the disjuncture between confident official claims of quantitative certainty and the murkier reality: "The acknowledgment of ambiguity and imprecision in the presentation of data poses a task of considerable delicacy. The appropriate disclaimers may be made in technical appendices, while the basic mode of presentation says the opposite."[40] Starr notes that the political manipulation of statistics has typically been subtler than simply "outright fabrication," and that "more common techniques include the deceptive use of classifications and tolerance for methodological inadequacies that yield data with useful political effect."[41]

The growing popularity of quantification in the nineteenth century also brought attention to social problems that had not been counted before. The deployment of statistics, even if of highly questionable validity, was therefore an especially useful tool for reform movements. For instance, Cohen notes that, "temperance statistics" illustrate "how the inauguration of quantification corresponds to a new sensitivity to something that had existed before but that was now seen as something necessary to control."

---

35. James C. Scott, *Seeing Like a State: How Certain Schemes to Improve the Human Condition Have Failed* (New Haven: Yale University Press, 1998).

36. Porter, *The Rise of Statistical Thinking*, 23.

37. Peter Miller, "Governing by Numbers: Why Calculative Practices Matter," *Social Research* 68 (2001): 379–96.

38. There is some evidence to suggest that things have not improved appreciably in the intervening years. For instance, it was discovered in 2008 that Germany had two million fewer inhabitants than was previously believed, due to systematic and systemic inflation across Germany's *Länder*. See, for instance, "Statistik lässt Bevölkerung schrumpfen," July 22, 2008, http://www.sueddeutsche.de/wissen/90/303085/text/. The authors thank Lee Seymour for this insight.

39. Cohen, *A Calculating People*, 158–59.

40. Starr, "The Sociology of Official Statistics," 51.

41. Ibid., 38.

Temperance groups increasingly carried out surveys and published annual reports drawing public attention to drinking as a problem.[42]

In the case of prostitution, Cohen writes that, "Prostitutes had probably always existed in American cities, but it was not until the 1830s that someone attempted to specify the dimensions of the problem…" The key player was the New York Moral Reform Society: "Their figures were estimates, and there is no way the reader could evaluate them."[43] In his historical study of prostitution in New York City, Timothy Gilfoyle observes that, "few statistics were as inexact and divergent as those pertaining to the population of prostitutes," and that "clerics, purity reformers, and some proponents of prostitution tended to inflate statistics." Indeed, "aggregate figures often surpassed 20 percent of the total female population between sixteen and thirty years of age." Such inflated figures, he writes, projected "the false impression that New York was the site of an ongoing orgy. Sympathizers even admitted as much. In 1833, for instance, the *Journal of Public Morals* concurred that the figure of 10,000 prostitutes was surely exaggerated, but it nevertheless continued to employ that figure." In sharp contrast, "For political reasons, the police continually underestimated the total amount of prostitution in order to stem criticism by the city establishment and religious hierarchy."[44]

Not unlike today, historical episodes of criminalizing and prohibiting an activity made it much harder to measure with any accuracy—though this did not inhibit confident official statistical truth claims (and in some cases this seemed to actually invite statistical abuse, because the reported number of illicit activities were difficult to falsify). In the case of estimating the prevalence of drug use in the United States, Alfred Lindesmith notes that "After 1914, when addiction became a criminal act, counting addicts posed much the same difficulties that would be encountered in a census of racketeers. The only relevant figures available on a national basis are those pertaining to arrests, prosecutions, convictions, and commitments, and these are far from being complete or reliable."[45] Nevertheless, federal law enforcement officials repeatedly deployed numbers to claim that drug use had plummeted following the passing of the first national drug prohibition law in 1914—just as U.S. officials had in earlier years deployed highly inflated drug use statistics to generate support for implementing

42. Cohen, *A Calculating People*, 208–10.

43. Ibid., 207–8.

44. Timothy J. Gilfoyle, *City of Eros: New York City, Prostitution, and the Commercialization of Sex, 1790–1920* (New York: W.W. Norton, 1992), 57–59.

45. Alfred R. Lindesmith, *The Addict and the Law* (Bloomington: Indiana University Press, 1965), 99.

drug prohibition.[46] Harry Anslinger, the commissioner of the Federal Bureau of Narcotics, told a Senate subcommittee in 1955: "Before the passage of national control legislation [in 1914] there was one addict in every 400 persons in the United States. By World War I, this incidence had been reduced to about 1 in every 1,500 persons, and by World War II the incidence was found to be roughly 1 in 10,000..."[47] Lindesmith concluded that, "An analysis of the Narcotics Bureau's survey of addiction suggests that this enterprise may well be a public relations effort rather than a serious attempt at enumeration. Detailed descriptions of the methods employed have probably not been published because it is realized that they would not stand inspection."[48]

The politics of numbers has also been transformed—and arguably become more important—over time because of changes in communications technologies and the growing role and influence of the media. At the same time as statistics gained strength and credibility with the public, technology was making possible their dissemination in unprecedented ways. In the United States, for instance, widespread use of the telegraph by the mid-nineteenth century (nearly 50,000 miles had been laid in the east alone) meant that newspaper editors could get information from their correspondents with unparalleled speed. This resulted in an "obsessive demands for the 'scoop,' often resulting in instant as opposed to accurate news." If there was difficulty finding the news, it was to be fabricated, even if it meant elevating rumor or gossip into truth.[49] A growing reliance on numbers (however dubious) and a striking level of detail added credibility to questionable reportage, creating a kind of perceived, albeit false, precision. Though media has expanded far beyond newspapers and the telegraph has become obsolete, the imperatives to which such technology gave rise have clear parallels and echoes today. If anything, today's 24/7 media machine heightens demands for statistics from the field—despite the fact that their veracity quotient has not necessarily improved.

As the technological capacity to share statistics broadly and quickly grew, so too did opportunities and incentives to doctor them. Nothing illustrates this more than the politics of "body counts" in wartime. During the U.S. Civil War, Secretary of War Edwin M. Stanton routinely "dickered" with casualty figures. This included altering an account of Union

46. See especially David T. Courtwright, *Dark Paradise: A History of Opiate Addiction in America* (Cambridge, MA: Harvard University Press, 2001).

47. Quoted in Lindesmith, *The Addict and the Law,* 104.

48. Ibid., 121.

49. The editor of the *Chicago Times,* Wilbur Storey, sent the following order to one of his reporters: "Telegraph fully all news you can get and when there is no news send rumour." Hudson and Stanier, *War and the Media,* 23.

General Ulysses S. Grant's failure at Petersburg, Virginia, reducing the losses to about one-third of their actual number.[50] This incident of creative accounting was hardly unique to this battle or war. During World War I, politicization became as pervasive as statistics themselves. Reportedly once the Germans started altering their casualty figures, they "became so muddled in their own lies," that the truth will probably never emerge.[51] Even supposedly objective observers found themselves unwilling to report potentially damaging conflict statistics. In defending his decision not to reveal the death toll from the Battle at Mons (August 14–25, 1914), the editor of the *Times* declared: "Such silence was prudent...had it been known in England that France had lost more than a quarter of a million men from her regular army in the first month of fighting, British determination must have been gravely weakened."[52] Moreover, journalists were often not in a position to question official statistics. Correspondents covering the air war over Britain during World War II, for instance, had no option but to accept the official tallies provided by the Air Ministry, even though, as even the pilots knew, they were "hopelessly inflated" to heighten morale.[53]

Body count politics became particularly notorious during the Vietnam War, where powerful political pressures and bureaucratic incentives favored both overcounting the number of enemy casualties and undercounting the size of enemy forces. As Philip Knightley put it: "It became a war like no other, a war with no front line, no easily identifiable enemy, no simply explained cause, no clearly designated villain on whom to focus the nation's hate, no menace to the homeland, no need for general sacrifice, and therefore, no nation-wide fervor of patriotism." Thus, it also became a "war in which military success had to be measured in numbers—weapons captured, villagers relocated, areas searched, areas cleared...and the body count—until only computers became capable of digesting and understanding it all, and machines took over decisions on life and death."[54] In fact, to some extent, the war in Vietnam became all about numbers. As Alain Enthoven and Wayne Smith note:

> The incentives for field commanders clearly lay in the direction of claiming a high body count. Padded claims kept everyone happy; there were no penalties for overstating enemy losses, but an understatement could lead to sharp questions as to why U.S. casualties were so high compared with the results

---

50. Phillip Knightley, *The First Casualty: The War Correspondent as Hero and Myth-Maker from the Crimea to Iraq* (Baltimore: Johns Hopkins University Press, 2004), 27.
51. Ibid., 116.
52. Quoted in ibid., 116.
53. Ibid., 259.
54. Ibid., 418.

achieved. Few commanders were bold enough to volunteer the information that they had lost as many men in an engagement as the enemy—or more. The net result of all this was that statistics regarding body counts were notoriously unreliable. Off-the-record interviews with officers who had been a part of the process revealed a consistent, almost universal pattern: in a representative case, battalions raised the figures coming in from the companies, and brigades raised the figures coming in from the battalions. In addition, something had to be (and was) put in for all the artillery and air support, which the men on the ground could not check out to give the supporting arms their share of the "kill."[55]

In his memoir, *War of Numbers,* the former CIA intelligence officer Sam Adams details the internal debates over what numbers to use in official estimates of the Vietcong. He argues that U.S. military and intelligence officials grossly and systematically understated the size of enemy combatants, and were keenly aware of—and concerned about—how the numbers would play out in the press.[56] The writer Peter Smith echoed these sentiments in recalling that:

> Back in the day, whenever the networks ran out of angles for covering the war in Vietnam, whenever there was no progress in the negotiations on the shape of the negotiation table at Henry Kissinger's stalled peace talks with the North Vietnamese in Paris, the nightly news would reduce the war to body counts. Numbers based on the premise that if we kill more of them (than they do of us), we're making progress. As if there were a finite number. As if, once we kill this many of them, the ones who are still living will sue for peace. As if the networks could develop a graphic—a Dead-O-Meter to appear on a screen over the shoulder of some latter day [Edward R.] Murrow where we could all track the progress toward peace.[57]

More than three decades later, body counts continue to be wrapped up in politics, as the current conflict in Iraq amply demonstrates. The most significant politics of numbers debate in the Iraq conflict has surrounded the measurement of civilian, rather than combatant, casualties and how and when such statistics have been released.[58] For instance, a small firestorm

55. Alain C. Enthoven and K. Wayne Smith, *How Much Is Enough? Shaping the Defense Program, 1961–1969* (Santa Monica, CA: RAND, 2005), 295.

56. Sam Adams, *War of Numbers: An Intelligence Memoir* (South Royalton, VT: Steerforth Press, 1994), 96–97.

57. Peter Smith, "Iraq Body Counts: The Ultimate Vietnam Flashback," *Huffington Post,* June 25, 2007, http://www.huffingtonpost.com/peter-smith/iraq-body-counts-the-ult_b_53692.html. See also Knightley, *The Last Casualty;* and Joshua Green, "The Numbers War," *Atlantic Monthly* (May 2006): 36–37.

58. See, for instance, Bialik, "Counting the Civilian Dead in Iraq."

erupted after a research team from Johns Hopkins published their controversial claim just weeks before the 2006 U.S. Congressional elections that more than 600,000 Iraqi noncombatants had died as a result of the war. A number of observers charged that the timing was hardly incidental, but rather specifically designed to influence the outcome of the elections.[59] The *National Journal* devoted an issue to the politics of body counts in Iraq, and the cover story "Data Bomb," largely to the timing issue.[60] There has also been a wide-ranging, and at times quite heated, debate over the reliability of the methodology employed in the Hopkins study, with criticism coming from both ends of the political spectrum. And, in a rare move, in early 2009 the American Association of Public Opinion Researchers (AAPOR) voted to censure the study's primary investigator after he failed to respond to requests for details about his research techniques and the study's underlying assumptions.[61]

As these wide-ranging illustrations suggest, the problems of the politicization of numbers in the realms of transnational crime and conflict are hardly new. But they have arguably expanded and become more important over time, with growing statistical fetishism and a corresponding sense that everything that really matters can and should be quantified. Unfortunately, public and professional scrutiny and interrogation of such numbers has not correspondingly expanded.[62]

Well-meaning professionals may inadvertently make these problems still worse, by assuming someone else will do the scrutinizing for them. For instance, Pulitzer Prize-winning author John McPhee has admitted, "In the comfortable knowledge that the fact-checking department is going to follow up behind me, I like to guess at certain names and numbers early on, while I change and re-change and listen to sentences, preferring to

59. Similar charges were levied two years before, when the first results of an earlier version of the study were published just weeks before the 2004 presidential election. At the time, Les Roberts, a Johns Hopkins epidemiologist and lead author on the original study, admitted he was opposed to the war and wanted the study to be published before the election so that "both candidates would be forced to pledge to protect civilian lives in Iraq." Bialik, "Counting the Civilian Dead in Iraq."

60. Neil Munro and Carl M. Cannon, "Data Bomb," *National Journal*, January 5, 2008.

61. The AAPOR noted that their Code of Professional Ethics and Practices calls for researchers to disclose their methodology when survey findings are released so they can be independently evaluated and verified. The AAPOR stated that Burnham's failure to cooperate with the probe into his study's methodology "violates the fundamental standards of science, seriously undermines open public debate on critical issues and undermines the credibility of all survey and public opinion research." Quoted in "Author of Shocking Iraq Study Accused of Bad Ethics," *Associated Press*, February 5, 2009.

62. See Donna M. Carlon, Alexis A. Downs, and Stacia Wert-Gray, "Statistics as Fetishes," *Organizational Research Methods* 9, no. 4 (2006): 475–90.

hear some ballpark figure or approximate date than the dissonant clink of journalistic terms." McPhee goes on to suggest that he then leaves it to the fact-checker to ensure that the "correct" number appears in print.[63]

Yet the existence of an invented number almost perforce means a fact-checker is going to begin (and quite often end) his or her search by "checking" to see if the number that is there can be verified. Although it may be findable, that does not mean that it will be correct. As Frederick Mosteller put it, "When we look up a number in more than one place, we may get several different answers, and then we have to exercise care. The moral is not that several answers are worse than one, but that whatever answer we get from one source might be different if we got it from another source."[64]

The Political Psychology of Numbers

The politicization of numbers has been enabled and aggravated by a variety of human psychological and cognitive tendencies that cannot be readily overridden, even if and when better numbers become available. In other words, the brain is partly to blame for why humans have proven to be such numerical dupes. For one thing, there is the problem of what cognitive scientists refer to as "anchoring effects"—the human tendency to fixate on numbers they have heard, even if those numbers are arbitrary or wrong. The idea is that during normal decision making, humans anchor on specific values and subsequently adjust to that value to account for other elements of the circumstance. Once an anchor is set, there is a bias toward it. Repeated experiments have confirmed the stickiness and enduring power of this tendency.[65]

Still more problematic is that, as psychological studies indicate, humans tend to anchor most strongly on the first number to which they are exposed, especially in cases where that number is "shocking and precise—like say, 601,027 violent deaths in Iraq."[66] Even when such numbers are presented only as central estimates within a wide range of possibilities, humans tend to ignore the range, focusing instead on the "lovely, hard number in the middle." This is so, at least in part, because humans are "terrible at dealing with uncertainty, and besides, headlines seldom

63. John McPhee, "Checkpoints," *New Yorker,* February 9, 2009, 59.

64. Frederick Mosteller, "Assessing Unknown Numbers: Order of Magnitude Estimation," in Fairley and Mosteller, *Statistics and Public Policy,* 165.

65. See, for instance, Amos Tversky and Daniel Kahneman, "Judgment under Uncertainty: Heuristics and Biases," *Science* 185 (September 1974): 1128–30.

66. Megan McArdle, "Body Counting," *Atlantic Monthly* (April 2008): 26.

highlight margins of error."[67] Add to this tendency what Best suggests is a fetishism for statistics, combine it with the public's general innumeracy, and it is hardly surprising that potentially dubious numbers become widely disseminated "social facts"—things that are deemed to be "true" because they are widely believed to be true.[68]

Further worrying is the fact that when information supports a person's preconceived notions, he or she is less apt to question it, while when the opposite is true, he or she can be quite adept at summarily dismissing it.[69] MRI imaging demonstrates that this tendency is heightened when the issues at hand are ones about which people feel strongly, such as statements with political valence. These cognitive biases are not solely found among advocates of particular numbers. The *Lancet* article's "central estimate" of Iraqi casualties, for instance, has been said to exert "a gravitational pull on even its harshest critics who seem to be mentally benchmarking their estimates by how much they differ from the 601,027 figure."[70]

Furthermore, once people proffer or adopt numbers, they will have strong tendencies to try to confirm them, a psychological idiosyncrasy that can create motivated biases even in previously disinterested parties.[71] As Megan McArdle points out, "By the time we've finished affirming the figure's plausibility, it has become ours, and we'll fight to defend it. Being challenged—say, arguing with a skeptical friend—now makes us dig in." As laboratory experiments have repeatedly shown, once someone has adopted a figure, they will continue to "recruit evidence" in support of that number. Eventually one ends up "surrounded by a little army of facts that support the theory."[72] Research shows that these tendencies can be further exacerbated, even subconsciously, when people have material reasons for wanting certain numbers to be correct; for instance, if one wants to catalyze a policy shift, satisfy extant government or private donors, or generate enthusiasm for action by new ones.[73]

---

67. McArdle, "Body Counting"; and Tversky and Kahneman, "Judgment under Uncertainty."

68. Best, *More Damned Lies and Statistics*. On social facts and their construction, see John R. Searle, *The Construction of Social Reality* (New York: Free Press, 1995).

69. Robert Jervis, *Perception and Misperception in International Politics* (Princeton: Princeton University Press, 1979), 143–54; and Robert J. MacCoun, "Biases in the Interpretation and Use of Research Results," *Annual Review of Psychology* 49 (1998): 272–73.

70. McArdle, "Body Counting."

71. Robert Jervis, Ned Lebow, and Janice Gross Stein, *Psychology and Deterrence* (Baltimore: Johns Hopkins University Press, 1985).

72. McArdle, "Body Counting."

73. See, for instance, Teresa Isabelle Daza Campbell and Sheila Slaughter, "Understanding the Potential for Misconduct in University-Industry Relationships: An Empirical View," in *Perspectives on Scholarly Misconduct in the Sciences,* ed. John M. Braxton (Columbus: Ohio State University Press, 1999).

A Preview of the Chapters in This Volume

Peter Andreas sets the stage for the chapters that focus on global crime. Andreas emphasizes that the illicit nature of certain cross-border flows enables and facilitates a politics of numbers that is defined by speculation, distortion, and sometimes even outright fabrication, and that policy debates and media reporting are typically part of the problem rather than solution. This reflects not only cynical manipulations by political actors, but also these actors' everyday coping strategies in a broader policy arena that demands quantification. This imperative to generate numbers prioritizes bad data over no data and privileges simple and visible metrics of policy "progress" and "success" that can be highly misleading. The first part of Andreas's chapter focuses on the production and proliferation of numbers regarding the size and magnitude of various illicit flows, ranging from the trade in endangered species to counterfeit goods. The second part of the chapter evaluates the metrics used to measure policy effectiveness, focusing on the case of the U.S.-led "war on drugs."

The next chapter provides a view from the field from UNESCO's David A. Feingold, who has spent most of the last several decades on the ground in Southeast Asia. This chapter challenges the conventional wisdom about the organized nature and prodigious scale of human trafficking enterprises in this region of the world. Feingold punctures the accepted wisdom that human trafficking is a rapidly growing form of modern day slavery, and argues that most trafficking is simply migration gone terribly wrong. The bulk of the chapter is devoted to an examination of the policy imperatives that give rise to statistical inflation and narrative embellishment in the human trafficking realm.

In chapter 4, H. Richard Friman turns to the realm of foreign policy and international diplomacy, critically examining the standard metrics used by the United States to determine whether foreign countries are sufficiently cooperating with U.S.-promoted campaigns to combat illicit drugs and human trafficking. Each year, with great fanfare, the U.S. Department of State releases assessments of foreign compliance—essentially handing out passing and failing grades. Friman explores these compliance certification systems on three dimensions: *inclusion,* which refers to the criteria used to determine whether a country is on the rating list; *ranking,* which refers to the criteria that are used to determine the country's placement in categories on the rating lists; and *effectiveness,* which refers to the criteria that are used to determine the overall impact of the rating and ranking process. He further argues that these processes are based on vague and subjective standards for inclusion as well as underspecified criteria for ranking, which have facilitated the influence of broader U.S. political considerations.

Moreover, although foreign governments have responded to the certification process, the actual changes in category/tier rankings raise questions for prominent claims concerning policy effectiveness.

Moving to a more multi-sited and hybrid macro- and micro-level of analysis, Kay Warren offers a case study of the politics of numbers in the sex trafficking trade between Colombia (the sending state) and Japan (the recipient). Specifically, Warren examines key sites of intervention to combat human trafficking along the routes between Colombia and Japan that have been used to channel women workers to Japan's sex entertainment industry since the early 1980s. This regional history has become part of a much larger international project to develop and enforce a new set of anti-trafficking norms negotiated at the United Nations in 1999–2000. The role of enforcer of these norms has been embraced by the U.S. State Department, which has created an international monitoring system to measure compliance. The first part of Warren's chapter examines this monitoring system, which systematically deploys statistics in widely circulated annual reports to make the case for the existence of an urgent human trafficking crisis. The second part focuses on the illusiveness of counting by government bureaucracies, the process through which women who have been trafficked have returned to Colombia, and women's narrative constructions of their own experiences as migratory laborers abroad.

The volume then moves to examine the politics of numbers in the realm of armed conflict. Focusing in particular on the politicization of numbers surrounding the dead and displaced, Kelly M. Greenhill critically examines both the origin of a variety of conflict-related statistics and their concrete measurable outcomes. Drawing on a variety of cases from the Middle East, Central Africa, and the Balkans, she demonstrates how and why such politicization matters and outlines a variety of negative policy consequences to which such politicization can give rise. These recur around the globe and across cases, and include the misallocation of limited resources; the compromised conduct of and/or efficacy of military operations; muddied evaluations of policy success and failure; and the creation of inflammatory political ammunition, which can be exploited by virulent nationalists and other enterprising actors. The chapter also addresses the perplexing fact that although dubious statistics are often quickly and unquestioningly adopted, they can become quite difficult to dislodge and discredit once they have taken root.

In the following chapter, Lara J. Nettelfield closely examines the particular case of the politicization of casualty statistics from the 1992–95 Bosnian War. Although conventional wisdom holds that between 200,000 and 250,000 people perished in the three-and-a-half-year war in Bosnia-Herzegovina, the Sarajevo-based Research and Documentation Center's project on population losses revealed that the number was close to half of the original estimate. As a result, some Bosnian elites vehemently attacked the project, its architects, and its findings. Nettelfield's detailed study traces how the early casualty estimates became fused with narratives about the war and argues that the hostile reaction to the revised estimates is not as surprising as it might initially seem.

Politicization in the realm of armed conflict is not limited to the inflation of numbers. Sometimes numbers are systematically deflated, or no counting is done at all. In striking contrast to the Bosnian case, the chapter by John Hagan and Wenona Rymond-Richmond on the crisis in Darfur is a powerful illustration of the deliberate undercounting of atrocities. Darfur has been labeled the "ambiguous genocide." A key source of ambiguity about this genocide derives from the failure of U.S. government agencies to meaningfully hold the government of Sudan accountable for the death toll in Darfur. More specifically, Hagan and Rymond-Richmond argue that the U.S. State Department and the U.S. Government Accountability Office have been key sources of low and uncertain estimates of the scale of mortality in Darfur. The effect of increasing uncertainty about mass atrocities in Darfur has been to reduce the public sense of urgency about stopping the alleged genocide and holding its architects accountable.

Winifred Tate's detailed examination of paramilitaries in Colombia provides another illustration of strategic undercounting and underreporting, but of a very different sort than in Darfur. Throughout the 1990s and into the early 2000s, Colombian paramilitary groups linked to government security forces played a central role in cocaine trafficking as well as carrying out brutal massacres as they moved into new areas of the country. U.S. policymakers debating a multi-billion dollar aid package largely glossed over and discounted the exploits of these groups, despite the fact that the stated aim of the package was to fight narcotics and strengthen democracy. Tate argues that this striking *absence* of counting in this context can only be adequately explained by considering the ways in which particular explanatory narratives are deployed by policymakers to explain violence statistics and drug production in the debates over U.S. policy toward Colombia.

The final case study critically evaluates the numbers and metrics used in efforts to counter terrorist financing—one of the most oft-cited and highly touted "success stories" of the "global war on terror." In their chapter, Sue Eckert and Thomas J. Biersteker focus on issues surrounding the utility of the frozen assets/designations methodology; political considerations underlying claims of policy success; obstacles to accurate measures (such as government classified information and intelligence); the discursive placement of qualitative and quantitative indicators in policymakers' statements; and alternative considerations regarding the effectiveness of policies to counter terrorist financing.

The concluding chapter underscores what we have learned and why it matters, identifies some of the policy pathologies that emerge from the contributors' collective findings, and points to unanswered questions and directions for further research.

2

The Politics of Measuring Illicit Flows and Policy Effectiveness

Peter Andreas

By definition, illicit transnational flows—such as migrant smuggling, drug trafficking, and money laundering—take place in the shadows and are thus inherently difficult to measure. For the most part, this is the domain of the invisible and the clandestine. There are no quarterly business reports, monthly job growth figures, annual trade balance statistics, and foreign direct investment numbers. To make matters worse, the actors and activities in the illicit world are not only hard to "see," but most are actively attempting to avoid being noticed, reported, and quantified. The success of a smuggling operation, for example, depends on not being detected and thus is designed to be as hidden as possible. This inevitably creates monumental measurement problems. Yet the preoccupation with quantification is as strikingly evident in policy debates about the illicit world as it is in the licit world. This is reflected in both the attempts to measure the size and magnitude of various illicit flows and the effectiveness of policy measures to combat them.

This chapter examines how numbers related to illicit flows and policy efforts to combat these flows are produced, perpetuated, and consumed. The chapter argues that illicitness makes possible a politics of numbers that is particularly susceptible to speculation, distortion, and sometimes even outright fabrication that is rarely questioned or challenged in policy debates and media reporting. To some extent, this reflects cynical manipulations by politicians and bureaucrats, but more importantly it reflects these actors' coping strategies and conundrums in a policy arena defined by a quantification fetish. The imperative to quantify prioritizes bad data over no data (or limited data) and promotes simple and visible metrics of policy "progress" and "success" that are highly ambiguous and misleading. What counts is what is counted—even if the actual process of counting is of questionable validity. The very act of counting makes the invisible at least appear visible, and therefore accessible for public debate. The first part of the chapter examines the creation and proliferation of numbers about the size and magnitude of a range of illicit flows. The second part critically evaluates the standard metrics used to measure policy effectiveness in the case of the U.S.-led international "war on drugs."

Producing and Perpetuating Mythical Numbers

The objective here is not to come up with more appropriate quantitative measures and techniques to calculate illicit flows and develop improved metrics of policy effectiveness.[1] Rather, the point is to demonstrate that the official numbers (from government offices and agencies and international organizations such as the UN and INTERPOL) are highly problematic yet go largely unchallenged because they serve multiple interests and functions that inhibit more skeptical scrutiny. In fact, all too often, little effort is made to try to explain where the official numbers come from and why these numbers should be considered remotely credible.

This pattern is illustrated in the case of international drug trafficking. As required by Congress, the U.S. State Department produces the annual *International Narcotics Control Strategy Report*, which estimates illicit drug production by other countries. Yet as the economist Peter Reuter points out, "No detail has ever been published on the methodology of these estimates, beyond the fact that they are generated from estimates of growing area, crop per acre, and refining yield per ton of raw product; the information sources, even the technology used to produce them (for area estimates) are classified." He concludes that the estimates "show inexplicable inconsistency over time and across sectors of the industry. Some numbers are simply implausible."[2] Some numbers are also noticeably missing, reflecting the importance of noncounting or selective counting. Most notably, although cannabis production around the world is regularly reported, no estimate is given for U.S. production levels.

---

1. For a critical discussion of measurement problems in the case of black markets, see the collection of articles in the *Economic Journal* 109 (June 1999). Also see Philip Mattera, *Off the Books: The Rise of the Underground Economy* (New York: St. Martin's Press, 1985), esp. ch. 4.

2. Peter Reuter, "The Mismeasurement of Illegal Drug Markets: The Implications of its Irrelevance," in *Exploring the Underground Economy*, ed. Susan Pozo (Kalamazoo, MI: Upjohn Institute, 1996), 65.

Similarly, in the 1990s the United Nations Drug Control Program (UNDCP) often reported the global annual value of the illicit drug trade to be $500 billion—making it one of the largest industries in the world. This number was picked up in the press and recycled through so many stories that it took on a life of its own, becoming a widely accepted and used figure. Some scholars perpetuated the problem by using this number in their own work, which was then reused by other scholars, repeating and further extending the recycling pattern found in the media.[3] R. T. Naylor recounts confronting a senior UN anti-drug official who used the $500 billion figure at a 1990 conference on drug trafficking:

> I diplomatically suggested to him that to get such a number, he and his colleagues must have not only included the value of every donkey owned by every campesino in the Andes but priced those donkeys as if they cost as much as a pickup truck. His response was to huff away. But he returned a while later, perhaps mellowed by cocktails, to suggest that although there were problems with the number, it was great for catching public attention.[4]

The UNDCP later lowered the estimate to $400 billion, reporting that this figure represented approximately 8 percent of international trade. Yet closer scrutiny reveals that this number is not actually a trade estimate but rather an estimate of retail-level expenditures (sale price on the street)—which, as Reuter notes, are considerably higher given the value-added in consumer countries (and the estimate is further inflated because it relies on U.S. drug prices, which are typically higher than elsewhere).[5] Francisco Thoumi, an economist and former UNDCP consultant "questioned several UNDCP members about the procedure that led to this figure, and the best explanation that they could offer was that they surveyed an array of estimates made in different parts of the world and came up with approximately $365 billion, a figure that was rounded up to $400 billion." He asks: "If they had arrived at $335 billion, would they have rounded it down to $300 billion?"[6]

---

3. This unfortunately includes H. Richard Friman and Peter Andreas, "Introduction: International Relations and the Illicit Global Economy," in *The Illicit Global Economy and State Power,* ed. Friman and Andreas (Lanham, MD: Rowman & Littlefield, 1999), 2. The authors cite Paul Stares, *Global Habit: The Drug Problem in a Borderless World* (Washington, DC: Brookings Institution Press, 1996), 2, 123–24. They note that other analysts have come up with a much lower figure, but this is buried in an endnote (of course, I blame my co-author for this).

4. R. T. Naylor, *Wages of Crime* (Ithaca: Cornell University Press, 2002), x.

5. Peter Reuter and Victoria Greenfield, "Measuring Global Drug Markets: How Good Are the Numbers and Why Should We Care about Them?" *World Economics* 2 (2001): 160.

6. Francisco E. Thoumi, "The Numbers Game: Let's All Guess the Size of the Illegal Drug Industry!" *Journal of Drug Issues* 2, 1 (2005): 190.

At the same time, drug numbers that fail to sufficiently impress are sometimes discarded. For instance, in the late 1990s, the Financial Action Task Force (FATF) began an effort to determine the size of the illicit global economy, with the first step focusing on the illicit drug trade. Reuter was hired to come up with an estimate. Thoumi writes that, "The resulting study is probably the most serious attempt to ascertain the size of the world illegal drug market and resulted in an estimated range between $45 and $280 billion. Unfortunately, after an internal debate at FATF it was decided not to publish the study because some country members expected a larger figure."[7]

Some official numbers reflect the old practice of "guesstimating." In his classic 1971 essay on "mythical numbers," Max Singer writes that, "Mythical numbers may be more mythical and have more vitality in the area of crime than in most areas." He points to the case of gambling:

> In the early 1950s the Kefauver Committee published a $20 billion estimate for the annual "take" of gambling in the United States. The figure was "picked from a hat." One staff member said: "We had no real idea of the money spent. The California Crime Commission said $12 billion. Virgil Petersen of Chicago said $30 billion. We picked $20 billion as the balance of the two."[8]

The same sort of "guesstimates" are evident today, but at the global level (illicit transnational flows of money, drugs, and so on).

Mythical numbers need not rely on their creators to be perpetuated and legitimated. The announcement of an impressive sounding number can generate substantial media attention, which further legitimates the number and stimulates its circulation—and the original source of the number can become lost through repetition in media accounts.[9] At the time, skeptical assessments of the number are not as newsworthy and tend to receive much less attention.

This dynamic is evident in the case of sex trafficking (examined in more detail in the Feingold, Friman, and Warren chapters in this volume). The U.S. government has estimated that between 600,000 and 800,000 people are trafficked across international borders annually—with this

---

7. Thoumi, "Numbers Game," 191. For a critique of FATF counting methods in the case of drug money, see Petrus C. Van Duyne and Michael Levi, *Drugs and Money: Managing the Drug Trade and Crime-Money in Europe* (London: Routledge, 2005), 107–9; and Petrus Van Duyne, *Organized Crime in Europe* (Commack, NY: Nova Science, 1996), ch. 6.

8. Max Singer, "The Vitality of Mythical Numbers," *Public Interest* 23 (1971): 3–9, fn 1.

9. David Luckenbill describes this process as "number laundering." Joel Best, *Damned Lies and Statistics: Untangling Numbers from the Media, Politicians, and Activists* (Berkeley: University of California Press, 2001), 35.

number used and reused in media reporting (including in the *Los Angeles Times, New York Times, Washington Post, NPR,* and *Boston Globe*). The Government Accountability Office (GAO) subsequently published a study casting serious doubt on this official estimate, stating:

> The U.S. government agency that prepares the trafficking estimate is part of the intelligence community, which makes its estimation methodology opaque and inaccessible. During a trafficking workshop in November 2005, the government agency provided a one-page overview of its methodology, which allowed for only a very limited peer review by the workshop participants. In addition, the U.S. government's methodology involves interpreting, classifying, and analyzing data, which was performed by one person who did not document all of his work. Thus the estimate may not be replicable, which raises doubts about its reliability.[10]

Though the U.S. government trafficking estimate received widespread media attention when it was announced, the GAO report questioning the validity of the estimate was virtually ignored by the media.[11]

This reflects a larger problem in media reporting. As Jack Shafer argues, "Reporters have so much faith in the pure power of numbers that many will inject into a piece any ones available as long as they 1) are big; 2) come from a seemingly authoritative source; and 3) don't contradict the point the reporter is trying to make."[12] He points to the identity theft issue to illustrate this, noting that, "The magic number for journalists covering the identity theft beat has been $48 billion—the estimated losses suffered by identity theft victims—which carries the Federal Trade Commission's imprimatur. Since its arrival in 2003, the number has appeared in hundreds of news stories."[13] Fred H. Cate, the director of the Center for Applied Cybersecurity Research at the University of Indiana, argues that if these numbers matched reality, half of the banking industry's $103 billion in profits in 2005 would disappear.[14]

Sometimes reporters, hungry for a number, cite a pundit or expert as the source of a large and impressive sounding number even though it is not

10. Committee on the Judiciary and Chairman, Committee on International Relations, U.S. House of Representatives, Government Accountability Office, "Human Trafficking: Better Data, Strategy, and Reporting Needed to Enhance U.S. Antitrafficking Efforts Abroad," Report to the Chairman, July 2006, 13.

11. Jack Shafer, "More Mythical Numbers: The GAO Debunks the Official Human-Trafficking Estimates," *Slate,* August 16, 2006.

12. Jack Shafer, "The (Ongoing) Vitality of Mythical Numbers: Does ID Theft Really Cost $48 Billion a Year?" *Slate,* June 26, 2006.

13. Ibid.

14. Quoted in ibid.

at all clear that the person quoted is the original source or would be in a position to come up with this figure on their own. For instance, a July 27, 2008 front-page story in the *New York Times* reported that "the FARC [Colombian guerilla group] still collects $200 to $300 million a year by taxing coca farmers and coordinating cocaine smuggling networks, according to Bruce Bagley, a specialist on the Andean drug war who teaches at the University of Miami." Apparently, for the *New York Times*, it is sufficient that an "expert" or "specialist" (in this case a respected university professor with regional expertise) is willing to provide and vouch for a number that supports the point of the article. No study is mentioned, and no questions are asked about where the number came from and how it was derived.[15] Of course, it is possible that when the journalist interviewed him, Bagley actually provided information on the origins and rationale for the number and may have even included qualifiers and caveats that suggest it is really more of a guesstimate, at best. But in its final published form, the article presents the number with unquestioned confidence, asserting it as "fact."

Sometimes, however, a "fact" turns out to be pure fiction. Take, for example, the claims of a "$20 billion-a-year" Internet child pornography business. This number was reported in the *New York Times* as well as in a press release for a congressional hearing on the subject. Finding the original source of the number produced many twists, turns, and dead-ends. When asked how the number made its way into a congressional hearing, a congressional staffer claimed the number came from the National Center for Missing and Exploited Children, a child protection advocacy group. The president of the group was then contacted, and he indicated that the source was actually the consulting firm McKinsey & Co. A McKinsey spokesperson said the number came from a report by the international advocacy group, End Child Prostitution, Child Pornography and Trafficking of Children for Sexual Purposes. That report (which noted that estimates range from $3 billion to $20 billion) actually listed the Federal Bureau of Investigation (FBI) as the original source. Yet when contacted, an FBI spokesperson insisted that the Bureau had never used this number.[16]

New technologies, most notably the Internet, further enable the proliferation of questionable numerical claims. Consider, for instance, a recent Tennessee anti-methamphetamine campaign. In 2005, the state's attorneys general created a website called "Meth Is Death," which asserted that, "99% of first-time meth users are hooked after just the first try"; "only 5% of meth addicts are able to kick it and stay away"; and "the life expectancy

15. Simon Romero, "Cocaine Sustains War in Rural Colombia," *New York Times,* July 27, 2008.

16. Carl Bialik, "Measuring the Child-Porn Trade," *Wall Street Journal,* April 18, 2006.

of a habitual meth user is only five years." The problem with these numbers is that, if true, it would mean that hundreds of thousands of young
people are dying every year—which fortunately is not the case. James W.
Kirby, executive director of the Tennessee District Attorneys General Association, acknowledges that it should have stated that 99 percent of meth
addicts were hooked from their first use, not that 99 percent of people who
try meth get hooked from the first use. "That is a little bit misleading,"
Kirby conceded. "It came out as a typo." Realizing that the numbers could
not be backed up, the state changed the website—but the old site remained
accessible. The numbers apparently came from MMA Creative, the public
relations firm that created the website. According to Mike McCloud, the
president and chief executive of the company, the numbers "were gathered
from various local and national sources about two years ago. Unfortunately, I can't even point you to some of the sites we researched back then
because they don't even exist today."[17]

The estimates regarding the size of the illicit trade in wildlife also reveal
the pattern of numbers taking on a life of their own—but in this case inflated by being misquoted from the start (conflating the size of the illegal
wildlife trade with all wildlife trade). As one critic has commented:

> There is also no doubt that the smuggling of illegal wildlife products is a
> multi-billion dollar business. However, the $20 billion figure so often cited
> as an estimate for the value of such trade does need to be re-examined. Using
> data from the early 1990s, TRAFFIC, the wildlife trade monitoring network
> of the World Wildlife Fund and IUCN, originally generated that estimate for
> the value of all wildlife trade, both legal and illegal, excluding commodities
> like timber and fish. The figure gained wide currency and was frequently
> quoted—and ultimately misquoted—as the value for illegal trade alone. The
> true value of illegal wildlife trade may, by now, indeed be that much. But we
> really don't know the exact number.[18]

Probing the source and proliferation of particular numbers can also
reveal striking inconsistencies in media reporting and policy debates.
For example, the CNN anchor Lou Dobbs, who has been a proponent
of tougher border controls, has in some reports spoken of "the toll that
20 million illegal aliens take on the infrastructure of the United States and
on local, state, and federal taxpayer budgets," while on other broadcasts
he has cited a range between 11 and 20 million. The inconsistency in the

17. Carl Bialik, "A Bad Meth Stat Lingers On," *Wall Street Journal,* March 11, 2006.
18. From "Re: 'Taking Animal Trafficking out of the Shadows," *Innovations* 2 (2007): 214,
http://www.mitpressjournals.org/doi/abs/10.1162/itgg.2007.2.1-2.214?cookieSet=1&
journalCode=itgg.

alleged number of illegal immigrants in the United States has even provided material for Comedy Central's Stephen Colbert. He noted that on a
Sunday political talk show, Senator Arlen Specter mentioned "11 million
undocumented aliens," but thirty minutes later on a different political talk
show, Senator Ted Kennedy used the "12 million figure." Colbert's comment: "One million illegals snuck into this country in half an hour! That
is alarming. At that rate, the entire population of Mexico would be here in
three days. Congress, get to work on that fence."[19]

Official numbers about the illicit world are sometimes further insu-
lated from public scrutiny because sources of the estimates originate from
within the intelligence community—which means that much of the data
and methodology is classified and therefore inaccessible. This is obviously
not conducive to public discussion, scrutiny, and debate over measurement
and methodology. The implicit message from the intelligence community
is clear even if not necessarily persuasive: "trust me, if you knew what I
know, you'd agree," and the half-joking comment, "I could tell you, but
then I'd have to kill you." In these cases, government agencies have a convenient rationale for not revealing sources, methodologies, and data collection techniques. This problem particularly afflicts the security-related
realms of the illicit world such as transnational terrorism and nuclear
smuggling, but is also evident in the generation of numbers related to issues such as sex trafficking and the drug trade.

What purposes do these often highly questionable numbers serve? In
a series of essays building on and extending Singer's original article on
"mythical numbers," Reuter argues that drug-related mythical numbers
have "continued vitality" but are essentially irrelevant because the official estimates have little bearing on the policy decision-making process.
He suggests that, "the numbers are in fact just decorations on the policy
process, rhetorical conveniences for official statements without any serious
consequences."[20]

Reuter makes a persuasive case that the drug trade numbers are grossly
overstated and unsupportable and that there is no constituency (except
perhaps drug dealers!) to seriously challenge the figures. Yet he is less
convincing in arguing that the numbers are essentially irrelevant and dismissing them as "just decorations" and "rhetorical conveniences." These
decorative and rhetorical roles can in fact matter a great deal in this policy
realm. After all, counterfactually speaking, what would happen if these
"mythical numbers" were not generated in the first place and were not

19. Carl Bialik, "Fuzzy Math on Illegal Immigration," *Wall Street Journal*, April 5, 2006.
20. Reuter, "Mismeasurement of Illegal Drug Markets," 64. Also see Reuter, "(Continued) Vitality."

available as "decorations" in drug policy debates and decisions on anti-drug funding? The specific numbers may not matter; what matters is that the numbers are big and appear in need of serious and sustained policy attention. Politically speaking, if there are no numbers there is no problem demanding urgent policy action. The specific numbers may have little influence on policy decisions, but given the policy obsession with quantification it seems that the absence of any attention-grabbing numbers would certainly be noticed and missed—and is thus consequential. Rather than simply dismissing the symbolic, decorative purpose of inflated numbers as irrelevant, it would be more analytically fruitful to take such political symbolism seriously in making sense of the politics of numbers in this policy domain.[21]

In addition, regardless of their questionable validity, official estimates of the size and magnitude of various illicit flows are not only part of the policy evaluation process but also provide ammunition in shaping the broader public debate and awareness of a problem. Most important, they are tools in constructing a dominant narrative of transnational crime as a large and growing global threat. As Deborah Stone reminds us, "numbers are commonly used to tell a story. Most obviously, they are the premier language for stories of decline and decay. Figures are invoked to show that a problem is getting bigger and worse."[22] Nowhere is this more strikingly evident than in the use of "scary numbers"[23] about illicit flows. For journalists, pundits, and policy analysts, big and scary estimates of the size of illicit flows help to draw attention to a problem and sound the alarm bells.

A few popular books illustrate this pattern. Take, for instance, Moises Naim's, *Illicit: How Smugglers, Traffickers and Copycats Are Hijacking the Global Economy.*[24] For Naim, the editor of *Foreign Policy,* the alarming numbers he uses support the underlying message of his provocative book: the illicit global economy is big, getting bigger, and requires a much bigger policy response. Naim has no incentives to question the numbers, and if he did not have these numbers to draw on—ranging from statistics about human trafficking to money laundering to counterfeiting—he would

---

21. Indeed, in other writings, Reuter has stressed the consequences of quantification and its deleterious impact on the policy process. See Peter Reuter, "The Social Costs of the Demand for Quantification," *Journal of Policy Analysis and Management* 5 (1986): 807–12.

22. Deborah Stone, *Policy Paradox: The Art of Political Decision Making* (New York: Norton, 1997), 172.

23. Joel Best devotes a chapter to the phenomena of "scary numbers" in *More Damned Lies and Statistics* (Berkeley: University of California Press, 2004).

24. Moises Naim, *Illicit: How Smugglers, Traffickers and Copycats are Hijacking the Global Economy* (New York: Doubleday, 2005).

not have been able to write the same book and tell the same story. This is evident in his depiction of the counterfeiting business:

> Since the early 1990s, according to INTERPOL, trade in counterfeits has grown *eight times* the speed of legitimate trade. Twenty years ago, commercial losses around the world due to counterfeiting were estimated in the $5 billion range; today they are around $500 billion. That puts the cost of counterfeiting between 5 and 10 percent of the total value of world trade, on a par with, say, the GDP of Australia.[25]

Equally eye-catching are the statistics Naim uses regarding money laundering: "The rule of thumb to estimate the scope of money laundering today is between two and five percent of world GDP, or $800 billion to $2 trillion. Some estimates run as high as 10 percent of global GDP."[26] Naim does not scrutinize the plausibility of these dramatic numbers: "All of the numbers in this book come from the most reliable sources possible—usually international organizations and governments or nongovernmental organizations whose work is generally deemed to be serious and reliable."[27]

Illicit has received widespread attention (reflected in numerous media interviews, op-eds in leading papers, speaking engagements, book reviews). *National Geographic* has even produced a documentary based on the book. Virtually none of the reviews of the book raise an eyebrow regarding Naim's uncritical use of official numbers and estimates.[28] It is as if the reliability of the data really does not matter—yet without these alarming numbers the edifice on which the book is built starts to crumble.

Another striking case is the book by Tim Phillips, *Knockoff: The Deadly Trade in Counterfeit Goods: The True Story of the World's Fastest Growing Crime Wave.*[29] The very title of the book depends on a provocative but unsubstantiated measurement claim—that counterfeit goods represent "the world's fastest growing crime wave." Phillips, a business journalist, rarely even cites the sources of the estimates he uses on the size of various counterfeiting activities. His numbers presumably come from the many

25. Naim, *Illicit*, 112.
26. Ibid., 137.
27. Ibid., 11.
28. See, for example, the review by William Wechsler and Richard N. Cooper in *Foreign Affairs* 85 (2006). The only exception I found is R. T. Naylor, "Marlboro Men," *London Review of Books*, March 22, 2007.
29. Tim Phillips, *Knockoff: The Deadly Trade in Counterfeit Goods: The True Story of the World's Fastest Growing Crime Wave* (London: Kogan, 2005).

business and trade groups that have sprung up to combat and draw attention to these problems. Not mentioned in the book is the possibility that the numbers may be influenced by the agendas of the companies that produce them to draw public attention and mobilize policy action. As an OECD (Organization for Economic Cooperation and Development) report on intellectual property crime observes, "Many of the anti-counterfeiting organizations are lobby groups and have an incentive to present exaggerated figures that may bias the true picture."[30] A remarkably unchallenged numerical move in the domain of intellectual property theft, for example, is to cite sales of counterfeit goods as full-price lost sales of legitimate goods. This falsely and misleadingly presumes that if knockoff CDs, DVDs, computer software, and Rolex watches were not available then the buyers of these goods would be purchasing the real thing. The result is grossly inflated figures regarding how much these illicit goods cost legitimate industry. It is simply implausible that the typical buyer of a $50 fake Rolex would instead spend $5,000 on the genuine item.

These books are not isolated cases but rather are representative of a growing genre of popular "global crime" books written since the early 1990s that have the same basic storyline: the illicit global economy is booming, it is unprecedented, and it is a grave and growing threat urgently in need of public concern and policy attention.[31] Moreover, it is viewed as increasingly connected to the clandestine world of transnational terrorism.[32] The narratives in these accounts both depend on and further legitimate official estimates regarding the size and significance of various illicit global flows. This is not to suggest that the illicit global economy is not a serious problem and should not be treated as a major public policy concern, but to stress that the numbers are often highly suspect but nevertheless popularized and rarely critically scrutinized, and that there are strong incentives to accept and reproduce rather than challenge and critique them. For the most part, the numbers are presented and embraced as uncontested "facts" and objective "evidence."

30. Organization for Economic Cooperation and Development, *The Economic Impact of Counterfeiting* (Paris: OECD, 1998), 27.
31. These include, for example, Jeffrey Robinson, *The Laundrymen: Inside the World's Third Largest Business,* 2nd ed. (New York: Pocket Books, 1998); Jeffrey Robinson, *The Merger: The Conglomeration of International Organized Crime* (New York: Overlook, 2002); Misha Glenny, *McMafia: A Journey through the Global Criminal Underworld* (New York: Knopf, 2008); Claire Sterling, *Thieves' World: The Threat of the New Global Network of Organized Crime* (New York: Simon and Schuster, 1994).
32. See especially John Robb, *Brave New World: The Next Stage of Terrorism and the End of Globalization* (Hoboken, NJ: Wiley, 2007). Robb asserts, without providing any source, that there is a global criminal GDP of $1 to $3 trillion, and is growing at a rate of "seven times the rate of legal global trade" (149).

As these books illustrate, the numbers alone are not enough—they require building a carefully crafted storyline around them. The numbers are used to help frame a particular narrative about the nature, size, and growth of the illicit global economy. The story gives the numbers meaning and brings them to life, while the numbers give the story apparent credibility. The same is true in the presentation of the numbers in official policy debates and in media reporting. Without the numbers there is no press conference or news report.

Quantifying Policy Effectiveness: The Case of Drug Control

If measuring illicit flows is inherently difficult, so too is the task of continuously demonstrating the effectiveness of policing efforts targeting such flows. This creates a formidable challenge for politicians and law enforcement agencies coping with the imperatives to "do something" and "show results." This is especially pronounced in the case of the most politically charged "hot button" illicit flows, such as drug trafficking, that generate public outrage and moral condemnation. This stimulates demands for "feel good" quantifiable indicators demonstrating "progress," political determination, and moral resolve (even if not always "success"). The indicators and metrics of effectiveness highlighted in the official evaluation process and funding mechanism tend to maximize symbolic value and image effect, but may do little to actually curb the illicit activity.

The politics of numbers in the case of the U.S.-led "war on drugs" means that a failing and flawed policy can be politically and bureaucratically successful. The standard measures of effectiveness become embedded and institutionalized within these agencies, as evident in the case of the U.S. federal law enforcement apparatus. As one U.S. military analyst has explained it:

> Historically, the federal LEAs [Law Enforcement Agencies] have justified their budgets and articulated their effectiveness by parading arrest, seizure and prosecution statistics before Congress. The importance of these statistics is ingrained in the values of those making up the law enforcement rank and file. They are taught to investigate crime, make arrests, confiscate contraband, and prosecute criminals. They are promoted to their organization's executive levels by adhering to these values.[33]

33. Major Craig L. Carlson, "Measures of Effectiveness—The Key to a Successful National Drug Control Strategy," *Military Review* 71 (1991): 90–94.

Moreover, as John Walsh points out, "the agencies with a stake in demonstrating success are themselves compiling and presenting the data."[34]

Law enforcement agencies not only have a powerful bureaucratic incentive not to question the numbers and what they measure, but in fact jockey for position against each other in generating and claiming credit for these numbers:

> LEAs compete for congressional appropriations by displaying caseload statistics. These statistics provide MOEs [Measures of Effectiveness] and help justify future budgets. The budget argument's bottom line is: Agency X made more arrests and had more drug seizures than agency Y; therefore agency X should get a higher percentage of congressional appropriations. Each LEA's financial survival rests on its ability to express its effectiveness.[35]

This dynamic can generate such fierce interagency competition and "turf wars" that different agencies sometimes claim credit for the same seizure or arrest, sometimes resulting in double counting. For example, the bureaucratic imperative to produce and claim credit for numbers helps to explain the age-old rivalry between Customs and Border Patrol agents along the U.S.-Mexico border.[36]

The ambiguity of the most popular measures of effectiveness is a source of great frustration for those charged with the task of combating illicit drug flows. Yet this very ambiguity also provides a mechanism to manipulate and distort the evaluation process, obscure and gloss over failure, and rationalize more funding and a continued escalation of drug enforcement. The convenient ambiguity of the numbers is evident in crop eradication, seizures, and border interdiction statistics, which can be interpreted as evidence of success or failure (depending on the particular "spin" of the analysis). "Going to the source" to target drug crops such as marijuana, coca, and opium poppy in foreign countries has for decades been a cornerstone of the U.S.-led drug war. Fighting drugs, it is commonly assumed, is easiest at the point of production abroad. Eradication numbers are therefore frequently used as evidence of policy effectiveness. As Thoumi points out:

> Forced and voluntary crop eradication statistics are frequently used to show "success" of repressive policies. Those data are misleading because the variable

34. John Walsh, *Are We There Yet? Measuring Progress in the U.S. War on Drugs in Latin America* (Washington, DC: Washington Office on Latin America, December 2004), 9.

35. Carlson, "Measures of Effectiveness," 90–91.

36. See Peter Andreas, *Border Games: Policing the U.S.-Mexico Divide* (Ithaca: Cornell University Press, 2000).

measured is not a good indicator of policy success. There is no doubt that if coca is wiped out from the face of the earth, cocaine would not be produced, except synthetically. However, because most eradication leads to crop displacement, acreage eradicated is not a good measure of policy success. A much better indicator would be cocaine retail prices and purity measures.[37]

There is also a tendency to exaggerate the monetary value of eradicated drug crops. Walsh observes that, "U.S. drug control agencies routinely inflate the significance of their achievements by expressing the value of drug crops destroyed or drugs captured in terms of the price that the drugs might have fetched on U.S. streets." He notes that the State Department has claimed as "riveting fact" that its eradication efforts in 2001 and 2002 "took $5 billion worth of cocaine, at street value, off the streets of the United States."[38] Yet because of the pricing structure in the supply line, in which most of the added value of cocaine is within the consumer country, "quantities of cocaine worth $5 billion on U.S. streets would be worth no more than $50 million at the cultivation stage. While eradication is indeed a heavy blow to coca farmers, traffickers' business is not jeopardized, and the disruption of production registers barely, if at all, in U.S. prices."[39] U.S. officials understandably (but misleadingly) stress the $5 billion figure rather than the $50 million figure.

The ambiguity of the numbers and potential for misleading interpretations is equally evident in the case of seizing and interdicting drugs at and beyond U.S. borders. Walsh points out that "larger and more frequent drug seizures are often presented as evidence of policy success, and lauded as a testament to more vigorous enforcement, but they may simply reflect increased drug production and trafficking. Or they may be the result of more enforcement and more drugs in circulation—the seizure statistics themselves provide no clue."[40]

This extreme ambiguity allows for a great deal of creative interpretation. Naim, for example, points to the dramatic growth in seizures as a sure sign of a booming illicit drug economy and rapidly declining law enforcement capacity: "During the 1990s the number of reported drug seizures worldwide, which had been stagnant at around 300,000 per year, more than quadrupled to 1.4 million in 2001." He then argues that "This explosion should come as no surprise, for the entire legal and technological apparatus of globalization has made the illicit drug trade faster, more efficient,

37. Thoumi, "Numbers Game," 196.
38. Quoted in Walsh, *Are We There Yet?* 15.
39. Ibid., 15.
40. Ibid., 9.

and easier to hide."[41] Although globalization has no doubt benefited the illicit drug trade, as Naim goes to great lengths to emphasize, it is not at all clear that these seizure statistics represent evidence of a dramatic growth in drug smuggling in just a few years. After all, if it was that much easier to hide illicit drugs in 2001 than in the 1990s (and that much harder for law enforcement to detect), as Naim claims, why would one expect a sharp rise in seizures?

Law enforcement agencies typically tout rising seizure numbers as an indicator of policing prowess and evidence that they are doing a good job. Interdicting and seizing more drugs en route has long been highlighted as a key indicator of the effectiveness of U.S. drug control policy. As noted by the State Department in 2006: "Our long-standing international campaign to curb the flow of cocaine and heroin to the United States advanced significantly during the year.... Drug seizures set new records for cocaine interdiction in the Western Hemisphere."[42]

The U.S. drug enforcement strategy has placed great faith in the assumption that pushing seizure levels up can eventually put drug traffickers out of business. According to the White House Office of National Drug Control Policy (ONDCP):

> In 2001, U.S. government and partner nations seized or otherwise interdicted more than 21 percent of the cocaine shipped to the United States, according to an interagency assessment. When added to the additional 7 percent that is seized at our borders or elsewhere in the United States, current interdiction rates are within reach of the 35 to 50 percent seizure rate that is estimated would prompt a collapse of profitability for smugglers unless they substantially raise their prices or expand their sales to non-U.S. markets.[43]

The ONDCP message is clear: we are making progress, success is just around the corner, and the battle can be won if we just fight harder. In its 2005 report, the ONDCP boasts that law enforcement successfully removed about half of the world's cocaine supply from the market in 2003; the report does not mention that this failed to prompt the expected collapse in the market and a sharp rise in prices. The report also makes no claim that there has been a decline in cocaine use despite record seizure levels.[44]

41. Naim, *Illicit*, 77.

42. U.S. Department of State, "International Narcotics Control Strategy Report 2006," 2006), http://www.state.gov/p/inl/rls/nrcrpt/2006/#.

43. Quoted in Matthew B. Robinson and Renee G. Scherlen, *Lies, Damned Lies, and Drug War Statistics: A Critical Analysis of Claims Made by the Office of National Drug Control Policy* (Albany: State University of New York Press, 2007), 113.

44. Ibid., 122–23.

Intensified interdiction efforts tend to reroute rather than deter drug trafficking—such rerouting can, in turn, provide a further rationale to expand interdiction. In the 1980s, for example, U.S. law enforcement pressure on cocaine shipments entering via the Caribbean pushed the trade to the southwest border. Coast Guard Admiral Paul Yost testified before Congress: "The more money that you spend on it, the more success you are going to have in the interdiction area.... We did that in the Caribbean for the last two years, and I'm sure that what we're about to do on the southwest border will also be extremely successful. It is also going to be extremely expensive, and the success expense ratio is going to be a very direct one."[45] Measuring such interdiction "success" is politically tricky. At a 1987 Senate hearing held in Nogales, Arizona, senator Pete Domenici (R-NM) provided a strikingly candid summary of the situation:

> Now, I understand that we're shooting at floating targets. I mean, you do well in the Southeast and they [the traffickers] move to the Southwest. We'll load up the Southwest and what happens next? Nonetheless, we have to continue the war on drugs. And for us to sustain the resources, you have to have a few victories of significant size that are measurable. We have to take that to the floor and to the committee and tell them we put a billion seven more and it's doing something. And it can't only be measured by manpower, it has to be measured in results.[46]

Customs Commissioner William Von Raab offered the following reply in defense of his rapidly growing agency: "We're just about 1 year into Operation Alliance [the federal interdiction initiative on the Southwest border]. The seizures, which are your typical measure of success, are impressive. Operation Alliance totals 250,000 pounds of marijuana and about 16,000 pounds of cocaine; that's very good." The commissioner asserted that, based on seizure levels, interdiction had improved ten times in the previous five years. Pleased to hear that some progress was being made in controlling the border, none of the committee members questioned what these measures of success actually measured.[47] At the same hearing, Von Raab acknowledged that "there is good news and bad news" in increased drug seizures. "The good news is that we are catching more drugs because we are getting better at doing our job. We have more resources. The

45. Testimony of Admiral Paul Yost, U.S. Coast Guard, before the House Select Committee on Narcotics Abuse and Control, "U.S. Narcotics Control Efforts in Mexico and on the Southwest Border, 99th Congress," July 22, 1986, 34.
46. See Senate Subcommittee, Southwest Border Law Enforcement and Trade, August 19, 1987, 25.
47. Ibid., 25, 191, 200.

bad news is that we are catching more because more is coming across." He concluded that "we are winning the battles, but I am not sure we are winning the war.... However, I am extremely comfortable with our performance."[48]

U.S. Customs officials have long acknowledged that seizures at U.S. border ports of entry represent only a small percentage of the overall flow of drugs. Nevertheless, seizures have traditionally been the leading instrument used by Customs agents to justify their mission, fend off political attacks, and assure continued funding. In other words, there is a bureaucratic imperative to generate seizures in order to project a positive impression of enforcement effort—regardless of what these seizures actually mean. When Customs Commissioner George Weise appeared on *Nightline* in May 1997 to defend his agency against charges of lax border inspections, he pointed to the substantial increase in drugs that had been seized in commercial cargo—even though such an increase could simply indicate that concealment in commercial cargo was becoming an increasingly popular smuggling method.[49]

When cocaine seizure levels subsequently declined, customs officials predictably reacted with alarm. A December 22, 1997 National Treasury Employees Union memo declared that new enforcement efforts were necessary, "the objective being to increase our seizures so customs and the union don't get their heads handed to them by the politicians in Washington when the budget meetings start in March."[50] The low seizure levels did indeed provoke political grumbling. Representative Ron Packard (R-CA) commented: "These are not the results we expected. If interdiction is down, the American people deserve some answers." To pacify and impress such critics, Customs launched a new and more intensive operation, promising that it would "dramatically increase drug seizures."[51]

Most politicians simply accept rather than challenge the numbers game in seizure statistics. There are occasional exceptions. Senator John McCain (R-AZ) once noted its questionable credibility in unusually blunt terms:

> The measures of success that are being made public have virtually no practical meaning. For example, efforts to assist seizures are measured in terms of the amount of drugs seized, with no effort to relate such data to the percentage of total drugs that get through, or to whether seizures have any meaningful impact on the main smuggling networks.... Another equally meaningless

48. Ibid., 191, 202.
49. ABC News, *Nightline*, May, 22 1997.
50. Quoted in *Los Angeles Times*, February 4, 1998.
51. Quoted in ibid.

measure of capability is to report the number of detections, arrests, or inter-
cepts, with no attempt to relate this to the number of successful crossings or
actual convictions, or whether such actions have any real effect on the flow
of drugs.[52]

Another popular measure of drug policy effectiveness is the disruption
and dismantling of trafficking organizations. The 2004 ONDCP report
boasts that "The U.S. Government's master list of targeted trafficking organizations is shorter this year, thanks to the elimination of eight major
trafficking organizations during the past fiscal year.... Another seven organizations were weakened enough to be classified as 'significantly disrupted.'" Yet as Matthew Robinson and Renée Scherlen point out, "We
have no way of verifying such claims or analyzing the data on which they
are based because ONDCP does not offer any evidence."[53] The 2005
ONDCP report similarly documents the number of trafficking organizations disrupted and dismantled. But as Robinson and Scherlen note, the
report is silent on the issue of replacement: Do other traffickers simply take
their place, taking advantage of the market opening?[54]

In its 2005 report, the ONDCP also highlights the increase in drug-
related asset forfeiture: "DEA's [Drug Enforcement Administration] asset
seizures are up from $383 million during fiscal year 2003 to $523 million
in 2004, and the number of seizures valued at more than $1 million rose by
more than half."[55] However, there is no explanation for how or why these
numbers matter in achieving U.S. anti-drug objectives. Asset forfeiture, it
seems, is treated as a goal in and of itself rather than a means to an end.

The political importance of drug war statistics has been further enhanced by the annual certification process ritual, in which the State Department grades the anti-drug performance of foreign drug producing and
exporting countries (for a more detailed discussion, see Friman's chapter
in this volume). Countries labeled as noncooperative can be "decertified,"
resulting in material and nonmaterial penalties: aid cutoffs, votes against
loans from multilateral lending agencies, loss of trade preferences, and the
stigma of being branded a "narco-state." Alternatively, the president can
decertify a country but opt for a national security waiver—meaning that
the material penalties are not imposed but the stigma of the decertification
label remains.

52. Quoted in J. F. Holden-Rhodes, *Sharing the Secrets: Open Source Intelligence and the
War on Drugs* (Westport, CT: Praeger, 1997), 190.
53. Robinson and Scherlen, *Lies, Damned Lies*, 115.
54. Ibid., 123.
55. Ibid.

In reality, only a few countries are ever fully decertified, and these tend to be countries Washington has few ties to, such as Iran and Syria. Nevertheless, the certification process has powerfully conditioned the politics of drug war numbers. By establishing an annual review process that commands political attention and media coverage, the law guarantees that the anti-drug performance of foreign countries will be on Washington's radar screen. It reinforces the supply-side focus of U.S. anti-drug efforts, deflecting attention away from domestic demand for drugs and toward foreign supply.

Most important for this analysis, the certification process and its focus on foreign supply reduction has reinforced political and bureaucratic incentives to rely on misleading measures of cooperation. For example, because the certification process rewards the most immediate and visible operational "successes," such as arrests and seizures, drug-exporting countries tend to prioritize the law enforcement efforts that generate these results. Policy measures that have longer term but less visible and quantifiable effects, such as judicial reform, may be neglected. Regardless of what the drug war statistics actually indicate, a positive image of effort is what gets a passing grade in the certification game. As one U.S. official has candidly remarked in the case of Mexico, "If I were a Mexican official, I would do the same thing: give the Americans the statistics that will make them happy."[56] These statistics serve as ammunition to pacify Congressional critics. In 1997, the Clinton White House happily reported to Congress that "In each year since 1994, Mexico has increased the quantity of illegal drugs seized and led the world in destruction of illegal drug crops."[57]

Finally, it should be emphasized that questionable drug war statistics can also serve larger foreign policy objectives, as was the case in U.S.-Mexico relations and the political campaign for passage of the North American Free Trade Agreement (NAFTA) in the early 1990s. During Mexican president Carlos Salinas's six-year term in office, drug-related arrests nearly doubled, and prominent traffickers were jailed. Seizure levels rose sharply, prompting Mexican officials to boast that they were confiscating more drugs than any other country in the region. During Salinas's first year in office the government seized more drugs than in the previous six years combined.[58] During Salinas's term in office the State Department offered glowing reviews of Mexico's anti-drug record. Robert Gelbard, the State Department's top drug control official, told the Senate Foreign Relations

---

56. Author interview, Narcotics Affairs Section, U.S. Embassy, Mexico City, July 17, 1997.
57. White House Office of National Drug Control Policy, Report to Congress, Vol. 1, United States and Mexico Counterdrug Cooperation (Washington, D.C., September 1997), 3.
58. U.S. Department of State, "Department of State Dispatch," November 26, 1990, 294.

Committee in August 1995 that, under Salinas, "Mexican authorities seized over 247 metric tons of cocaine, made over 100,000 drug-related arrests, and eradicated 147,000 hectares of opium poppy and marijuana crops." Gelbard concluded that "these successes represent a substantial level of effort and a credible demonstration of political will."[59] As hoped, Mexico's anti-drug performance helped preserve the upbeat mood in U.S.-Mexican relations on the eve of the NAFTA vote.[60]

Ironically, the operational achievements of the U.S. and Mexican anti-drug campaigns during this time were actually aided by the size of the illegal drug trade. Well-publicized increases in seizures and arrests on both sides of the border were partly made possible by the fact that there were large quantities of drugs to seize and large numbers of smugglers to arrest. Similarly, record eradication levels were facilitated by bumper crops of marijuana and opium poppy. Moreover, impressive drug enforcement statistics masked the fact that the Mexican crackdown was selective: old guard smugglers were targeted, while the business of others was left untouched. Thus, record arrest and seizure statistics during the Salinas years did not lead to less smuggling but simply created openings for more aggressive and entrepreneurial smugglers on the rise.

Distorted evaluations and misleading indicators of effectiveness are not new in U.S. drug war politics. In 1973 the National Commission on Marijuana and Drug Abuse pointed out that the drug control "funding mechanism is so structured that it responds only when 'bodies' can be produced or counted. Such a structure penalizes a reduction in the body count, while it rewards any increase in incidence figures and arrest statistics with more money. Those receiving funds have a vested interest in increasing or maintaining those figures. The statistics, in turn, fuel public and bureaucratic concerns, and assure that the problem continues to be defined incorrectly." These kind of figures, concluded the commission, "are dramatic, but do not really tell what is happening." Increased numbers of arrests, for instance, "may simply mean more violators, rather than more effective enforcement." Similarly, "the quantities of drugs seized may reflect only the size of the illegal market."[61]

More than three decades later, the reliance on misleading measures of effectiveness persists, but the political stage on which they are displayed has

---

59. Testimony of Robert Gelbard, Assistant Secretary of State for International Narcotics and Law Enforcement Matters, Senate Committee on Foreign Relations, *The Drug Trade in Mexico and Its Implications for U.S.-Mexican Relations*, 104th Cong., 1st session, August 8, 1995, 67.

60. See Andreas, *Border Games*, 56–61.

61. National Commission on Marihuana and Drug Abuse, "Drug Use in America: Problem in Perspective, Second Report," Washington, D.C., 1973, 282, 227.

significantly expanded. In 1972 only two Senate committees and one House committee held hearings on proposed drug legislation; by the mid-1980s, drug policy cut across the jurisdiction of some twenty-four congressional committees and subcommittees. Consequently, congressional hearings have become an increasingly important forum for evaluating and promoting the federal anti-drug effort. Each hearing follows the same basic routine: the chair delivers an opening statement about the scourge of drugs, insisting that we must do more to stop drugs from crossing the nation's borders. Other committee members then offer their own variations on the same theme. These are followed by testimonies from drug enforcement officials, highlighting what their agencies have accomplished and what they hope to accomplish if more resources are forthcoming from Congress. Each agency is concerned only about showing the success of its discrete mission, rather than with the viability of the policy as a whole. Each has its own way of measuring and justifying its performance: Customs highlights seizures and arrests at the border ports of entry; the Drug Enforcement Administration prioritizes the capture of major traffickers; and the State Department stresses levels of bilateral cooperation. Poor results are blamed on mismanagement and insufficient resources. Improved results are assumed to come from more and better enforcement and international cooperation. And so the numbers game continues—regardless of its relationship to reducing the domestic availability of drugs or levels of drug consumption.

The drug war numbers game does not go entirely unchallenged. A 2001 National Research Council study on the role of research in drug policy concluded that it "is unconscionable for this country to continue to carry out a public policy of this magnitude and cost without any way of knowing whether and to what extent it is having the desired effect."[62] In 2003, the Office of Management and Budget concluded that the Drug Enforcement Administration "is unable to demonstrate its progress in reducing the availability of illegal drugs in the U.S." And in 2003 and 2004, the Office of Management and Budget gave the Coast Guard a "results not demonstrated" rating on drug interdiction, noting that there is "no clear link between the annual goal of total amount of drugs seized and the long-term goals of reduction in use."[63] Yet such skeptical assessments are rare and receive relatively little attention in the policy debate.

Given the importance of the numbers game in fighting drugs, it is understandable how some of the producers of the numbers can become deeply cynical about their work. One DEA agent describes his desk job in the

62. Quoted in Walsh, *Are We There Yet?* 16.
63. Quoted in ibid., 16.

Latin American unit at headquarters: "The other half of the job is makin' up fact sheets and briefing papers—you know, statistical bullshit, how we're winnin' the war—so one of these clowns can go on TV or testify before Congress." When asked where he got the statistics, he laughed. "Outta yer head, where else?"[64]

Conclusion

To "make crime count," Kevin Haggerty reminds us, "involves transforming crime and the criminal justice system into something that can be counted."[65] Nowhere is this more evident than in the effort to quantify illicit cross-border flows and efforts to police such flows—however misleading and distorting such quantitative endeavors may be. This chapter has provided a brief sketch of the use and abuse of problematic "data" about various illicit transnational flows, and the politics of measuring policy effectiveness in the case of international drug control.

Illicit flows are both fascinating and frustrating to study. The poor quality of the data is no doubt an important part of the explanation for why more researchers do not study the illicit world. The subject matter obviously does not lend itself to the type of "large N" quantitative studies that are increasingly favored by many mainstream journals in various disciplines, including political science and sociology. A typical tenure-seeking economist or international relations scholar will understandably opt to focus on legal trade and foreign direct investment patterns rather than the illicit drug trade and narco-investment patterns. The availability of data and the quality of the data (rather than, say, an interesting research question or empirical puzzle) tends to drive research projects in disciplines that increasingly privilege and reward quantitative work. For more qualitatively oriented scholars, such as ethnographers, the poor quality of the aggregate data is much less consequential, but access to interview subjects and other research materials in the illicit world presents its own distinct obstacles and challenges, including potentially finding oneself in risky and even dangerous situations.[66]

64. Michael Levine with Laura Kavanau-Levine, *Big White Lie: The CIA and the Cocaine/Crack Epidemic* (New York: Thunder's Mouth Press, 1993), 129.

65. Kevin D. Haggerty, *Making Crime Count* (Toronto: University of Toronto Press, 2001), 3.

66. Though field research on illicit flows can be difficult, it is not impossible. For some recent examples of the type of research possible in this area, see Kamal Sadiq, *Paper Citizens: How Illegal Immigrants Acquire Citizenship in Developing Countries* (New York: Oxford University Press, 2009); and Ko-Lin Chin, *The Golden Triangle: Inside Southeast Asia's Drug Trade* (Ithaca: Cornell University Press, 2009).

These practical limitations are the Achilles heel of research in this area. But while bad data and their highly politicized nature understandably inhibit more quality scholarship on illicit flows, it is the political use and misuse of such data in the policy evaluation process and in media reporting that should attract much more public scrutiny and scholarly inquiry. The point here is not that we should throw up our hands in frustration and conclude that the illicit world should be ignored and cannot be studied simply because it cannot adequately be quantified. Doing so would be the equivalent of the drunkard looking for his keys under the lightpost because it is the only place he can see.

3

Trafficking in Numbers

THE SOCIAL CONSTRUCTION
OF HUMAN TRAFFICKING DATA

David A. Feingold

—I didn't have any accurate numbers, so I just made this one up.
Studies have shown that accurate numbers aren't any more useful
than the ones you make up.
—How many studies showed that?
—Eighty-seven.

Dilbert

Statistics are like a bikini. What they reveal is suggestive, but
what they conceal is vital.

Aaron Levenstein

I have researched the issue of human trafficking for over a decade. In
that time, I have seen it move from a relatively arcane subject of study
and concern to a favorite topic for college term papers, movies, and MTV

The author thanks the editors, Peter Andreas and Kelly M. Greenhill, the Watson Institute
for International Studies at Brown University, and his fellow participants for stimulating and
insightful comments. This chapter is part of ongoing research into the trade in minority girls
and women from Yunnan, China; Burma (Myanmar); and Laos into Thailand. Research for
this project has been conducted under grants from the John D. and Catherine T. MacArthur
Foundation, the Else Sackler Foundation, and the Spunk Fund, Inc. The project has received
ongoing support from the United Nations Educational, Scientific and Cultural Organization
(UNESCO). The UNESCO Trafficking & HIV/AIDS Project, which I direct, has received
support from the UN Inter-Agency Project on Human Trafficking in the Greater Mekong
Sub-region (UNIAP), the United Nations Joint Programme on HIV/AIDS (UNAIDS), the
Asian Development Bank (ADB), the U.S. Centers for Disease Control, and the U.K. Embassy, Bangkok. Earlier research on opium production, trade, and use was conducted under
grants from the U.S. National Institute of Mental Health (NIMH), the National Institute on
Drug Abuse (NIDA), and the National Endowment for the Humanities (NEH). The author
thanks these organizations for their generous support. The ideas presented in this chapter do
not purport to represent the views of any of these institutions.

specials. I have watched as the topic of human trafficking has evolved from being a source of surprise for many officials, to being labeled "the number three illicit industry, behind drugs and small arms," to being labeled "second only to illegal drugs" in terms of criminal profit.[1] The value of the global trade in persons has been estimated by the United Nations Office on Drugs and Crime (UNODC) to be $7 billion annually and by the United Nations Children's Fund (UNICEF) to be $10 billion. The International Labour Organization (ILO) estimates the total illicit profits of trafficked forced laborers at just under $32 billion for one year, or about one-tenth of the estimates for the drug trade.[2] Except for a brief explanation by the ILO, it is not clear how these figures were derived. It is crystal clear, however, that in the case of human trafficking, no one really knows the true value of the trade. The trafficking field is best characterized as one of numerical certainty and statistical doubt. Trafficking numbers provide the false precision of quantification, while lacking any of the supports of statistical rigor.

This chapter analyzes how information on human trafficking comes to be constructed as data, and how these data do—or do not—inform policy. Based on research on trafficking in the Mekong region, the chapter explores the perpetuation of trafficking myths and the disjunction between international policies and trafficking realities. The chapter seeks to understand human trafficking as a process, rather than an event, and proposes an alternative epidemiological approach to tracking and comprehending a shifting phenomenon.

Illicit Economies: Some Similarities, But Significant Differences

Human trafficking is often likened to drug trafficking. The analogizing of human trafficking networks to drug trafficking networks has both a rhetorical and administrative appeal for many governments and international agencies. Were it true, it would mean that "kingpins" could be targeted, networks disrupted, and a few high profile cases could act as a deterrent to lessen the problem. This is an enforcement-based model that is well understood, even if few of the victories in the Drug War have led to any sort of lasting peace. Despite a gradual commitment to "alternative development"— sometimes more apparent than real—drug control is still seen as a law enforcement issue. It is not surprising, therefore, that the problem tends to

1. Wildlife trade advocates have been making competing claims for the number two spot, but do not seem to have gained traction so far.
2. David A. Feingold, "Think Again: Human Trafficking," *Foreign Policy* 150 (2005): 26–32.

get personified. A "kingpin" will be designated, and the belief promulgated that his capture will strike an irreparable blow to the drug trade. This has certainly not proved to be the case in the so-called Golden Triangle of opium in Southeast Asia. The decline of one "King of Opium" has only led to the rise of another.[3] Nevertheless, it is clear that the trade in illicit drugs flows through a variety of sophisticated and adaptive networks.[4]

Despite the quest for likely criminal masterminds of human trafficking, their existence remains elusive. Lo Hsing-han, Khun Sa, or any of the subsequent players in the Burmese drug trade did not traffick in people—jade, yes, but not people. In fact, with the exception of Thai women smuggled to Japan through Yakuza—Japanese organized crime—networks, most human trafficking is undertaken less by organized crime than by disorganized crime—at least in the Mekong region. If anything, networks such as the *Luk Moo* (Piglets) and the *Kabuankarn Loy Fah* (Floating in the Sky) have become less significant in the last decade.[5] Zhang and Chin draw similar conclusions from their study of Chinese human smuggling into the United States:

> Contrary to widely held conceptions about Chinese organized crime, most smugglers of human beings are otherwise ordinary citizens whose family networks and fortuitous social contacts have led them to take part in a profitable trade…They are loosely connected and form temporary alliances to carry out smuggling operations. With the exception of a shared commitment to money, there is little that holds them together.[6]

Trafficking: Modern Day Slavery, or Migration Gone Wrong?

A nearly endless string of international meetings have concluded that trafficking is "a modern form of slavery" and a "world-wide scourge," reducing what once might have been an insightful metaphor to a cliché.[7]

---

3. It was the arrest of Lo Hsing-han by Thai authorities in 1973 that allowed Khun Sa to gain control of the Shan opium trade. Similarly, Khun Sa's retirement had very limited impact on the scope of the drug trade.

4. For a discussion of these networks in the opium trade, see David A. Feingold, "Kings, Princes and Mountaineers: Ethnicity, Opium and the State on the Burma Border," paper presented at the Social Science Research Council Beyond Borders Conference, Centre d'Etudes et de Recherches Internationales (CERI), Paris, July, 2000.

5. David A. Feingold, "Sex, Drugs, and the IMF: Some Implications of 'Structural Readjustment' for the Trade in Heroin, Girls, and Women in the Upper Mekong Region," *New Cargo: The Global Business of Trafficking in Women (a special issue of Refuge)* 17 (1998): 4–10.

6. Sheldon Zhang and Ko Lin Chin, "Chinese Human Smuggling in the United States of America," *Forum on Crime and Society* 1 (2001): 31–52.

7. Though this phrase has become something of a cliché through repetition, it was not when first used in 1993 in an Asia Watch report. Asia Watch, *A Modern Form of Slavery: Trafficking Burmese Women and Girls into Brothels in Thailand* (New York: Asia Watch, 1993).

The identification of trafficking with chattel slavery—in particular, the transatlantic slave trade—is tenuous at best. In the eighteenth and nineteenth centuries, African slaves were kidnapped or captured in war. They were shipped to the New World into life-long servitude, from which they or their children could rarely escape. In contrast, although some trafficking victims are kidnapped, for most in the Mekong region, trafficking is migration gone terribly wrong.[8] Most leave their homes voluntarily—though sometimes coerced by circumstance—in search of a materially better or more exciting life.[9] Along the way, they become enmeshed in a coercive and exploitative situation. However, this situation rarely persists for life; nor, in Southeast Asia, do the trafficked become a permanent or hereditary caste.

Moreover, the term *slavery* in English refers to a variety of complex social and political relationships that existed in various societies in different parts of the world at different times, which entitled or allowed one person or group of people to exercise control over another person or group of people. The institutions of slavery in China and Southeast Asia were quite different from that in Africa at the time of the transatlantic trade, as well as at different historical periods.

F. W. Mote's discussion of social categories in China under the Southern Song Dynasty (1127–1279) highlights the complexity of applying the current understanding of *slavery* to China:

> China indeed had bound servants, but they...were not legally confined to that status; they could work their way out of it. There were also still poorer people; the very poor in China might become so desperate in times of famine or disorder that they would "sell" children, even occasionally adults, to richer neighbors who would take them into their families as servants or, in some cases, wives, or even (usually by deceiving the parents) to be reared in houses of prostitution. In neither the Chinese legal definition nor the popular consciousness, however, were such miserable humans chattel; they were not mere property. Their status is sometimes mistranslated as "slave," but that misrepresents the situation.[10]

Mote goes on to note that they had basic rights and could "quite realistically" work their way out of the situation.[11]

8. David A. Feingold, *Trading Women*, 77-minute edition (Philadelphia: Ophidian Films, 2005), documentary film.

9. For an interesting discussion of the complexity and limitations of the slavery metaphor as applied to Britain, see Julia O'Connell Davidson, "Will the Real Sex Slave Please Stand Up?" *Feminist Review* 83 (2006): 4–22.

10. Frederick W. Mote, *Imperial China: 900–1800* (Cambridge: Harvard University Press, 1999), 366.

11. For another view, see also Edwin G. Pulleybank, "The Origins and Nature of Chattel Slavery in China," *Journal of Economic and Social History of the Orient* 1 (1958): 185–220.

In addition, the patterns of the end of slavery in various societies were quite diverse as was the impact of the end of slavery as well. In Thailand, for example, an unintended consequence of the abolition of slavery was a large-scale increase in prostitution as former female slaves sought to support themselves.

Yet, regardless of the analytic accuracy of equating trafficking with "modern day slavery," there can be no question of its advocacy-related appeal. Trafficking is clearly the flavor of the month, forcing its way up the public agenda. Funding has poured into combating trafficking. NGOs that previously cared for battered women refashioned themselves as "trafficking NGOs" to heighten their attractiveness vis-à-vis funding. Some "faith-based" groups had full faith that, given sufficient funding, they could come up with a divine plan to end the problem. Many Beltway bandit companies, whose previous experience was not getting things built in Iraq or only occasionally detecting explosives at airports, desperately hunted for consultant resumés to lend credibility to their newly minted trafficking expertise.[12] The *Washington Post* revealed that "the Bush administration has paid the public relations firm, Ketchum, $12 million as part of the government's outreach program" to find victims of trafficking.[13]

A new trafficking bill, the "William Wilberforce Trafficking Victims Protection Reauthorization Act of 2008" (H.R. 3887), which passed the House, would have remedied any shortage of victims. In the words of the *Washington Post*, the new "anti-human trafficking bill would send the FBI agents on the trail of pimps"[14] and in essence federalize prostitution prosecutions.[15] The Department of Justice objected to the bill for several reasons, most significantly because of the expansion of federal responsibility into law enforcement areas traditionally reserved for states. For their pains, they were accused by Ambassador John Miller, former head of the State Department Office to Monitor and Combat Trafficking in Persons office, of being "blind to slavery."[16]

---

12. I—and a number of people I know in the field—have been contacted by such companies.

13. Jerry Markon, "Human Trafficking Evokes Outrage, Little Evidence," *Washington Post,* September 23, 2007.

14. Jerry Markon, "Human Trafficking Bill Would Send FBI Agents on Trail of Pimps," *Washington Post,* November 29, 2007.

15. A related Senate Bill (S.3601), which is less expansive, was pending. On July 9, 2008, the Department of Justice sent a twelve-page letter to Sen. Patrick Leahy, Chairman of the Judiciary Committee, outlining its critique of the Senate version of the bill. The bill that eventually became law was more limited.

16. John Miller, "The Justice Department Blind to Slavery," *New York Times,* July 11, 2008, op-ed.

No Number Too High: Counting on Sex

Early on, *prostitution* was frequently conflated with trafficking. Exaggerated numbers abounded. In 1997, the organization End Child Prostitution, Child Pornography, and Trafficking of Children for Sexual Purposes (ECPAT) claimed there were 800,000 child prostitutes in Thailand (a figure that, to their credit, they now disown).[17] Other NGOs and journalists were claiming that there were 4 million sex workers in Thailand. However, had this number been correct, it would have meant that 24 percent of the female population of Thailand between the ages of ten and thirty-nine was engaged in commercial sex work—an unlikely proposition at best.[18]

As is the current case with overall trafficking numbers, there was a fear that any attempt to indicate that the figures for children in prostitution were inflated might lead to less willingness to address what was a very real and significant problem. I have been at many meetings with international organizations, activists, and NGOs where people have discussed the "advocacy value of numbers" and their importance for "mobilization." There is no area of trafficking that attracts more attention than child trafficking, and no area can compete for attention with child trafficking for sexual exploitation. Children—considered by the UN Convention on the Rights of the Child as anyone under eighteen years of age—are, by definition, innocent victims. This legally designated innocence shields us from the vexing questions of agency, motivation, consent, and the nature and extent of exploitation that frequently complicate adult victim identification. Governments tend to demand a clear line between illegal, economic migrants, on the one hand, and innocent trafficking victims on the other hand. They are uncomfortable with gray areas. Therefore, policies said to address the uniquely repellant sexual trafficking of children are sheltered from critical evaluation.[19] Moreover, there is often great reluctance to accept data that calls into question the scale and trend of the problem.

In a very important study, Simon Baker found that demographic changes in Northern Thailand had led to families investing more in girls' education and, contrary to what was frequently asserted, more girls than boys went on to secondary school. Also contrary to common assertion, the number

---

17. Despite the best efforts of the current incarnation of ECPAT, it still reappears in print from time to time.

18. See David A. Feingold, "The Hell of Good Intentions: Some Preliminary Thoughts on Opium in the Political Ecology of the Trade in Girls and Women," in *South China and Mainland Southeast Asia: Cross Border Relations in the Post-Socialist Age*, ed. Grant Evans (New York: St. Martin's Press, 2000).

19. It must be noted that a number of countries do not even provide adequate victim protection to children.

of underage female sex workers had decreased.[20] "The number of Northern Thai children at risk of becoming victims of child prostitution has declined substantially over the last 20 years. Thai children are fewer both in absolute numbers and as a proportion of the total population, and are better educated than two decades earlier. Girls, who would have sought employment, including in the sex industry, are now far more likely to be studying."[21]

In 2000, many NGOs expressed concern that Baker's findings would undermine their attempts to mobilize support for attacking child prostitution. Others felt that it could be used to diminish pressure on Thailand to comply with U.S. Trafficking in Persons (TIP) standards. Baker notes, "It must be stressed that the views expressed in this report are controversial. At a presentation to a group of NGO officials working with children in Chiangwat Chiang Rai the findings were attacked. At the beginning of the meeting only one person out of 25 people thought that the number of children entering prostitution was declining. The difference between the views of the 24 people and what is expressed in this report are marked."[22]

Numbers No One Can Count On

In 2003, I initiated the UNESCO Trafficking Statistics Project with Cecilia Khilstrand. We began this project because we were constantly beset by oft-repeated and contradictory numbers, cited without provenance or methodology. At the time, I wrote for the UNESCO website, "When it comes to statistics, trafficking of girls and women is one of several highly emotive issues which seem to overwhelm critical faculties."[23] Numbers take on a life of their own, gaining acceptance through repetition, often with little inquiry into their derivations. Journalists—bowing to the pressures of editors—demand numbers, any numbers. Organizations feel compelled to supply them, lending false precision and spurious authority to many reports. The UNESCO Trafficking Statistics Project is a first step toward clarifying what we know, what we think we know, and what we do not know about trafficking.[24]

---

20. Simon Baker, *The Changing Situation of Child Prostitution in Northern Thailand: A Study of Chiangwat Chiang Rai* (Bangkok: ECPAT International, 2000), 30; and Simon Baker, *"Child Labour" and Child Prostitution in Thailand: Changing Realities* (Bangkok: White Lotus, 2007).

21. Baker, *"Child Labour,"* 125.

22. Ibid.

23. Illicit drug production, trafficking, and use are others.

24. The UNESCO Trafficking Statistics Project is available at http://www.unescobkk.org/index.php?id=1022.

The object of the project is to collect published statistics on trafficking and related issues (commercial sexual exploitation, labor exploitation and forced labor, forced marriage, undocumented migration, etc.), and attempt to trace them back to their original source. In addition, we attempt to ascertain the empirical and methodological bases for the numbers—where possible.

Over the years, what we have found in the trafficking field could be called numerical certainty and statistical doubt. That is, bald statements are made with great force: "There are 1.2 million children in sexual slavery" (UNICEF)[25]; "5,000 girls are trafficked each year between Nepal and India" (numerous sources)[26]; "600,000 to 800,000 people are trafficked worldwide each year" (U.S. government).[27] However, there is almost never any indication as to either the provenance or the basis for the figures.

Before the U.S. government lowered its figures from 700,000 to 2 million people trafficked worldwide to 600,000 to 800,000 people, Pino Arlacchi, the former head of UNODC, gave a speech. In what was a very bad day for trafficking victims, he stated that the number of trafficking victims was 4 million. In the subsequent reports using this statistic, the figure was attributed to him; then, to UNODC; and finally, it became, the UN estimates. Figure 3.1 compares worldwide estimates that clearly show the broad range of figures.

Does It Matter?

An obvious question is: do global trafficking numbers matter? And if yes, at what order of magnitude do they make a difference? Even given the lip service paid to "evidence-based programming" and "results-based management," would policy be significantly different if the true figure at one point in time were 600,000, rather than 800,000—or even 4 million persons? Moreover, if the experience of the period from 1997 to the present

25. The UNICEF figures are repeated in a variety of places, slightly modified, e.g., "Factsheet: Child Protection": "An Estimate 1.2 Million Children Are Trafficked Every Year"; and UNICEF Press Centre, "Facts on Children" (updated 2008): "According to the latest estimates in for 2002, some 1.2 million children are trafficked worldwide every year." (This is more than the State Department figure for children and adults combined.)

26. This figure derives from a 1986 NGO seminar, was published in the *Times of India* on January 2, 1989, and has been cited ever since. It may or may not have been correct in 1986, but is unlikely to have remained the same for two decades—particularly in light of an article in the March 5, 2005 edition of the *Times of India,* which claimed that women trafficking was "growing by leaps and bounds." Arun Kumar Das, "Women-Trafficking Growing by Leaps and Bounds," *Times of India,* March 5, 2005.

27. U.S. Department of State, *Trafficking in Persons Report 2006* (Washington, DC: GPO, 2006).

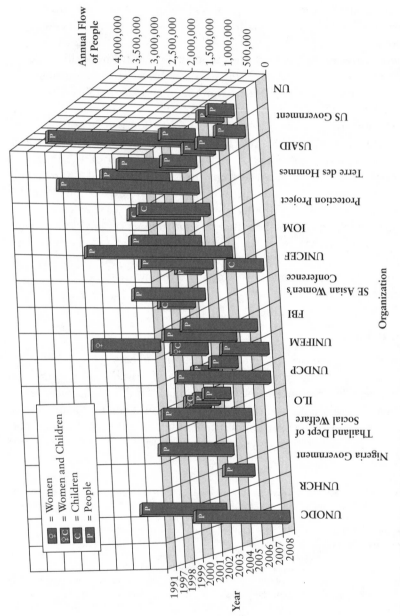

Figure 3.1. Worldwide trafficking estimates by organizations
Source: UNESCO Trafficking Project, www.unescobkk.org/culture/trafficking

(2009) has shown anything, it is that trafficking and related issues must be dealt with regionally, rather than with a one-size-fits-all global approach. The situation in Moldova is not that of Burma; the problems of Indonesia do not neatly map onto those of Thailand.

> The question of whether global estimates of the scale of trafficking in humans serve any serious policy purposes should be posed. For other serious crimes, such as homicide, assault, or rape, global estimates are usually not given even though there are considerable problems with the data in some regions of the world. The global estimates on the numbers of persons involved in trafficking are always vague and cannot serve as a reliable knowledge base for policy planning. Thus it remains questionable whether this type of information is needed at all.[28]

I believe it is quite clear that global estimates of trafficking do not "serve any serious policy purposes." However, they do serve a socio-political purpose: to advocate for and justify the expenditure of resources. These data are not policy responsive. Sanghera (among others) has pointed out that regardless of upward or downward adjustment of figures, the "problem is always 'rapidly increasing.'"[29] Here is one more example from the website of an otherwise reliable NGO:

> The UN estimates that approximately 1 million girls [not women] are forced into the commercial sex industry each year. This is occurring in almost every country, including the United States. These girls are sold by their families for money, tricked into going with the promise of a job or marriage, or kidnapped and forcefully taken away. They are taken to brothels where they are raped and abused into submission and then are forced to have sex with as many as 30 men each day, usually without any type of protection. According to UNICEF statistics, the sex trafficking industry exploits children alone to the tune of $10 billion a year.[30]

Questions abound: Where did these figures come from? How were they derived? If 1 million girls are forced into the sex industry each year, how many leave? For how long have 1 million girls each year been forced into the sex industry? Ten years? Twenty? Thirty?

---

28. Kristiina Kangaspunta, "Mapping the Inhuman Trade: Preliminary Findings of the Database on Trafficking in Human Beings," *Forum on Crime and Society* 3 (2003): 84.

29. Jyoti Sanghera, "Unpacking the Trafficking Discourse," in *Trafficking and Prostitution Reconsidered: New Perspectives on Migration, Sex Work, and Human Rights*, ed. Kamala Kempadoo, Jyoti Sanghera, and Bandana Pattanaik (Boulder, CO: Paradigm, 2005).

30. The Population Media Center, http://www.populationmedia.org/issues/child-protection/.

The search for global data can best be characterized as the pursuit of the unknowable by the unknowing. It would be hoped that local figures would be more accurate, at least in the United States. Given that few countries have the same commitment to attacking trafficking as the United States, coupled with the resources to act on that commitment, one would expect that data in the United States would be equal or superior to other countries. The United States has "mobilized political will at the highest level," and has dynamic and active civil society support, a legal framework in place, relatively uncorrupt federal judiciary and prosecutorial service, and an engaged public media—all the elements that it seeks but rarely finds in its partner countries abroad. Even individual U.S. states are passing laws to outlaw trafficking, although in some cases it seems unlikely that they are addressing much of an unmet need. Nevertheless, there is little basis for confidence in U.S. local figures.

In fairness, the U.S. government has been trying to refine its guesstimates. At the beginning of the decade, the State Department's report "estimated that 45,000 to 50,000 people were trafficked into the United States each year and forced into labor or prostitution. Those estimates dropped over the following years, first from 18,000 to 20,000 in State's 2003 report, and then from 14,500 to 17,000 in the 2004 and 2005 reports."[31]

However, if we assume that trafficking into the United States has not increased significantly in the face of dramatically stepped up efforts to counter it, it is not unreasonable to assume that the level of trafficking has been approximately the same from 1999 to 2009. This should mean that there are somewhere between 145,000 and 200,000 victims of human trafficking in the United States.

Certainly, there have been many attempts to portray the country as awash in trafficked women. Rarely is there as much excitement about exploited migrant farm workers. The *frisson* of sex slaves down the street in suburbia is too good to pass up. In 2004, the *New York Times Magazine* titillated their Sunday readers with Peter Landesman's story, "The Girls Next Door."[32]

After noting that cybernetworks like KaZaA and Morpheus "have become the Mexican border of virtual sexual exploitation," Landesman gives us the following memorable scene:

> I had heard of one Web site that supposedly offered sex slaves for purchase to individuals. The [Immigration and Customs Enforcement] agents hadn't heard of it. Special Agent Don Daufenbach, I.C.E.'s manager for undercover

31. Jack Shafer, "The Sex-Slavery Epidemic That Wasn't: Revisiting the Numbers behind the New York Times Magazine's Sex-Slave Story," *Slate,* September 24, 2007.

32. Peter Landesman, "The Girls Next Door," *New York Times Magazine,* January 25, 2004.

operations, brought it up on a screen. A hush came over the room as the agents leaned forward, clearly disturbed. "That sure looks like the real thing," Daufenbach said. There were streams of Web pages of thumbnail images of young women of every ethnicity in obvious distress, bound, gagged, contorted. The agents in the room pointed out probable injuries from torture. *Cyberauctions for some of the women were in progress; one had exceeded $300,000.*[33]

I have no doubt that the images were repugnant; the more so if trained observers believed the images to be representations of actual sadistic behavior. However, there are some other questions that come up. For example, how exactly does the cyberauction work on this sexual eBay? First, for eBay to maximize profit, an auction must attract as many potential bidders as possible. To do that, it must be as public as possible, unless one pictures some James Bond style auction to select rich evildoers. If the auction is public, why does law enforcement not shut it down? As far as we know, the owners of the site and the bidders were not prosecuted. On a more mundane level, how do you pay $300,000 at a cyberauction—a really big PayPal account? Finally, and not to put too fine a point on it, it would be an interesting ethnomethodological experiment to waive a certified check for $300,000 on a university campus to see if one could acquire two (or more) willing slaves for the same price.

The point here is that the mere mention of "trafficking" and "sex slavery" seems to dull critical sensibility—even for the fact-checked *New York Times*. As with other moral panics, people are so appalled by the enormity of the crime that they do not question whether it is occurring—and if so, whether it is occurring on the scale that is alleged.[34]

What has been spoken of privately by government officials and social service providers has now become public. In September 2007, the *Washington Post* published a story called "Human Trafficking Evokes Outrage, Little Evidence." As a result of its investigation, it maintained: "None of the estimates offered by activists—or the government—now seem remotely accurate. The *Post* reported that despite dispatching 42 Justice Department task forces to address the human-trafficking problem, only 1,362 victims of human trafficking brought into the United States have been identified since 2000. Efforts to reach victims of sex slavery continue."[35]

Whenever questions are raised about the inadequacy of human trafficking numbers, the response is that trafficking is a hidden phenomenon

33. Ibid. (emphasis added).

34. See also Ronald Weitzer, "The Social Construction of Sex Trafficking: Ideology and Institutionalization of a Moral Crusade," *Politics and Society* 35 (2007): 447–75.

35. Markon, "Human Trafficking Evokes Outrage."

because it is illegal. There is no question that research on underground trades—whether drugs, guns, or girls—is difficult, particularly when quantitative or extensive research is the focus.[36] However, this is often used to justify accepting whatever bizarre notions are put forward as fact. For example, after the 2004 Asian Tsunami, there was a hew and cry about orphans trafficked from Indonesia's Aceh Province and other areas affected by the Tsunami into prostitution. I was contacted by CNN, two units at ABC, and a producer for Oprah—all of whom heard, "it was happening." In fact, investigations by the UN have yet to identify a single confirmed case of sex trafficking in these areas.[37]

In a similar vein, the 2006 World Cup in Germany produced another candidate for "The Chicken Little Award." NGOs warned against "40,000 women being trafficked" into Germany to fulfill the base desires of soccer fans. At the time, a Google search of "trafficking + World Cup" produced some 1.9 million hits. A female member of the Swedish parliament called on the Swedish team to boycott the Cup. Porta-potty brothels were allegedly being set up to service the rabid fans.

Typical in tone was an op-ed in the *Washington Post* written by workers for the Polaris Project, saucily titled, "Soccer with a Side of Slavery":

> As the 2006 World Cup games get underway in Germany, tourists and soccer fans are being joined at the various competition venues by denizens of an international world of crime where human beings are bought and sold for profit. Human trafficking is the third-largest criminal industry in the world, after arms and drugs. While soccer fans anticipate the excitement of the games, many of us in the anti-trafficking movement are deeply troubled by the expected surge of sex trafficking in Germany to meet the demand for commercial sex associated with the World Cup. It is estimated that more than 40,000 women and children will be imported to Germany during the month-long competition to provide commercial sex in the "mega-brothels," "quickie shacks," other legalized venues and vast underground networks that exist in Germany.[38]

Congress called on the State Department to take action. The State Department dispatched local Foreign Service officers to investigate. They

---

36. Though it is not within the bounds of this chapter to elaborate on my ideas on intensive versus extensive research methodologies, I should note that I prefer this distinction to the more common one of "qualitative" versus "quantitative." Many ethnographic studies use quantitative indicators, but these have the advantage of being deeply contextualized. See, for example, Lisa R. Taylor, "Dangerous Trade-Offs: The Behavioral Ecology of Child Labor and Prostitution in Rural Northern Thailand," *Current Anthropology* 46 (2005): 411–31.

37. Feingold, "Think Again."

38. Katherine Chon and Derek Ellerman, "Soccer with a Side of Slavery," *Washington Post,* June 10, 2006.

found that it was easier to get bratwurst than sex at most of the places being set up. The origin of the endlessly repeated figure of 40,000 was never clear, but if repetition equaled veracity, it was the most reliable number around.

A detailed study by the International Organization for Migration (IOM)[39] found no evidence of any increase in either prostitution or trafficking as a result of the World Cup.[40] The report concluded, "the estimate of 40,000 women expected to be trafficked was unfounded and unrealistic."[41]

The activists claimed that the lack of trafficking in Germany was only because they raised the alarm. Similarly, I was at a meeting where a representative from UNICEF claimed that tsunami orphans were not trafficked because UNICEF raised the alarm.

The IOM report also pointed to structural reasons why trafficking for the World Cup was unlikely: "Trafficking in human beings is a process that requires prior logistics and investment on the part of the traffickers— possibly a short and one-time event like the World Cup in Germany was not perceived as sufficiently profitable for the traffickers in this respect."[42]

Past cries of wolf have not proved discouraging, however. The 2008 Beijing Olympics attracted alarming warnings of girls to be trafficked to satisfy lustful sports fans. The same warnings are being issued about the 2010 World Cup in South Africa. "Criminals see gold at Olympics—organized crime, adept at human trafficking, aims to flood Beijing with prostitutes," warns the *Toronto Star*. "It's not just the gymnasts, grapplers and jumpers who are worth watching at this summer's Beijing Olympics," a British organized crime expert says. "It's also the prostitutes—or lack of them."[43] Given the extreme security measures China took to control even legitimate access to the Olympics and surrounding venues, the flood was more likely a trickle. Visa restrictions were notably tightened, even for UN personnel; long-planned international meetings were cancelled or postponed; and in some areas, local officials were instructed not to travel outside of their province. Of course, it might have turned out that a torrent of trafficked women would wash over Beijing, but it seemed unlikely. There is no evidence it took place. Moreover, this emphasis on forced prostitution and sexual exploitation, though attention grabbing, diverts attention from the

---

39. International Organization for Migration, *Trafficking in Human Beings and the World Cup in Germany* (Geneva: IOM, 2007).

40. "Report: No Rise in Human Trafficking in Germany Due to World Cup," *Associated Press*, July 15, 2006.

41. IOM, *Trafficking in Human Beings*, 5.

42. Ibid., 6.

43. "Criminals see gold at Olympics—Organized Crime, Adept at Human Trafficking, Aims to Flood Beijing with Prostitutes," *Toronto Star*, May 4, 2008.

very real human costs of population displacement by the Olympics and other mega-projects in China.

Regardless of what might—or might not—have happened in Beijing that summer, London is already steeling itself for its own trafficking blitz in 2012. Nigel Morris wrote for *The Independent*, "The London Olympics are being targeted by criminal gangs behind the multi-billion pound international trade in sex slaves and illegal workers, police have warned."[44]

How the police became privy to this targeting knowledge is said, of course, to involve sources and methods that cannot be divulged. However, given that the London Olympics were five years off when the article was written, the above-mentioned criminal gangs seem better attuned to long-horizon strategic planning than many corporate CEOs. Fortunately, with so much advanced warning, the authorities should be well placed to fight the traffickers in the streets and on the beaches—and, perhaps, even at the airports and train terminals. Yet, regardless of the severity, scale, or reality of the problem, one can be quite sure that the response will be judged to have been a very fine hour, indeed.

The tragic and deadly cyclone that struck Burma in May 2008 led to a virtual replay of the tsunami trafficking scenario. According to an *Agence France-Presse* report, a spokeswoman for UNICEF said that "the most vulnerable" families without access to aid could "be tempted to sell their children."[45] The same story said that "aid groups had also warned that traffickers are targeting youngsters in crowded camps." The story was repeated widely around the world.

The reality was quite different. Because the storm destroyed both roads and boats in the area, the worst affected areas of the delta were inaccessible. It is therefore not clear to whom the children could be sold—even assuming that the parents were willing. In fact, there was no evidence that the sale of children was taking place. Investigation by various agencies turned up one suspicious recruitment that took place in one Rangoon township—not in the hardest hit region.

Yet despite little or no evidence for any increased trafficking due to the cyclone, the story was certainly good for fund-raising. Take, for example, this e-mail appeal sent out by the *Not For Sale* campaign:

> *The Crisis in Burma continues....* Today in Myanmar, 2.5 million people cling to survival after the disaster that hit two weeks ago. The latest state

---

44. Nigel Morris, "London Olympics Targeted by Trade in Sex Trafficking and Illegal Workers," *The Independent*, March 24, 2007.

45. "Child Cyclone Victims Open to Risks of Disease, Other Abuse: UN," *Agence France-Presse*, May 16, 2008.

television update in former Burma has declared the death toll after the May 2nd cyclone to be 77,738 people. Another 55,917 are still reported missing. Thousands swarm the roadsides of a country void of the foreign aid it so desperately needs. Children, destitute and orphaned, are picked up by vicious traffickers prowling the disaster area.

This week, David Batstone travels to Myanmar to approach the crisis situation. Last Fall, Not For Sale partnered with Thai Abolitionist Kru Nam to build a shelter for 125 kids rescued out of the sex trade industry. Today, she implores us to intervene again as Burmese children trafficked into Thailand are being rampantly sold.... *It's time to build a shelter, and it's time to act fast.* Not For Sale, this week, has partnered with a foundation that will match EVERY DOLLAR we donate, up to $25,000. Our goal is to raise $50K in the next two weeks. The shelter will be on the border between former Burma and Thailand, and will provide the critical care necessary to rescue Burmese orphans out of slavery. Kru Nam's village, as is, cannot support one of the growing needs in this crisis. But together, we believe we can raise enough money that can. *DONATE now. Every dollar you give is worth two. Join the call to action in this crisis.*

How "the vicious traffickers" were managing to "prowl the disaster area" and extract the children is not made clear, especially because both rare news footage and relief agency reports showed how difficult it was to move through the region. It is also unclear how aiding Kru (Teacher) Nam's shelter on the Thai border—however worthy it might be—will be of much use to children in the disaster zone that are unlikely ever to reach it.[46] Kru Nam's shelter is outside of Mae Sai, the northernmost town in Thailand. To traffic children from the delta of Lower Burma to the north of Thailand would be difficult at most times; given the disruption of transport and infrastructure caused by the cyclone, it is highly problematic.

This is not to question the sincerity of the majority of those claiming to be concerned with providing protection to potentially vulnerable populations, although some of the crusading rhetoric can seem more than a bit self-serving. More significant, however, there is frequently a flight from complexity. There seems to be an almost overwhelming craving for a simple narrative of innocence debauched, a wrong that can be righted by the apprehension of an evildoer.[47] As noted above, most governments crave certifiably innocent victims—those without agency, easily identifiable and easily distinguishable from detested (but often necessary) economic

---

46. In a later e-mail, the Not For Sale campaign announced that it had reached its goal.

47. For a more detailed discussion of trafficking discourses, see David A. Feingold, "Virgin Territory: Ethnographic Insight, Public Policy, and the Trade in Minority Women in Southeast Asia," in *Ethnography and Policy: What Do We Know about Trafficking?*, ed. Carole Vance (Santa Fe: School of American Research, 2007).

migrants. It has been very difficult to educate governments to accept that consent—even eagerness—to cross a border illegally does not constitute consent to all subsequent acts of exploitation.

For the United States, it has been both politically more expedient and emotionally more rewarding to focus on trafficking for sexual exploitation, rather than for labor exploitation. Under the influence of a politically well-connected "abolitionist" lobby, *prostitution* has been conflated with *trafficking;* a crusade against the former is seen as synonymous with a victory against the latter. NGOs and researchers funded by the United States were told to avoid the terms *sex work* and *sex worker* in favor of *prostitution* and *prostituted women*.[48] Some very dubious numbers have been generated to support this emphasis on sex trafficking over trafficking for labor[49]—numbers that seem less about informing policy than about confirming political decisions.[50] It should be noted, however, that in 2008, for the first time, an ambassadorial-level appointment was made to the State Department's TIP Office specifically tasked to focus on labor trafficking. Moreover, responding to past criticism, the 2008 TIP Report places new emphasis on labor trafficking. This emphasis is likely to be expanded under the Obama administration.

However, old numbers—like old habits—die hard. At the Briefing on the Release of the eighth annual *Trafficking in Persons Report* in Washington on June 4, 2008, Ambassador Mark P. Lagon, Director of the Office to Monitor and Combat Trafficking in Persons, stated:

> These are forms of human trafficking. They are, in fact, forms of modern-day slavery. Estimates of the number of victims vary widely. According to the U.S. intelligence community, approximately 800,000 people are trafficked across international borders each year. About 80 percent of them are female. Up to half are minors. These figures do not include millions who are trafficked for purposes of labor and sexual exploitation within national borders as well.

Two years after the Government Accountability Office (GAO) issued a critical report, the numbers have not changed.[51] The report was highly

---

48. I have been told this by a number of researchers and NGOs that prefer to remain anonymous to protect their funding. It should be noted that many program officers see this almost Confucian attempt at "rectification of names" to be both silly and counterproductive to effective countertrafficking efforts.

49. Feingold, "Think Again."

50. Sonia Stefanizzi, "Measuring the Non-Measurable: Towards the Development of Indicators for Measuring Human Trafficking," in *Measuring Human Trafficking: Complexities and Pitfalls*, ed. Ernesto Ugo Savona and Sonia Stefanizzi (New York: Springer, 2007), 45–53.

51. Committee on the Judiciary and Chairman, Committee on International Relations, House of Representatives, and Government Accountability Office, *Human Trafficking: Better*

critical of the U.S. government's gathering, analysis and use of data related to human trafficking. The report points to the questionable basis of the widely quoted figure of 600,000–800,000 persons trafficked across borders worldwide:

> The U.S. government estimates that 600,000 to 800,000 persons are trafficked across international borders annually. However, such estimates of global human trafficking are questionable. The accuracy of the estimates is in doubt because of methodological weaknesses, gaps in data, and numerical discrepancies. For example, the *U.S. government's estimate was developed by one person* who did not document all his work, so the estimate may not be replicable, casting doubt on its reliability. Moreover, country data are not available, reliable, or comparable. There is also a considerable discrepancy between the numbers of observed and estimated victims of human trafficking. The U.S. government has not yet established an effective mechanism for estimating the number of victims or for conducting ongoing analysis of trafficking related data that resides within government entities.[52]

The report goes on to identify weaknesses in the data:

> *Estimate not entirely replicable.* The U.S. government agency that prepares the trafficking estimate is part of the intelligence community, which makes its estimation methodology opaque and inaccessible. During a trafficking workshop in November 2005, the government agency provided a one-page overview of its methodology, which allowed for only a very limited peer review by the workshop participants. In addition, the U.S. government's methodology involves interpreting, classifying, and analyzing data, which was performed by one person who did not document all of his work. Thus the estimate may not be replicable, which raises doubts about its reliability.[53]

The UNESCO Trafficking Statistics Project had been inquiring about the basis for the U.S. government's figures for some time before finally receiving a copy of the same one-page overview of the methodology, which said that the U.S. government filled in missing data using a Markov chain Monte Carlo method, as was widely done in the health sciences. Though the last point is true, people working in bio-medical research have much better data to which to apply the method. A statistician colleague of mine remarked that this seemed less of a clarification than an attempt to "baffle them with science."

Data, Strategy, and Reporting Needed to Enhance U.S. Anti-trafficking Efforts Abroad (Report to the Chairman) (Washington, DC: GPO, 2006).
   52. Ibid., 2–3 (emphasis added).
   53. Ibid., 13.

The GAO also points out that the estimate is:

based on unreliable estimates of others. The biggest methodological challenge in calculating an accurate number of global trafficking victims is how
to transition from reported to unreported victims. The U.S. government does
not directly estimate the number of unreported victims but relies on the estimates of others, adjusting them through a complex statistical process. It essentially averages the various aggregate estimates of reported and unreported
trafficking victims published by NGOs, governments, and international organizations, estimates that themselves are not reliable or comparable due to
different definitions, methodologies, data sources, and data validation procedures. Moreover, the methodologies used to develop these estimates are
generally not published and available for professional scrutiny.[54]

As noted above, a significant problem is that the majority of trafficking statistics are developed by NGOs and agencies for the purpose of
advocacy, rather than the result of serious research. Furthermore, I have
found that many NGOs—overstretched and underfunded (particularly,
in developing countries)—are untrained in research and believe that it
diverts them from their primary tasks of advocacy or delivery of social
services.

Governments in much of the world are frequently reluctant to share
data among their own ministries, much less with outsiders. Data access requires long-term investment in building relationships.[55] Governments are
particularly unwilling to share data that they feel may reflect negatively on
them and be used against them.

In 2006, the U.S. TIP report put the Lao People's Democratic Republic
in Tier Three (the lowest possible ranking).[56] Although Laos does have a
trafficking problem, it is certainly less severe than many other countries
in the region. However, Laos had several factors working against it. First,
it was a communist country, without political clout, that was of little use
to the United States. Second, Laos was essentially penalized for doing the
right thing: because Laos allowed research to be conducted where previously little research on trafficking had been carried out and that research
found more trafficking than had been anticipated, it was portrayed as a
country with a growing trafficking problem that was not being addressed.
Third, a lack of capacity—a widespread problem in all areas in Laos—was

54. Ibid.
55. UNESCO is the only external agency with access to Lao census material down to the
village level (1985–2005), as well as sex service venue data for Thailand (1998–2009).
56. *Trafficking in Persons Report 2006.*

conflated with lack of will. In fact, Laos has been very willing to cooperate on anti-trafficking initiatives.[57]

The GAO also addressed the vexing question of internal trafficking, which in many countries exceeds cross-border trafficking (for example, in China):

> *Internal trafficking data not included.* The U.S. government does not collect data on internal trafficking, which could be a significant problem in countries such as India, where forced labor is reportedly widespread. According to the 2005 *Trafficking in Persons Report,* many nations may be overlooking internal trafficking or forms of labor trafficking in their national legislations. In particular, what is often absent is involuntary servitude, a form of severe trafficking. The report also noted that the TVPA [Trafficking Victims Protection Act] specifically includes involuntary servitude in the U.S. definition of severe forms of trafficking. Nonetheless, the U.S. government estimate does not account for it, because it only collects data on offenses that cross national borders.[58]

This is an accurate but somewhat unfair critique. The Chinese government, for example, sees its major problem as trafficking within China for purposes of forced marriage, forced labor, or forced adoption, rather than movement across international boundaries. However, the Palermo Protocol and most other relevant international instruments deal almost exclusively with cross-border trafficking. The TIP law in the United States does not address internal trafficking; hence, the State Department is not tasked to examine it.

Another issue that inhibits effective data gathering is the lack of agreement on what constitutes trafficking, and even where there is agreement, how to identify victims. Although international legal definitions are—in theory—universal, their understandings and interpretations are not, nor are the ways in which they articulate with real world experience. Article 3, subparagraph (a) of the Trafficking Protocol reads:

> "Trafficking in persons" shall mean the recruitment, transportation, transfer, harbouring or receipt of persons, by means of threat or use of force or other forms of coercion, of abduction, of fraud, of deception, of the abuse of power or of a position of vulnerability or of the giving or receiving of payments or benefits to achieve the consent of a person having control over

---

57. For an insightful comparison of the U.S. government "certification" process for human trafficking and narcotics control, see Friman's chapter in this volume.

58. *Human Trafficking,* 13.

another person, for the purpose of exploitation. Exploitation shall include, at a minimum, the exploitation of the prostitution of others or other forms of sexual exploitation, forced labour or services, slavery or practices similar to slavery, servitude or the removal of organs.

There have been extensive critiques of both the opacity and ambiguity of the Protocol as a legal document.[59] In fact, it reads as if it had been drafted by a rather unhappy and fatigued committee, attempting to wrangle groups of testy ideological elephants into the same tent.[60]

The Global Alliance Against Trafficking in Women (GAATW) has developed a somewhat more pragmatic and effective definition. The group defines trafficking in women as "all acts involved in the recruitment and/ or transportation of women within and across national borders for work or services by means of violence or threat of violence, abuse of authority or dominant position, debt bondage, deception or other forms of coercion."[61] The definition is easily broadened to include men.

The lack of clear agreement among the agencies of various governments and among researchers, as well as NGOs, inhibits the development of comparable data at the most basic level. In addition, there are significant methodological problems and disagreements as to how they should be addressed.[62]

The 2006 GAO report has attempted to summarize the methodologies, key assumptions, and limitations of data from the ILO, IOM, UNODC, and the U.S. government (see table 3.1).

The table presents three points relevant to our discussion. First, UNODC has labeled its report "Trafficking in Persons: Global Patterns," when, in fact, it is not a study of patterns of trafficking, but patterns of reporting

---

59. See, for example, Janie Chuang, "The United States as Global Sheriff," *Michigan Journal of International Law* 27 (2006): 437–94.

60. I understand this is a fairly apt description of what actually took place.

61. GAATW, *Human Rights and Trafficking in Persons: A Handbook* (Bangkok: Global Alliance Against Traffic in Women, 2000), 26.

62. See, for example, Guri Tyldum and Anette Brunovskis, "Describing the Unobserved: Methodological Challenges in Empirical Studies on Human Trafficking," in *Data and Research on Human Trafficking: A Global Survey,* ed. Frank Laczko and Elzbieta Gozdziak (Geneva: IOM, 2003), 17–34; Frank Laczko and Marco Gramegna, "Developing Better Indicators of Human Trafficking," *Brown Journal of World Affairs* 10 (2003): 179–94; Frank Laczko, "Data and Research on Human Trafficking: A Global Survey," *International Migration* 43 (2005): 5–16; Nicola Piper, "A Problem by a Different Name? A Review of Research on Trafficking in South-East Asia and Oceania," *International Migration* 43 (2005): 203–33; and Simon Baker, Allan Beesey, and Thomas M. Steinfatt, "Measuring the Number of Trafficked Women in Cambodia: Part-I of a Series," paper presented at the "Human Rights Challenge of Globalization in Asia-Pacific-U.S.: The Trafficking in Persons, Especially Women and Children" conference, University of Hawaii-Manoa, Honolulu, 2002.

Table 3.1. Four organizations' methodologies: Key assumptions and limitations

	U.S. government	ILO[a]	UNODC[b]	IOM[c]
Methodology	(A) Average of aggregate estimates of reported and unreported victims (B) Data augmentation to fill in missing values[d]	Estimation based on two extrapolations: (A) Estimation of all reported victims[e] (B) Estimation of all reported and unreported victims[f]	(A) Assignment of a score of 1 each times a country is reported by a different institution (B) Coding gender, age, and type of trafficking victims,[f] using the same technique	n.a.
Key assumptions	For (A)—underlying data of total victims are reliable and comparable; For (B)—technical conditions for the procedure are plausible	For (A)—technical conditions for then procedure are met; For (B)—the ratio of the average duration of a case divided by the probability of being reported is greater than or equal to 10	For both (A) and (B)—how much a country is affected by the trafficking problem depends on the frequency of it being reported to different institutions	n.a.
Limitations	Internal trafficking not studied -subject to very limited peer review -may not be replicable	-limited to sources in 11 languages	-no information about the number of victims -no measure of the severity of the problem -internal trafficking not studied	-data limited to the countries where IOM has a presence -confidentiality of victim assistance -may not be generalizable

(*Table 3.1.—cont.*)

U.S. government	ILO[a]	UNODC[b]	IOM[c]
-cannot be used for time series studies -not based on reliable country level data			

Source: GAO analysis of U.S. government, ILO, UNODC, and IOM data (2006).

[a] For a detailed discussion, see Patrick Belser, Michaelle de Cock, and Mehran Ferhad Mehran, "ILO Minimum Estimate of Forced Labour in the World," Geneva, April 2005, http://www.ilo.org/wcmsp5/groups/public/---ed_norm/---declaration/documents/publication/wcms_081913.pdf.

[b] For a detailed discussion, see UNODC, "Trafficking in Persons Global Patterns," Vienna, April 2006, http://www.lastradainternational.org/lsidocs/90%20Trafficking%20in%20Persons%20-%20Global%20Patterns%20(UNODC).pdf.

[c] For a detailed discussion, see IOM, "Data and Research on Human Trafficking: A Global Survey," Geneva, 2005, http://www.nswp.org/pdf/IOM-GLOBAL-TRAFFICK.PDF.

[d] The data augmentation is performed using Monte Carlo Markov chain simulations with Bayealan inference. Making use of plausible values for unknown information, the technique replaces missing data under a wide range of conditions to reflect uncertainty in the open source information regarding the type of trafficking, age group, gender, country of origin, and destination.

[e] The estimation procedure uses the capture-recapture method. Two random samples of reported human trafficking cases are independently drawn and the counts of common and different cases between the two samples are used to estimate the total number of reported trafficking cases.

[f] Under the most conservative assumption, the minimum estimate corresponds to assigning to the probability of being reported a value of 1.

on trafficking using content analysis.[63] Though analyzing patterns of reporting on trafficking might be quite useful, it should not be confused
with analyzing patterns of trafficking. Unfortunately, this example of
overextrapolated conclusions is not unique. In February 2009, UNODC
issued a "Global Report on Trafficking in Persons."[64] It is based solely
on self-reports by 155 governments of prosecutions under human trafficking statutes; prosecutions that are surprisingly sparse, given the resources
and attention given to the issue. The report also emphasizes that "Criminal
justice data alone cannot give a sense of the scale of human trafficking
flows."[65] The limitations of the study were clearly delineated at the local
"roll-out" of the report at a UNODC press conference in Bangkok. However, a UNODC press release, announcing the issuing of the report in New
York, states: "According to the report, the most common form of human
trafficking is sexual exploitation."[66] In fact, the report only documents
that 79 percent of prosecutions is for sexual exploitation, and there is no
reason to believe (and good reasons not to believe) that prosecutions are a
microcosm of the range of trafficking.

Second, trafficking is a process, not a discrete act. For example, a Shan
woman flees her village to escape being press ganged by the Burmese army.
At this point, she is an internally displaced person. Then, without money,
she seeks a job in a town on the Burma side of the Thai border. If encountered then, she might be seen as an internal economic migrant. If she
crosses the border without proper papers, she becomes an undocumented
or illegal migrant. If she is deceived and exploited, she becomes a trafficking victim. As noted above, although some victims are quite literally
kidnapped from their homes, for most, trafficking is linked to a migration
event gone awry.

Third, trafficking is a dynamic phenomenon, the patterns of which
evolve through time. These patterns change not only in response to varying labor demands at destinations, but also in relation to changing social,
economic, and cultural patterns at points of origin. For example, the flow
of migrants in any region is known to be influenced by ecological, political, and social changes in source areas. The land taxation policy in the dry
zone of Burma led to an increase in migrants from that region to Thailand
starting about 1998. The opium eradication policy being pursued in Laos
has had the unintended consequences of exacerbating food insecurity and

63. UNODC, *Trafficking in Persons: Global Patterns* (Vienna: UNODC, 2006), esp. ch. 4.
64. Ibid.
65. Ibid., 11.
66. UNODC, "Denial and Neglect Undermine the Fight against Human Trafficking,"
Press Release, New York, February 12, 2009.

promoting both drug use and resettlement to unproductive areas.[67] Re-settlement, under such conditions, has the effect of pushing people out of their communities, making them more vulnerable to trafficking and other forms of exploitation. Conversely, increased communication, education, and expanded knowledge of the wider world often provoke a desire to see and experience that world. Tai Lue from Xishuangbanna in Yunnan, China, often see Thailand as a place of opportunity, wealth, and excitement. Sharing a closely related language as well as ethnic identity, most are more attracted to temporary migration to Thailand than to cities in China, where they feel alienated and at a competitive disadvantage to Han Chinese.[68]

At present, there is considerable concern about the impact of the global economic crisis on the patterns and extent of trafficking. On the one hand, the job opportunities in destination countries are dropping, making them less attractive to migrants. On the other hand, the conditions in source countries may become sufficiently desperate that people will attempt to flee regardless of perceived opportunity. Moreover, the pressure on profit margins is likely to increase the demand for cheap and docile labor.

Venues and Vulnerability

Changes in customer tastes and venue choices also influence both the scale and nature of trafficking. I have noted elsewhere that Thailand does a census of sex service venues each year, and that there are twenty-four categories plus a twenty-fifth—"other."[69] These range from direct sex venues, that is, brothels, to indirect venues, including karaokes and bars.

---

67. For a summary of the negative impact of development strategies on highland people, see David A. Feingold, "One Size Does Not Fit All: Ethno-linguistic Minorities and Inclusive Growth," paper presented at the Asian Development Bank's "Forum on Inclusive Growth in the New Asia and Pacific," Manila, 2003. For the impact of resettlement, see, for example, Cornelia Kammerer, "Of Labels and Laws: Thailand's Resettlement and Repatriation Policies," *Cultural Survival Quarterly* 12 (1998): 7–12; C. Alton and Houmphanh Rattanavong, "Service Delivery and Resettlement: Options for Developmental Planning," unpublished report for the Vientiane Lao PDR, UNDP, 2004; Olivier Evrard and Yves Goudineau, "Planned Resettlement, Unexpected Migrations and Cultural Trauma: The Political Management of Rural Mobility and Interethnic Relationships in Laos," *Development and Change* 35 (2004): 937–62; Chris Lyttleton et al., *Watermelons, Bars and Trucks: Dangerous Intersections in Northwest Lao PDR: An Ethnographic Study of Social Change and Health Vulnerability along the Road through Muang Sing and Muang Long* (Vientiane: Institute for Cultural Research of Laos and Macquarie University, 2004); and Laurent Romagny and Steve Daviau, "Synthesis of Reports on Resettlement in Long District, Luang Namtha Province," unpublished report (Vientiane: Action Contre la Faim Mission in Lao PDR, 2003).

68. Heather A. Peters, communication with the author, 2003.

69. See Feingold, "The Hell of Good Intentions."

In direct sex venues, only sexual services are sold, and the women have little or no choice in customers. In indirect venues, sometimes referred to as secondary prostitution, sex is sold secondary to some other activity. In general, women perceive these as much better working conditions. Trafficked women in the sex industry are more likely to end up in a brothel.

The UNESCO Trafficking Project, which I direct, has been working with the Thai Ministry of Public Health to map sex venues and sex workers since 1997. Since at least that time, there has been a steady decline in the number of brothels in Thailand, and an increase in karaokes.[70]

For the first time in a decade, 2007 data show an increase in brothels and a decrease in karaokes (see table 3.2 and figure 3.2). This shift is not a result of changes in either definitions or sampling. However, it is not yet clear whether this is a temporary aberration or a trend. If it continues, it indicates both a significant reversal in customer preferences, as well as a possible risk factor for an increase in trafficking. Again, it is important to be clear: not all brothel-based sex workers are trafficked, but women trafficked for sex are more likely to end up in a brothel.

Toward an Epidemiology of Trafficking

My own view is that what is necessary is a sentinel surveillance epidemiological approach to studying trafficking, similar to that used to track HIV and AIDS. A classic approach of epidemiology is to characterize disease by "time, place, and persons."[71] To simplify, for diseases like polio or TB, the aim is to identify and count every case. With HIV, because of rights issues and expense of mass testing, a sentinel surveillance approach is used. Though not best for absolute numbers, if well constructed, it provides an excellent monitor of trends through time. If we are to be able to move toward policy that is both informed by and responsive to the fluid nature of trafficking and migration, we must base that policy on the results of research, rather than produce research results to justify policy. If we are to have truly effective prevention, we must have a very clear notion of what it is that we are trying to prevent. Too often, governments' initial response to trafficking is to focus on controlling migration, rather than controlling coercion, deception, and exploitation. In particular, the understandable desire to protect women and children often results in the equation of the two. Adult women are infantilized, protected from trafficking by depriving them of the right to unsupervised movement. Burma, for

---

70. The exception was 1998, when some changes were made in methodology.

71. David E. Lillienfield and Paul D. Stolley, eds., *Foundations of Epidemiology*, 3rd ed. (Oxford: Oxford University Press, 1994), 3.

Table 3.2. Distribution of sex service venues in Thailand in 1997–2007

Year	Brothel	Accommodation	Bar	Disco/ Nightclub	Karaoke	Massage and sauna	Food and beverage	Hairdresser	Call girl	Street walker	Other
1997	643	287	1,106	171	1,087	767	3,229	108	42	57	74
1998	682	340	1,217	99	1,210	924	3,284	135	33	34	57
1999	634	388	1,371	134	1,439	1,018	3,161	153	30	33	69
2000	625	423	1,444	149	2,165	1,212	3,514	83	22	46	104
2001	603	462	1,937	159	3,397	1,282	3,312	191	22	40	75
2002	595	481	1,791	136	4,301	1,364	3,102	186	27	37	70
2003	563	444	1,864	102	4,693	1,369	2,833	209	17	41	94
2004	369	582	1,969	132	4,888	1,317	3,175	281	8	28	98
2005	390	751	1,892	169	5,471	1,331	3,256	443	10	29	91
2006	363	824	1,833	131	5,624	1,316	2,692	465	8	42	100
2007	518	975	1,348	115	5,227	1,344	2,460	536	10	47	268

Source: Ministry of Public Health © UNESCO, 2007.

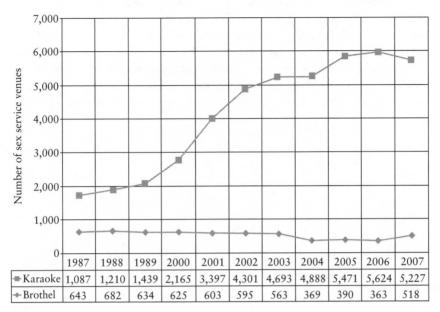

	1987	1988	1989	2000	2001	2002	2003	2004	2005	2006	2007
Karaoke	1,087	1,210	1,439	2,165	3,397	4,301	4,693	4,888	5,471	5,624	5,227
Brothel	643	682	634	625	603	595	563	369	390	363	518

Figure 3.2. Distribution of sex service venues in Thailand, 1997–2007
Source: Ministry of Public Health © UNESCO, 2007

example, is one of many countries that restrict the right of adult women under a given age (in this case, twenty-six) to travel in border regions without permission of their husbands or parents.[72]

To reiterate, trafficking is a process, not an event. If we are to be able to have any long-term impact on the problem, we must use research to identify the most cost-effective areas for intervention. Identifying and ameliorating structural vulnerabilities—such as lack of legal status for hill people in Thailand—is essential in this regard. Analyzing the unintended consequences of well-meant but ill-conceived migration or development policies is vital to a comprehensive approach, which avoids fixing one problem while exacerbating another.

Compared with the complex nature of prevention, prosecution may seem a relatively simple area to track. However, although prosecution can be essential for a sense of justice ("bad people should be punished for doing bad things"), there is no nation in which prosecution can be shown to have reduced the aggregate amount of trafficking—including the United States.

---

72. It should be noted that this regulation was instituted to protect them from trafficking, and is not a holdover of customary law.

Since 2000, global resources expended to fight trafficking have grown exponentially. Although it is possible to point to improved legal frameworks, better international cooperation, and improved treatment for victims in some countries, there is a sharp disjunction between these actions and the perception of an ever-worsening problem. In a world of scarce resources, I believe it is only a matter of time before "trafficking fatigue" sets in, and people ask why we have spent so much to achieve so little.

4

Numbers and Certification

ASSESSING FOREIGN COMPLIANCE IN COMBATING

NARCOTICS AND HUMAN TRAFFICKING

H. Richard Friman

Since 1987, the U.S. Department of State has assessed and certified select foreign government compliance with U.S. counternarcotics efforts and reported the results in the annual *International Narcotics Control Strategy Report (INCSR)*.[1] Since 2001, the Department of State has released the annual *Trafficking in Persons Report (TIPR)* comprising an assessment of foreign government compliance with U.S. priorities in combating human trafficking. Scholarship on these and other rating and ranking systems reveals that controversy and certification go hand in hand. Mark Chinen argues that U.S. certification systems have been created with the intent of increasing congressional influence over the Executive and enhancing foreign compliance with the U.S. control agenda, and have evidenced only limited success in both areas.[2] Oded Löwenheim places the U.S. efforts in the context of a broader rise of "international governance indicators" that reproduce "structures of power and authority in the international system."[3]

The author thanks Alex McShiras, Alexandria Innes, and Julian Lee for their research assistance.
    1. The *INCSR* predates this certification function. See the discussion of the 1981 International Security and Development Cooperation Act and especially the Department of State Authorization Act for FY 1984 and FY 1985, in Harry L. Hogan, "Federal Laws Relating to the Control of Narcotics and Other Dangerous Drugs, Enacted 1961–1985: Brief Summaries," Congressional Research Service, January 15, 1986, http://digital.library.unt.edu/govdocs/crs/permalink/meta-crs-8414, 1.
    2. Mark A. Chinen, "Presidential Certification in U.S. Foreign Policy Legislation," *International Law and Politics* 31 (1999): 217–306.
    3. Oded Löwenheim, "Examining the State: A Foucauldian Perspective on International 'Governance Indicators,'" *Third World Quarterly* 29 (2008): 255–74.

This chapter explores the politics of numbers used by the United States to assess foreign compliance in efforts against narcotics and human trafficking. Politicization of numbers has been extensive in official estimates of the extent of illicit flows.[4] Drug trafficking figures are notorious for their politicization, and prominent estimates of the extent of human trafficking are problematic at best.[5] In contrast to the politics of estimating illicit flows, the politics of numbers used in the certification systems of foreign compliance remains understudied.

To address this gap, this chapter explores certification systems on three dimensions: *inclusion,* referring to the criteria used to determine whether a country will be on the rating list; *ranking,* referring to the criteria that are used to determine the country's placement in categories on the rating lists; and *effectiveness,* referring to the criteria that are used to determine the overall impact of the rating and ranking process. These dimensions serve as a framework for a focused, structured comparison of the U.S. narcotics and human trafficking certification processes. The chapter argues that these processes are based on vague and subjective standards for inclusion as well as underspecified criteria for ranking that have facilitated the influence of broader U.S. political considerations. Moreover, although foreign governments have responded to the certification processes, the actual changes in category/tier rankings raise questions for prominent claims concerning effectiveness.

Certification and Narcotics

In a climate of escalating concern over illegal drugs and domestic political posturing by members of Congress and the Executive over the extent to which the Reagan administration was responding to threat to the United States, Congress passed the Omnibus Drug Enforcement, Education and Control Act of 1986 (Anti-Drug Abuse Act of 1986, ADAA).[6] Among its provisions, the 1986 ADAA amended the Foreign Assistance Act (FAA) of 1961 adding a certification process for drug exporting and transit countries. Such steps were intended to increase both foreign cooperation with U.S. drug control efforts and political pressure on the Reagan

---

4. See chapter 2 in this volume.

5. General Accountability Office (GAO), *Human Trafficking: Better Data, Strategy, and Reporting Needed to Enhance U.S. Antitrafficking Efforts Abroad,* GAO-06-825 (July 2006), 10–21.

6. John C. McWilliams, "Through the Past Darkly: The Politics and Policies of America's Drug War," in *Drug Control Policy: Essays in Historical and Comparative Perspective,* ed. William O. Walker, III (University Park: Pennsylvania State University Press, 1992), 5–41, esp. 24–25.

administration to adopt a tougher foreign policy approach against drug trafficking.[7] The certification process incorporated the "threat of linkage strategies," holding financial assistance, support in multilateral lending institutions, and preferential trade agreements hostage in the absence of requisite compliance by foreign governments.[8]

In 1971 and 1972, Congress had amended the FAA by adding Section 481 authorizing the president to conclude drug control agreements and provide countries with economic and military assistance. Section 481 also authorized suspension of such assistance under the following conditions: "when the President determines that the government of such country has failed to take adequate steps to prevent narcotic drugs and other controlled substances (as defined by the Comprehensive Drug Abuse Prevention and Control Act of 1970) produced or processed, in whole or in part, in such country, or transported through such country, from being sold illegally within the jurisdiction of such country to United States Government personnel or their dependents, or from entering the United States unlawfully."[9]

Amendments to the FAA during the early to mid-1980s expanded the provisions of Section 481 culminating in certification provisions introduced under the 1986 ADAA. Of note for this chapter, the Department of State Authorization Act, Fiscal Years 1984 and 1985 passed in November 1983, and the 1986 ADAA amended Section 481 to require an annual report by the president to Congress on U.S. international drug control policy. The report was to include the identification of and detailed information concerning "those countries which are significant or indirect sources of illicit narcotics and psychotropic drugs and other controlled substances significantly affecting the United States."[10] Under the amended FAA, the report's findings were to serve as the basis for congressional deliberations over sanctions including cutting "50 percent of United States assistance allocated for such" countries in the current fiscal year (and 100 percent in subsequent years), and voting against financial assistance in multilateral institutions including the World Bank and regional development banks.[11]

7. Chinen, "Presidential Certification," 220.

8. Maria Celia Toro, "Unilateralism and Bilateralism," in *Drug Policy in the Americas*, ed. Peter H. Smith (Boulder, CO: Westview Press, 1992), 314–28, esp. 318.

9. Rafael F. Perl, "International Narcotics Control and Foreign Assistance Certification: Requirements, Procedures, Timetables and Guidelines," CRS Report for Congress, 88–130 F, February 11, 1988, 12 (note 2).

10. See FAA, Section 481 (e)(1–7). Department of State Authorization Act Fiscal Years 1984 and 1985 (P.L. 98–164, November 22, 1983), *U.S. Code, Congressional and Administrative News*, 97 Stat. 1053–1056; Perl, "International Narcotics Control," 16–17.

11. Section 481 (h)(1)(A-B), in Perl, "International Narcotics Control," 9, 18–19. See also Raphael Francis Perl, "Congress, International Narcotics Policy, and the Anti-Drug Abuse Act of 1988," *Journal of Interamerican Studies and World Affairs* 30 (1988): 19–51.

Such steps would be taken unless it was "determined" and "certified" by the president that: "during the previous year the country has cooperated fully with the United States, or has taken adequate steps on its own, in satisfying the goals agreed to in an applicable bilateral narcotics agreement with the United States," and, in "preventing" drugs "from being sold illegally" to U.S. personnel/dependents, transporting drugs into the United States, and "preventing and punishing the laundering in that country of drug related profits or drug related monies."[12] The amended FAA added another path to certification. Specifically, in those cases where the country "would not otherwise qualify for certification" under the above provisions, the president can certify "the vital national interests of the United States require the provision of such assistance."[13] For the national interest waiver, Congress required that the president provide a "full and complete description of the national interest placed at risk" weighed against the risk of the absence of the country "to cooperate fully with the United States in combating narcotics or to take adequate steps to combat narcotics on its own."[14] If unsatisfied, Congress was empowered by the amended FAA to "disapprove a Presidential determination of certification" by joint resolution within a specified time frame, and if necessary override a presidential veto of the resolution with a two-thirds majority.[15]

In addition to financial assistance programs, the ADAA introduced trade sanctions for noncompliance by amending the Trade Act of 1974. For example, the act's Title VII, Section 802 empowered the president to deny preferential tariff treatment and to increase tariffs on "any or all...dutiable products" up to 50 percent for "every major drug producing country and every major drug transit country...to the extent considered necessary."[16] However, such steps would not apply if the president determined and certified to the Congress that the country in question had met the full cooperation or adequate thresholds noted in the FAA provisions.[17]

In effect, by the late 1980s, the United States had introduced a rating and ranking system to assess foreign compliance in counternarcotics efforts. In practice, the certification process has been rife with controversy since its introduction. Congressional critics have questioned presidential certifications

12. FAA, Section 481 (h)(2)(A)(i) (I), in Perl, "International Narcotics Control," 18–20.
13. FAA, Section 481 (h)(2)(A)(i)(II)(i-ii), in Perl, "International Narcotics Control," 20.
14. FAA, Section 481 (h)(2)(B)(i-ii), in Perl, "International Narcotics Control," 20.
15. Perl, "International Narcotics Control," 8.
16. Trade Act of 1974, Title VIII, Section 802(a), in Perl, "International Narcotics Control," 26.
17. Trade Act of 1974, Title VIII, Section 802(b), in Perl, "International Narcotics Control," 26–29. The threat of trade sanctions ended with the 2002 amendments to the FAA, which refocused the sanctions on financial steps.

and national interest waivers. Countries targeted by the certification process have challenged the determinations as politically driven and downplayed the role of extensive U.S. demand in driving the drug trade.[18]

Inclusion

Although the *INCSR* narrative explores a wide array of countries, the narcotics certification process applies to only those countries that meet the thresholds of what has become known as the "majors list."[19] Since 1987 a total of thirty-two countries have been included on the majors list (table 4.1). As defined by the amended FAA, the list entails "those countries which are significant or indirect sources of illicit narcotics and psychotropic drugs and other controlled substances significantly affecting the United States." However, the criteria for determining inclusion have been underspecified at best.

The narcotics provisions in the Department of State Authorization Act passed in November 1983 stem from an amendment to the Senate version introduced by Paula Hawkins (R-FL), a vocal critic of the Reagan administration's limited steps against the drug trade.[20] Passed unanimously by the Senate in October and, with no counterpart in the House, incorporated into the final act, these provisions included amending the 1961 FAA to define a "major illicit drug producing country" as one producing "five metric tons or more" of opium/derivatives or 500 metric tons of coca or marijuana per fiscal year.[21] The origins of these specific thresholds are not addressed in the legislative history of the act and the numbers received little attention on their introduction.[22] Those major U.S. aid recipients seen

18. For example, see United States Information Agency, "U.S. Anti-Drug Policy: Certification Criticized; 1999 Drug Control Strategy Praised," March 3, 1999, http://www.fas. org/irp/news/1999/03/wwwh9m03.htm; Council on Hemispheric Affairs, "Decertifying the Uncertifiable: Deeply Flawed Certification Process is a Hemispheric Joke and Deserves to be Junked," Memorandum to the Press, February 28, 1998, http://www.coha.org/NEW_PRESS_ RELEASES/New_Press_Releases_1998/98.08_Deeply_Flawed_Certification_Process_is_a_ Hemispheric_Joke.htm; Bill Spencer et al., "Foreign Policy in Focus: Drug Certification," *Foreign Policy in Focus* 3 (1998), http://www.drugpolicy.org/library/spencer2.cfm.

19. Other majors lists have emerged as part of amendments of the FAA that focus on precursor chemical source countries and money laundering countries. Only the narcotics majors list is explored here.

20. "State Department Bill," 151. For brief mentions of Senator Hawkins role, see Rensselaer W. Lee III, "Latin American Drug Connection," *Foreign Policy* 61 (1985–86): 144; Bruce Michael Bagley, "U.S. Foreign Policy and the War on Drugs: Analysis of Policy Failure," *Journal of Interamerican Studies and World Affairs* 30 (1988): 192.

21. P.L. 98-164, Title X, Section 1003 (b)(i). See also Section 481 (h)(5)(i)(2), in Perl, "International Narcotics Control," 22.

22. "International Narcotics Control," *U.S. Code, Legislative History,* P.L. 98-164 (1983), 1612–1613. *Congressional Quarterly Weekly Report* overviews of the progress of the reauthorization act through Congress during 1983 either ignore the narcotics issue or

Table 4.1. Narcotics majors list by country, 1987–2008

Country	Year	Country	Year
Afghanistan	1987–2008	Iran	1987–1998
Aruba	1998–1999	Jamaica	1987–2008
Bahamas	1987–2008	Laos	1987–2008
Belize	1987–1999	Lebanon	1987–1997
Bolivia	1987–2008	Malaysia	1987–1998
Brazil	1987–2008	Mexico	1987–2008
Burma/Myanmar	1987–2008	Morocco	1987–1993
Cambodia	1996–2000	Nigeria	1987–2008
China	1992–2005	Pakistan	1987–2008
Colombia	1987–2008	Panama	1987–2008
Dominican Republic	1996–2008	Paraguay	1987–2008
Ecuador	1987–2008	Peru	1987–2008
Guatemala	1992–2008	Syria	1987–1997
Haiti	1996–2008	Thailand	1987–2004
Hong Kong	1987–1999	Venezuela	1992–2008
India	1987–2008	Vietnam	1996–2005

Source: Memorandum of May 12, 1987 from Ronald Reagan delegating to the Secretary of State the responsibility for submitting the first report and certification, 52
Federal Register 20053 (1987); Presidential Determination, Certification for (Major)
Narcotics Producing and Transit Countries, *Federal Register* (1988–2000); Presidential Determination on Major Drug Transit or Major Illicit Drug Producing Countries
(2001–2007), available at http://www.state.gov/p/inl/rls/nrcrpt/2008/vol1.

by analysts as likely targets of the legislation—such as Pakistan, Thailand,
Colombia, Bolivia, Mexico, and Jamaica—easily exceeded the thresholds.
For example, production estimates for Pakistan and Thailand in 1983
were seven to twelve times the opium threshold, while Mexican production was over three times the figure. Bolivia and Colombia were producing
an estimated twenty-two to eighty times the coca thresholds while Mexico
and Jamaica were producing an estimated five to ten times the marijuana
thresholds.[23]

At the risk of speculation, at least two potential explanations can be offered for the opium thresholds. First, Section 481 of the FAA as introduced

---

note it in passing. For example, see "Foreign Aid Bills Reported; Stage Set for Policy Debate," *Congressional Quarterly Weekly Report*, June 18, 1983, 1227–34. A more detailed
discussion of the narcotics issue appears in "State Department Bill," *Congressional Quarterly
Almanac 1983*, 151.

23. "State Department Bill," 151. Lee, "The Latin American Drug Connection," 143–44.
The production figures are from the Department of State, "International Narcotics Control
Strategy Report Summary," February 1, 1985, cited in Ted Galen Carpenter, "The U.S. Cam-
paign against International Narcotics Trafficking: A Cure Worse Than the Disease," *Cato
Policy Analysis* 63 (1985): 13.

in the early 1970s explicitly noted the goal of promoting U.S. and foreign cooperation with the 1961 United Nations Single Convention on Narcotic Drugs and its goals of limiting licit and eliminating illicit drug production. Article 24, Paragraph 2 of the Convention, as amended in 1972, uses five tons as a threshold for the introduction of stricter approval practices for licit opium exports. Those countries seeking to export over five tons annually must gain the approval of the UN Economic and Social Council and specify the exact amount of exports as well as country controls and export destinations. Those seeking to export less than this threshold require approval of the International Narcotics Control Board, and must provide the aforementioned information with the exception of the exact amounts of exports.[24]

A second possible explanation for the selection of a five-ton threshold in the amended FAA appears in an unpublished paper by the U.S. Bureau of Narcotics and Dangerous Drugs (BNDD) intelligence staff from October 1970. The paper includes BNDD estimates of licit and illicit opium production in metric tons for twelve countries and a category of "other." Five to ten metric tons is the estimate of production for the lowest opium producing explicitly country noted on the list, Mexico. Although the extent of circulation of the paper is unclear, the paper is cited in detail with the complete reproduction of the opium data tables in an edited volume released by the Ford Foundation's Drug Abuse Survey Project in 1972.[25]

If these explanations do in fact account for the five metric ton threshold in the amended FAA, the origins of the 500 metric ton standard for coca or marijuana are less readily apparent. No coca or cannabis threshold appears in the amended UN Single Convention. Nor are these products addressed in the BNDD opium production paper. Although other intelligence estimations may have informed the numerical choice, in the absence of information concerning such sources, the FAA threshold appears to stem from simply multiplying the opium standard by a factor of 100.

During the 1990s, the criteria for determining major drug producing countries changed. The International Narcotics Control Correction Act of 1994 amended the definition of major drug producing country in Section 481 of the FAA shifting from quantities of drugs produced to hectares

24. United Nations, Single Convention on Narcotics Drugs, 1961 as amended by the 1972 Protocol amending the Single Convention on Narcotics Drugs, 1961, http://www.incb.org/pdf/e/conv/convention_1961_en.pdf.

25. John F. Holahan with Paul A. Henningsen, "The Economics of Heroin," in *Dealing with Drug Abuse: A Report to the Ford Foundation,* ed. Patricia Wald et al. (New York: Praeger, 1972), 255–99, esp. table 4–1 on page 259. The BNDD paper as cited by Holahan is also used in the classic work on international drug control by Kettil Brunn, Lynn Pan, and Ingemar Rexed, *The Gentlemen's Club: International Control of Drugs and Alcohol* (Chicago: University of Chicago Press, 1975).

"cultivated or harvested during a year."[26] This practice as well as the specific numerical thresholds have remained in place ever since. As noted in the 2008 *INCSR,* these threshold figures are "1,000 or more hectares" of "illicit opium poppy" or "illicit coca," or "5,000 hectares or more of illicit cannabis" unless such production is determined by the president to "not significantly affect the United States."[27] As noted by Representative Lee Hamilton (D-IN), chair of the House Committee on Foreign Relations, in the report concerning the act, the shift from "potential production" figures in terms of metric tons to hectares of cultivation was intended to add precision. Where "differences in yield rates and other variables" made the tonnage figures "not precise," Hamilton states that the hectare figure "is more readily quantifiable through a variety of means."[28] This argument appears in greater detail in the *INCSRs* of April 1994 and March 1995.[29] Citing the use of similar methods to measure licit crops in the United States for "more than a decade and a half," the Department's Bureau for International Narcotics Matters draws a distinction in its narrative between hectare figures that are known "with reasonable certainty" and yield figures "that are only approximations... [and] should not be treated as hard data."[30]

This still begs the question of why the hectare thresholds for major drug producing countries were set at 1,000 or more for opium and coca and 5,000 or more for cannabis, and have remained at these levels since 1994. The prioritization of cocaine relative to heroin during the late 1980s and into the 1990s in U.S. drug control policy helps to explain why the coca and opium thresholds converged, but is less helpful in accounting for the choice of the specific figure of 1,000 hectares.[31] Although the 1994 Act was

26. Chinen, "Presidential Certifications," 235 (note 75).

27. U.S. Department of State, "International Narcotics Control Strategy Report," http://www.state.gov/p/inl/rls/nrcrpt/2008/vol1/html/100772.htm, introduction. See also Chinen, "Presidential Certifications," 235–36 (note 75).

28. U.S. Congress, House, Committee on Foreign Affairs (CFA), *International Narcotics Control Correction Act of 1994: Report (to Accompany H.R. 5030)* (Washington, DC: U.S. GPO, 1994), 3–4.

29. The shift to hectares was made on the recommendation of the Bureau of International Narcotics Matters in consultation with members of the intelligence community. Author's correspondence with former staff member of the Committee on Foreign Relations, February 3, 2009.

30. United States, Department of State, Bureau of International Narcotics Matters, *International Narcotics Control Strategy Report April 1994* (Washington, DC: U.S. GPO, 1994), 14–17; U.S. Department of State, Bureau of International Narcotics and Law Enforcement Affairs, *International Narcotics Control Strategy Report March 1995* (Washington, DC: U.S. GPO, 1995), 21–22. For a critique of hectare estimates, see John M. Walsh, "Are We There Yet? Measuring Progress in the U.S. War on Drugs in Latin America," *Drug War Monitor,* December 2004, 10–12.

31. The U.S. focus on Central and South America, and the ability to verify hectares under cultivation by using aerial assets played an important role in the shift to the hectare standard.

intended to bring U.S. reporting and certification practices in line with the 1988 United Nations Convention against Illicit Traffic in Narcotic Drugs and Psychotropic Substances, no such thresholds appear in the Convention. U.S. government estimates of opium and coca cultivation for 1993 and 1994 prominently noted in the introduction to the 1995 *INCSR* do little to suggest the logic of the thresholds.[32] The figures for opium producers reveal a range of countries between 2 and 150 times the hectare threshold, with only Colombia and Guatemala hovering at slightly over the 1,000 hectare threshold for net (after eradication) cultivation in 1991. For Andean cocaine producers such as Bolivia, Peru and Colombia, cultivation figures range from between 49 to 109 times the hectare threshold.[33]

In the 1994 report, Hamilton notes that the change in the standard for major marijuana producers was intended to "allow the executive branch more flexibility to exclude countries the activity of which does not have a significant impact on the United States." Hamilton points explicitly to the case of Morocco where despite being a major cannabis producer the drugs were either consumed locally or sent to Europe instead of the United States.[34] Although helpful in explaining the origins of the qualifier of significance, this explanation does not explain the choice of numerical threshold.[35] In contrast, the *INCSR* tables reveal that the only country hovering at 5,000 hectare level for cannabis during 1993 (5,050 hectares cultivated, and 5,000 net) and 1994 (5,000 hectares cultivated and 4,986 net) was Colombia. Given Colombia's prominence in coca (over 20,000 hectares net from 1992 to 1994) and thus its unlikelihood of falling off the majors list it is not clear why Colombia would be used to set the cannabis threshold.[36] Regardless of their origins, the numerical thresholds for

---

Author's correspondence with former staff member of the Committee on Foreign Relations, February 3, 2009.

32. The logic at the time, according to one former official, was that the thresholds, albeit "arbitrary," were seen by the "anti-drug community" as the minimum area that would produce levels capable of fueling U.S. drug abuse. Author's correspondence with Department of State officials, March 5, 2009.

33. In 1987, Bolivia's estimated hectares in production of coca stood at over 60 times the threshold and Peru's at almost 166 times the threshold in 1988. See Elena Alvarez, "Coca Production in Peru," in *Drug Policy in the Americas,* ed. Peter H. Smith (Boulder, CT: Westview Press, 1992), 81; and Flavio Machicado, "Coca Production in Bolivia," in *Drug Policy in the Americas,* ed. Peter H. Smith (Boulder, CT: Westview Press, 1992), 89.

34. CFA, *International Narcotics Control Correction Act of 1994,* 3–4.

35. Official statements by the Moroccan government in 1993 noted 50,000 hectares under cultivation. Department of State, *International Narcotics Control Strategy Report March 1995,* 433.

36. In 1993 Colombia had 5,050 hectares cultivated and 5,000 net (after eradication), and in 1994 5,000 hectares cultivated and 4,986 net. Department of State, *International Narcotics Control Strategy Report March 1995,* 26.

cannabis, opium poppy, and coca cultivation have remained unchanged since the 1990s.[37]

In contrast to the thresholds used to determine major drug producing countries, the criteria for "major drug transit country" lacked any explicit numerical standards. Introduced into the FAA by the 1986 ADAA, the provisions defined a major drug transit country as one:

> that is a significant direct source of illicit narcotic or psychotropic drugs or other controlled substances significantly affecting the United States; through which are transported such drugs or substances; or through which significant sums of drug-related profits or monies are laundered with the knowledge or complicity of the government.[38]

The exact thresholds for "significant" were not defined in the 1986 ADAA, nor were levels of production or transshipment that might be significantly affecting other countries included in certification considerations. Growing congressional concerns with the certification process after the release of the Reagan administration's first certification list in 1987 led to new calls in the Anti-Drug Abuse Act of 1988, including "requiring the president to establish numerical standards and guidelines for determining which countries are major illicit drug transit nations."[39] However, over twenty years later, little progress had been made in this regard.

Finally, it is important to note that advanced industrial countries are conspicuously absent from the majors list. The introduction sections in the annual *INCSR* containing the annual certification announcements on rare occasions have noted the president's special concern with advanced industrial countries—such as the Netherlands (regarding MDMA [Ecstasy] and other synthetics, from 2003 to 2005), and Canada (regarding marijuana and border controls, from 2003 to 2006).[40] However, such countries have not been included on the majors list. Advanced industrial countries are

37. Once established, the numbers became institutionalized. Neither Congress nor officials in the State Department's Bureau of International Narcotics Matters (later the Bureau of International Narcotics and Law Enforcement Affairs) sought to reopen the issue. Author's correspondence with Department of State officials, March 5, 2009.

38. Section 2005 (c) (3)(5), Anti-Drug Abuse Act of 1986 (P.L. 99–570), *U.S. Code, Congressional and Administrative News* (99th Cong. 2nd Session, 1986), 100 Stat 3207–3263. See also Section 481 (h)(5)(i)(5), in Perl, "International Narcotics Control," 22.

39. Other proposed changes to the certification process included the addition of country specific compliance criteria (including progress in crop eradication, drug production, and cooperative enforcement efforts) for Bolivia, Peru, Mexico, Pakistan, Laos, Afghanistan, India, and Turkey. Perl, "The Anti-Drug Abuse Act," 36–39.

40. The one other country noted in the introduction sections, and also not formally included in the designation and certification process, has been North Korea (in 2002, and the 2004–6 reports).

discussed in the context of precursor chemical and money laundering controls but actions in these areas in and of themselves are not used in the certification process. The irony is that Congress and the Executive have both argued since the 1980s that the narcotics trade is a global challenge that affects the national security of the United States and have sought to pressure developed and developing countries alike to increase compliance with the U.S. control agenda. These arguments have intensified since the September 11, 2001 terrorist attacks, emphasizing the threat of drug traffickers and terrorist organizations with global reach. In effect, illegal drug production and transshipment everywhere significantly affect the United States.[41] Yet such arguments have yet to inform the drug certification process.

Ranking

Under the language of the amended FAA, countries on the majors list are designated and certified by the president as falling into three broad categories: cooperating fully (a category that included cooperating fully or the government taking adequate steps on its own); merited a national interest waiver; or not certified, which were subject to congressional sanction. These latter two categories changed with amendments to the FAA by the 2002 Foreign Relations Authorization Act (FRAA). Section 706 of the FRAA replaced the category of noncertified countries with a new category of countries that have "failed demonstrably within the previous 12 months to make substantial efforts to adhere to [their] obligations under international counter-narcotics agreements and to take the counter-narcotics measures set forth" by the FAA. The national interest waiver category was also amended to include countries that had failed demonstrably but where continued U.S. financial assistance to such countries was "vital to the national interests of the United States."[42]

The standards for placement of countries into these categories have been distinguished by vague and subjective thresholds since the inception of the certification process. Standards such as "cooperating fully," "adequate steps," "substantial efforts," and "failing demonstrably" remain underspecified in the FAA. Although numerical thresholds help to determine the majors list, the legislation contains no specification of annual or other reductions

---

41. For example, see H. Richard Friman, *NarcoDiplomacy: Exporting the U.S. War on Drugs* (Ithaca: Cornell University Press, 1996); Peter Andreas and Ethan Nadelmann, *Policing the Globe: Criminalization and Crime Control in International Relations* (New York: Oxford University Press, 2006).

42. Modifying Section 489(a)(1) of the FAA. U.S. Congress, *Legislation on Foreign Relations Through 2002* (Washington DC: U.S. GPO, 2003), 189–90. See also Julie Ayling, "Conscription in the War on Drugs: Recent Reforms to the U.S. Drug Certification Process," *International Journal of Drug Policy* 16 (2005), 376–83.

of yield/hectare numbers necessary for governments to reach certification status. Instead, considerations of progress are more broadly defined, including "whether the actions of the government have resulted in the maximum reductions in illicit drug production which were determined to be achievable," as reported by the president and based in part on the control steps planned by the government in question.[43] As a result, the politics of numbers in ranking has been distinguished by the relative absence of numbers. Political controversy has focused more on the number of countries that have been ranked in the different categories each year, and especially on the certification status of specific countries of congressional concern.

In 1987—the first year of implementation of the new rating and ranking provisions—President Reagan certified nineteen countries for fully cooperating with the United States or taking adequate steps on their own to implement bilateral narcotics control agreements, certified two countries on national interest grounds, and withheld certification for three countries for failing to meet the requisite thresholds. Those certified were "the Bahamas, Belize, Bolivia, Brazil, Burma [Myanmar], Colombia, Ecuador, Hong Kong, India, Jamaica, Malaysia, Mexico, Morocco, Nigeria, Pakistan, Panama, Paraguay, Peru and Thailand." Those receiving national interest waivers were Laos and Lebanon; and those not certified were "Soviet-occupied Afghanistan," and Iran and Syria (deemed state sponsors of terrorism by the then secretary of state George Shultz).[44] As table 4.2 shows, since 1987 few governments have ever been rated as noncertified or failing demonstrably—never more than six countries. Moreover, those that fall into this category tend to be the subject of broader U.S. political concerns beyond questions on compliance in counternarcotics. Most countries on the majors list over the past 30 years have been certified, including those that have posed the greatest challenge to U.S. drug control efforts. Table 4.2 also reveals that certification through national interest waivers has been relatively rare, with the exception of the seven waivers granted by the Clinton administration during 1994 and 1995.

The overall number of countries being certified has been less controversial than the rating and ranking of specific countries. For example, critics of the Reagan administration that had pushed hard for the certification process reacted with disappointment to the first round of certifications, and introduced resolutions in the Senate that challenged the designations for Panama, Mexico, and the Bahamas as fully cooperating. The Mexico and Bahamas resolutions failed to garner requisite Senate support while

43. For example, see Section 481(2)(e)(4) and 481(3).
44. Perl, "International Narcotics Control," 19 (notes 15 and 16), 20 (note 18).

Table 4.2. Annual narcotics certification of majors' list countries, totals by ranking category, 1987–2008

Year	Total Number Reviewed	Certified	National Interest Waiver	Not Certified
1987	24	19 (79.2%)	2	3
1988	24	17 (70.8%)	3	4
1989	24	17 (70.8%)	1	6
1990	24	19 (79.2%)	1	4
1991	24	19 (79.2%)	1	4
1992	27	22 (81.5%)	1	4
1993	27	22 (81.5%)	2	4
1994	26	15 (57.75%)	7	4
1995	26	15 (57.7%)	7	4
1996	30	22 (73.3%)	2	6
1997	30	22 (73.3%)	2	6
1998	29	20 (69.0%)	4	2
1999	27	21 (77.8%)	4	2
2000	24	20 (83.3%)	2	1
2001	23	20 (87.0%)	2	1
2002	23	21 (91.3%)	1	1
2003	23	20 (87.0%)	2	1
2004	23	21 (91.3%)	0	1
2005	22	21 (95.5%)	0	1
2006	20	18 (90.0%)	1	1
2007	20	18 (90.0%)	1	1
2008	20	18 (90.0%)	1	1

Note: Countries added to the review: in 1992—China, Guatemala, Venezuela; in 1996—Cambodia, Dominican Republic, Haiti, Vietnam.
Source: See table 4.1

the Panama resolution passed by only one vote. Because none of these efforts was taken up by the House, the Reagan administration's certifications went unchanged.[45] Following the certification process in 1988, the Senate successfully passed a resolution on Mexico but again the measure was not taken up by the House.[46] Presidential certification of Mexico during the mid-1990s despite high profile issues of corruption and drug trafficking once again sparked a congressional backlash. However, as in 1988 Congress failed to muster the votes necessary for decertification.[47]

45. Elaine Shannon, *Desperados: Latin Drug Lords, U.S. Lawmen, and the War America Can't Win* (New York: Signet, 1989), 482–96; Perl, "International Narcotics Control," 10.
46. The time period was initially set at thirty days. Perl, "International Narcotics Control," 10; Raphael F. Perl, "Narcotics Certification of Drug Producing and Trafficking Nations: Questions and Answers," *CRS Report for Congress,* March 27, 2000, 5; Shannon, *Desperados,* 482–96.
47. Spencer, "Drug Certification"; Council on Hemispheric Affairs, "Decertifying the Uncertifiable."

The Department of State's certification recommendations and the inability of Congress to overturn these recommendations reflected the efforts of administration officials. During the late 1980s, for example, Drug Enforcement Administration (DEA) and Customs officials stressed cooperative efforts underway with the Bahamian government as ruling against decertification. Support from the U.S. ambassador to Mexico Charles Pilliod and Attorney General Edwin Meese influenced the ranking process for Mexico despite growing frustration within the DEA, Customs, and Department of State over the actions of the Mexican government. In the case of Panama, officials from the DEA, Central Intelligence Agency, and National Security Council emphasized the role of General Manuel Noriega as a strategic asset in intelligence operations despite growing evidence of corruption, repression, and drug trafficking. But by 1988 the combination of Panamanian government's response to political unrest and formal indictments in Florida against General Noriega for drug trafficking created growing political liability for the Reagan administration. As a result, Panama was added to the decertification category.[48]

Effectiveness

The effectiveness of the certification system in counternarcotics remains controversial. As argued by U.S. presidential administrations since the system's inception, certification has resulted in greater narcotics control efforts abroad. The threat of decertification conveys U.S. "seriousness" on the issue to foreign governments, leading them to do what they would otherwise not do—signing treaties, adopting legislation, and engaging in enforcement steps (such as eradication efforts, crackdowns on production facilities, and trafficking networks)—often at great political and economic cost.[49] Critics of the certification process challenge the "seriousness" claim by pointing to the uneven application of certifications and the use of waivers as undermining the system's legitimacy and credibility, and the shortcomings of the supply-side focus of the certification process.[50] Critics also question the effectiveness of such efforts, and the use of hectare and yield

48. See discussion in Shannon, *Desperados*, 482–96; Bagley, "U.S. Foreign Policy," 192; "The Senate Foreign Relations Committee and the War on Drugs," in *Drugs in the Western Hemisphere: An Odyssey of Cultures in Conflict*, ed., William O. Walker III (Wilmington, DE: Scholarly Resources, 1996), 198–201.

49. See discussion in Chinen, "Presidential Certifications," 266–67; Carpenter, "Declaring an Armistice in the International Drug War"; Ayling, "Conscription in the War on Drugs," 378.

50. Spencer, "Drug Certification"; Carpenter, "Declaring an Armistice in the International Drug War"; Rafael Perl, "Drug Control: International Policy and Approaches," CRS Issue Brief for Congress, September 8, 2003.

estimates as well as interdiction/seizure data as indicators of progress. As summarized by Congressional Research Service analyst Rafael Perl, "efforts to significantly reduce the flow of illicit drugs from abroad into the United States have so far not succeeded."[51] Ultimately, however, the certification system assesses the extent to which governments are cooperating with the United States more than it assesses the extent to which these cooperative efforts are successful in curtailing the drug trade.

If, as administration proponents have argued, the certification process leads governments on the majors list to act, one should see these efforts reflected in changes in their certification status. As table 4.3 shows, this has not been the case. Of the three countries that were first ranked on the majors list as decertified, Iran and Syria were dropped from the list with little sense that cooperation with the United States had led to them ceasing to meet the criteria of the majors list. The third country, Afghanistan, became certified only following regime change in the early 1990s, only to lose certification with the rise of the Taliban and regain it in the aftermath of invasion and the ongoing consolidation of the U.S.-backed government.[52] Those countries that were first ranked as certified by national interest waiver have either gone through dramatic swings of status (the noncertification, certification, waivers, and certification path of Laos) or were removed from the majors list (Lebanon after eleven years).

Those countries that were initially ranked as certified and lost their rankings reveal greater diversity. Three countries recovered status after one year: Bolivia and Peru from 1994 to 1995, and Guatemala from 2003 to 2004. Four countries took a longer path back to certification lasting between three and six years: Colombia and Nigeria from 1994 to 1999, Pakistan from 1996 to 1999, and Haiti from 1999 to 2005. Two countries struggled to return and hold onto certified status: Panama from 1988 to 1996 and Paraguay from 1998 to 2000. Other governments never recovered (Burma), were removed from the list (Cambodia), or it is too early to determine their future at the time of this writing (Venezuela). Finally, of those governments that were initially ranked as certified and have retained this status, six are no longer on the list despite their continued role in drug production/transshipment: Aruba, Belize, China, Hong Kong, Thailand, and Vietnam. Those that remain on the majors list continue to draw

51. Walsh, "Are We There Yet"; Raphael Perl, "Drug Control: International Policy and Approaches," CRS Issue Brief for Congress, February 2, 2006, summary.

52. Afghanistan remains certified despite the country's continued prominence as the source of opium for over 92 percent of the world's heroin. United Nations Office on Drugs and Crime, "World Drug Report," 2007, 7, 195–200, http://www.unodc.org/unodc/en/data-and-analysis/WDR-2007.html.

Table 4.3. Changes in narcotics certification status, 1987–2008

	Move to certified status	National interest waiver	Not certified/ failed demonstrably	Removed
1987		Laos Lebanon	Afghanistan Iran Syria	
1988		Laos Lebanon Paraguay*	Afghanistan Iran Panama* Syria	
1989	Paraguay**	Lebanon	Afghanistan Burma* Iran Laos** Panama Syria	
1990	Laos** Panama***	Lebanon	Afghanistan Burma Iran Syria	
1991		Lebanon	Afghanistan Burma Iran Syria	
1992		Lebanon	Afghanistan Burma Iran Syria	
1993		Afghanistan*** Lebanon	Burma Iran Syria	
1994		Afghanistan Bolivia* Colombia* Laos* Lebanon Panama* Peru*	Burma Iran Nigeria* Syria	Morocco*
1995		Afghanistan Bolivia Colombia Laos Lebanon Panama Peru	Burma Iran Nigeria Syria	
1996	Bolivia** Laos** Panama** Peru**	Lebanon Pakistan*	Afghanistan** Burma Colombia** Iran Nigeria Syria	

(*Table 4.3.—cont.*)

	Move to certified status	National interest waiver	Not certified/ failed demonstrably	Removed
1997		Lebanon Pakistan	Afghanistan Burma Colombia Iran Nigeria Syria	
1998		Cambodia* Colombia*** Pakistan Paraguay*	Afghanistan Burma Iran Nigeria	Lebanon** Syria***
1999	Colombia** Pakistan**	Cambodia Haiti* Nigeria*** Paraguay	Afghanistan Burma	Iran*** Malaysia*
2000	Nigeria** Paraguay**	Cambodia Haiti	Afghanistan Burma	Aruba* Belize* HK*
2001		Afghanistan Haiti	Burma	Cambodia**
2002	Afghanistan**	Haiti	Burma	
2003		Guatemala* Haiti	Burma	
2004	Guatemala*	Haiti	Burma	
2005	Haiti**		Burma	Thailand*
2006		Venezuela*	Burma	China* Vietnam*
2007		Venezuela	Burma	
2008		Venezuela	Burma	

Note: Coding: *prior status as certified; **prior status as waiver; ***prior status as not certified; ****prior status as not reviewed.
Source: See table 4.1.

varying degrees of congressional concern for their rankings: for example, Mexico, Jamaica, and the Bahamas attracting greater attention than Brazil, Ecuador, and India. In short, even metrics generated by the narcotics certification process raise questions as to the effectiveness of the approach.

Certification and Human Trafficking

During the 1990s, a wide ranging coalition of religious leaders, women's rights groups, government officials, and others brought increased attention to the issue of human trafficking, and especially the threat of trafficking of women and children for sexual exploitation.[53] These efforts resulted in the addition of the Palermo Protocol—to Prevent, Suppress, and Punish Trafficking in Persons, Especially Women and Children—to the 2000 United Nations Convention against Transnational Organized Crime.[54] Within the United States, these efforts culminated in the Victims of Trafficking and Violence Protection Act of 2000 (better known as the Trafficking Victims Protection Act, or TVPA), and facilitated its reauthorization in 2003, 2005, and 2008. As in the case of narcotics control, members of Congress turned to legislative measures as a means to address foreign efforts against trafficking and to hold the executive branch to task in prioritizing the issue.[55] The TVPA certification process entails annual reports by the Department of State regarding the extent of cooperation by foreign governments and incorporates threats of financial sanction in the absence of requisite compliance. Unlike the narcotics case, the certification process in human trafficking adds moral sanction through incorporating "name and shame" into a tier ranking system.[56]

The TVPA focuses on "severe forms" of human trafficking, defined as:

> sex trafficking in which a commercial sex act is induced by force, fraud or coercion, or in which the person induced to perform the act has not attained 18 years of age; or the recruitment, harboring, transportation, provision, or obtaining of a person for labor or services, through the use of force fraud or coercion for the purpose of subjection to involuntary servitude, peonage, debt bondage, or slavery.[57]

In addressing the challenge of severe forms of trafficking, the TVPA calls on the United States to "promote cooperation" through bilateral and multilateral efforts, and introduces a certification mechanism to facilitate

53. For a discussion of the continued role of these coalitions, see Feingold's chapter in this volume.

54. For example, see Victor Malarek, *The Natashas: Inside the New Global Sex Trade* (New York: Arcade, 2003); Allen D. Hertzke, *Freeing God's Children: The Unholy Alliance for Global Human Rights* (Lanham, MD: Rowman & Littlefield, 2004); Joyce Outshoorn, "The Political Debates on Prostitution and Trafficking of Women," *Social Politics* 12, no. 1 (Spring 2005): 141–55; Anthony DeStefano, *The War on Human Trafficking: U.S. Policy Assessed* (New Brunswick, NJ: Rutgers University Press, 2007).

55. Hertzke, *Freeing God's Children*, 317–35; DeStefano, *War on Human Trafficking*; and Janie Chuang, "The United States as Global Sheriff: Using Unilateral Sanctions to Combat Human Trafficking," *Michigan Journal of International Law* 27 (Winter 2006): 450–56.

56. On the dynamics of name and shame, see Margaret E. Keck and Kathryn Sikkink, *Activists Beyond Borders: Advocacy Networks in International Politics* (Ithaca: Cornell University Press, 1998), 23–29.

57. TVPA Section 103(8). Victims of Trafficking and Violence Protection Act of 2000 (TVPA 2000), http://www.state.gov/g/tip/rls/61124.htm. This focus differs from the broader definition of trafficking found in the Palermo Protocol.

these efforts.[58] Section 110(b) of the TVPA requires that the secretary of state submit an annual report to Congress that addresses "the status of severe forms of trafficking in persons," and includes assessments for each country "to which the minimum standards for the elimination of trafficking are applicable" concerning their level of compliance.[59] Responding to this requirement, the Department of State released the first *TIPR* in 2001.

Section 110(b) of the TVPA specifies three possible levels of compliance: those countries "whose governments fully comply" with the minimum standards; those countries "whose governments do not yet fully comply with such standards but are making significant efforts to bring themselves into compliance"; and those countries "whose governments do not fully comply with such standards and are not making significant efforts to bring themselves into compliance."[60] The 2003 Trafficking Victims Protection Reauthorization Act (TVPRA) added a "special watch list" covering those countries that had improved their level of compliance from the "previous annual report," and those countries that were making significant efforts to comply with the minimum standards but exhibited characteristics that distinguished them in a negative way from other countries making such efforts.[61]

In those cases where the president determines that a foreign government is not making significant efforts to comply, the TVPA allows for the withholding of "non-humanitarian, non-trade-related assistance." The threat of economic sanction includes aid provided under the 1961 FAA and the 1976 Arms Export Control Act, and the withholding of U.S. support for funding through multilateral development banks and the International Monetary Fund.[62] As in the case of drug certification, the TVPA empowers

58. TVPA, Section 102(24) and Section 110.

59. TVPA, Section 110(b). Section 104(a) also amends the annual Country Reports on Human Rights reporting requirements under Section 116(f) and 502B of the FAA of 1961 for recipient of U.S. economic and/or security assistance "that is a country of origin, transit or destination for victims of severe forms of trafficking in persons."

60. TVPA, Section 110(b)(1), Section 110(b)(3).

61. TVPA 2003 Reauthorization Act, Section 6(3)(A). As specified under Section 107 of the Wilberforce Act, amending Section 110 (b)(3), "countries on the special watch list for 2 consecutive years" after the act comes into force are automatically placed into the third category of noncompliant governments—what the Department of State has labeled Tier 3. This placement can be waived by the president for up to two years with the provision of "credible evidence" presented to Congress of efforts to comply. William Wilberforce Trafficking Victims Protection Reauthorization Act of 2008, 14–15, http://www.state.gov/g/tip/laws/index.htm.

62. TVPA, Section 103 (7), Section 110(d). Examples of exclusions from FAA sanction include narcotics-related assistance, refugee assistance, NGO development assistance, and antiterrorism assistance.

the president to waive sanctions if "in the national interest of the United States."[63]

Acting under the TVPA, by the early 2000s the United States had introduced a rating and ranking system to assess foreign compliance in efforts against human trafficking. As in the case of narcotics, the certification process in human trafficking has been rife with controversy since its introduction. National interest waivers, however, have been less controversial than the Department of State's rating and ranking of countries in the annual *TIPR*. Critics including the governments of countries targeted by the certification process have challenged the U.S. determinations as politically driven, noting among other concerns the tendency of allies to fare better than adversaries in the annual reports.

Inclusion

As specified by the 2000 TVPA, the "minimum standards for the elimination of trafficking" apply to "the government of a country of origin, transit, or destination for a significant number of victims of severe forms of trafficking."[64] In the December 2008 reauthorization of the TVPA Congress changed this specification by removing the qualifier of "significant number of victims."[65] In both the original and amended definitions, the range of inclusion into the *TIPR* certification process is broader than that found in the case of narcotics. Destination countries are addressed in addition to source and transit countries. There also is no requirement that the trafficking in persons must significantly affect the United States.

From 2000 to 2008, the TVPA offered no criteria, numerical or otherwise, to determine what comprised a "significant number of victims." In the political deliberations leading up to the TVPA, this terminology first appears in the Trafficking Victims Protection Act of 1999 (H.R. 3244) as introduced by Representative Christopher Smith (R-NJ) on November 8, 1999.[66] Although Senator Paul Wellstone (D-MN) and others were instrumental in bringing the idea of U.S. anti-trafficking legislation to fruition through resolutions and proposed legislation in 1998 and 1999, Smith played the more influential role in the addition of certification systems to assess foreign compliance into the TVPA.[67] Section 4 of H.R. 3244 requires that the Department of State add assessments on human trafficking to the

63. TVPA, Section 110(d)(4). The president also can waive sanctions if "necessary to avoid significant adverse effects on vulnerable populations, including women and children." TVPA, Section 110(d)(5)(B).

64. TVPA 2000 Section 108(a).

65. Wilberforce Act, 14.

66. The Trafficking Victims Protection Act of 1999, http://thomas.loc.gov/cgi-bin/query/F?c106:5:./temp/~c1061iI6qk:e38607.

67. DeStefano, *War on Human Trafficking*, 32–37.

Annual Country Reports on Human Rights Practices, for origin, transit and destination countries "with a significant number of victims of severe forms of trafficking." Section 8 adds the same threshold of inclusion to the definition of "minimum standards" for the elimination of trafficking, and H.R. 3244 uses Section 8 as the basis of its call in Section 10 for a new annual reporting and certification process focused on foreign government compliance with such standards.[68] The idea of holding foreign governments to "minimum standards" for the elimination of trafficking had appeared in legislation introduced by Smith earlier in March. Section 5(b) of the Freedom from Sexual Trafficking Act of 1999 (H.R. 1356) called for the secretary of state to submit annual reports to Congress "on the status of international sexual trafficking" that would include a list of all countries that had failed to meet the minimum standards.[69] However, with H.R. 3244 and the language of "significant number" the thresholds for inclusion had become narrower.

The question of the criteria for thresholds of inclusion does not appear to be a point of contention between the bill's supporters and opponents. For example, the greater concerns of the Clinton administration were focused on the entire idea of a new reporting/certification system and the system's threat of sanctions.[70] By late November 1999, the FY 2000 Consolidated Appropriations Act (P.L. 106–113) backed by the administration had adopted the idea of adding human trafficking to Annual Country Reports on Human Rights Practices. Section 597 of the act amended Section 116 of the 1961 FAA by requiring the addition of a list of *all* trafficking source, transit, and destination countries and an assessment of steps by the governments of those countries "to combat trafficking."[71] By May 2000, the Clinton administration was arguing, albeit unsuccessfully, that such steps made H.R. 3244's additional reporting/certification system unnecessary.[72] Ultimately, both measures would appear in the final TVPA.[73]

68. Section 4 and Section 8 H.R. 3244, http://thomas.loc.gov/cgi-bin/query/F?c106:2:./temp/~c106ADX0gb:e19385. The reasons for the addition are not addressed in the House report on the bill. The concept of a "significant trafficker" is also introduced in Section 11 (Actions against Significant Traffickers in Persons), but the criteria for significant once again are not specified.

69. H.R. 1356, The Freedom from Sexual Trafficking Act, March 25, 1999, http://thomas.loc.gov/cgi-bin/query/F?c106:1:./temp/~mdbs4qXudy:e11112.

70. DeStefano, *War on Human Trafficking*, 37.

71. P.L. 106–13 (November 29, 1999), Appendix B 113 Stat. 1501A—126–127, http://frwebgate.access.gpo.gov/cgi-bin/getdoc.cgi?dbname=106_cong_public_laws&docid=f:publ113.106.pdf.

72. White House, Office of Management and Budget, H.R. 3244, Trafficking Victims Protection Act of 2000, May 9, 2000, http://www.whitehouse.gov/omb/legislative/sap/106-2/print/HR3244-h.html.

73. See Section 104(a) and (b) of the 2000 TVPA requiring the assessment of government efforts on human trafficking to be included in the Annual Country Reports on Human

In the absence of steps to clarify the language of a "significant number of victims," Department of State officials developed their own threshold for inclusion. As discussed in the methodology section of the *TIPR*, this threshold is met where the country is a source, transit, or destination for "generally on the order of 100 or more victims."[74] The origins of this figure lie in the data collection and analysis processes of the first report. Drawing on questionnaires sent to U.S. embassies seeking information on trafficking levels and government responses and following extensive internal discussions, officials in State's Bureau of International Narcotics and Law Enforcement concluded that "only numbers in the hundreds or higher were considered significant."[75] Beginning with the 2002 *TIPR* this language was tightened to the "100 or more" standard.

The Government Accountability Office's (GAO) 2006 review of the *TIPR* process notes problems with the threshold including determining whether such victims were subject to *severe* forms of trafficking and the absence of supporting data in many cases demonstrating that the thresholds had been met.[76] This still begs the question of why the figure was set and remained at 100 persons, rather than at a lower or higher level.

From the outset, the view that even one victim of trafficking was one victim too many informed the agency's internal discussions. Five years later as observed by the GAO, "Some State officials have suggested abandoning the threshold of 100 victims and including all countries in the report."[77] Whether due to some combination of a natural breakpoint in the embassy data collected in 2001, the allure of a round number, or a negotiated compromise, the threshold of significance has allowed the Department of State's Office to Monitor and Combat Trafficking in Persons (G/TIP) to engage in broad country coverage in the application of anti-trafficking efforts. Eighty-two countries were tier ranked in 2001, 90 in 2002, 116 in 2003, 131 in 2004, 142 in 2005, 149 in 2006, 151 in 2007, and 153 countries in the 2008 *TIPR*.

The William Wilberforce Trafficking Victims Protection Reauthorization Act of 2008, signed into law by President George W. Bush on December

---

Rights Practices. These provisions applied to all countries receiving U.S. economic or security assistance.

74. This specific language was first introduced in the 2005 report. From 2002 to 2004, the language was "on the order of one hundred or more." U.S. Department of State, *Trafficking in Persons Report 2005*, http://www.state.gov/g/tip/rls/tiprpt/2005/46606.htm.

75. U.S. Department of State, *2001 Trafficking in Persons Report*, http://www.state.gov/g/tip/rls/tiprpt/2001/3929.htm; DeStefano, *The War Against Trafficking*, 119; Author's correspondence with Department of State officials, May 20, 2008.

76. U.S. GAO, *Human Trafficking*, 30.

77. Author's correspondence with Department of State officials, May 20, 2008; U.S. GAO, *Human Trafficking*, 30.

23, 2008, expands this coverage even further.[78] Section 106 of the Wilberforce Act amends Section 108(a) of the TVPA by removing "a significant number" of victims from the criteria for inclusion. The minimum standards for elimination of trafficking under the amended language thus will apply to "the government of a country of origin, transit, or destination for victims of severe forms of trafficking."[79] In effect, with this amendment the Department of State no longer needs its numerical baseline to establish a threshold of significance. The presence of any number of trafficking victims becomes the criteria for inclusion.[80]

Ranking

For those countries that meet the threshold of inclusion, the TVPA requires the secretary of state to assess and report to Congress the extent of government compliance with the minimum standards for the elimination of trafficking. These standards are specified in detail in Section 108(a):

(1) The government of the country should prohibit severe forms of trafficking in persons and punish acts of such trafficking; (2) For the knowing commission of any act of sex trafficking involving force, fraud, coercion, or in which the victim of sex trafficking is a child incapable of giving meaningful consent, or of trafficking which includes rape or kidnapping or which causes a death, the government of the country should prescribe punishment commensurate with that for grave crimes, such as forcible sexual assault; (3) For the knowing commission of any act of a severe form of trafficking in persons, the government of the country should prescribe punishment that is sufficiently stringent to deter and that adequately reflects the heinous nature of the offense; (4) The government of the country should make serious and sustained efforts to eliminate severe forms of trafficking in persons.

The specific criteria for "determinations" regarding the minimum standards under the fourth category are extensive and address various dimensions of prosecution of trafficking in persons, victims' protections, and prevention measures. Seven broad criteria were introduced under this category in the 2000 TVPA. The 2003 TVPRA amended these criteria in

---

78. For other ramifications of the Wilberforce Act, see Feingold's chapter in this volume.

79. Wilberforce Act, 12.

80. At the time of this writing it is still too early to determine the impact this shift will have on the *TIPR*. As noted by Department of State officials (Author's correspondence from April 6, 2009), the changes in inclusion would take effect in the 2009 *TIPR*. Yet the terminology of significant number of victims also appears in other areas such as the Tier 2 Watch List discussed below.

part by adding three new ones; the 2005 and 2008 TVPRA amended the criteria still further.[81]

As noted above, the 2000 TVPA specified three levels of compliance with the minimum standards for the elimination of trafficking while the 2003 TVPRA added the special watch list as a monitoring category. In practice, Department of State officials have recast the three levels as ranked tiers in the annual *TIPR*. Tier 1 consists of those countries "whose governments fully comply" with these standards, Tier 2 of those "whose governments do not yet fully comply with such standards but are making significant efforts" to do so, and Tier 3 of those "whose governments do not fully comply with such standards and are not making significant efforts" to do so.

The 2004 *TIPR* incorporated the special watch list with an additional twist. G/TIP introduced a new ranked certification level falling between Tier 2 and Tier 3 known as the "Tier 2 Watch List." This list consists of countries on Tier 2 where:

> The absolute number of victims of severe forms of trafficking is very significant or is significantly increasing; there is a failure to provide evidence of increasing efforts to combat severe forms of trafficking in persons from the previous year, including investigations, prosecutions and convictions of trafficking crimes, increased assistance to victims and decreasing evidence of complicity in severe forms of trafficking; or the determination that a country is making significant efforts to bring themselves into compliance with minimum standards was based on commitments by the country to take the additional steps over the next year.[82]

Although drawing on the broader special watch list provisions, the Tier 2 Watch List was not mandated by the 2003 TVPRA.

The Section 108 standards for placement of countries into the tiers are in some ways clearer than those used for narcotics certification. For example, the first two standards require assessing whether trafficking either is or is not prohibited by law, and whether punishment for trafficking offenses is or is not commensurate with that for other grave crimes. Beyond these minimum standards, however, the criteria become problematic. The third standard requires assessing whether governments are taking steps "sufficiently stringent to deter" trafficking. Yet all countries subject to

---

81. For details on these criteria, see TVPA 2000 Section 108 (b); Trafficking Victims Protection Reauthorization Act of 2003, Section 6(d), http://www.state.gov/g/tip/rls/61130.htm; Trafficking Victims Protection Reauthorization Act of 2005, Section 104 (b)(1), http://www.state.gov/g/tip/rls/61106.htm; William Wilberforce Trafficking Victims Protection Reauthorization Act of 2008, http://www.state.gov/g/tip/laws/index.htm.

82. TVPA 2003 section 6(3)(A).

assessment under the *TIPR* are distinguished by a "significant number of victims" suggesting that they have failed to deter trafficking.

The fourth standard of "serious and sustained efforts" against severe trafficking leads to the greatest potential for subjective application. The "indicia of serious and sustained efforts" are especially vague in that there are no criteria in the TVPA as amended as to what levels of performance on these indicators count as either serious or sustained. Of particular note are requirements that the government "vigorously" engages in investigation and prosecution and "achieves appreciable progress" in eliminating trafficking when compared to the preceding year—criteria, which in the absence of more precise metrics, lie in the eye of the beholder.[83] Further problems appear in the absence of any clear sense as to how the ten indicia, increased to eleven with the Wilberforce Act, let alone the four standards, are to fit together. When pressed by the GAO in 2006 for failing to fully follow the TVPA criteria in tier placements, the official Department of State response was that Congress did not specify that the criteria for assessing a government's "serious and sustained efforts" to deal with trafficking *must* be used, only that they *"should"* be considered.[84]

Those countries whose governments do not meet the standards of Tier 1 face additional ranking criteria that broadly focus on the extent to which they are engaged in the "significant efforts to comply" necessary for a Tier 2 ranking. Section 110(b)(3) posits that the secretary of state "shall consider" three criteria in this determination: the "extent to which the country" is a destination, transit or source country for severe trafficking; "the extent of noncompliance with the minimum standards," especially those involving government complicity in trafficking; and the measures "reasonable to bring the government into compliance" given its "resources and capabilities." The level of "extent" of trafficking or compliance necessary to demonstrate significant efforts remains unclear. Similar problems appear in the levels of "significance," "significantly increasing," and "significant efforts" necessary for placement on the Tier 2 Watch List instead of on Tier 3. In effect and even more than the case of narcotics certification, the politics of numbers in ranking has been distinguished by the absence of numbers.[85]

---

83. Governments are to take steps such as protecting victims, adopting education and awareness measures, cooperating with other governments, participating in extradition, monitoring of migration patterns, data provision, systematic monitoring of efforts, public assessment, and demand reduction (including that linked with sex tourism and foreign deployment in peacekeeping missions). TVPA Section 108(b); 2003 TVPRA Section 6(d); 2005 TVPRA Section 104(b).

84. U.S. GAO, *Human Trafficking*, 55–56.

85. As the *TIPR* applied the criteria in practice critics noted the relative absence of data linked to the tier placements including details on the numbers of trafficking victims and

Political controversy has focused more on patterns in the placement of countries in the *TIPR* ordinal tiers.[86] Placement in Tier 3 has been relatively rare. Tier 3 placements declined from a high of twenty-three countries in 2001 to fifteen countries in the first year of sanctions determinations in 2003 (see table 4.4). Since 2004 and the introduction of the Tier 2 Watch List, an average of only 9.1 percent of all countries ranked appear on Tier 3. A positive interpretation of this trend is that the threat of a Tier 3 ranking has led governments to extensive shifts in policy and practice, but such claims must be approached with caution. Placement on Tier 1 has been larger than that of Tier 3 but is still overshadowed by the Tier 2 and Tier 2 Watch List rankings. Table 4.5 offers a more detailed breakdown of countries by their initial rankings in the *TIPR* process. This initial placement has been dominated by Tier 2 rankings, with Tier 1 rankings heavily comprised of advanced industrial countries and U.S. political allies and the presence of such countries in Tier 3 being relatively rare.

On July 12, 2001, the Department of State released the first *TIPR* placing twelve countries in Tier 1, forty-seven in Tier 2, and twenty-three in Tier 3. Those certified as meeting the minimum standards for elimination of trafficking were Austria, Belgium, Canada, Colombia, Germany, Hong Kong, Italy, the Netherlands, Spain, Switzerland, Taiwan, and the United Kingdom.[87] Critics questioned placement of Germany and the Netherlands on Tier 1—despite extensive prostitution and widespread roles as destination countries—as being shaped by broader U.S. political considerations.[88] By 2004, critics of Tier 1 rankings were also pointing to the absence of laws and protections for victims of labor trafficking in, for example, Germany, Sweden, and the United Kingdom.[89] In contrast, the Tier 3 rankings

---

prosecutions. See Malarek, *The Natashas*, 199–200. The 2003 TVPRA sought to address these shortfalls by requiring the provision of data by governments as part of the amended criteria under the fourth minimum compliance standard.

86. For a related discussion see chapters 3 and 5 in this volume.

87. *TIPR* 2001.

88. Changes in the Wilberforce Act focused on the issue of reducing demand for commercial sex, creating the possibility that these rankings may change in the future. For example, Section 106(2)(D) of the Wilberforce Act (2008, 14) modifies the TVPA Section 108(a)(4) provisions, as listed under Section 108(b) for "determining serious and sustained efforts" as part of the minimum standards to eliminate trafficking. Under the 2005 TVPRA (Section 104(b)(1)(A)), Congress had added the need to address the demand for commercial sex acts and sex tourism to the measures to prevent trafficking listed under Section 108(b)(3). The Wilberforce Act removes this change and moves the issue of demand for commercial sex to a separate category, Section 108(b)(11). Thus, in the absence of "serious and sustained efforts to reduce the demand for commercial sex acts and participation in international sex tourism by nationals of the country" a government will fail to meet the minimum standards for the elimination of trafficking, and will be ineligible for a Tier 1 ranking.

89. Chuang, "United States as Global Sheriff," 476–88.

Table 4.4. *TIPR* rankings by tier, 2001–2008

	Tier 1	Tier 2	Tier 2 WL	Tier 3	Total
2001	12 (14.6%)	47 (57.3%)	n.a.	23 (28.1%	82
2002	18 (20.0%)	53 (58.9%)	n.a.	19 (21.1%)	90
2003	26 (22.4%)	75 (64.7%)	n.a.	15 (12.9%)	116
2004	25 (19.1%)	54 (41.2%)	42 (32.1%)	10 (7.6%)	131
2005	24 (16.9%)	77 (54.2%)	27 (19.0%)	14 (9.9%)	142
2006	26 (17.5%)	79 (53.0%)	32 (21.5%)	12 (8.1%)	149
2007	28 (18.5%)	75 (49.7%)	32 (21.2%)	16 (10.6%)	151
2008	29 (19.0%)	70 (45.8%)	40 (26.1%)	14 (9.2%)	153

Source: U.S. Department of State, *Trafficking in Persons Report*, 2001–2008.

of Israel and South Korea in 2001 initially appeared to counter claims of political favoritism in the *TIPR* placement. However, the meteoric rise of South Korea to Tier 1 status and Israel's ranking to Tier 2 status the following year strengthened arguments of a biased process.[90] Venezuela's fall from Tier 2 in 2004 to join political pariahs such as Cuba and Burma on Tier 3 raised similar concerns as the shift came in the context of increasing tensions between presidents George Bush and Hugo Chávez.

As revealed by the GAO in 2006, political bargaining over tier rankings within the Department of State was undermining the credibility of the ranking process. Tensions between the narrow issue focus of the Trafficking Office and the broader political concerns of State's Regional Bureaus over proposed placements resulted in greater weight being placed on political concerns and disagreements being resolved at times by bargaining. In the case of the latter, the GAO noted the practice of "'horse trading' whereby the Trafficking Office agrees to raise some countries' tier rankings in exchange for lowering others."[91] Political bargaining between Congress and the Executive over ranking reveals a different pattern than that found in the narcotics certification process. Congressional resolutions calling for the reclassification of specific rankings and legislative efforts comparable to the narcotics efforts against Mexico and Panama to move countries into different tiers have failed to emerge. Instead, political efforts in Congress have focused more on using the TVPRA to raise the bar for higher tier rankings and on seeking personnel changes at the upper levels of the Department of State's Trafficking Office.[92]

90. Malarek, *The Natashas*, 188–208; DeStefano, *War on Human Trafficking*, 111–27.
91. U.S. GAO, *Human Trafficking*, 32–33.
92. Part of the difference lies in the specifics of authorizing legislations for the two processes. On the issue of personnel change see the push to replace the first director of the office Ambassador Nancy Ely-Raphael. Hertzke, *Freeing God's Children*, 317–35.

Table 4.5. Countries coded by their initial tier ranking in the annual *Trafficking in Persons Report*, 2001–2008

Tier 1 (20)	Tier 2 (91)	Tier 2 WL (13)	Tier 3 (34)
Australia, Austria, Belgium, Canada, Colombia, Denmark, Germany, Hong Kong, Ireland, Italy, Luxembourg, Mauritius, Netherlands, New Zealand, Norway, Portugal, Spain, Switzerland, Taiwan, United Kingdom	Albania, Angola, Algeria, Argentina, Bangladesh, Benin, Bolivia, Brazil, Brunei, Bulgaria, Burkina Faso, Burundi, Cambodia, Cameroon, Chad, China, Chile, Costa Rica, Cote D'Ivoire, Croatia, Czech Republic, Dominican Republic, East Timor (Timor-Leste), Egypt, Equatorial Guinea, El Salvador, Estonia, Ethiopia, Finland, France, Gambia, Georgia, Ghana, Guinea, Guinea-Bissau, Guatemala, Haiti, Honduras, Hungary, India, Jamaica, Japan, Jordan, Kenya, Kuwait, Kyrgyzstan (Kyrgyz Republic), Laos, Latvia, Libya, Lithuania, Macedonia, Malawi, Malaysia, Mali, Malta, Mexico, Moldova, Mongolia, Morocco, Mozambique, Nepal, Nicaragua, Niger, Nigeria, Oman, Panama, Philippines, Poland, Rwanda, Senegal, Serbia (and Montenegro), Sierra Leone, Singapore, Slovak Republic, Slovenia, South Africa, Sri Lanka, Syria, Sweden, Tanzania, Thailand, Togo, Tunisia, Uganda, Ukraine, Uruguay, Venezuela, Vietnam, Yemen, Zambia, Zimbabwe	Azerbaijan, Central African Republic, Cyprus, Djibouti, Fiji, Macau, Madagascar, Mauritania, Montenegro, Papua New Guinea, Paraguay, Peru, Republic of Congo	Armenia, Afghanistan, Bahrain, Belarus, Belize, Bosnia-Herzegovina, Burma, Cuba, Democratic Republic of Congo, Ecuador, Gabon, Greece, Guyana, Iran, Indonesia, Israel, Kazakhstan, Lebanon, Liberia, North Korea, Pakistan, Qatar, Romania, Russia, Saudi Arabia, South Korea, Suriname, Sudan, Tajikistan, Turkey, UAE, Uzbekistan, Federal Republic of Yugoslavia

Source: U.S. Department of State, *Trafficking in Persons Report,* 2001–2008.

Effectiveness

As in narcotics, the effectiveness of the certification system in human trafficking is controversial. The Department of State response to the GAO inquiry emphasized that the *TIPR* has served to "raise awareness and motivate action" on human trafficking worldwide.[93] Awareness of the issue of human trafficking clearly has increased but campaigns by the United Nations, international and local nongovernmental organizations, national governments, and the media also have played important roles. Action has been motivated by the *TIPR*'s threats of shame and sanction.[94] In Thailand, for example, "government agencies are very sensitive to the grading they are awarded and strive to provide positive information to those responsible for its compilation."[95] Legislation, enforcement, cooperation with nongovernmental organizations, and other steps taken by countries such as Turkey, Greece, Jamaica, and Japan in the face of name and shame and sanction threats were highlighted by the Department of State in 2006 as *TIPR* success stories in response to the GAO critique.[96] In the Balkans, governments have developed National Action Plans and regional cooperative initiatives in areas of prosecution, prevention, and protection.[97] Yet the extent to which steps taken in the rush to avoid poor rankings have been properly conceived and well executed remains a point of concern.[98] Prosecution has tended to receive greater prioritization in the ranking process and, in turn, in the response of foreign governments. But even foreign governments included as success stories by the Department of State, have been slow to fully implement steps against trafficking.[99]

Numerical indicators of progress from 2003 to 2007 as highlighted in the 2008 *TIPR* consist of regional data on prosecutions and convictions of traffickers as well as the introduction of new or amended trafficking legislation. The overall numbers have increased with a total of 32,985 prosecutions, 17,194 convictions, and 152 legislation changes during the five-year

93. U.S. GAO, *Human Trafficking*, 51.
94. The actual full use of sanctions against Tier 3 countries has been the exception rather than the rule, applied more to countries already isolated by U.S. policy—such as Burma, Cuba, and North Korea. Tier 3 countries such as Saudi Arabia and Kuwait have typically been waived from sanctions.
95. Anne Gallagher, "Human Rights and Human Trafficking in Thailand: A Shadow TIP Report," in *Trafficking and the Global Sex Industry*, ed. Karen Beeks and Delila Amir (Lanham, MD: Lexington Books, 2006), 141. On trafficking, the *TIPR*, and Thailand also see Feingold's chapter in this volume.
96. U.S. GAO, *Human Trafficking*, 57. On Japan, also see Warren's chapter in this volume.
97. Friman and Reich, *Human Trafficking*.
98. DeStefano, *War on Human Trafficking*, 125–26.
99. On Japan for example, see Kevin Bales, *Ending Slavery: How We Free Today's Slaves* (Berkeley: University of California Press, 2007), 111–13.

Table 4.6. *Trafficking in Persons Report* Highlighted Impact Indicators, 2003–2007

	Region	Prosecutions	Convictions	New or amended legislation
2003	Africa	50	10	3
	East Asia & Pacific	1,727	583	1
	Europe	2,231	1,469	14
	Near East	1,004	279	4
	South and Central Asia	2,805	447	0
	Western Hemisphere	175	27	2
	TOTAL	7,992	2,815	24
2004	Africa	134	29	7
	East Asia & Pacific	438	348	3
	Europe	3,270	993	20
	Near East	134	59	1
	South and Central Asia	2,764	1,541	1
	Western Hemisphere	145	56	7
	TOTAL	6,885	3,026	39
2005	Africa	194	58	12
	East Asia & Pacific	2,580	2,347	5
	Europe	2,521	1,792	12
	Near East	112	104	3
	South and Central Asia	1,041	406	0
	Western Hemisphere	170	59	9
	TOTAL	6,618	4,766	41
2006	Africa	170	51	3
	East Asia & Pacific	1,321	763	3
	Europe	2,950	1,821	7
	Near East	295	187	2
	South and Central Asia	629	275	0
	Western Hemisphere	443	63	6
	TOTAL	5,808	3,160	20
2007	Africa	123	63	5
	East Asia & Pacific	1,074	651	4
	Europe	2,820	1,941	7
	Near East	415	361	1
	South and Central Asia	824	298	4
	Western Hemisphere	426	113	7
	TOTAL	5,682	3,427	28
Total		32,985	17,194	152

Note: Western Hemisphere figures exclude the United States.
Source: U.S. Department of State, *Trafficking in Persons Report,* 2008, 45–50.

period (see table 4.6). The table also reveals that prosecutions peaked in 2003, and convictions and legislation in 2005. The 2008 *TIPR* figures offer little insight into the nature of the offenses prosecuted, the lengths of sentences, and content of the legislation. Patterns in reducing the number of trafficking victims remain even less clear. The 2008 *TIPR,* citing U.S. government backed research, estimates that 800,000 persons are victims of international trafficking each year. Despite eight years of *TIPR* influence, however, this figure has changed little. In the 2001 and 2002 *TIPR* reports the official U.S. estimate was 700,000 persons, in 2003 the figure increased to 800,000 to 900,000 persons, from 2004 to 2006 the number decreased to 600,000 to 800,000, and in the 2007 and the 2008 *TIPR* the number changed to the upper end of this range at 800,000 persons.[100]

Ultimately as in the case of narcotics, the certification system assesses the extent to which governments are cooperating with the United States more than it assesses the extent to which these cooperative efforts are successful. Movement up in tier ranks is presented in the *TIPR* as an indicator of progress in cooperation with U.S. diplomatic efforts.[101] The reports explicitly note that "no country placement is permanent" and thus "all countries must maintain and increase their efforts to combat trafficking" in order to retain their high tier rankings or improve their positions.[102] The *TIPR*'s narrative sections offer brief insights into specific steps taken by countries in the areas of prosecution, prevention, and protection. However, the tier rankings and shifts in tier rankings are the focal point of the annual reports.

Table 4.7 reveals that out of the 138 countries that were not initially classified in Tier 1 in the *TIPR* process only 12 have made enough progress in the eyes of the Department of State to be moved up to Tier 1 and have remained ranked at this level. South Korea is the only country to have moved from an initial ranking of Tier 3 to Tier 1. In 2008 Madagascar became the first country initially ranked on the Tier 2 Watch List to make the transition to Tier 1. Table 4.7 also reveals that nine other countries moved up from their initial Tier 2 rankings to Tier 1, but have failed to remain

---

100. *TIPR 2008,* 7.

101. For example, the introduction to the 2002 *TIPR* offered a brief summary of movement of countries in tier rankings compared to the prior year. Since 2005, the reports have included summary figures concerning the number of special watch list countries that had moved up or down from the baseline of tier rankings in interim assessments as well as compared to the prior year. The Wilberforce Act provisions limiting time spent on the Special Watch List also will increase the focus on movement over time. Phone interview with Department of State official, March 10, 2009.

102. This statement appears in each of the reports, with "including the United States" appearing since 2004.

Table 4.7. Movement to (and subsequently from) Tier 1 ranking, by country and year of reclassification, 2002–2008

Rise to Tier 1 and remain (12 countries)	Rise to and subsequent fall from Tier 1 (8 countries)	Rise, fall, and return to Tier 1 (1 country)
Croatia (2008), Czech Republic (2002), Finland (2006), France (2002), Georgia (2007), Hungary (2007), Lithuania (2002), Madagascar (2008), Poland (2002), Slovenia (2007) South Korea (2002), Sweden (2003)	Benin (2003, fall since 2004), Czech Republic (2002, fall since 2006), Ghana (2003, fall since 2005), Malawi (2006, fall since 2008), Morocco (2003, fall since 2008), Nepal (2005, fall since 2006), Singapore (2006, fall since 2007), the UAE (2003, fall since 2004)	Macedonia (2002, fall 2005–2007, return 2008)

Source: U.S. Department of State, *Trafficking in Persons Report,* 2001–2008.

at this level.[103] Granted, movement up to Tier 1 is a high threshold for assessing progress in U.S. diplomacy,[104] although because the TIP process has been in place for eight years it would be reasonable to hold the process to this standard.

Lowering the bar does reveal a more positive outcome. Since 2004, Tier 2 Watch List countries have received special scrutiny in annual and interim assessments of their efforts toward compliance with the minimum standards. In 2004, forty-five countries were placed on the inaugural Tier 2 Watch List. Table 4.8 traces the subsequent *TIPR* rankings for these countries through the 2008 report. Of the forty-five countries, only India and Russia have failed to move off the Tier 2 Watch List, and only Qatar has fallen to a Tier 3 ranking. Three countries—Croatia, Madagascar, and Malawi—eventually advanced to Tier 1 status. Twenty-eight countries have moved up to Tier 2 and remained at this level, six countries have fallen back in rank and recovered, and ten countries have fallen back and not recovered. In short, movement off the Tier 2 Watch List as a standard for assessing the effectiveness of the certification process yields more positive results.

103. By comparison, five of the twenty countries initially listed as Tier 1 have fallen from this ranking: Canada (2003), Taiwan (2003–8), Switzerland (2004–5), Mauritius (2004–8), and Portugal (2006–8).

104. All the more so since the minimum standards for the elimination of trafficking also have increased with the TVPRA of 2003 and 2005, and Wilberforce Act of 2008.

Table 4.8. Changes in tier ranking by countries originally listed on the 2004 Tier 2 watch list, 2005–2008

No rise (2 countries)	Fall to Tier 3 (1 country)	Rise to Tier 1 (3 countries)	Rise to Tier 2 and remain (28 countries)	Subsequent fall from Tier 2 to Tier 2 WL (10 countries)	Subsequent fall to from Tier 2 to Tier 3 (0 countries)	Subsequent fall and recover to Tier 2 (6 countries)
India, Russia	Qatar (2005, since 2007)	Croatia (2008, rise to Tier 2 in 2005), Madagascar (2008, rise to Tier 2 in 2005), Malawi (2006, rise to Tier 2 in 2005),	2005 (19): Cyprus, Estonia, Ethiopia, Gabon, Georgia, Guyana, Japan, Laos, Mauritania, Nigeria, Pakistan, Paraguay, Senegal, Serbia (and Montenegro), Tanzania, Thailand, Turkey, Vietnam, Zambia 2006 (4): Greece, Philippines, Sierra Leone, Suriname 2007 (4): Belize, Bolivia, Ecuador, Jamaica 2008 (1): Mexico	Azerbaijan (2008), Côte D'Ivoire (2008), Cyprus (since 2006), Democratic Republic of Congo (2008), Dominican Republic (since 2007), Gabon (2008), Guatemala (since 2007), Guyana (since 2007), Tajikistan (2008), Zimbabwe (2008)		Honduras (fall to WL in 2007, recover in 2008), Kazakhstan (fall to WL in 2007, recover in 2008), Kenya (fall to WL in 2006, recover in 2008), Laos (fall to Tier 3 in 2006, return 2007), Mauritania (fall to WL in 2006, return in 2008), Peru (fall to WL in 2006, return in 2008)

Note: In 2004, Ecuador, Guyana, and Sierra Leone were initially ranked at Tier 3 but shifted to the Tier 2 Watch List on subsequent presidential reassessment.
Source: U.S. Department of State, *Trafficking in Persons Report, 2001–2008.*

Conclusion

Certification systems assessing foreign government compliance have emerged as a high profile component of U.S. foreign policy. A structured, focused comparison of the certification systems in narcotics and human trafficking reveals that the politics of numbers is not limited to estimates of illicit flows but also appears in efforts to assess patterns of foreign compliance. Insights into the latter lie in exploring certification systems on the dimensions of inclusion, ranking, and effectiveness.

Both of the cases explored in this chapter reveal vague and subjective standards for inclusion. Although numerical thresholds exist for country inclusion on the narcotics majors and severe forms of human trafficking lists, only the former is specified by legislation and both lack identifiable justification for the specific threshold levels. Despite being the gateway into the certification process, these thresholds have attracted little attention in congressional deliberations or from the broader challenges of critics. Analysts have pointed extensively to the shortcomings of hectare and yield analysis but not the absence of justification for the actual numerical thresholds in the FAA or for that matter the qualifier that the country's drug activities must significantly affect the United States. The GAO and others have taken the Department of State to task for contending that countries have in fact met the 100 victims of human trafficking threshold but tend not to question the arbitrariness of the threshold itself. The result in practice has been a certification system in narcotics focused on the behavior of a small number of countries and a certification system in human trafficking with global reach.

The standards for ranking countries in the narcotics and human trafficking certification systems reveal a politics of numbers that largely eschews numbers as criteria for placement. Both ranking systems rely instead on an array of criteria and indicia that are vague at best when viewed in isolation and have been overshadowed by broader political concerns when selectively combined. Terms such as substantial, significant, serious, and fully complying/cooperating are overused and underspecified in the authorizing legislation. This has allowed U.S. national security considerations as interpreted and contested by officials within the Department of State and the Executive branch more broadly to influence the ranking process. It is in this context that the politics of numbers in the broader debate over ranking has shifted to emphasizing the numbers of countries that fall into the certification categories/ordinal tiers, and the rankings of particular countries of concern.

Given these issues in inclusion and ranking it is little surprise that determinations of the effectiveness of the narcotics and human trafficking certification systems have been mired in controversy. Both certification systems have raised the political profiles of drug and human trafficking and increased the legislative, enforcement, and other steps taken by foreign governments. These steps also have been distinguished by an array of problems in content, implementation, and impact. It is in this context that neither the falling numbers of countries on the narcotics majors list nor the high levels of certification for those that remain are assuring indicators of effectiveness. Similarly, little assurance is found in the increasing numbers of countries on the human trafficking list and the low levels of those that have improved to, and held onto, the highest tier ranking—a ranking that certifies meeting only the minimum standards for the elimination of the trade in human beings.

5

The Illusiveness of Counting "Victims" and the Concreteness of Ranking Countries

TRAFFICKING IN PERSONS
FROM COLOMBIA TO JAPAN

Kay B. Warren

Just a year after the Palermo Protocol established the international legal language to criminalize human trafficking in 2000, the U.S. State Department set up the international monitoring system that uses statistics—particularly estimates of the total number of victims per year—to make the case for interventions to combat trafficking as a global crisis. With an expanding interest in simple quantitative variables that can be tallied and graphed, the Office to Monitor and Combat Trafficking in Persons (G/TIP) created the dominant country-by-country schema to measure compliance with this new generation of international norms and punish noncompliance.[1] This

The author thanks Peter Andreas and Kelly M. Greenhill for the opportunity to participate in this collaboration. Andreas offered especially insightful feedback and cogent questions for which I am very grateful. I have been involved in field work and archival research related to this topic from 2003 to 2006 in Japan and from 2006 to 2009 in Colombia and Washington, D.C. This multi-sited research project has been funded by a Senior Research Fulbright; an Abe Fellowship from the Center for Global Partnership in Tokyo, the Social Science Research Council, and American Council of Learned Societies; the Rockefeller Center for Latin American Studies at Harvard University; the Center for Latin American and Caribbean Studies at Brown University; the Watson Institute for International Studies; and Brown University.

1. For analysis of the production of international norms designed to criminalize human traffickers rather than their victims, see Kay Warren, "The 2000 UN Human Trafficking Protocol: Rights, Enforcement, and Vulnerability," in *The Practice of Human Rights: Tracking Between the Global and the Local,* ed. Mark Goodale and Sally Merry (Cambridge: Cambridge University Press, 2007), 242–69.

chapter examines the U.S. monitoring system in action,[2] particularly with regard to the Pacific Rim trafficking route from Colombia to Japan via which women workers have been channeled to Japan's sex entertainment industry since the early 1980s.

This analysis asks: What makes counting—whether it be victims, prosecutions of traffickers, or return migrants—such an important yet illusive aspect of efforts to combat human trafficking as a transnational crime? What insights emerge about "the politics of numbers" when the standardizing object of the U.S. anti-trafficking monitoring system, designed to promote legal and policing reforms in addition to auditing compliance, is compared with diverse state policies and practices throughout the world?[3]

The elephant in the room is the international consensus—well established by 2005 and forcefully argued in 2006 by the U.S. Government Accountability Office and affirmed by other multilateral organizations—that there are really no reliable or credible statistics on the number of people who are internationally trafficked.[4] The 2008 TIP Report attempts to remedy this by citing a range of radically different estimates from the ILO and the U.S. government but the amazing differences between the estimates only underscore this foundational problem.[5]

The TIP Report's country rankings have become an alternative front for intensive numerical analysis by governments, NGOs, and academic experts as countries are arrayed each year on what amounts to a four-tiered ladder. For instance, at meetings sponsored by Vital Voices with the NGO community after the release of the report, the head of the TIP Report group, Mark Taylor, has routinely spent the major part of his always impressive presentation characterizing the bigger picture of how many countries in aggregate have moved up and down the rankings at different levels. Taylor did so at the expense of going into detail on the dilemmas of specific cases or the paradox of the heterogeneous situations in which the top tier

---

2. The Bush administration committed $528 million of programmatic funding—fiscal years 2001–7—for an abolitionist framing of the problem. As the G/TIP director during the Bush period, Mark Lagon, reported in the 2008 TIP Report, the goal of U.S. policy was "not to mitigate, or regulate, but rather to eliminate human trafficking." U.S. Department of State, *Trafficking in Persons Report 2008* (Washington, DC, 2008), 2.

3. For anthropological perspectives on the politics of numbers and audit culture, see Jean Comaroff and John L. Comaroff, "Figuring Crime: Quantifacts and the Production of the Un/Real," *Public Culture* 18 (2006): 209–46; Charles Briggs with Clara Mantini-Briggs, *Stories in the Time of Cholera: Racial Profiling during a Medical Nightmare* (Berkeley: University of California Press, 2004); and Marilyn Strathern, ed., *Audit Cultures: Anthropological Studies in Accountability, Ethics and the Academy* (London: Routledge, 2000).

4. U.S. GAO, *Human Trafficking: Better Data, Strategy, and Reporting Needed to Enhance U.S. Antitrafficking Efforts Abroad*, GAO-06–825 (Washington, DC: U.S. Government Accountability Office, 2006).

5. *Trafficking in Persons Report 2008*, 7.

of high achievers find themselves. His virtuoso performance argues for the rigorousness of the process, the science of this audit, while running out of time for a wide array of other issues that might be addressed.

To further justify these rankings and establish their urgency, the TIP reports feature narrative portrayals, most often in the form of third-person "testimonies"[6] of victimization. In 2008, these human interest stories of "modern-day slavery" included a much wider range of issues than the earlier reports. Over the years, the TIP Report seems to have come of age, with direct and effective responses to its critics. Photo collages of profiles are designed to dramatize the human cost of trafficking by concentrating on archetypal victims who stand for particularly vulnerable categories of people.[7] Although the 2008 Report opens with iconic images of innocent young women tricked into prostitution, it also covers women working outside the sex industry and the exploitation of men in a variety of situations. As the introduction continues with cases from many parts of the world, women are cast as exploiters—not just as victims—and children, especially young boys, are a major focus of concern. Trafficking is identified as a domestic and international issue, a change from earlier reports that focused on cross-border trafficking. The text offers a flood of different kinds of forced labor situations: North Korean refugees, boy victims of commercial sexual exploitation, child sex tourism, street children, migrant workers, child trafficking victims, products made by forced labor, and forced begging. Despite the growing concern in the TIP Report with a wider range of coercive and exploitative work situations, the common thread across the great majority of these cases of trafficked people from Romania, Lithuania, Mexico, China, Brazil, India, China, South Africa, Thailand, Bangladesh, the Philippines, and Senegal continues to be sexual exploitation.

The ironic juxtaposition of these two modes of knowledge production is striking. Ranking is constructed as a rigorous evidence-based process that focuses on numerical facts. The vignettes are designed to stir up moral outrage about these crimes and to challenge "compassion fatigue"[8] that plagues news coverage of violence in faraway places. Ironically, the often demeaned subjective and anecdotal evidence is, in effect, shoring up a numerical edifice with uncertain foundations. In the end, it is the rankings

6. This contrasts with wider testimonial literatures on violence and exploitation, which seek to present accounts in the speaker's voice.

7. Interestingly, the 2008 TIP Report states: "The photographs on this Report's cover and most uncaptioned photographs in the Report are not images of confirmed trafficking victims, but are provided to show the myriad forms of exploitation that help define trafficking and the variety of cultures in which trafficking victims are found," 4.

8. Susan D. Moeller, *Compassion Fatigue: How the Media Sell Disease, Famine, War and Death* (London: Routledge, 1999).

and their reputational consequences that capture the attention of many governments, including Colombia and Japan.

This chapter advances two lines of argumentation. First, it documents and discusses the consequences of the multi-sited production and circulation of international norms and discursive constructions of trafficking that are crafted as abstractions in the UN Protocol to Prevent, Suppress, and Punish Trafficking in Persons, Especially Women and Children (also known as the Palermo Protocol) and then knowingly replicated in altered form in distinctive national situations. Second, it examines the strange alchemy of comparison in TIP report audits where, despite being repeatedly discredited, certain facts and representations have particular powers and effects. They can be used tactically to stigmatize countries in ways that make them increasingly susceptible to political leverage and international coalitional politics despite the apparent indifference or lack of political will of recalcitrant countries to conform to these norms. The issue is what form this pressure takes and what it actually produces. What "counts" in this monitoring regime as compliance? Given the notoriously weak enforcement powers associated with international legal frameworks, what does actually change when countries capitulate and conform to TIP auditing policies?[9]

This chapter's multi-sited approach builds on the discussion of the mix of numerical and narrative knowledge produced in the process of monitoring human trafficking and the critiques of the TIP reports by trafficking activists in and outside the United States.[10] This analysis demonstrates how the process of monitoring takes on a life of its own, giving countries new identities to which they respond in strategic ways. Of special interest are the ways in which the very process of measurement in the field distorts and obscures that which is being measured.[11] The chapter goes on to discuss how Colombia and Japan, paired in this discourse as "a source country" and "a destination country," have responded to their relative rankings and appropriated the TIP schema for their own ends. The chapter then considers

9. My larger investigation, which I draw from for this analysis, has involved participant observer research and interviews at a series of meetings and conferences between 2007 and 2009 with U.S. State Department officials involved in the TIP report process, including the TIP report rollout meetings and the NGO meetings to critically review each new report. For the Japan-Colombia comparison, I attended anti-trafficking meetings and conferences and conducted interviews with government officials, NGO activists, and researchers in Japan between 2004 and 2006 and in Colombia between 2007 and 2009.

10. For a more ethnographic treatment of human trafficking and foreign aid for Japan and Colombia, see Kay B. Warren, "Trafficking in Persons: A Multi-Sited View of International Norms and Local Responses," in *Japanese Aid and the Construction of Global Development,* ed. David Leheny and Kay B. Warren (London: Routledge, 2010).

11. This is an interesting example of the Heisenberg principle.

telling slippages between the monitoring system and the on-the-ground realities of people's lives and bureaucratic practices in Colombia. At issue are return migrants' resistance to seeing themselves as "victims" and the criminal justice system's ambivalence about standardized modes of counting that fail to take bureaucratic functions into account. The chapter ends with a consideration of the ways national policy in Colombia has recently moved from the innocent victim paradigm to a neoliberal imaginary that emphasizes the collective vulnerability of some populations along with the capacity and responsibility of individuals to make their own choices about effective versus dangerous choices in labor migration.[12] This reorientation, shaped by worldwide neoliberal trends in governance, social welfare, and development policies, may well foreshadow a decline in the focus on women and adolescents involved in sex trafficking per se and, perhaps, resurgence in labor migration perspectives that are concerned with a much wider array of transnational workers on the move and their connections with their home countries.

Background on Human Trafficking

To understand the development of transregional human trafficking networks and the Pacific Rim route from Colombia to Japan, it is important to retrace the Palermo Protocol's journey from its birthplace amid much debate in Vienna, Austria, to Washington, D.C., and the rest of the world.[13] Of particular importance are the political and moral interests involved in the development of international legal norms to criminalize human trafficking through the 2000 Palermo Protocol, which forms part of the UN Convention on Transnational Organized Crime.[14] The legal definition of human trafficking stresses the international recruitment and transportation of individuals, "especially women and children," as the protocol repeatedly states, which involves some form of coercion to facilitate exploitation for financial gain. The definition has been read in two common ways. First, in the wide construction, as any form of labor that meets the legal standards,

---

12. See Wendy Brown, *Edgework: Critical Essays on Knowledge and Politics* (Princeton: Princeton University Press, 2005).

13. For the New York node in the production of gendered international norms, see Sally Engle Merry, *Human Rights and Gender Violence: Translating International Law into Local Justice* (Chicago: University of Chicago Press, 2006).

14. United Nations General Assembly, "UN Convention against Transnational Organized Crime," 2000; "UN Protocol to Prevent, Suppress and Punish Trafficking in Persons, especially Women and Children," 2000; and "UN Protocol against the Smuggling of Migrants by Land, Sea and Air," 2000, http://www.uncjin.org/Documents/Conventions/dcatoc/final_documents_2/index.htm.

whether it be agricultural labor, domestic work, mining, or child soldiers. In practice, however, many anti-trafficking campaigns have focused on women and children recruited for sexual exploitation. Here we see traces of the process through which a genealogy of central issues is consolidated. Debt bondage—that is, control over persons through inflated debts for transportation, travel documents, and job placement—is a very common form of trafficking in either the wide or the narrow construction.[15]

The history of U.S. commitments to anti-trafficking politics across the Clinton and Bush administrations shows how anti-trafficking politics became anti-prostitution policies as abolitionists challenged labor rights perspectives on human trafficking.[16] While the Bush administration pursued as national policy the neoabolitionist goal of eradicating prostitution globally, advocates of labor rights for migrants caught in trafficking networks have challenged the contours of this framing with some success. In the 2000s, the Department of Justice prosecuted cases dealing with different forms of labor. It has been fascinating to follow the clash of state policies, the separate streams of feminist perspectives that inform them historically, and the differing constructions of human rights discourse in anti-trafficking campaigns. These ongoing debates are significant because of their major effect on the practice of the U.S. State Department's international monitoring system.

The challenge for anti-trafficking research is to follow campaigns across major world regions to see how national governments and social movements reinterpret international norms for their own ends in distinctive cultural and economic contexts. As in the TIP Reports, there is a media dimension to this inquiry. In pursuing anti-trafficking projects, government bureaucracies and NGOs have become avid producers and appropriators of popular culture—circulating stories and scenarios that represent victimizers and the traumatic experiences of those who are victimized—in order to publicize their anti-trafficking efforts and reach wider publics. The circulation of media, including documentaries and fictional portrayals of trafficking, doubles as a way to raise public awareness about this new crime category and aid prevention efforts targeted at categories of people defined as "vulnerable" or "at risk" to the deceptive promises of international labor recruiters. The TIP Report and U.S. Congressional hearings

15. See Ann Jordan, "The Annotated Guide to the Complete UN Trafficking Protocol," International Rights Group, Washington, DC, 2002, http://www.walnet.org/csis/papers/UN-TRAFFICK.PDF.

16. For the abolitionist view of the protocol, see Janice Raymond, *Guide to the New UN Trafficking Protocol* (North Amherst, MA: Coalition against Trafficking in Women, 2001).

for the periodic renewal of the Trafficking Victims Protection Act (TVPA) actively appropriate and contribute to popular culture.

In the case of the Colombia-Japan trade, the asymmetry between the two countries' economic situations created the conditions of possibility for their reciprocal relationship as sending and receiving countries linked by organized crime networks. In the 1980s, this notorious current of trafficking was created to bring women as sex workers and men as foot soldiers for criminal gangs specializing in robbery and other criminal activities.[17] At that historic conjuncture, the Japanese economy moved into its "boom" period during which the Japanese entertainment industry and Japanese tourism expanded greatly. For its part, Colombia suffered a serious recession that left many in debt with few employment options. With the allure of easy money, criminal networks, and a culture of heightened consumption, the Medellín-based regional drug economy began to expand in the midst of growing political violence. It was at this point that Koichi "Sony" Hagiwara, a Japanese entrepreneur, travel agent, and college graduate who majored in Latin American Studies, moved from Japan to Colombia to organize a human trafficking network tied to the Yakuza—Japanese organized crime. After building ties with networks of Colombians and Peruvians for the Latin American side of the business, Sony moved back to Japan to head his own thriving enterprise. In 2002, he was arrested and prosecuted in Japan for trafficking related offenses in what was the first trial and conviction of a trafficker of Colombian women for sexual exploitation to Japan.

My ethnographic project brings this history up to date with an examination of human trafficking networks in contemporary Colombia, their regional focus, and recruitment practices. There would seem to be built-in tension in Colombian migrant imaginaries of international labor migration as a way for women to be able to afford to buy a house and consumer goods for their families; women's roles as local labor recruiters for criminal networks; and women workers' experiences of dislocation, traumatic violence, and cultural alienation in Japan.

Colombian and Japanese governments have responded to growing international pressures that focus on standardized legal and policing reforms, prevention programs, and social services to assist those who have been internationally trafficked. In this package of reforms, one sees the larger role that U.S. foreign policy plays in both countries, not only in criminalizing human trafficking but also in matters such as standardizing legal systems,

---

17. It is revealing that the highly gendered modes of recruitment of youths for transnational sex work and criminal gangs are not questioned in an integrated way.

regional security, and the war on drugs. By contrast, significant currents of U.S. politics under the Bush presidency—such as the religious right's abolitionist position, which informed anti-trafficking monitoring—appear not to have found traction in either Colombia or Japan. For their part, a new generation of policymakers in Colombia is promoting "healthy" labor migration for Colombians of all classes, while Japan maintains its preoccupation with the "national security threat" that foreigners as criminals represent and the consequent urgency of controlling the entry of foreign workers. The disjuncture between these two objectives is reflected in new patterns of labor migration and trafficking, which are redirecting Colombians away from Japan to Hong Kong, Singapore, and Spain. In this globalized commerce, women trafficked from still other countries, such as China, will be brought to Japan to take their places.

Ranking Countries

Before country compliance could be evaluated and ranked, there had to be victims of harm. As this analysis argues, counting "victims" of human trafficking is a complex and illusive process. Anthropologists Jean Comaroff and John Comaroff argue that the most over generalized and least qualified numbers travel the best. The widely cited U.S. government global estimate of 600,000 to 800,000 trafficking victims each year is a case in point.[18] This number has been used in congressional testimonies and government reports as a measure of a global tragedy—the human cost of rising rates of transnational crime at this historical conjuncture of globalized commerce, illicit trade, and vast movements of migrant labor across world regions. This estimate is designed to index a crisis and focus international attention and public awareness on the urgent need for monitoring and international intervention.

The U.S. Department of State's TIP reports anchor the wider crisis to country rankings based on their compliance with "minimum standards" to combat human trafficking nationally. These standards are outlined in the U.S. TVPA, passed in 2001 and recertified in 2003, 2005, and 2008.[19] The monitoring and ranking of discrete countries throughout the world is a fascinating and ironic move because trafficking is a transnational crime, following on the heels of illicit commerce in drugs and arms. This

18. This was the most common estimate cited in TIP Reports before 2008.
19. The William Wilberforce Reauthorization Act of 2008, which passed the House and Senate without objection on December 10, 2008, and was signed by President Bush on December 23, 2008, set appropriations for 2008–11.

illicit commerce—which has many completely legal components[20]—freely crosses borders and world regions through ever-changing circuits to escape police and immigration authorities. Traffickers routinely bestow new nationalities and identity papers on those who are trafficked as they move toward their destinations. In the mid-2000s, Colombians were frequently given new identities in Peru, which complicated the process of attributing nationalities to these labor migrants. No matter what the consequences are, it is still national governments and countries that count in this monitoring regime.

The minimum standards used to measure country compliance include the prohibition and punishment of severe forms of trafficking, punishments commensurate with country standards for grave crimes, punishments prescribed to deter and reflect the heinous nature of the offences, and efforts to eliminate severe forms of trafficking. This crime and punishment paradigm becomes more diffuse as one reviews the criteria the U.S. G/TIP office employs to determine a country's status in the four-tiered international monitoring system:

- Does a government provide data on investigations, prosecutions, convictions, or sentences showing vigorous prosecutions according to the country's capacity? Or, at the very least does the country make a good will effort to collect data?
- Does the government protect victims and encourage their participation in criminal prosecutions of traffickers? Does it free victims from prosecution for crimes committed as a result of being trafficked? Does it develop alternatives to deportation when victims want to stay?
- Has the government adopted prevention measures and public education programs that reach out to potential victims?
- Does the country collaborate transnationally in criminal prosecutions?
- Does the country have extradition processes?
- Does the country monitor immigration and emigration patterns, use this evidence in investigations and prosecutions, and recognize victim rights to return to their own country or choose to leave it?[21]

---

20. Among them, conventional travel and banking, including wire transfers which facilitate transnational commerce. See Carolyn Nordstrom, *Shadows of War: Violence, Power, and International Profiteering in the Twenty-First Century* (Berkeley: University of California Press, 2004).

21. I derived this set of questions to represent the major themes covered by "minimum standards for the elimination of trafficking in persons" from the longer statement of TVPA policies commonly included in TIP Reports. See, for example, *Trafficking in Persons Report, 2008*, 284–85.

The problem, however, is that reliable comparable data across states does not exist, and, in fact, there is no consensus on the appropriate methodology to gather such data. One might argue that there is little incentive for countries to make these issues more transparent. But the story is much more complex than incentives, consensus building, or promoting rational action.

In fact, if one examines the TIP Reports in any detail, the rankings are as much about "national reputation" as actual evidence-based objective hierarchies of compliance. This index contrasts with the Comaroffs' treatment of crime statistics as "an index of 'national worth'—at least in the global marketplace, where southern politics must meet northern scrutiny with respect to democratization, stability, creditworthiness, and the like."[22] In the context of human trafficking, Japan was seen—at the height of the anti-trafficking activism in 2004—as the outlier country from the global north in a state of denial about the implications of new international anti-trafficking norms for its estimated $100 billion a year sex entertainment industry which is built, in great part, on women trafficked from different parts of the world.

In this case, the country with the world's second largest economy, a special national security relationship with the United States, and pride in its status as a major international foreign aid donor did not pass the test of the international/Western system of monitoring human rights abuses. Japan did not institutionally meet the minimum standards because it failed to formally recognize the newly defined crime of human trafficking until 2004. To increase the pressure, a new sub-tier in the TIP report was created for countries like Japan—Tier 2 "watch list"—which signaled the imminent danger of falling into Tier 3, occupied by countries like North Korea, Burma, and Cuba. The Japanese government was publicly stigmatized by this ranking and the possibility of a continuing downward spiral. Increasing pressure was applied at international meetings at the 2004 UN University in Tokyo by the U.S. embassy in Tokyo, East Asian feminist NGOs, and the Colombian embassy in Tokyo—as the BBC cameras rolled and Ministry of Foreign Affairs officials were interrogated by the audience of activists. Japanese officials were put on the spot by pointed questioning from the heads of East Asian anti-trafficking NGOs, who purposefully violated Japanese norms of decorum to reveal the institutionalized indifference of bureaucrats who handled visa applications that facilitated certain forms of trafficking. Their superiors witnessed these confrontations and saw the strength of the anti-trafficking consensus of major actors at these

22. Comaroff and Comaroff, *Figuring Crime*, 224.

meetings, including the U.S. embassy. This was an extremely awkward moment for the host country.

Annual visits from the G/TIP delegation made it clear that this pressure was not going to abate without policy reform. By the end of the year, Japanese officials took the required step of drafting an action plan to come into full compliance with the TIP framework and directly addressed each of the minimum standards in ways that demonstrated the good intensions required by the U.S. monitoring apparatus. In particular, they reformed their entertainment visa system, which had offered the Philippines 60,000 entertainment visas each year, and took steps to stop criminalizing trafficking victims. To demonstrate its commitment, the Japanese government produced anti-trafficking media for international circulation. In 2005, Japan regained its Tier 2 status, though for many officials that was still not enough for a major international donor.

Colombia is an interesting case because from the onset of the TIP reports it achieved a Tier 1 ranking despite the fact that since the 1980s it has been a major source country for human trafficking and drug trafficking. Its institutional strategy was a very interesting one. Colombian lawyers pursued institutional reforms including a very detailed analysis of the national legal system and, through UNODC-Colombia and the national congress, spent several years debating and revising their legal code so that it incorporated Colombian readings of international norms from the Palermo Protocol. They also revitalized the inter-institutional agency within the government to combat trafficking. Finally, the Colombian embassy in Tokyo with its well-known activist officials had a long history of helping women who had been trafficked to Japan and served as an eager ally pressuring the Japanese government to reform its legal and policing systems. Colombians were seen as ideal collaborators with the U.S. embassy, its anti-trafficking Labor Attaché Ann Kambara, and U.S. monitoring personnel, and lauded for emphasizing the three Ps to combat trafficking: prevention, prosecution, and protection.

The concreteness of these national rankings, which have a history of being based on country narratives rather than statistical monitoring, cannot really obscure their politicized, constructed nature. Many have pointed out that Tier 3 included a Bush administration enemies list to which Venezuela was added in 2005. Moreover, the United States continued to escape its own discipline of being ranked until the Obama administration broached the issue in 2009.[23]

---

23. See U.S. Department of Justice, "Attorney General's Report to Congress and Assessment of the U.S. Government Activities to Combat Trafficking in Persons," 2008, which was designed as an annual accounting to compensate for the U.S. failure to rank itself in the TIP Reports.

Monitoring by ranking creates an imaginary of concreteness through which law and order established through state policy is able to defeat criminal disorder. Yet, as we turn to the illusiveness of counting "victims" in Colombia, the picture becomes much more complicated. In this case, carefully contextualized anthropological and sociological research reveals the limits of standardized monitoring and interesting patterns of resistance to the discipline mandated by the U.S. anti-trafficking scheme.

Counting "Victims" in Colombia

Few would deny the traumatic experiences of women who return to Colombia from sexually exploitative work in Japan. Their accounts of suffering extremely harsh and demeaning labor conditions are harrowing. Yet their stories often detail women's continual efforts to improve their situations however marginally or reach out to others for mutual assistance. Some are able to move from highly restrictive confinement and debt bondage sex work to other kinds of jobs in organized crime networks, but many are not. A few are able to escape to small firms doing outsourced assembly work in Japan. Some hear that the Colombian embassy in Tokyo offers refuge and help to women who want to escape their illegal status as visa overstayers and go home; others are arrested, jailed, and summarily deported as criminals by the Japanese authorities.

Upon their return, the women are met at El Dorado International Airport in Bogotá by agents of the Colombian office of DAS-Interpol and immediately transferred to representatives of the International Organization for Migration (IOM) or the Fundación Esperanza—both major NGOs with substantial experience in victim services who help returned migrants with the immediate transition. They are offered short-term counseling, health screening, clothing, and a place to stay to get their bearings. Some find longer-term support from local organizations that work on women's issues. Then, overwhelmingly, these women disappear. Some return to the regions where they lived previously. For a variety of reasons, few, if any, feel they can return to their families or home communities. They seek to evade the moral stigma of sex work, the fact that they betrayed their families with promises of remittance earnings that never came, and, for those who fled without paying off their debt to their captors, the realistic fear that they will be found and punished by Colombian gangs affiliated with the Colombia–East Asian trade.

Women who have worked in Japan agree at least in part with women's organizations that advocate "closing the chapter" on the confusion and brutality of their exploitation so far from home. Some NGOs put this idea at the center of their therapeutic regime. At local centers that offer counseling services, women are able to share their experiences in private sessions with supportive nonjudgmental social workers. If they choose to, they have the opportunity to keep in touch with other women who have been trafficked.

Women back from Japan—where brutal working conditions are made more difficult by gaps in language, culture, and cuisine—generally avoid long-term active contact with sympathetic women's organizations, even when they have had good experiences and have gone through substantial therapy. If remaking the world involves closing the chapter and exploring new options, then they choose to leave these memories with the others. Nevertheless, they do worry about situations in which they might relive the past. For the wider publics they serve, these organizations can be important conduits to educational, work, and social support networks. Yet, the women drift away, occasionally getting in touch with friends at the centers, or disappearing and becoming a history without a known ending.

No one in the social service networks in Colombia or Japan seems to know what happens to the women who do not return. There are no reliable surveys or ethnographic studies. Are these women able to learn Japanese and adapt to Japanese food and culture? What do they do for a living? How do they make sense of their lives? Do they go elsewhere? In these fluid situations, counting victims—generating quantifacts, as the Comaroffs[24] call them—inevitably seems to be an incomplete process. The experience of being trafficked and being anti-trafficking service providers at the sending or receiving nexuses along this Pacific Rim route appears to trump the process of standardized state-centric monitoring from Washington.

Most telling is the evidence that in general women who return to Colombia do not consider themselves "victims." They see themselves as caught in very troubled circumstances, with jobs that did not work out, at great distances from home. But they tend not to adopt the identity of "victim" in its all-encompassing sense. Rather this term of reference serves as an NGO and international donor shorthand for these women. The continued repetition of this shorthand—in the Palermo Protocol and anti-trafficking activism—overdetermines a particular construction of the "other," as one defined by her need of external assistance from these organizations. Yet this framing is not an unproblematic ally of women's self-perceptions. Colombian women have not, up to this point, created organizations to channel demands as "survivors" of transnational trafficking, although this has happened in other parts of the world.

If one turns to the Colombian state, the production of quantitative hard data—that is, crime statistics dealing with human trafficking—has its own

24. Ibid.

institutional complexities. Mónica Hurtado,[25] a well-known Colombian social science researcher, was given the task in 2005 of working with different state agencies to generate the first compilation of statistics across key governmental organizations involved in combating trafficking, investigating crimes, prosecuting traffickers, and providing victim services. Her assignment was funded by the International Labour Organization (ILO) and carried out with the blessing of the Colombian government's fourteen member Inter-Institutional Agency to Combat Trafficking. She was charged with working with the National Police Humanitas section, which specialized in trafficking issues, the Colombian office of DAS-INTERPOL, the National Attorney General's office, and IOM-Colombia. The Attorney General's office decided not to provide data for the study, which meant that the final report lacked data on prosecutions and the outcomes of judicial cases brought against traffickers in Colombia. It may be the case that these statistics were unavailable because between 2003 and 2005 relatively few cases had moved past the initial investigation phase during which the Fiscalía de la Nación decided if there was adequate evidence to proceed to arrests and to prosecutions. The open question is how many cases have made their way since these early years to trial and finally after a possible appeal to a final verdict so they might be counted in the present.

Nevertheless, Hurtado's findings are very helpful in terms of giving us a window on how the production of statistics is institutionally mediated in Colombia.[26] It became apparent from Hurtado's research that different institutions in the state apparatus and their collaborators collect incommensurate kinds of data according to their functions and interests. In practice, they have different engagements with "trafficking." The National Police focus their investigations on criminal operations, which may include one or more traffickers. DAS-INTERPOL undertakes individual investigations of traffickers or victims, which are used by the Attorney General's office to decide whether the evidence is strong enough to pursue prosecution. IOM focuses its assistance efforts on individual women who have been victimized and returned to Colombia. One can see some of the reasons here for the lack of consensus on domestic practices to combat trafficking and the difficulties inter-institutional agencies have in imagining ways to coordinate their activities. From this vantage point, the state is hardly a unitary political form; its production of knowledge remains organizationally based in a way that has left limited grounds for collaboration or centralization.

25. Mónica Hurtado, *Dimensiones de la Trata de Personas en Colombia* (Bogotá, Colombia: OIM, 2006).

26. Hurtado, *Dimensiones de la Trata de Personas.*

First Generation and Second Generation State Policy in Colombia

From 2003 through 2008, the Colombian state's discourse underwent a striking shift in the way it portrays women's vulnerability to trafficking. First generation policy framings focused attention on images of innocent women from the coffee growing countryside regions, like the Eje Cafetero, who were victimized by offers of high paying jobs outside Colombia. This framing imagined the worthy victim as one who is betrayed by the bait-and-switch tactics used by recruiters who offer poor women dream jobs to gain their interest in working abroad. Later when these women arrive at their destination, their new managers brutally reveal the ugly truth that they must work in forced prostitution to pay off tremendous debts, on the order of $30,000 to $40,000 they have allegedly incurred for travel and other expenses. The apparent goal of early anti-trafficking campaigns was to instill fear in those deemed most vulnerable.

Second generation policy framings focus on images of labor migrants who, with the help of carefully designed media from prevention campaigns, are able to weigh their options and decide for themselves if work offers are risky or not. With help from the state, they can learn the danger signs of bad faith labor recruiters and how to assess their offers of high paying jobs, marriage, or other forms of easy money outside the country. "Don't hurt your dreams" (No dañe a tus sueños) is the refrain in this anti-trafficking literature that circulates through airports, passport offices, and social service organizations. The goal is not to instill fear of migration or negate the dream of bettering one's economic situation but rather to educate people to make better employment decisions.

Here the imagery of young women's exceptional vulnerability is, in part, displaced by a wider workers' rights approach in which all Colombians are seen as having dreams—many of which might be fulfilled outside the country. In this case, trafficked women become a subset of much wider currents of cross-border labor migration; and the state identifies itself as a country that will produce large numbers of people whose future will take them outside the country.

It is clear that the central goals of the international campaign Colombia Nos Une (Colombia Unites Us), are preeminently class inflected ones. The government's larger campaign, as featured on the Ministry of Foreign Affair's website and other promotional materials, focuses on encouraging labor migrants, particularly the most successful professionals living in the United States, to feel more personally connected to Colombia. The goal is to encourage individuals to invest in their homeland by purchasing second homes in Bogotá, the nation's capital city with its cosmopolitanism, greater security, and vibrant consumer culture. It takes more than a few clicks to find any hint that trafficking is a concern for the nation. The number of clicks reveals the hierarchy of state concerns and hierarchies of value that rank the social worth of individuals.

Conclusions

As this chapter illustrates, human trafficking is a complex transnational formation of violence constructed and monitored as a particular kind of crisis. This analysis has addressed several major questions: What kinds of knowledge does the U.S. State Department's monitoring system generate in order to rank countries and measure their compliance with international anti-trafficking norms? What are the concrete effects of ranking? What makes the audit logic of counting victims and prosecutions such an illusive process in practice? What can be learned about the politics of numbers from divergent national practices that are designed to respond both to international anti-trafficking pressure and to domestic politics?

There are major debates about the scope of this crime and about the victims. The counting of victims is a multi-sited performance required by audit routines that derive their legitimacy from the UN anti-trafficking protocol and their institutional form from the U.S. State Department's G/TIP annual report system, which defines what compliance to international norms means in practice. As this study of the Colombia-to-Japan human trafficking pattern shows, the discipline of state-by-state monitoring is challenged by the fluidity of individual experiences and the practice of state bureaucracies and NGOs involved in the production of knowledge about transnational criminal enterprises in the domestic versus international arenas. Many of the "victims" named in international law do not see themselves as such; state policies define their status in continually changing ways, and many individuals simply disappear from scrutiny along their labor migration routes.

Ironies abound in anti-trafficking technologies of counting victims in the Palermo Protocol's language of vulnerability: "especially women and children." For those who do return to Colombia, the common fear is that they will become victims of violence at the hands of Colombian enforcers for any debts unpaid. The fear of retaliation and the moral economy of family consumerism, which is betrayed by the common failure of these migrants to send sufficient remittances to their families, mean that it is impossible for many women to go home. It is clear from this overview that much is happening to these women at the precise time in their lives when they are counseled by specialized NGOs to "turn the chapter" on their former lives and move past their memories of sexual exploitation and trauma abroad.

To do justice to the politics of counting human trafficking victims, it is important to see this situation from the viewpoint of those who search for work across borders, as well as from the perspectives of state bureaucracies, audit cultures, and international crime control and legal norms. It is also important to recognize that much of the concern with counting human trafficking abroad shifts attention away from coercive patterns of labor recruitment and debt bondage on the domestic scene of the countries involved in this transnational commerce. This pattern of displacement of one set of issues by another set of preoccupations is another facet of the politics of human trafficking.

This chapter has illustrated the illusive character of counting when numerical signifiers and what is signified are relentlessly uncoupled from the social and political contexts of labor migration and the subjectivity of labor migrants—all in a way that Jean Boudrillard would find quite telling. For the auditors of the trafficking crisis, counting is part of a larger bureaucratic reporting system elaborated by the U.S. State Department, which seeks to standardize legal and criminal justice procedures as represented in the U.S. Trafficking Victims Protection Act and to use rankings for multiple political projects, far beyond the norms of the Palermo Protocol. For others, counting becomes a performance designed to please auditors once a year. For NGOs that must continually compete for international funding, counting mediates their mission of providing services for particular classes of vulnerable migrant laborers, be they individuals considering transnational migration, those caught in terrible working conditions abroad, or undocumented migrants being forcefully repatriated. For their part, the ultimate objects of current technologies of counting repeatedly disappear and often reject the rationales for being counted first of all as "victims."

One can ask if more thorough methodologies for counting would make a difference in international responses to human trafficking. But that framing raises the reality of the limited accountability for states from the global north or south that are subject to this scrutiny. The incentive for states to more aggressively limit the power of organized crime involved in human trafficking or to promote domestic job creation for those facing economic insecurity is repeatedly undercut by the fact that human trafficking is seen as a discrete, low priority issue in the face of other economic and political dilemmas clamoring for attention. This is the ranking that really counts. The bottom line is: there is too little funding currently available from domestic and international sources in countries such as Colombia—with its challenging patterns of low intensity warfare, political violence, drug trafficking, displacement, and growing poverty—to mount more comprehensive efforts given the current understanding of the issue as trafficking for sexual exploitation. The recent shift in the government's construction of labor migration as a higher priority issue for public policy seems to support this conclusion in provocative ways.

6

Counting the Cost

THE POLITICS OF NUMBERS
IN ARMED CONFLICT

Kelly M. Greenhill

The phrase "truth is the first casualty of war" has been so long recognized and oft-uttered that it has become something of a truism about the power of information and the politics of persuasion during periods of conflict. Does it actually matter, then, if the truth about casualties is itself one of war's primary victims?

It has long been popular in some circles to argue that a drive for statistical accuracy in conflict environments is unnecessary, misguided, or even dangerous. What is most germane are not facts on the ground, so the argument goes, but rather the aims and objectives of those producing and promulgating the data. In other words, good intentions trump bad numbers. While recognizing the powerful incentives that can give rise to this "intentions-based" position, this chapter offers a strenuous rebuttal to it. Drawing on evidence from a variety of contemporary conflicts—and focusing in particular on statistics surrounding the dead and the displaced—this chapter argues that a failure to at least strive for statistical accuracy in the realm of warfare can prove demonstrably counterproductive and enduringly damaging, from political, humanitarian, juridical, and scholarly perspectives. This is particularly true because—for reasons outlined in the introductory chapter of this volume—politicized conflict statistics tend to be sticky and resistant to updating, and sometimes even take on lives of their own.

The author thanks Rich Friman, Lincoln Greenhill, Corbin Lyday, Lara Nettelfield, and participants in the Belfer Center's Intrastate Conflict Program seminar series at Harvard University for helpful comments on earlier versions of this chapter.

Consider the following example surrounding the toll war ostensibly takes on children. It not only offers compelling evidence of the resilience of conflict-related magical numbers, but also powerfully demonstrates the facility with which such dramatic "social facts"—that is, things that are deemed to be "true" simply because they are widely believed to be true—can be adopted and widely disseminated.[1] This single, but far from singular, example also serves as a useful preamble to the case studies and discussion that follow.

An Illustrative Myth

As of this writing, a briefing paper on the website of the British nongovernmental organization (NGO) Campaign Against Arms Trade (CAAT) authoritatively asserts: "In the last decade child victims of armed conflict include 2 million children killed, 4–5 million children disabled, 12 million children left homeless, more than 1 million children orphaned or separated from their parents, [and] some 10 million children traumatized."[2] These are arresting and terrible statistics, mustered with the best of intentions, to catalyze support for programs designed to alleviate human suffering and mitigate conflict-related misery. Not surprisingly, CAAT is not alone in deploying them. These selfsame figures appear on the websites of numerous other NGOs, international organizations (IOs), and intergovernmental organizations (IGOs). They have likewise been cited in a plethora of impassioned speeches,[3] embedded in myriad NGO, IO, and IGO reports, documents, and press releases,[4] and published in wide variety of journalistic

1. On social facts and their construction, see John R. Searle, *The Construction of Social Reality* (New York: Free Press, 1995).
2. Campaign Against Arms Trade, "Paying the Price: How the Arms Trade Impacts on Children Around the World," http://www.caat.org.uk/campaigns/paying-the-price/briefing.php.
3. See, for instance, the speech by the Honourable Lloyd Axworthy, Minister of Foreign Affairs, to the G-8 Foreign Ministers' Meeting, June 9, 1999, http://w01.international.gc.ca/MinPub/Publication.aspx?lang=eng&publication_id=377168&docnum=99/40; and Carol Bellamy, "Speech to the Arco Forum at Harvard's Institute of Politics, John F. Kennedy School of Government," February 19, 2003, available at: http://www.unicef.org/media/media_9326.html.
4. See, for instance, British American Security Information Council, "Putting Children First: Building a Framework for International Action to Address the Impact of Small Arms on Children," http://www.crin.org/docs/resources/publications/BitingtheBullet11.pdf; Amnesty International, *In the Firing Line—War and Children's Rights* (London: AI, 2001); Olara A. Otunnu, *Children in Conflict: The Many Faces of Suffering* (New York: United Nations, 1999); and Rachel Harvey, *Children and Armed Conflict: A Guide to International Humanitarian and Human Rights Law* (Montreal: International Bureau for Children's Rights, 2001), www.essex.ac.uk/armedcon/story_id/000044.pdf.

outlets, scholarly journals, and books.[5] In short, these figures have been embraced as facts. Indeed, they even appear as part of an online quiz for students wishing to learn about life on the frontlines of war.[6] But are these dramatic and gripping numbers about childhood victims of war accurate? Probably not.

The websites, speeches, and publications that include sources for these statistics—and many do not—most often cite either (a report produced by) the United Nations Children's Fund (UNICEF), Graca Machel's *The Machel Review 1996–2000: A Critical Analysis of Progress Made and Obstacles Encountered in Increasing Protection for War-Affected Children*, and/or one of a number of reports compiled by Olara Otunnu, the former UN Under-Secretary General and Special Representative for Children and Armed Conflict. At first glance, the fact that these disparate sources all reported similar statistics would seem to bolster the credibility of the numbers. However, all roads ultimately lead back to a single source, UNICEF, since the Machel and Otunnu reports themselves cite the United Nations Childrens' Fund as the source of their data.[7] A search of UNICEF's website yields the same alarmingly large, and remarkably round, numbers. But the footnote supporting these figures simply states that "UNICEF has compiled the estimates from a diversity of sources," with nary a source nor a method of obtaining said information identified.[8] This omission alone ought to give consumers of conflict-related statistics pause, but it is potentially but the tip of an iceberg.

5. See, for example, Peter W. Singer, *Children at War* (New York: Pantheon Books, 2005); and Karin Arts and Vesselin Popovski, eds., *International Criminal Accountability and the Rights of Children* (Cambridge: Cambridge University Press, 2006).

6. Frontline Connection, "Fun Zone: Information Zone Quiz," http://frontline.worldvision. org.nz/funzone_quiz.asp.

7. Graça Machel, *The Machel Review 1996–2000: A Critical Analysis of Progress Made and Obstacles Encountered in Increasing Protection for War-Affected Children* (New York: Macmillan, 2001), 5. Also available at http://www.un.org/children/conflict/english/the-machel-study-1996.html, 7. For Reports on Children and Armed Conflict to the UN General Assembly, see http://www.un.org/children/conflict/english/reports.html.

8. UNICEF, "State of the World's Children 1996: Children in War," http://www.unicef. org/sowc96/1cinwar.htm; and UNICEF, "Children in Conflict and Emergencies," www.unicef. org/protection/index_armedconflict.html. As no official datasets on armed conflicts, genocides, or core human rights abuses existed when these 1996 reports were compiled, it is unclear whence many of these statistics could have come. What wartime casualty data does exist has only been gathered systematically since 2002 and is acknowledged to be of questionable reliability. See Human Security Centre, *Human Security Report 2005* (Vancouver: University of British Columbia, 2005), pt. II. A partial exception is the 1998–2002 dataset gathered by the World Health Organization. However, there are numerous uncertainties surrounding these data, which have had to be adjusted downward on occasion (e.g., in 2002, by about one-third). Moreover, these data would not yet have been available at the time the 1996 report was compiled.

For one thing, the UNICEF report in question dates from 1996; thus the decade to which it refers is 1986–96, not 1999–2009. Some of the authors, politicians, and practitioners who employ these statistics make note of this temporal boundary, but at least as many do not.[9] (Those failing to make this distinction include former UNICEF director Carol Bellamy, who in a 2003 speech at Harvard University declared two million had been killed in the *last decade*.[10]) Moreover, those who do bound the "last decade" timeframe tend to say "during the 1990s," instead of noting that the real decade in question was 1986–96, not 1990–2000. Might this distinction make a difference?

Leaving aside the question of whether the estimates were valid in 1996, in the intervening years, the aggregate number of conflicts in the world plummeted from a post–World War II high of more than 50 in 1992–93 to under 30 a decade later.[11] Might the conflicts raging in the 2000s have been correspondingly more deadly than their predecessors, such that the aggregate numbers of victims did not budge even though the number of conflicts almost halved? Possibly, if improbably, particularly since the extraordinary bloodbath that was the Rwandan genocide took place in 1994. In any case, we would need to know what sources UNICEF employed in 1996 in order to evaluate this proposition, which we do not.

What we do know is that the same UNICEF report further declared: "the increasing number of child victims is primarily explained by the higher proportion of civilian deaths in recent conflicts....In the later decades of this century the proportion of civilian victims has been rising steadily: in World War II it was two-thirds, and by the end of the 1980s it was almost 90 percent."[12] Like its aforementioned counterparts, this stunning figure has been widely adopted and broadly disseminated by scholars, policymakers, and the media alike. The only problem is that it too appears to have little basis in reality. Rather, this magical number can be traced back to widespread misquotation and misinterpretation of Christa Ahlström and Kjell-Åke Nordquist's *Casualties of Conflict* and Ruth Sivard's *World Military and Social Expenditures*—both cited in the aforementioned 1996 UNICEF report.[13]

9. See, for instance, Stephen Leahy, "Prosecuting Child Soldiers for Their Own Safety," http://stephenleahy.net/non-environmental-journalism/prosecuting-child-soldiers-for-their-own-safety/; and Lisa Schlein, "UN Reports Children Increasingly Vulnerable in Armed Conflict," *VOA News*, September 29, 2006.

10. Bellamy, "Speech to the Arco Forum."

11. *Human Security Report 2005*, 22. This decline came after the number of conflicts had risen steadily from the late 1970s to mid-1990s (23.)

12. *The State of the World's Children 1996*.

13. Christa Ahlström and Kjell-Åke Nordquist, *Casualties of Conflict—Report for the World Campaign for the Protection of Victims of War* (Uppsala: Uppsala University, Department of Peace and Conflict Research, 1991); and Ruth L. Sivard, *World Military and Social Expenditures*, 14th ed. (Washington, DC: World Priorities, 1991).

Ahlström and Nordquist's volume included the claim that "nine out of ten victims (dead *and* uprooted) of war and armed conflict today are civilians."[14] An explicit reference to those "uprooted" by conflict makes plain that the authors' definition of "victim" included refugees and other displaced (but still living) persons. As such, it also implied a rather less dramatic civilian casualty figure—namely, about 67 percent—which was consistent with earlier decades' estimates. On the book jacket, however, the parenthetical phrase "dead and uprooted" was omitted, leaving only the statement that "nine out of ten victims of war and armed conflict today are civilians."[15] As a result, many readers equated victim with fatality, and a new social fact was born. This figure was so widely embraced that, ironically enough, even the United Nations High Commissioner for Refugees (UNHCR)—whose very *raison d'être* is the care and protection of living displaced people—adopted it.[16]

This social fact's "validity" was further reinforced by the assertion in Sivard's text that "in 1990 [the proportion of civilian to combat deaths] appears to have been close to 90%." However, Sivard's estimate included war-related famine deaths, which are—to quote the 2005 *Human Security Report*—"not what most people have in mind when they talk about civilians being *killed* in war." The *Report* further concluded, "The only claim we can make with any confidence is that the oft-cited 90% civilian death rate for the 1990s is a myth."[17] Nevertheless, this mythical social fact also continues to be widely cited and replicated. In contrast, a competing estimate proffered by the International Committee of the Red Cross in 1999, suggesting that between 30 and 65 percent of conflict casualties are civilians has been, at least relatively speaking, largely ignored.[18]

Furthermore, some of the actors who employ the more dramatic statistics have embroidered or added greater specificity to these already shocking figures. In some cases, what was previously a ballpark "estimate" has

14. *Casualties of Conflict*, cited in the *Human Security Report 2005*, 75.

15. *Human Security Report 2005*, 75.

16. *The State of the World's Children 1996*.

17. Sivard, *World Military and Social Expenditures*, quoted in *Human Security Report 2005*, 75 (inset). Moreover, because no global data on deaths caused by war-related famine and disease exist, the authors of the *Human Security Report* note, it is impossible to ascertain the origin of her statistics or how she reached her conclusions.

18. International Committee of the Red Cross, *Arms Availability and the Situation of Children in Armed Conflict* (Geneva: ICRC, 1999). http://www.icrc.org/Web/eng/siteeng0. nsf/html/p0734?OpenDocument. See also Jonathan Hall, Erik Melander, and Magnus Öberg, "The 'New Wars' Debate Revisited: An Empirical Evaluation of the Atrociousness of 'New Wars," Uppsala Peace Research Papers no. 9, Department of Peace and Conflict Research, Uppsala University, 2006; and the *Human Security Report 2005*. Somewhat ironically, the ICRC report, released a decade ago—that is, *before* the Marcel and Otunnu reports of the early 2000s—includes a detailed discussion of its methodology and data sources.

become the low-end assessment. Consequently, it is now common to see claims that "in the last decade," "at least" or "more than" two million were killed, five million were disabled, and so on.[19] At least one author further upped the ante in declaring that the two million killed had been "deliberately murdered," as if their deaths as a consequence of conflict were not horrible enough.[20] And in the preface for special issue of a journal on children and war, Otunnu declared that of the 90 percent of civilian victims of war since 1990, 80 percent "were women and children who fell victim to the 'misuse' of small arms and light weapons."[21] No sources were provided for any of these elaborations.[22]

Does It Matter?

For students of the politics of numbers, the irregular provenance and widespread propagation of the aforementioned statistics may sound disturbingly familiar and not especially surprising, particularly given the paradoxical nature of the environment from which such numbers emanate. On the one hand, we live in a world in which things that are not measured, for all intents and purposes, do not exist. Because funding and policy decisions tend to driven by the perceived size and significance of a problem, advocates and activists are compelled to package their claims as "facts"—social or otherwise—by including numbers, and the most compelling ones at that.[23]

19. For the use of "at least," see, for example, Anatole Ayissi, "Protecting Children in Armed Conflict: From Commitment to Compliance," *Disarmament Forum* 3 (Special Issue on Children and Security) (2002): 9. For the use of "more than," see, for instance, Julia Freedson, "The Impact of Conflict on Children—The Role of Small Arms," in *Disarmament Forum* 3 (2002). For a fantastically hyperbolic extrapolation of how the figures mean that "half the children on earth today" are "a people on the run from wars that take the lives of their brothers and sisters," see Stephen Khan, "At Risk: 1,000,000,000 of the World's Children," *Independent*, December 10, 2004.

20. Ayissi, "Protecting Children in Armed Conflict."

21. Ibid., 3–4.

22. In "The Impact of Conflict on Children," Freedson cites a report by Rachel Stohl et al. as the source for the slightly more ambiguous claim that "some estimates put civilian casualties of war as high as 80–90%—a large portion are women and children killed by small arms." However, Stohl has argued that although these weapons are undoubtedly responsible for many deaths, it is unclear how many children are killed "directly by small arms," as "child fatalities by small arms are rarely specifically noted. It is also extremely unusual that injuries and deaths from small arms are reported and codified." Rachel Stohl, "Targeting Children: Small Arms and Children in Conflict," *Brown Journal of World Affairs* 9 (2002): 283. Thus, the source of the 80 percent killed by small arms remains a mystery.

23. Lynn Smith, "Putting a Spin on the Truth with Statistics and Studies," *Los Angeles Times*, June 6, 2001.

On the other hand, the numbers actors want (or need) to identify can be very difficult to acquire or even ascertain, particularly under fire, in remote locations and in the midst of social and political disorder—that is, in the context of armed conflict. In the absence of real data, therefore, figures are often simply invented. If those producing the numbers believe the issue at hand is a big problem that warrants greater resources and attention, they want a big number; if not, they want a small one.[24] Moreover, actors may possess what they perceive to be good reasons to dissemble; thus even when good statistics *can* be had, they may not be shared. Consequently, depending on one's outlook, agenda, and choice of methodology, measurements of the same phenomena can be astonishingly divergent.[25] Estimates of the numbers of Iraqis who died between March 2003 and March 2008, for instance, have ranged from as low as 82,000—itself a sizable number, 1.4 times U.S. losses in Vietnam—to well over one million—or about 550 people per day in the first five years after the invasion.[26]

Faced with the nearly inescapable conclusion that conflict-related statistics will tend to be suspect—and the fact that the size of some problems probably cannot reasonably be known—do the source, size, and ultimate credibility, of such statistics actually matter? Should we be concerned, in other words, if conflict-related social facts are often not facts at all, but rather politically motivated, socially constructed inventions? Might it matter if, for example, the vast majority of those dying in wars today are not "murdered" by small arms, but rather succumb to preventable diseases or fall victim to starvation? Or if more lives might be saved by pursuing perpetrators of violence than by protecting civilians from their depredations?[27]

The Good Intentions Paradox

One school of thought, which I call the *intentions-based* position, says, effectively no. Because "everyone knows" conflict statistics are unreliable, uncertain, and subject to wide margins of error, consumers of these numbers mentally correct for such uncertainties and take these figures with a grain of salt. Moreover, the argument goes, the veracity of such statistics

---

24. Ibid.

25. For an analogous argument that examines conflicting (and shifting) assessments of the rate of civil war recidivism—and the implications of these divergent estimates—see Astrid Suhrke and Ingrid Samset, "What's in a Figure? Estimating Recurrence of Civil War," *International Peacekeeping* 14 (2007): 195–203.

26. See, for instance, Jonathan Steele and Suzanne Goldenberg, "What Is the Real Death Toll in Iraq?" *Guardian*, March 19, 2008.

27. See, for example, Taylor Seybolt, *Humanitarian Military Intervention: The Conditions for Success and Failure* (Oxford: Oxford University Press, 2007).

is ultimately insignificant, if the underlying sentiment that motivates their adoption and promulgation is sound.[28] Put another way, if the policy being bolstered by potentially unreliable figures is ultimately a "good" or "virtuous" one, then the fact that they might be inflated or deflated is irrelevant.[29] Some intentions-based advocates go farther still, asserting that accurate counting is not just unnecessary; it is downright objectionable. Migration expert Barbara Harrell-Bond has argued, for instance, that "the requirement to count refugees leads to highly undesirable, oppressive consequences" for the displaced.[30]

The most extreme version of the intentions-based position suggests that using misleading statistics should not simply be condoned, but actually encouraged, if it mobilizes public opinion in the appropriate direction. This is not a new idea. As journalist Claude Cockburn declared in the midst of the Spanish Civil War: "the public has no right to the truth," at least until "they have exerted themselves to alter the policy of their bloody government....This isn't an abstract question. This is a shocking war."[31] Similarly, but more recently, Balkans scholar Mark Almond suggested vastly inflated figures were used in Kosovo because:

> Self-righteous people very often feel that it is not a sin for them to tell untruths because it's in a good cause...[B]ecause there are no pictures of what's really going on in Kosovo, we have to tell people. And the temptation is to say, "We know the Serbs are awful, we know they've been awful in the past, so they must be awful now, although we don't know exactly what they're doing, so let's reach into the drawer of atrocities from previous wars and find the worst we possibly can."[32]

Another version of the intentions-based position rejects compiling or reporting numbers altogether. One reason is the belief that seeking objective data on the horrors of war and its victims could "abstractify," dehumanize, and consequently drain such issues of the emotional impact

---

28. See, for instance, Daniel Pearl and Robert Block, "Body Count: War in Kosovo Was Cruel, Bitter, Savage; Genocide It Wasn't," *Wall Street Journal*, December 31, 1999.

29. See "Clinton Gave Exaggerated Kosovo Atrocity Figures," *USA Today*, July 1, 1999; Jerry Markon, "Human Trafficking Evokes Outrage, Little Evidence," *Washington Post*, September 23, 2007; and numerous examples cited in Phillip Knightley, *The First Casualty: The War Correspondent as Hero and Myth-Maker from the Crimea to Iraq* (Baltimore, MD: Johns Hopkins University Press, 2004).

30. Barbara Harrell-Bond et al., "Counting the Refugees: Gifts, Givers, Patrons and Clients," *Journal of Refugee Studies* 5 (1992). Similar arguments are made by John Telford in *Counting and Identification of Beneficiary Populations in Emergency Operations: Registration and Its Alternatives* (London: Overseas Development Institute, 1997).

31. Quoted in Knightley, *The First Casualty*, 213.

32. *Sydney Morning Herald*, April 24, 1999.

that mark them as worthy of special concern. A further rationale in support of the rejectionist position is the fact that measurement can reveal numbers that may be politically inconvenient.[33] Finally, some actors may resist counting—as a number of British Parliamentarians did during World War II—because such statistics could be used to measure progress and "give aid and comfort" to a country's adversaries.[34] This logic can be compelling and helps explain why politicized, magical numbers are often embraced with alacrity and seemingly little circumspection.

Why Politization Matters

Yet, issues and problems do not simply *exist;* they are defined at least in part by what we want to *do* about them. Numbers are key in determining what to do and how to respond to those issues about which we care. Thus, for a variety of distinct reasons the veracity and ultimate credibility of conflict statistics often does matter, sometimes enormously. This is not to suggest that good numbers are always attainable, only that pretending—as the intentions-based position perforce must—that (at least ballpark) accuracy does not matter is a position that is misguided and potentially dangerous.

On the *political* front, statistics shape both public and closed-door policy debates. They serve to legitimize some positions and undercut others; consequently, they have tremendous implications for a wide range of security-related policies. Although "impressively arranged numbers" can help leaders bolster claims about anything from budget deficits to an insurgency's "last throes," politicized data also "have a way of supplying a false—and [often] very perishable—sense of authority."[35] In the context of conflict itself, prevailing estimates of the scale of violence, its complexion, and its measurable consequences undeniably play a role in shaping policy priorities and objectives. Operating under false pretenses compromises the ability of both politicians and their polities to assess what their priorities and goals should be, and how and when they may need to be revisited or revised. The U.S. experience during the first years of its post-2003 occupation of Iraq offers food for thought in this regard.

33. See, for instance, Karen DeYoung, "Experts Doubt Drop in Violence in Iraq: Military Statistics Called into Question," *Washington Post,* September 6, 2007.

34. Herbert F. Spirer, Louise Spirer, and A. J. Jaffe, *Misused Statistics* (New York: Marcel Dekker, 1998), 231. Similarly, as far back as 1753, members of the House of Lords refused to permit a census of the British population, for fear it would "reveal to potential enemies how small an army the British could muster" (230).

35. After all, the 1968 Tet Offensive was devastating to President Lyndon Johnson's Vietnam policy not because it was a military success, but because "of the jarring counter it delivered to the official story line." Joshua Green, "The Numbers War," *Atlantic Monthly* (May 2006): 36–37.

On the *humanitarian* front, IOs, IGOs, and NGOs rely on statistics to guide their responses to humanitarian emergencies in the midst of conflict. Aid agencies and advocacy groups use numbers to determine client needs, to bolster and support funding requests, to make decisions about how and where to deploy finite resources, and to lobby for action. As the intentions-based position suggests, politicized numbers can help garner attention and catalyze diplomatic and military action. But numbers that are fictitious and thus divorced from actual on-the-ground requirements can give rise to counterproductive outcomes and hurt the very people they are designed to help. As the case studies examined in this chapter illustrate, at best, inaccurate numbers can lead to wasted resources and effort where such expenditures are unnecessary; at worst, they may result in too few supplies and personnel being deployed where they are required most acutely.

From a *juridical* perspective, accurately estimating the number of war-related victims, including casualties, refugees, and internally displaced persons is vital for providing services during conflicts and in administering justice (whether restorative or retributive) after the fighting stops. Numbers and patterns of deaths and population displacement are used to hold perpetrators to account and to help ensure that victims and survivors receive reparations and/or other forms of recompense. Thus, politicization and systematic inflation or deflation of war-related statistics can exercise pernicious effects even long after a conflict ends. The truth about numbers matters still further because "good history" is believed to be key to effective political healing.[36] Absent a shared understanding of true costs of a conflict, local and regional political entrepreneurs can continue to exploit related issues for decades to come. Recurrent cycles of mass killing in central Africa and the Balkans offer ample evidence of this dynamic in action.

Finally, from a knowledge-gathering, scholarly perspective, historical data are critical in interpreting past events and making predictions about what we are likely to observe in the future. Conflict statistics are a key component of the data that allow scholars and practitioners to accurately gauge relationships between cause and effect and understand the political and social processes that lead to—and follow from—violence. To the extent that the available data are false or flawed, they compromise actors' abilities to accurately analyze historical events and draw useful lessons from them.

So, how do these abstract concerns play out in the real world, in the arena of intra- and interstate politics? In particular, how does this kind of

---

36. See, for instance, Barry Posen, "The Security Dilemma and Ethnic Conflict," *Survival* 35 (1993): 27–47; and Stephen Van Evera, "Hypotheses on Nationalism and War," *International Security* 18 (1994): 5–39.

politicization affect policy outcomes and people on the ground in conflict zones? Focusing specifically on the politicization of numbers surrounding the dead and the displaced, the balance of this chapter tackles these questions through the lens of a series of contemporary case studies—namely, the conflict and refugee crisis in eastern Zaire in the mid-1990s, the Battle of Jenin in the Palestinian territories in 2003, and the 1998–99 Kosovo crisis.[37] Taken together and individually, these cases illustrate how the politics of numbers in the realm of conflict can have very real and quite significant political, humanitarian, legal, and scholarly consequences. The chapter concludes with a discussion of the broader implications and generalizability of the chapter's findings.

To be clear, this is not to suggest that statistical politicization will *inexorably* engender pernicious consequences. Nor should the argument herein be construed as reinforcing the misguided idea that everything can and should be counted, or that numbers are by definition appropriate proxies for measuring progress. However, the global, diverse, and interconnected nature of the cases discussed herein—considered in tandem with the cases of Bosnia, Darfur, and Colombia examined elsewhere in this volume—demonstrate that neither are the consequences of politicization generally benign nor is embrace of an "intentions-based" position generally defensible. As Michael Blastland and Andrew Dilnot bluntly put it: "Everyone pays for this [cavalier or even hostile] attitude [towards numbers] in bad policy, bad government, gobbledygook news, and it ends in lost chances and screwed-up lives."[38]

The Politics of Numbers in (Military) Action

Rwandan Refugees in Eastern Zaire

At the conclusion of the cold war, there was a great deal of optimism in some circles that its end would facilitate the collection and dissemination of more accurate statistics, in part because the United Nations High Commissioner for Refugees (UNHCR) and other international organizations and agencies were to be liberated from some of the political pressures to which they were subjected during that decades-long ideological struggle.[39]

---

37. See chapter 11 in this volume for a comprehensive examination of the potential policy implications of statistical politicization.

38. Michael Blastland and Andrew Dilnot, *The Numbers Game: The Commonsense Guide to Understanding Numbers in News, in Politics and in Life* (New York: Gotham, 2008), xii.

39. This case draws heavily on the insights shared by refugee expert and Africa specialist, Jeff Crisp in "Who Has Counted the Refugees? UNHCR and the Politics of Numbers," *New Issues in Refugee Research* 12 (1999).

Nevertheless, events in eastern Zaire in late 1996 would soon undercut this optimism and demonstrate that geopolitical interests would, at least under some conditions, continue to impinge on issues surrounding the definition, scope, and magnitude of cross-border population movements.[40] In the interest of eschewing greater involvement in the region, and sidestepping demands that it interpose itself between combatants in the midst of ongoing conflict, the United States actively downplayed and "downsized" the scope of the ongoing Great Lakes refugee crisis. This episode of statistical politicization was a success insofar as it allowed the United States to eschew a mission it was reluctant to undertake. But from a humanitarian and possibly also a longer-term juridical perspective, the verdict reads rather differently.

Having grown weary of cross-border attacks back into Rwanda by militarized Hutu refugees operating out of camps in Zaire, in the fall of 1996, Rwandan Patriotic Army (RPA)/Armee Patriotique Rwandaise (APR) forces backed (and then covertly joined) an offensive by Laurent Kabila's Alliance des Forces Democratiques pour la Liberation du Congo-Zaire (AFDL) forces into Zaire and into the camps along the border. Following the incursion, the camps were cut off from humanitarian aid and supplies. In short order, media reports began circulating about the danger of disease and imminent starvation of those still sheltering within the camps. As fears and publicity mounted, so did calls for international action. In response, the UN Security Council authorized a multinational intervention force. The Canadian-led UN mission—which was to include 4,000 U.S. troops—was tasked with overseeing protection and provision of food aid for the refugees. However, at just about this same time, the refugees began streaming back across the border into Rwanda. After more than two years in exile, within a matter of a few days, approximately half a million Rwandans suddenly left eastern Zaire and returned to their country of origin. Then, just as suddenly, the mass self-repatriation ended, encouraging some observers—and especially U.S. government and Rwandan officials—to declare the crisis in the Great Lakes region of Africa effectively over. In short, almost before the ink was dry on the UN Security Council resolution, the operation was declared by some as moribund and unnecessary.[41]

However, it quickly became evident that the real story was more complicated than it had first appeared. Contrary to prevailing claims that all of the

40. Crisp, "Who Has Counted the Refugees?"; and Jo Ellen Fair and Lisa Parks, "Inspecting African Bodies: Television News Coverage and Satellite Imaging of Rwandan Refugees," paper presented at the Sixth Annual African Studies Consortium Workshop, October 2, 1998, http://www.africa.upenn.edu/Workshop/joelisa98.html.

41. Stephen Handelman, "Canada to Halt African Mission," *Toronto Star,* December 14, 1996, A1; Brian McGrory, "U.S. Will Reassess Rwandan Mission; Refugee Exodus Could Alter Plans," *Boston Globe,* November 18, 1996.

Rwandan refugees had gone home, evidence began to emerge that some-where between 350,000 and 700,000 remained in eastern Zaire, where they were being hunted down and killed by AFDL and RPA/APR forces.[42] Relief agencies reported that hundreds of thousands of refugees had not only been displaced from the camps following the rebel attacks, but also that many were "lost" and could not be located. Despite an upsurge in U.S. television news coverage, the true scale and scope of the crisis remained largely hidden.[43] As a result, agencies such as Refugees International and Human Rights Watch called for the use of satellite images and aerial pho-tography as a way of locating and tracking the missing as well as "making visible" conditions in the region.[44] The operative logic was that the images from above would both pinpoint lost refugees for relief workers and pro-vide a graphic display of their living conditions for Western television view-ers. The belief was that the satellite images would reinvigorate support for the military mission; in the end, however, it did exactly the opposite.

When pictures were eventually taken, both UN and U.S. officials ex-amined them. But the United States and the UN came away with widely divergent interpretations of the data: whereas UN officials said they lo-cated 750,000 refugees in the pictures, U.S. officials claimed they saw al-most none.[45] At a November 23, 1996, press conference, the U.S. military summarily dismissed UN estimates, claiming the photos showed only one significant cluster of Rwandans in eastern Zaire. The U.S. interpretation further served to reinforce the Rwandan government's contention that the refugee numbers had been inflated from the outset—that is, since the af-termath of the 1994 genocide. The Rwandan president's political adviser "challenge[d] the UNHCR to give us proof of where those refugees are. Nowhere do the American satellite photographs show up any significant refugee concentrations."[46]

---

42. AFDL and RPA forces, with the support of Rwanda, had originally attacked refu-gee camps—and later dispersed groups of refugees—in eastern Zaire. They did so largely in response to repeated cross-border attacks by ex-FAR (*Forces Armees Rwandaises*) and *Interahamwe* forces, which had been using the camps as bases and recruitment centers. Many of those residing in the camps were Hutu who had fled Rwanda in the summer of 1994, fol-lowing the genocide.

43. Lionel Rosenblatt, "Unless U.S. Galvanizes International Action, Central Africa Will Explode," Refugees International Report no. 8, 1996. See also Fair and Parks, "Inspecting African Bodies."

44. Refugees International, "Presidential Leadership Needed to Save One Million Refu-gees," press release, November 1996; cited in Fair and Parks, "Inspecting African Bodies."

45. Fair and Parks, "Inspecting African Bodies."

46. Johan Pottier, "The 'Self' in Self-Repatriation: Closing Down Mugunga Camp, East-ern Zaire," in *The End of the Refugee Cycle: Refugee Repatriation and Reconstruction*, ed. Richard Black and Khalid Khoser (Oxford: Berghahn Books, 1999), 148.

A senior Oxfam official, who had (along with his staff) viewed the self-same satellite and aerial photos three days before, in turn disputed U.S. and Rwandan claims, declaring the photos, "confirmed, in considerable detail, the existence of over half a million people, distributed in three major and numerous minor agglomerations." Others' refusal to acknowledge as much left him "bound to conclude that as many as 400,000 refugees and unknown numbers of Zairian displaced persons have, in effect, been air-brushed from history."[47] For his part, Lionel Rosenblatt, President of Refugees International—one of the key figures who had lobbied for the acquisition of aerial images at the outset—concurred. "Obviously, it's not factual to say that few refugees are left in eastern Zaire. Both Washington and Kigali have declared victory, but we're still missing 600,000, maybe 700,000, refugees who two weeks ago were wards of the international community."[48]

A separate statement by UNHCR—which suggested similarly large numbers of displaced remained in Zaire—was angrily dismissed by the Rwandans. Officials in Kigali declared everyone knew that UNHCR "had a habit of exaggerating its figures, so why would anyone want to believe them this time round?"[49] The U.S. versus UNHCR "feud over the figures," as Joel Boutroue has called it, escalated further when the United States— through its embassy in Kigali—announced that it was taking over the counting of Rwandan returnees. Thereafter, the United States produced daily estimates of returnee figures that were routinely at least 100,000 persons higher than UNHCR's.

U.S. officials further argued that there were also reasons to doubt that those who still remained in Zaire were genuine refugees—as opposed to soldiers and militia members who had been responsible for the 1994 genocide. As one U.S. general put it, "What is a refugee? There's fighting going on in eastern Zaire and that fighting has displaced Zairians who could in some loose terms be called refugees, so you can see there could be difficulties." Another argued, "It's very difficult to know how many refugees are where, what kind of condition they are in and what their intentions are." Thus, they concluded, not only were there many fewer displaced people than had been claimed, but also still fewer of them were actually refugees.[50] Soon thereafter, the United States announced that—consistent with Rwandan government claims—UNHCR's figures were indeed inflated, and

47. Cited in Crisp, "Who's Counting the Refugees?"
48. Bradley Graham and Stephen Buckley, "U.S. Sharply Cuts Back Africa Force," *Washington Post*, November 20, 1996.
49. Pottier, "The 'Self' in Self-Repatriation," 149.
50. Ibid.

no refugee groupings of note remained in Zaire.[51] (The fact that UNHCR was known to provide unreliable [read politicized] numbers on occasion meant some of those able to provide hard evidence to the contrary were self-deterred from sharing it.)[52]

In an impassioned plea to save the now-threatened UN mission, and in support of more aggressive and expanded military action, the European Union's humanitarian aid commissioner, Emma Bonino, turned the numbers issue on its head, asking in a speech to the European Parliament, "How many lives have to be in danger...to justify a deployment of troops?"[53] France, Belgium and Spain, the UNHCR, and NGOs on the ground asserted that, "Military action was still [very much] needed to find and protect 700,000 'missing' Rwandans."[54] UN Special Envoy Raymond Chrétien likewise beseeched observers not to "think only of what you see on the television screens. There is a huge number of refugees that are absolutely invisible but are still very much in eastern Zaire."[55] But it was too late.

Although the Clinton administration had never been particularly enthusiastic about the mission, it was the official "decline" in refugee numbers that provided the administration with the political cover it felt it needed to justify its reduced commitment and ultimate withdrawal from the Security Council-backed operation. Indeed, U.S. military officials later stressed the importance of the "timely distribution and evaluation" of aerial data as critical in preventing "the unnecessary deployment of a multinational force."[56] The "success" of the repatriation and low refugee estimates allowed National Security Adviser Anthony Lake to declare first that the need for international military intervention in eastern Zaire had shrunk, and then that it had disappeared altogether. "Every day we have seen movements that are encouraging. It's sorting itself out."[57] Even before the images were publicly released, U.S. Secretary of Defense William Perry

51. Joel Boutroue, "Missed Opportunities: The Role of the International Community in the Return of the Rwandan Refugees from Eastern Zaire," Rosemary Rogers Working Paper no. 1, 1998, 61.

52. Crisp, "Who's Counting the Refugees?"

53. John Lichfield, "'Missing' Rwandan Refugees Fall Prey to Whim of Big-Power Rivalry," *Independent*, November 22, 1996.

54. Ibid.

55. Tim Harper, "Rescue Plan for Zaire in Jeopardy," *Toronto Star*, November 18, 1996.

56. "Military: Operation Guardian Assistance," http://www.globalsecurity.org/military/ops/guardian_assistance.htm. See also U.S. Department of Defense report to Congress, "U.S. Military Activities in Rwanda, 1994—August 1997," http://www.dod.mil/pubs/rwanda/index.html.

57. Alan Cowell, "African Aid Effort Mired in Dispute Over Scope of Mission," *New York Times*, November 23, 1996.

declared that the repatriation had "caused Washington to rethink its role in the force." After all, "we are not the Salvation Army."[58]

This outcome prevailed despite the fact that "the information provided by the U.S. government was contradictory at times, and its source was unclear, since aerial photographs [of returnees] were taken inside Zaire and then only along specific routes."[59] Nevertheless, the deflated numbers stuck, and in the space of a few days, the originally proffered 4,000 troops fell to 2,000, then to 1,000, then to a token 200. This meant that the critical logistical roles to be played by U.S. troops—including securing the airport at Goma, keeping transportation lines to and from the airport open (so that aid could be distributed quickly and efficiently), and providing intelligence—were left unfilled, largely crippling the skeleton force that remained.

Although the UN still declared the mission a success, the assessment of those on the ground was far less charitable. According to James Orbinski, head of Médecins Sans Frontières in Goma, it was "anything but a success. The mission set out with the intention of providing secure access to a population in danger and it has not done that.... There are still hundreds of thousands of refugees who have not crossed over into their homeland and are still being coerced by *Interahamwe* militias and the former Rwandan army and still being chased at the same time by rebel forces." And as deputy field director for the Irish NGO Concern Willa Addis put it, "To be perfectly frank, I don't actually know what they did and that in itself is telling.... [The] impact level on the ground for the refugees, as far as I'm aware, has been zilch."[60]

Arguably still more important, from a humanitarian perspective, the political wrangling over the "dwindling numbers" of refugees begat a material failure to accurately measure them. This in turn meant that the quantity of humanitarian supplies subsequently provided were inadequate to feed and provide clean water and medical care for the significant number who remained displaced. For instance, in the camps at Tingi Tingi, where a mortality surveillance system had been in place since the outset of the crisis, there was a "clear and constant deterioration" of the health status of the refugees from December 1996—soon after the release of the satellite data—primarily "due to the absence of adequate food supplies" and

58. Harper, "Rescue Plan for Zaire in Jeopardy."

59. Boutroue, "Missed Opportunities," 61. He notes that French counts largely comported with UNHCR's, not U.S./Rwandan estimates (61, note 195).

60. Alan Thompson, "African Rescue Mission Receives Scathing Reviews," *Toronto Star*, December 22, 1996.

disease.[61] By the end of February 1997, Congolese rebel forces reached Tingi Tingi, and most of the remaining refugees fled still further west. Others reportedly hid in the forest and came back some days later, and many disappeared altogether.[62]

Groups of refugees were again located in May 1997, on the eastern bank of the Congo River. After a final attack on the camps, they crossed over toward Congo-Brazzaville.[63] Debate still remains over how many remained alive at that point and what happened to them thereafter. Some say few actually made it to the western side of what was by that time the Democratic Republic of Congo, arguing instead that those still missing were killed as part of a retaliatory genocide by the AFDL and RPA/APR.[64] On the other side of the debate are those who believe most of the "missing" were subsequently repatriated back to Rwanda.[65] This issue is not simply one of academic importance. The Great Lakes region has been wracked by periods of episodic mass killings since the late 1950s and is still reeling from the after effects of the 1994 Rwandan genocide and a decade-long regional war. In light of the recurrent bloodlettings in this part of the world—and how those orchestrating these massacres have galvanized support for them— the truth about these numbers still fundamentally matters.[66]

61. Between December 27, 1996 (the first day of food distribution), and January 24, 1997, a daily average of 900 kilocalories per person was provided to the refugees in the camps (UNHCR recommends a daily ration of 2,100 kilocalories). High mortality rates were also explained by subsequent dysentery and cholera outbreaks.

62. Dominique Legros, Christophe Paquet, and Pierre Nabeth, "The Evolution of Mortality Among Rwandan Refugees in Zaire Between 1994 and 1997," in *Forced Migration and Mortality*, ed. Charles Keely and Holly Reed (Washington, DC: National Academies Press, 2001), 57–58.

63. Legros et al., "The Evolution of Mortality." See also "50,000 Refugees at Congo River After 1,000-Mile Trek in Zaire," *New York Times*, May 6, 1997.

64. Kisangani N.F. Emizet, "The Massacre of Refugees in Congo: A Case of UN Peacekeeping Failure and International Law," *Journal of Modern African Studies* 38 (2000): 163– 202. Likewise, Legros, Paquet, and Nabeth tracked the flight of Rwandans into the forests of then eastern Zaire and discuss mortality at various stages of the migration. By their final estimates, only about 20 percent of the original refugee population remained; the rest were either dead or missing (65).

65. Great Lakes Center for Strategic Studies, "Fact Finder Bulletin on Claims That Rwandan Army and AFDL Killed 230,000 Refugees in 1996–1997," 2006 (As of September 2009, this organization appears defunct.), www.glcss.org/php/bulletins/Fact%20Finder%20Bulletin %201001%202006%20Refugees%201996%201997.pdf. The *Bulletin* argues: "Professor Emizet's number of 232,000 refugees killed was never accurate because the UNHCR only reported 173,000 missing refugees in 1997. Of this number, 132,329 have either been repatriated to Rwanda, are waiting to be repatriated or estimated by UNHCR to be still in hiding. This leaves an approximate balance of 40,671 refugees that remain missing or some portion of that number presumed dead."

66. See, for instance, Benjamin Valentino, *Final Solutions: Mass Killing and Genocide in the Twentieth Century* (Ithaca: Cornell University Press, 2004).

The Battle of Jenin

Information critical to the conduct of successful military operations is often enveloped in what is known as "the fog of war."[67] To the extent one can control this "fog," it can be both tactically and strategically useful to obscure from one's opponents the true toll his actions have taken and how that toll might affect relative capabilities. However, as Israeli Defense Forces and their government were to be painfully reminded both during and long after the conclusion of Operation Defensive Shield, adversaries are not the only audience for conflict-related statistics. And if the fog of war (controlled or otherwise) means good data are obscured or simply cannot be acquired, bad—and operationally damaging—data may be substituted, sometimes to catastrophic effect.

The controversy over what became known as "the Jenin Massacre" arose after Israeli Defense Forces (IDF) conducted military operations in the Palestinian refugee camp in Jenin, between April 3 and April 11, 2002. Israeli forces targeted Jenin, after charging that the camp had "served as a launch site for numerous terrorist attacks against both Israeli civilians and Israeli towns and villages in the area," including the dispatch of several dozen suicide bombers since the start of the Second Intifada.[68] Operation Defensive Shield was launched in early April, specifically, in retribution for a Passover suicide bombing in Netanya, which claimed the lives of twenty-eight Israelis.[69]

In the context of the operation, the Israeli army decided to block all media access to Jenin. The IDF's stated reason for restricting access was:

> [the] need to preserve freedom of operation. Journalists and cameramen chasing after a picture or a story could impede military operations in the camp's narrow streets and had to be restricted. Furthermore, their presence in the battle scene endangered their lives. Cameramen were particularly vulnerable: Israeli helicopter pilots reported they misidentified television cameras as shoulder launched anti-aircraft weapons and could have easily targeted innocent journalists.[70]

The decision turned out to be a double-edged sword. Keeping journalists out of the area of operations provided the IDF with the greater opera-

---

67. As the term's progenitor, Carl von Clausewitz, put it: "The great uncertainty of all data in war is a peculiar difficulty, because all action must, to a certain extent, be planned in a mere twilight, which in addition not infrequently—like the effect of a fog or moonshine—gives to things exaggerated dimensions and unnatural appearance." Carl von Clausewitz, *On War,* trans. J. J. Graham (London: Kegan Paul, Trench, Trubner & Co., 1908), bk. 2, ch. 2, paragraph 24.

68. "Jenin's Terrorist Infrastructure," http://www.mfa.gov.il/MFA.

69. See, for instance, Ken Lee, "Jenin Rises from the Dirt," BBC News, June 24, 2003.

70. Gal Luft, "Urban Operations in Jenin Refugee Camp: The Israeli Experience," http://www.hks.harvard.edu/cchrp/Use%20of%20Force/October%202002/Luft_final.pdf.

tional freedom it sought; however, this was a benefit probably not worth its ultimate political and economic costs. The absence of reporters on the ground meant good information was hard to come by. With no credible journalists on the scene, international media outlets got their information from local Palestinian sources, who described widespread war crimes that the Israelis were allegedly trying to cover up. Consequently, false reports about a massacre of anywhere between 500 and 3,000 people appeared in some of the world's most reputable media.[71]

How and why was this myth created? At some point during the fighting, the IDF reportedly used loudspeakers to issue a demand that all men between the ages of sixteen and fifty turn themselves in. Many of the men who appeared were then rounded up by Israeli authorities for questioning. The rest were forbidden to return to the city, since the fighting in Jenin raged on. These men were instead temporarily transferred to nearby villages in the West Bank. However, because their families did not receive word from or about them, "rumors began to fly that they had been executed."[72] At the same time, another inflammatory rumor also began to spread, this one apparently a consequence of the IDF's decision to send three large air-conditioned supply trucks to Jenin, in which some Israeli reservists decided to sleep. After some Palestinians observed dozens of covered bodies lying in the trucks, they told reporters—who were themselves far from the scene—that the IDF had filled the trucks with Palestinian bodies.[73] Hearsay reports were treated as facts, which might—it was quickly added—be difficult to substantiate, as "recovering the bodies would be difficult because many buildings collapsed during bombardment."[74]

All of these rumors were later proven false. Indeed, a UN fact-finding committee established months after the event that the Palestinian death toll in Jenin was not in the thousands or even the hundreds, but rather totaled only fifty-two, of whom noncombatants numbered no more than twenty.[75] Human Rights Watch reported similar figures, as did the Palestinian Authority, which further acknowledged that most of those killed were combatants.[76] Twenty-three Israeli soldiers were also killed, which led

71. See, for instance, "Jenin 'Massacre' Evidence Growing," BBC News, April 18, 2002.
72. Ibid.
73. Luft, "Urban Operations in Jenin Refugee Camp."
74. "Jenin 'Massacre' Evidence Growing."
75. "Report of the Secretary-General, Prepared Pursuant to General Assembly Resolution ES-10/10 (Report on Jenin)," http://www.un.org/peace/jenin/.
76. Human Rights Watch, "Israel, the Occupied West Bank and Gaza Strip, and the Palestinian Authority Territories," May 2002, http://hrw.org/reports/2002/israel3/israel0502-01.htm#P49_1774; Tom Gross, "How the Media Made 'Jeningrad,'" *Courier Mail*, June 8, 2002.

Abdel Rahman Sa'adi—an Islamic Jihad member—to quip, "This was a massacre of the Jews, not of us."[77]

By the time the truth was established, however, the "Jenin Massacre" had become a social fact, already anchored in the minds of millions, and both short- and long-term damage was done.

Before the myth's debunking, credible media sources published a variety of very troubling assertions, predicated on "facts" that ultimately proved to be bogus. The *Guardian*'s lead editorial proclaimed Israel's actions in Jenin "every bit as repellent" as Osama bin Laden's attack on New York on September 11, 2001.[78] A leading columnist for London's *Evening Standard* asserted: "We are talking here of massacre, and a cover-up, of genocide."[79] For her part, Janine di Giovanni, the London *Times* correspondent in Jenin opined, "Rarely in more than a decade of war reporting from Bosnia, Chechnya, Sierra Leone, Kosovo, have I seen such deliberate destruction, such disrespect for human life." Di Giovanni further suggested that the refugees "she had earlier interviewed escaping the West Bank city 'underestimated the carnage and the horror.'"[80] Small wonder then that the casualty figures got inflated.

Hyperbole abounded elsewhere as well. "Amid the ruins, the grisly evidence of a war crime," was the headline for the April 17 report from the *Independent*'s Jerusalem correspondent, Phil Reeves. He reported that, "a monstrous war crime that Israel has tried to cover up for a fortnight has finally been exposed.... The sweet and ghastly reek of rotting human bodies is everywhere, evidence that it is a human tomb. The people say there are hundreds of corpses, entombed beneath the dust."[81] Moreover, the *Guardian*, the *Independent*, the *Telegraph,* and the *Times* all quoted the same solitary "witness," Kamal Anis, who claimed that he saw "Israeli soldiers heap 30 bodies beneath a half-wrecked house."[82] "When the pile was complete, they bulldozed the building, bringing its ruins down on the corpses," according to Anis, "then they flattened the area with a tank."[83]

---

77. Quoted in "Claims of Massacre Go Unsupported by Palestinian Fighters," *Boston Globe,* April 29, 2002.

78. Sharon Sadeh, "Media: How Jenin Battle Became a 'Massacre,'" *Guardian,* May 6, 2002, 7.

79. Quoted in Gross, "Jeningrad"; Sadeh, "Media."

80. Quoted in Bruce Wilson, "Stench of Jenin Begins to Rise in the West," *Daily Telegraph,* April 17, 2002, 29.

81. Phil Reeves, "Amid the Ruins of Jenin, the Grisly Evidence of a War Crime," *Independent,* April 16, 2002.

82. Sadeh, "How Jenin Battle Became a 'Massacre,'" 7.

83. Kenneth Lasson, "War of Words," *Global Journalist,* 2004, www.globaljournalist.org/magazine/2004-1/war-of-words.html.

Such imagery is hard to combat, particularly when correcting the record was treated with far less vim and vigor than reporting the initial "facts" about the thousands who had been slaughtered. As former IDF Lieutenant Colonel Gal Luft put it:

> Israel learned the hard way that mishandling and restricting the media can have strategic consequences and that the absence of Western media in Jenin contributed to distorted, often hostile, coverage. Influenced by the horror stories from Jenin, the international community mobilized to bring a premature end to the Israeli campaign, which was the exact response Israel wanted to avoid.[84]

In short, despite employment of a number of successful tactical innovations, the Israeli operation ultimately failed to achieve its military objectives. And, at the same time, the nature of the press coverage damaged the IDF's image and legitimacy.[85] For their part, Palestinian leaders declared the operation a "great victory against the Jews."[86] Whatever the truth of this statement on the military front, with respect to public opinion, their assessment was undoubtedly correct—a sentiment that has been echoed by Gideon Meir, deputy director general for Media and Public Affairs in Israel's Ministry of Foreign Affairs.[87]

What were the concrete costs? The negative image of Israel, particularly in the European press, "contributed to a sense of unease about doing business [t]here. There [was] a noticeable fall in business visitors—investors, analysts, and buyers. There [we]re questions about the ability of Israeli companies to supply goods to overseas customers, and concerns about fulfilling contracts for goods already sold."[88] There were also calls and moves by some organizations and individuals to boycott Israeli goods. Norway's labor union—whose members number nearly 20 percent of the country's population (about 900,000 people)—called for a boycott of Israeli goods, while Germany halted the supply of engines for Israel's Merkava tank.[89]

84. Luft, "Urban Operations in Jenin Refugee Camp."

85. Sergio Catignani, "The Israel Defense Forces and the Al-Aqsa Intifada: When Tactical Victory Meets Strategic Disappointment," European University Institute Working Paper Series, 2008, 10–11.

86. Gross, "Jeningrad."

87. Hirsh Goodman and Jonathan Cummings, eds., "The Battle of Jenin: A Case Study in Israel's Communications Strategy," Jaffee Center for Strategic Studies Memorandum 63, 2003, 31. Meir declared it "had an enormous impact on international public opinion."

88. Dan Propper, Chairman of the Osem Group of Companies, in Goodman and Cummings, "The Battle of Jenin," 29.

89. "Shield: A Post Mortem," *Insight: A Middle East Analysis*, June 2002, http://www.ujc.org/page.html?ArticleID=79160. (It should be noted that *Insight* is an avowedly pro-Israel publication.)

Others attempted to punish Israel by "showcasing" Israeli products so that consumers would be able to identify and avoid them easily. This strategy appears to have worked. The Israel Citrus Grower's Association reported that the export of oranges to Europe dropped 25 percent, following the operation in Jenin. The image hit was believed to have further contributed to the ongoing rise in anti-Semitism in Europe; in France, for instance, fifty-six synagogues and Jewish institutions were attacked within the month after Defensive Shield, a significantly greater number than in the period leading up to it.[90]

In addition, though the Palestinians did not succeed in internationalizing the conflict, Egypt withdrew its ambassador to Tel Aviv, Jordan delayed its appointment of an ambassador whose term expired, and the Gulf States and Morocco (at least, temporarily) cut economic ties with Israel. As Hirsh Goodman and Jonathan Cummings bluntly put it: "Clearly media ineptitude [and the politicization this facilitated] had strategic consequences for Israel in this war."[91]

Finally, even if one might argue that the measurable economic and diplomatic fallout was short term, the political psychological damage was not. According to Ephraim Kam, Deputy Head of the Jaffee Center for Strategic Studies:

> In the Palestinian mindset, Jenin is now associated with massacre, despite those reports having been partially corrected in the West. Even informed Palestinians express no doubt that there was indeed a massacre, just as there is a collective memory of 10,000 Palestinians massacred in "Black September" 1970, though the real number was closer to 1,000.[92]

The "Jenin massacre" has become a damaging social fact, even though it never occurred. This case provides further evidence in support of the proposition that the promulgation of bad numbers can have lasting and damaging consequences—both locally and farther afield—a conclusion that has been repeatedly borne out in the Balkans as well.

Kosovo

Politicized refugee and casualty statistics may also fulfill the political function of legitimizing action against a country that is responsible for the displacement or expulsion of its citizens.[93] Refugee statistics and (projected)

---

90. Goodman and Cummings, "The Battle of Jenin," 28; and "Shield: A Post Mortem."
91. Goodman and Cummings, "The Battle of Jenin," 10.
92. Ibid., 28.
93. Crisp, "Who Has Counted the Refugees?"

refugee movements were the central component of the political and public relations strategy NATO used to legitimize and maintain support for its actions in the then-Yugoslav province of Kosovo. Although what became known as the "Kosovo conflict" had been simmering throughout the 1990s, the crisis came to a low boil in mid-1998, following a brutal crackdown by the Serbs on the province's Albanian population, as part of their counterinsurgency campaign against Kosovar separatists, and especially the militant Kosovo Liberation Army (KLA).

Conflict-related statistics were routinely manipulated and politicized throughout the Kosovo crisis and beyond. The political and humanitarian implications of this strategy became clear with some alacrity; the juridical and scholarly consequences are still being felt as of this writing a decade later. In some cases, the numbers proffered were wildly and demonstrably unreliable as well as clearly politically motivated. In other cases, the numbers reported might have in fact been technically correct; however, they were reported in ways that suggested that they were not exactly what they seemed.

For instance, following the Yugoslav Army's 1998 summer offensive against the KLA, it was believed that several hundred thousand Kosovar Albanians had been displaced from their homes. With winter coming and few reliable statistics available, aid workers sounded the alarm about an impending humanitarian crisis.[94] "The prospect of tens of thousands of Kosovars starving or freezing during the coming winter, in the words of one pundit, 'concentrated the minds in Washington and elsewhere.'"[95] Drawing on warnings of the winter threat, President Clinton released a statement saying, "With more than 250,000 Kosovars displaced from their homes and the cold weather coming, [Yugoslav President Slobodan] Milosevic must act immediately...to prevent a major humanitarian disaster and restore peace in the region."[96] However—as the Organization for Security and Cooperation in Europe (OSCE) knew at the time—the vast majority of the displaced were living in other homes, not exposed to the elements, as Clinton's statement suggests.

Nevertheless, not only did the urgent humanitarian warnings and (misleading) prospect of a quarter of a million people freezing to death on western Europe's doorstep galvanize support for military action against

---

94. Abby Stoddard, *Humanitarian Alert: NGO Information and Its Impact on U.S. Foreign Policy* (Sterling, VA: Kumarian Press, 2007), 167.

95. David T. Buckwalter, "Madeleine's War: Operation Allied Force," *Case Studies in Policy Making and Implementation* (Newport: Naval War College, 2002), 12.

96. "Statement by President William Jefferson Clinton," September 23, 1998; cited in Stoddard, *Humanitarian Alert,* 168.

the Serbs, it also led to the misallocation of limited humanitarian assistance resources and prevented aid being delivered to locations where it was more desperately needed. In fact, when the NGO-run mobile health clinics supplied their epidemiological data to the World Health Organization in January 1999, the resulting morbidity report "looked not unlike what you might find in a typical stable population at that time of year." The most common diagnosis (accounting for 35 percent of total consultations and 50 percent of diagnoses for children 0–5) was respiratory infection, including common colds. However, in the period leading up to NATO's campaign in the spring of 1999, these findings were not widely reported in the press.[97]

What was widely reported were groundless figures about the numbers and nature of victims of Serb actions in Kosovo.[98] These included U.S. Secretary of Defense William Cohen's claim that "we've now seen about 100,000 military-aged [Albanian] men missing...they may have been murdered," while David Scheffer, U.S. ambassador at large for war crimes announced that as many as "225,000 ethnic Albanian men aged between 14 and 59" may have been killed. Then two weeks after air strikes began, the U.S. State Department said that it had reports of 3,200 killings and up to 100,000 Kosovars missing. For its part, the British Foreign Office, which had appointed a special investigator, claimed that deaths ran "probably to tens of thousands."[99]

Once the conflict ended in early June, death toll estimates hovered around 10,000, with the sometimes quite explicit promise of higher figures to come. As one report warned:

> During the NATO bombing of Kosovo, when Serbia controlled reporters' access to the region, journalists could document atrocities only by interviewing the ethnic Albanians who had fled to refugee camps. News reports of their accounts usually carried the words "could not be independently confirmed."

97. By way of contrast, the major cause of morbidity and mortality among populations in severe emergencies tends to be diarrheal diseases—which caused about 70 percent of the deaths of Kurdish refugees in northern Iraq and 90 percent of deaths among Rwandan refugees in Goma. "Statement by President William Jefferson Clinton," 168.

98. There was even disagreement over how many Kosovar Albanians were killed during the Serbs' brutal prebombing counterinsurgency campaign. In some media sources, numbers actually doubled (from 1,000 to 2,000) in the week after the failed talks at Rambouillet (Sid Balman, Jr., "Focus: Agreement in Principle Reached," *United Press International,* February 23, 1999). A March 3 report asserted that 2,000 had been killed, and the number of displaced was cited as 250,000 ("Yugoslav Army Continues Border Build-Up," *United Press International,* March 3, 1999). Yet UNHCR reported only 69,500 refugees several days *after* NATO bombing began.

99. Michael Binyon, Charles Bremner, Stephen Farrell and Anthony Loyd, "Serbs Have Murdered at Least 5,000," *Times,* May 7. 1999.

They can be now....The British Government now says that at least 10,000 ethnic Albanian civilians were killed in hundreds of massacres. An American official called this number "conservative in the extreme.[100]

Another quoted British officials as claiming, "by the hour" NATO troops were "uncovering evidence of savage wartime atrocities—mass murder, rapes, and torture—carried out against ethnic Albanian civilians by Serb soldiers and police in Kosovo....They estimated that more than 10,000 Kosovars were killed in at least 100 separate massacres."[101] For his part, Clinton decried evidence of "wholesale slaughter" by Serb forces as world leaders gathered for a G-7/G-8 summit whose agenda was dominated by the massive task of rebuilding the Balkans. Commenting on reports of 10,000 plus dead, he said, "It is a worse truth than we dared dream of." Blair concurred.[102]

What is curious is that this figure was already being bandied about and widely published nearly a month before the conflict ended. On May 7, 1999, the London *Times* reported that it had "learnt that President Milosevic's police and paramilitary forces have massacred at least 5,000 Kosovar Albanians and perhaps as many as 10,000....NATO announced yesterday that at least 4,000 people have been summarily killed and a further 100,000 men of military age have disappeared."[103]

Within days, the 10,000 death toll began appearing in newspapers worldwide, despite the fact that no investigators were yet on the ground inside the Yugoslav province.[104] To be fair, the 10,000 dead figure was much lower than many estimates proffered early on. Yet this number held fast even after investigators entered Kosovo in mid-June.[105] In fact, soon after hostilities ceased, British Foreign Office minister Geoffrey Hoon told reporters that *new* evidence suggested the number was at least 10,000, but would surely rise as investigators were able to access more of the province.

100. "The Horrors of Kosovo," *New York Times,* June 21, 1999.

101. Susan Milligan and Mary Leonard, "Crisis in Kosovo; Serb Atrocity Evidence Mounting," *Boston Globe,* June 18, 1999.

102. Martin Crutsinger, "Summit Talk Focuses on Milosevic," Associated Press, June 18, 1999.

103. "Serbs Have Murdered at Least 5,000."

104. See, for instance, "Milo Massacre Total Could Hit 10,000," *New York Post,* May 7, 1999.

105. One Associated Press report acknowledged, there were "no official estimates for the number of Kosovo Albanians killed by Serb security forces since NATO began bombing March 24," and reported that "refugees have reported hundreds of deaths." "Facts, Figures of Kosovo Crisis," Associated Press, June 3, 1999.

"Tragically, our estimates of the numbers of innocent men, women and children killed will almost certainly have to be revised upwards."[106]

But the widely reported "upwards of 10,000 bodies" were never found, nowhere close in fact. The U.S. Federal Bureau of Investigation team— which arrived in June to investigate what was called "the largest crime scene in the Bureau's forensic history"—departed several weeks later, having not found a single mass grave. A separate Spanish forensic team also returned home disenchanted soon thereafter. The head of its team complained angrily that he and his colleagues had become part of "a semantic pirouette by the war propaganda machines, because we did not find one— not one—mass grave."[107] In the words of Spanish pathologist Emilio Pérez Pujol, who exhumed bodies in both Rwanda and Kosovo, "Rwanda was a true genocide. Kosovo was ethnic cleansing light." In Pujol's sector of western Kosovo, for instance, the UN told him to expect as many as 2,000 victims. His team found just 187 corpses, none of which showed evidence to confirm local accounts of mutilations.[108]

As of November 1999, the number of bodies discovered was 2,108—not all of which were necessarily war crimes victims. Though more than 300 reported grave sites remained to be investigated at that point, the International Criminal Tribunal for the Former Yugoslavia (ICTY) had checked the largest reported sites first and found most contained no more than five bodies, suggesting intimate acts of barbarity rather than mass murder.[109]

How did this set of events, too, go so wrong? As in Jenin, politically motivated actors on the ground—in this case, the KLA—helped form the West's wartime image of Kosovo.[110] International human rights groups reported, for instance, that KLA officials served on the Kosovo-based Council for the Defense of Human Rights and Freedoms. And it was Council activists who were often the first to interview refugees arriving in Macedonia. Journalists later cited the Council's missing persons list to support theories about the death toll, and the U.S. State Department echoed these same estimates. But this number had to be taken on faith, because the Council reportedly refused to share its missing persons list.

106. John Ward Anderson and Molly Moore, "Kosovo's Albanians Returning In Droves; Serb-Led Offensive Took 10,000 Lives, Britain Estimates," *Washington Post,* June 18, 1999.

107. Pearl and Block, "Body Count."

108. Ibid.

109. Pearl and Block, "Body Count"; "Early Count Hints at Fewer Kosovo Deaths," *New York Times,* November 11, 1999.

110. See also "Chapter 3, Now the Refugees Are the War: NATO and the Kosovo Conflict," in Kelly M. Greenhill, *Weapons of Mass Migration: Forced Displacement, Coercion, and Foreign Policy* (Ithaca: Cornell University Press, 2010).

Within weeks, *USA Today* would report that many of the figures used by the Clinton administration and NATO to describe the wartime plight of the Kosovar Albanians were greatly exaggerated. Not only were far fewer killed, but "600,000 ethnic Albanians were not 'trapped within Kosovo itself lacking shelter, short of food, afraid to go home or buried in mass graves dug by their executioners,' [but also] Kosovo's livestock, wheat and other crops were still 'growing, not slaughtered wholesale or torched,' as widely reported."[111]

Then Pentagon spokesman Kenneth Bacon defended the Administration's position, saying "the best estimates available were used," that it was indeed appropriate to compare Milosevic to a World War II Nazi, and that "[even] if other war crimes turn out less than expected, 'I don't think you can say killing 100,000 is 10 times more morally repugnant than killing 10,000.'"[112] This is a defensible position, but then why inflate the numbers so egregiously in the first place?

One possible answer comes from Holly Burkhalter, former Washington director of Physicians for Human Rights. In early April 1999, Burkhalter read an essay on National Public Radio, in which she urged President Clinton to deploy ground troops to stop what she sincerely believed was a genocide in the making. She proclaimed that "if President Clinton avoids taking the painful action necessary to expel Serb forces from Kosovo, he will be remembered as the President on whose watch three genocides unfolded."[113] Burkhalter later admitted that on the issue of genocide in Kosovo, she "was wrong... but if you wait until it is proved to you six ways to Sunday, you haven't prevented it, have you?"[114] In a similar vein, a family friend of the Kosovar teenager, Rajmonda—whose claims that Serbs had tortured and killed her sister were shown to be false—declared, "If this small lie... made some kind of impact on what Western countries did in Kosovo, then it's worth it."[115]

In November 1999, the *Wall Street Journal* published the results of its own investigation, dismissing what it called "the mass-grave obsession." Instead of "the huge killing fields" some investigators were led to expect, they found "scattered killings [mostly] in areas where the separatist Kosovo Liberation Army had been active." In the end the reporters concluded NATO simply stepped up its claims about Serb killing fields when it "saw

111. "Clinton Gave Exaggerated Kosovo Atrocity Figures."

112. Ibid.

113. Holly Burkhalter, "Statement on Genocide in Kosovo," National Public Radio's *All Things Considered*, April 9, 1999.

114. Pearl and Block, "Body Count."

115. From a Canadian Broadcasting Company interview, quoted in Knightley, *The First Casualty*.

a fatigued press corps drifting toward the contrarian story: civilians killed by NATO's bombs."[116]

Although the Kosovo death toll has been adjusted downwards, even today, in many sources the 10,000 plus figure remains the accepted and authoritative figure.[117] Defenders of the 10,000 dead figure argue, among other things, that many of the missing bodies may have been dumped into rivers or been burnt. As Chief ICTY Prosecutor Carla Del Ponte put it, the number of bodies found:

> does not necessarily reflect the total number of actual victims, because we have discovered evidence of tampering with graves. There are also a significant number of sites where the precise number of bodies cannot be counted. . . . In these places, steps were taken to hide the evidence. Many bodies have been burned, but at those sites the forensic evidence is nevertheless consistent with the accounts given by witnesses of the crimes. The figures themselves may therefore not tell the whole story, and we would not expect the forensic evidence in isolation to produce a definitive total.[118]

There is probably some truth in the defenders' assertions; there were likely more victims than those who have been conclusively identified. However, since war's end, Kosovo's rivers have been dredged, most of the suspected mass graves have been searched, and still the body count remains less than half of the alleged 10,000 plus—to say nothing of the 100,000 figure.[119] (The ICTY declared the final number of bodies found in Kosovo's "mass graves" 2,788.) It is of course possible that many thousands of bodies were cremated, but even then some evidence should still be identifiable. Skeletal evidence tends to remain, even decades after burning (and even if that evidence has been doused with acid).[120] Kenneth Bacon and others have argued that it does not matter if the number is only 10,000. But what if the number were actually less than 4,000? At what point, if any, does the number matter?

It does matter, if for no other reason than the fact that it was reportedly the aforementioned *Wall Street Journal* article that helped Slobodan Milosevic discredit one of Carla Del Ponte's star witnesses, Halit Barani,

---

116. Pearl and Block, "Body Count."

117. See, for instance, Iain King and Whit Mason, *Peace at any Price: How the World Failed Kosovo* (Ithaca: Cornell University Press, 2006).

118. Institute for War and Peace Reporting, "Kosovo: Preliminary Statistics on the Death Toll," http://iwpr.net/?p=tri&s=f&o=252678&apc_state=henitri1999.

119. "No Bodies Found at Suspected Mass Grave Near Kosovo, Judge Says," Associated Press, June 8, 2007.

120. See, for instance, "Lost Romanov Bones 'Identified,'" BBC News, September 28, 2007.

former actor turned reporter. Of the claims outlined in the article, one of the most gruesome was that the Serb paramilitary had dumped 700 [some reports were as high as 1,500] bodies into the furnace at the Trepca mine, after having ground them into little pieces. As the article reported it:

> By late summer, stories about a Nazi-like body-disposal facility were so widespread that investigators sent a three-man French Gendarmerie team spelunking half a mile down the mine to search for bodies. They found none. Another team analyzed ashes in the furnace. They found no teeth or other signs of burnt bodies.... Mr. Berani doesn't completely stand by his story. "I told everybody it was supposition, it was not confirmed information."[121]

Whatever one's position on the legality or ultimate sagacity of NATO's 1999 bombing campaign, it is indisputable that before his four-year, multi-million dollar war crimes trial could be concluded, Milosevic died in his cell in the Hague. Although he died in prison, the former Yugoslav president was saved at least in part from conviction by the politicization of the conflict and the numbers to which it gave rise. More significant, and somewhat ironically, this inconclusive ending has provided additional succor to radicals who still maintain that the Serbs were the true victims of the 1990s wars. For whatever such political ammunition is worth, as virulent nationalists such as Tomislav Nikolić and Vojislav Šešelj still garner the support of a significant number of Serbs, this can hardly be the outcome the ICTY had hoped for.[122]

Conclusions and Implications

The preceding chapters in this volume advance our understanding of the politics of numbers by moving beyond borders and focusing on the politicization of statistics within the international illicit political economy. This chapter takes this expansion of our understanding a step further and examines how the politics of numbers we so frequently witness in the arena of transnational crime is echoed or replicated in the realm of armed conflict. It also tackles the question of whether and why politicization in this arena matters.

Armed conflict shares some of the same informational shortcomings and difficulties that mark data gathering vis-à-vis transnational crime. Logistical difficulties and a lack of transparency, coupled with compelling incentives to cite and deploy politicized numbers, can give rise to a variety of

121. Pearl and Block, "Body Count."
122. Nick Hawton, "Poll Leaves Serbs Split," BBC News, February 4, 2008.

distinct policy pathologies. Each can independently exacerbate the very suffering politicization is often undertaken to prevent as well as give rise to distinct political, humanitarian, juridical, and knowledge-impeding consequences.

Furthermore, these consequences often extend beyond what might be regarded as their normal shelf life. Consider, for instance, the persistence of the erroneous, yet seemingly ubiquitous, social fact that upward of 250,000 were killed during the 1992–95 Bosnian War. (The real number appears to be closer to 97,000.)[123] Although thoroughly discredited in the decade after the war ended, the inflated figure is still being casually cited and widely reproduced.[124] During the July 2007 Aspen Ideas Festival, for instance, former U.S. president Bill Clinton remarked:

> As awful as Iraq has been, fewer people have died there than would have died if the American military hadn't been there. You've got to be prepared for this. And all you have to do is look at Bosnia. Both Bosnia and Iraq are multi-ethnic, artificial creations of the demise of the Ottoman Empire at the end of World War I. We didn't do anything in Bosnia for three years, until sort of the blood lust was spent, NATO bombed them for a few days, we went to a peace agreement and made a deal. But before that deal was made, there were 250,000 dead people and two and a half million refugees. Iraq is four times as big. Nearly as I can tell, the death rate is three or four hundred thousand and two million refugees, which means you could have another six hundred thousand dead people and eight million more refugees if we disengage altogether before the process plays itself out and politics can assert itself.[125]

Thus it appears that, the difference between 100,000 and 250,000 still matters, as Clinton appeared to predicate his support for the Iraq war based on a flawed and inflated assessment of what a failure to act decisively wrought. Pointing out this flaw is not to suggest that a valid case could not be made for staying the course in Iraq. But if that case were based on playing the numbers game, it would be incumbent upon the actor making said case not to stack the deck.[126]

---

123. See Lara Nettelfield's chapter in this volume for details.

124. See, for instance, King and Mason, *Peace at any Price.*

125. Excerpt from "William Jefferson Clinton's July 2007 Speech at the Aspen Ideas Festival," http://www.youtube.com/watch?v=5hjCouO5fzU&feature=player_embedded.

126. Somewhat ironic, Clinton's fundamental argument comparing casualties in Bosnia and Iraq may have been bolstered by the fact that research by the World Health Organization suggests that the now famous *Lancet* study's death toll of well over 600,000 Iraqis had overstated mortality by about a factor of four. As both the Bosnia *and* Iraq tolls appear to have been inflated, by Clinton's logic, they may indeed be comparable after all. Iraq Family

To add insult to injury, inflated estimates of conflict casualties can serve to trivialize the very problems they were intended to highlight or combat. In her *Atlantic Monthly* essay on the controversy surrounding the Iraq body count, Megan McArdle observes the example of the *Lancet* study's critics, who:

> triumphantly waved the WHO results at their opponents. But even if "only" 150,000 people have been killed by violence in Iraq, that's a damn high price.[127]...Conversely, few of the study's supporters expressed much pleasure at the news that an extra 450,000 people might be walking around in Iraq. After a year and a half of bitter argument, all that anyone seemed interested in was proving they had been right. In counting we somehow lost track of the mountain of dead bodies piling up beneath our numbers.[128]

As Michael Berenbaum, director of the Holocaust Research Institute at the United States Holocaust Memorial Museum, argues, magnitude does matter. "The Holocaust has raised our tolerance for ordinary evil. This forces people to make their own plight more Holocaust-like."[129] It apparently also generates similar responses in some of those who seek to help those who find themselves struggling, oppressed, and/or living under duress. It is nevertheless essential that we undertake to measure and promulgate the actual "intensities of these events" "so that unlike events are not equated, and so that all inhumane behavior is not conflated and then flattened to the point where all such crimes are equal."[130] Moreover, because we live in a world of finite resources, choosing to address one set of issues—and to address them in a particular way—perforce means others will be shunted aside or ignored. If the numbers used to make these determinations are fundamentally flawed, more than resources will ultimately be misallocated.[131]

As Carl Sagan once put it, "Finding the occasional straw of truth awash in a great ocean of confusion and bamboozle requires intelligence, vigilance, dedication and courage. But if we don't practice these tough habits

---

Health Survey Study Group, "Violence-Related Mortality in Iraq from 2002 to 2006," *New England Journal of Medicine* 358 (2008): 484–93.

127. To their credit, the WHO researchers who critiqued the *Lancet* study took pains to note: "Although the estimated range is substantially lower than a recent survey-based estimate, it nonetheless points to a massive death toll, only one of the many health and human consequences of an ongoing humanitarian crisis." "Violence-Related Mortality," 485.

128. McArdle, "Body Counting," 28.

129. Quoted in Kenney, "The Bosnian Calculation Revisited."

130. Colin Tatz, *With Intent to Destroy: Reflections on Genocide* (London: Verso, 2003), 145.

131. See also Suhrke and Samset, "What's in a Figure?"

of thought, we cannot hope to solve the truly serious problems that face us...and we risk becoming a nation of suckers up for grabs by the next charlatan that comes along."[132] Sagan's admonition bears particular attention because the stickiness of social facts tends to be further magnified when coupled with consumers' psychological predispositions toward anchoring and demonstrable tendencies to unquestioningly adopt and replicate figures that emanate from "authoritative" sources.[133]

At the same time, it would be absurd and unfair to argue that somehow we are compelled to find a way to measure the unmeasurable. However, to the extent that we (as consumers, producers, and disseminators of statistics) can be more savvy and less credulous in our acquisition and utilization of these data, it is incumbent upon us to do so. It need not even be particularly difficult. There are several straightforward questions that can and should be regularly posed when presented with conflict-related statistics:

1. What is/are the source(s) of the numbers?
2. What definitions is/are the source(s) employing—for example, who is a combatant? What constitutes a combat-related death? Who is a refugee?—and thus what exactly is being measured?
3. What are the interests of those providing the numbers? What do these actors stand to gain or lose if the statistics in question are (or are not) embraced or accepted?
4. What methodologies were employed in acquiring the numbers?
5. Do potentially competing figures exist, and, if so, what do we know about their sources, measurements, and methodologies?

The political power of statistical information is destined to be a constant feature of conflict; the critical issue is how those who generate, employ, and simply consume these data react to that fact. This chapter opened with a truism about what happens to truth in war. It concludes by paraphrasing another truism: in the realm of conflict-related statistics, good intentions are not enough; they are misguided metrics that, however well meaning, as often as not, pave the road to hell.

132. Quoted in Spirer, Spirer, and Jaffe, *Misused Statistics*, 243.
133. See the introductory chapter in this volume for details.

7

Research and Repercussions of Death Tolls

THE CASE OF THE BOSNIAN
BOOK OF THE DEAD

Lara J. Nettelfield

In June 2007, the Sarajevo-based Research and Documentation Center (RDC) unveiled the initial results of "Human Losses in Bosnia and Herzegovina 1991–95," its multi-year project that sought to document all the deaths of the three-and-a-half-year war in Bosnia and Herzegovina (hereafter, Bosnia).[1] The project, which also came to be known as the Bosnian Book of the Dead (BBD), was motivated mainly by the fact that an accurate accounting of the victims still did not exist well over a decade after the war's end. Journalists, both local and international, consistently cited the figures of between 200,000 and 250,000 deaths, numbers that started to circulate during the war. The RDC's initial results revealed that the real number was close to half of the original estimate. Although this should have been welcome news across the country, in the year preceding the announcement of the findings, the Center's employees received numerous threats, local human rights activists were not forthcoming in their support of the project, and key stakeholders failed to show up for the presentation of the first round of the findings. This response raises the question: Why would a project based on the scrupulous collection of all forms of data about the war be such a controversial endeavor in a country in which the

1. The Research and Documentation Center website is http://www.idc.org.ba. The author was a guest of the RDC from 2003–2005 while she conducted her dissertation field research. She would like to thank: Robert Donia, Ewa Tabeau, Patrick Ball, Henrik Urdal, Linda Popić, Kate Doyle, Andrew Mack, and Kimberly Storr for helpful comments, and Sabiha Jukić for research assistance.

international community largely governs, and locally gathered facts are so glaringly absent? It is a question relevant not only for Bosnians, but also for those working in other postconflict zones who are attempting to apply scientific methodologies to questions about human rights violations, removing these issues from the realm of speculation to the realm of the scientific.

This chapter argues that the difficulty in producing and introducing new facts in transitional environments stems from the manner in which early scientific estimates about casualties become fused with narratives about victimhood and the character of a conflict. This makes it difficult for elites invested in older understandings to assimilate revised and more accurate information. Until the political forces that utilize older narratives and numbers no longer have a stake in the perceived accuracy of figures produced in times of transition, new scientific knowledge will encounter resistance. Similarly, narratives about the equality of victimhood can make postwar reintegration seem unwise. Recent studies in psychology can inform our understanding of the politics of the numbers of wartime casualty estimates in postconflict societies. Given that the use of quantitative analysis of human rights violations is quickly growing within societies that have suffered violent histories, this case study provides a useful history of one important effort, relevant for scholars and practitioners alike.[2]

Background

If you were to ask an average Bosnian citizen how many people died in the Bosnian war, it is likely that he or she will either tell you 200,000 or 250,000. This estimated number of deaths emerged early in the conflict and was subject to little scrutiny because the wartime environment made the attainment of precise figures impossible.

The exact origination of this number has been the source of some dispute, but almost all accounts point to the wartime foreign minister. A recent report in the Bosnian press reveals the origin of the figure as follows: President Alija Izetbegović, Foreign Minister Haris Silajdžić, and the commander of the Bosnian Army Sefer Halilović held a meeting in the summer of 1992 to decide what number would be used for public consumption.[3] President Alija Izetbegović suggested the number of 150,000 civilians killed

---

2. See, for example, Helge Brunborg and Ewa Tabeau, "Demography of Conflict and Violence: An Emerging Field," *European Journal of Population* 21 (2005): 131–44.

3. Bakir Hadžiomerović, "Pet Minuta" (Five Minutes), *Start* 223 (June 26, 2007). Halilović confirmed that this meeting took place.

by Serb nationalists, a figure that was agreed by all present at the meeting. However, during Silajdžić's first press conference after the gathering, he cited the figure of 250,000 Bosniak dead, adding an additional 100,000 deaths to the number previously agreed upon.[4]

International reporting reflected that confusion. After the first year of the war, for example, the *New York Times* reported that 150,000 had died; anticipating a grueling winter, forecasts estimated that up to 400,000 people could perish in the cold of the coming season. Other reports put the Bosnian government estimate at 134,000 as late as February 1993. Over the course of that spring, various estimates rose from 150,000 to 200,000.[5] Bosnian government officials allegedly stated in June 1993 that 200,000 had died.[6] Later in the conflict, that estimate floated upward until 250,000 became standard in most international and local reporting. Over time, this number hardened into conventional wisdom. Members of the local and international press quoted it, and it became the accepted truth about the number of casualties in the Bosnian war.[7]

Some international observers of the war, such as George Kenney, former head of the State Department's Yugoslav desk, questioned the estimate early on. Kenney resigned in 1992 to protest the Bush administration's policies in the region, the first of a string of high-level State Department officials to do so.[8] In an article for the *New York Times* magazine a few years later, he wrote that he was not convinced about the early estimates, stating: "Bosnia isn't the Holocaust or Rwanda; it's Lebanon."[9] He placed the estimate at between 25,000 and 60,000, arguing that the conflict did not qualify as "a unique genocide, as the United Nations and the Bosnian Muslims have charged."[10] Although his estimate was closer to the truth, the International Criminal Tribunal for the former Yugoslavia (ICTY), in the trial of Radislav Krstić, later found that genocide was committed against the Bosniaks after the fall of the Srebrenica enclave. Other estimates

---

4. Hadžiomerović, "Pet Minuta." In September 1993, Bosnian Muslim leaders voted to rename their community "Bosniaks" at the Second Congress of Bosniaks in Sarajevo. See Robert J. Donia, "The New Bosniak History," *Nationalities Papers* 28 (2000): 351–58.

5. John F. Burns, "As Deaths from Cold Rise in Sarajevo, UN Commander Appeals for Truce," *New York Times*, December 30, 1992. Two weeks earlier, the *New York Times* columnist A. M. Rosenthal had cited a figure of 100,000. See A. M. Rosenthal, "On My Mind; Deaths in Sarajevo," *New York Times*, December 1, 1992.

6. George Kenney, "The Bosnia Calculation: How Many Have Died? Not Nearly as Many as Some Would Have You Think," *New York Times Magazine*, April 23, 1995.

7. Some analysts argued that the 250,000 figure was perceived by some as a sort of a threshold after which military intervention could be justified.

8. See Laura Blumenfeld, "A Sense of Resignation: The Bosnia Dissenters, Three Young Men Cut Short Their Careers on Principle," *Washington Post*, August 28, 1993.

9. Kenney, "Bosnia Calculation."

10. Ibid.

from international sources were produced by the Stockholm International Peace Research Institute (SIPRI), which estimated 169,100 deaths for only the first eighteen months of the war. Reports by Cherif Bassiouni, chairman of the War Crimes Commission that set the foundation for the creation of the ICTY, offered the highest estimate of all international sources at 200,000.[11]

However, given that the 250,000 figure was in such wide use, the debate largely fell out of the public eye, that is, until the RDC started a project to document the wartime dead. No domestic organization had attempted such a detailed and comprehensive study. Some organizations had tried to initiate an effort, but stopped because of their perception that such a project would require millions of euros. There were some postwar estimates conducted by local organizations, including two by the Bosnian Institute for Public Health in early 1996, but their results differed by more than 100,000.[12] Most local documentation efforts were conducted along ethnic lines, which further inhibited a comprehensive study.

The initiators of the "Human Losses" project hoped such a documentation effort would be much more than an exercise in counting, although the primacy of the wartime figure meant that the press would often (erroneously) portray it solely as an exercise in quantification. They hoped an accurate accounting would memorialize the victims, prevent future manipulation, help in the prosecution of perpetrators, and, ultimately, create a more accurate picture of the war. They also hoped that the use of scientific methodologies and facts would alter the character of the discussion about this and related human rights issues inside Bosnia.

The RDC was well suited, if not well funded, to undertake such a mission. The Center is a nongovernmental organization registered on the state level in Bosnia.[13] It was formed on April 19, 2004 as the successor organization to the State Commission for Gathering Facts on War Crimes, which was established by the Presidency of the Republic of Bosnia and Herzegovina in April 1992. During the war, the Commission was tasked with collecting information about violations of international humanitarian law, and did so by gathering witness statements, taking pictures, and filming throughout the war. What is probably the largest single source of primary

11. Ewa Tabeau and Jacub Bijak, "War-Related Deaths in the 1992–1995 Armed Conflicts in Bosnia and Herzegovina: A Critique of Previous Estimates and Recent Results," *European Journal of Population/Revue Europenne de Demographie* 21 (2005): 187–215.

12. The Institute for Public Health Bulletin of January 1996 gave an estimate of 156,824; a second estimate in March 1996 was 278,800. Of the six post-war efforts, the lowest was the January 1996 one, the highest was 329,000.

13. This was a rarity at the time of registration as most NGOs in Bosnia and Herzegovina are registered on the entity level.

materials relating to wartime atrocities and violations of international humanitarian law in Bosnia was amassed. By their own estimates, the RDC has millions of pages of written documentation, including testimonies of surviving victims and eyewitnesses, in addition to audio and video materials. This documentation provided a strong base from which to launch the "Human Losses" project.

At the beginning of the war, incoming data related to violations of the laws of war was stored in a large database. Working with an experienced information technology specialist, the Commission created a relational database that captured the complexity of each document they processed. That meant if fifteen proper names were listed in one witness statement, each name would be cross-referenced in the database. Each document that was processed potentially contained names of witnesses, victims, and perpetrators. The data collection effort was conducted with an eye toward eventual criminal trials, though it predated the formation of the ICTY.

In April 2004, the RDC formally started its project, with funding from the Norwegian government. By the end of that first month, the project had 39,572 individual files, some of which represented duplicate entries. The process undertaken by the RDC involved collection of every possible source that documented individuals who had perished during the war: newspapers; military records; lists put together by concerned citizens; records from churches, mosques, and synagogues; official sources from defense ministries and police forces; and so on. The project was not advertised early on, but people who found out about it started to call from all over the country wanting to provide information. Staff members traveled to the farthest corners of the country for data, sometimes for meetings with people who wanted to hand over lists and sources anonymously. Many people felt the need to speak, but wanted to remain unidentified. Center staff also visited 400 gravesites all over the country, including military gravesites, taking pictures of each grave marker. Smaller databases put together by local NGOs were incorporated into the RDC database. Eventually the project holdings included over 60,000 photos. The collection also included war-era newspapers and magazines.[14] These various sources allowed them to not only assemble a chronology of wartime events, but the death notices (*smrtovnice*) published in local papers were an additional source of the identities of individuals who perished in the war.

14. On the role of the media, see Tom Gjelten, *Sarajevo Daily: A City and Its Newspaper under Siege* (New York: HarperCollins, 1995); Kemal Kurspahic and Kemal Acc, *As Long as Sarajevo Exists* (Stony Creek, CT: Pamphleteer's Press, 1997); and Kemal Kurspahic, *Prime Time Crime: Balkan Media in War and Peace* (Washington, DC: United States Institute of Peace Press, 2003).

Over time the database was reconstructed to address the increasing complexity of the data collection effort, such as the issue of duplicate names. The goal was to use the same technology in the RDC's partner organizations in Zagreb and Belgrade in order to facilitate analysis of common questions facing the region as a whole. The RDC also hoped this documentation effort would eventually serve as a model for other postconflict countries.

An intensive outreach campaign, launched in February 2005, bolstered the RDC's efforts in the field. Under the banner "Has Anyone Been Forgotten?" (*Da li Je Neko Zaboravljen?*), events were held all over the country, inviting Bosnian citizens to submit information about relatives and friends who perished in the war, or to verify information already in the database. Lists of individuals in the database were also printed in local newspapers. A television spot created by Sarajevo-based artist Faruk Šabanović aired all over the country, with many stations donating what was estimated to be 150,000 BAM worth of their time (1 BAM approximately equals €.50).[15] The spot encouraged Bosnians to "write, and send, so that no one is forgotten." The Center received numerous submissions by individuals; outreach meetings produced lists collected by people and organizations previously unknown. Visits to small towns and municipalities would uncover that some citizens had scrupulously documented the disintegration of their own communities as the war unfolded and populations were expelled.

The campaign had some effect. For example, between September and December 2005, 4,000 people submitted information for the database. At the start of the campaign, they had 86,000 individual names in their database. They increased that number by over 10,000, and added 20,000 photographs to their existing collection of 30,000.[16] The first major outreach event related to the project was a public presentation in Banja Luka in December 2005, which was well received and was followed by fifteen others around the country. The events allowed individual citizens to see (and to correct, if necessary) the information in the database—increasing the transparency of the project and the information collected, and, the RDC hoped, increasing trust in the findings. Still, their outreach effort was only a small portion of what was likely needed for a project that uncovered what turned out to be such controversial findings.

The project's database swelled with new pieces of information over the course of data collection, but when overlapping records were accounted for these new inputs did not result in a precipitous increase in the total number

---

15. Research and Documentation Center, "Project Results," 2007.
16. Ibid.

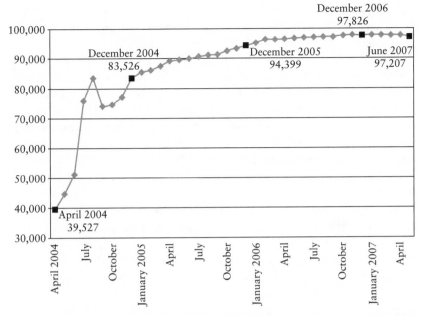

Figure 7.1. Cumulative number of killed and missing persons in project database, April 2004–June 2007
Source: Research and Documentation Center, 2007

of individuals in the database. Eventually, it was clear that researchers had likely documented close to the total number of deaths. Figure 7.1 plots the numbers of individual names in the database over the life of the project. Overlapping records were identified in late summer 2004, contributing to the decline in the figure. By June 2007, when the initial results were announced, they had identified over 97,000 unique deaths resulting directly from military activity during the war.

Numbers of Deaths in Southeastern European History

Debates over the numbers of casualties had long characterized discussions about political violence in the region. This was also an issue after World War II. When Josip Broz Tito's partisan forces emerged victorious, the subject of the war in general was largely banned from public discussion. The extent of human losses in the Socialist Federal Republic of Yugoslavia (SFRY) was a subject of controversy, but was not debated in Yugoslav society until Tito's death—more than thirty-five years after the end of the war—provided an opening for further inquiry and research. Over one

million people perished during World War II in SFRY, though, in the interest of securing more reparations from Germany, the postwar communist
government initially claimed that 1.7 million people were lost.[17] Once this
figure was submitted to the International Reparation Commission in Paris,
information about human losses was closely guarded by the state.[18] Many
analysts have argued that the leadership's lack of attention to atrocities
committed on all sides left many open wounds, unsettled scores, and un-
discovered facts in the region, especially in Bosnia, where so much fighting
took place. In addition, historical issues such as the number of deaths at
the Jasenovac concentration camp during World War II was a source of debate and discussion. Some progress had been made estimating the numbers
of deaths that occurred there and in other places, until rising nationalism
brought the return of inaccurate numbers. When nationalist parties came
to power on the eve of the Bosnian war, old (inflated) numbers circulated,
generating fear and distrust among local populations. The conduits of mis-
information were often academics. Historian Ivo Banac famously called
these individuals "para-historians."[19]

The Postwar Response of the Bosnian Serb Nationalists

Debates over the numbers of casualties in the 1990s characterized that
postwar period as well. Nationalist Bosnian Serb politicians were the primary source of manipulation of the figures, making outlandish claims
with relative impunity. To cite just one example: In March 2005, Pero
Bukejlović, then prime minister of the Republika Srpska (RS), one of Bosnia's two entities, charged at a conference of the Serb Democratic Party
(SDS) in Pale that, "perhaps a greater genocide was committed against the
Serbs in Sarajevo than against Bosniaks in Srebrenica." He added that the
RS government was "committed to prove that Serbs were the victim of
genocide."[20] This narrative of the equality of deaths, and kinds of crimes

---

17. Vladimir Žerjavić, *Population Losses in Yugoslavia, 1941–1945* (Zagreb: Hrvatski Institut za Povijest, 1997).
18. Ibid., 58.
19. For background on the role of historians, see Ivo Banac, "Historiography of the Coun-tries of Eastern Europe: Yugoslavia," *American Historical Review* 97 (1992): 1084–1104.
20. The government, of course, would not be competent to determine whether genocide occurred. See Aldijana Omeragić, "Nad Srbima u Sarajevu počinjen genocid veći nego u Sre-brenici" (A Bigger Genocide Was Committed Against the Serbs in Sarajevo Than in Srebrenica), *Oslobođenje*, March 26, 2005; "Bosnian Serb PM Says Sarajevo Serbs Suffered More Than Srebrenica Muslims," *Agence France Presse*, March 25, 2005; Anes Alic, "Bosnian Serbs Al-lege Sarajevo massacre," *ISN Security Watch*, January 5, 2005, http://listserv.acsu.buffalo.edu/cgi-bin/wa?A2=JUSTWATCH-L;N%2BQ4EQ;20050502085302–0400; and Lara J. Nettelfield,

committed against them (e.g., genocide) would characterize the postwar discourse on the part of Bosnian Serb nationalists.

The misuse of the numbers had transparent political goals. The nationalist elite continued to enforce the idea that Bosnian Serbs were a threatened minority who had suffered equal injustices, which continued to go unaddressed. Some observers argued that this was a conscious strategy of victimization used to slow down the wheels of reform, which threatened the existence of the entity level armed forces (which no longer exist), entity level police forces, and even the Republika Srpska itself. This perspective included a corollary opinion that further separation between the entities was necessary. The argument that all sides suffered equally in the war made Bosnia's further integration, first toward a more centralized state, and then into the European Union, seem premature and politically naive.[21]

This meta-narrative was challenged by the RDC and other (largely) Sarajevo-based activists. In 2005, the RS Ministry of Interior released the names of Serbs alleged to be killed in Sarajevo between 1992 and 1995. The initial list contained 2,435 names of killed Serbs and only 575 missing persons. RDC president Mirsad Tokača scrutinized the list and compared it with the project database, finding nine people listed twice on the first page alone.[22] Tokača argued that this was improvised and unprofessional work lacking transparent sources and necessary information.[23] The political use of fallacious numbers also had implications for reforms on the ground, as Tokača insisted that the list showed Bosnia's need for radical reform of its police forces.[24]

These debates took place largely without a reaction from the public in the RS. The Bosnian Serb public accepted—or at least did not react strongly against—such statements, despite their lacking any empirical basis. Still, that did not necessarily imply support or trust in the figures. At the same time, while nationalist politicians used numbers as a source of division in the country, family and survivors' associations of all ethnicities had increasing contact with each other, meeting at joint conferences and in some cases, pooling resources and information.

Courting Democracy in Bosnia and Herzegovina: The Hague Tribunal's Impact in a Post War State (New York: Cambridge University Press, 2010), esp. ch. 6.

21. Nettelfield, *Courting Democracy.*

22. M. Čulov, "Dupla imena na spiskovima 'ubijenih i nestalih' Srba" (Double Names on the Lists of Killed and Missing Serbs), *Jutarnje Novine,* April 22, 2005.

23. Ibid.

24. L. Sinanović, "Spisak Dokazuje da nam Treba Radikalna Reforma Policije" (The List Shows That We Need Radical Reform of the Police), *Dnevzi Avaz,* April 29, 2005.

There was no overwhelming response from this elite to the "Human Losses" project results, in part because the composition of the findings challenged their narrative of equal victimization. Yet the new figure of total casualties supported their narrative that the conflict was not as severe as the Bosnian government had claimed. On more nationalist websites frequented by primarily Bosnian Serbs, there were comments stating that the wartime government had purposefully inflated the figures to gain international sympathy.

The Bosniak Nationalist Elite Response

Postwar discussions in Sarajevo generally included estimates of between 200,000 and 350,000 wartime deaths. In some Bosniak circles there, the "Human Losses" project was viewed as a threat to the dominant narrative of the war, the future political goals of certain politicians, and the status of Bosniaks as the biggest victims of the war. The strong response illustrated just how strong their narrative of the war in Bosnia—that aggression was committed on the Republic of Bosnia and Herzegovina resulting in genocide—was fused to casualty estimates. The new figure presented by the RDC seemed to question the narrative of Bosniaks as the greatest victims of the war, despite the fact that this was in contrast to international jurisprudence about the war. In addition, the breakdown of figures largely supported the dominant narrative of Bosniak elite circles.

Interestingly, the importance of the numbers in these circles was in contrast to the findings at the ICTY, which found that genocide had occurred on Bosnian soil after the fall of the UN enclave in July 1995. In the judgment against Radislav Krstić at the appellate level, the accused was found guilty of aiding and abetting genocide. The Genocide Convention of 1948 defines the crime as "the intent to destroy, in whole or in part, a national, ethnical, racial or religious group." The trial chamber's judgment emphasized that to destroy part of a group constituted genocide, given the impact of the disappearance of this part of the Bosniak community on the survival of the community as a whole in the eastern enclave.[25] The intent was crucial, and not the numbers of killed per se. This decision was important, especially to many espousing a nationalist Bosniak perspective, because it was the only case to date that included the judgment of genocide, and therefore confirmed their argument about one of the defining characteristics

25. See Prosecutor vs. Krstić, Judgement, International Criminal Tribunal for the Former Yugoslavia, Case No. IT-98–33-A, April 19, 2004, http://www.icty.org/x/cases/krstic/acjug/en/krs-aj040419e.pdf.

of their narrative about the war. Despite the fact that the project findings only bolstered the dominant position that came out of Sarajevo, the response was strong and aggressive. It played out mostly in the local press.

The project provoked the ire of a small but vocal group in Sarajevo. Reactions to the project were not characterized by an interest in the material contained in the database or the documentation found. The RDC was forced to continuously defend the project and its preliminary findings. In Sarajevo, the debate reached a crescendo when Smail Čekić, a historian and founder of the Institute for Research on Crimes Against Humanity and International Law, claimed publicly both in the press and during a television interview that the "Human Losses" project was not "scientifically relevant" and used a "suspicious methodology."[26] The Institute, a part of the University of Sarajevo and largely funded by the cantonal government, conducts research solely about crimes committed against Bosniaks during the war. The attack illustrated the character of the discussion and the climate in Sarajevo faced by the project architects. Čekić was an influential commentator because of his role as an academic at the university. He enjoyed support among Bosniak survivors and family associations, especially those representing Srebrenica's victims.[27] When the RS government was forced to form a Commission to investigate the events surrounding the fall of the enclave, he was the individual chosen to represent their interests. Tokača was unequivocal in his response to Čekić's comments:

> People come to our offices, even from the other side of the Atlantic, to become acquainted with the work of our Center, and this never even occurred to Čekić. He did not even have the patience to wait until the end of the project, as everyone who pretends to be a scientific expert would be obligated to do, and then respond to it. Now just as we are making presentations and adding to our database across Bosnia and Herzegovina, Čekić, serving the known methods of people without arguments, spits on me, wishing to proclaim me a national traitor.[28]

The Sarajevo weekly *Dani* even protested the professor's poor behavior during a television show dedicated to the subject in its weekly ratings of

26. "Sedam Dana i Ljudi" (Seven Days and People), *Slobodna Bosna,* January 19, 2006; Merima Spahić, "Mirsad Tokača na napade Smaila Čekića: Ne zna ni gdje su nam prostorije" (Mirsad Tokača on the Attacks of Smail Čekić: He Does Not Know Where Our Offices Are), *Oslobođenje,* January15, 2006.

27. In Tuzla, the Women of Srebrenica, one of the largest groups representing the survivors of the massacre, held a protest against the RDC project and its findings. Their association's website is http://www.srebrenica.ba/index.en.php. RDC representatives later met with the association to discuss the findings.

28. Spahić, "Mirsad Tokača."

good and bad deeds. *Dani* editors argued, "Sometimes the good professor just doesn't know what he's talking about...[i]t's a shame that a university professor doesn't know the subject of discussion to such an extent."[29] This was more than a battle between two intellectuals in a small town, it was also a discussion about how the nascent state would settle disputes over its past, and utilize the best evidence to do so.

Attacks on the project continued in all forms, sometimes verging on the absurd. Dr. Rasim Muratović, an associate of Čekić's Institute, argued in an open letter to the editor of a Sarajevo newspaper that the Norwegians financed the project because they wanted to assert that "from 1991 to 1995 an aggression wasn't committed against the Republic of Bosnia and Herzegovina and that a genocide wasn't committed against the Bosniaks."[30] The author asked, "Would the strange Bosnian government support a project in Norway by the name of 'Population Losses of the White Bears of Svalbard 1992–1995' and find some Tokača to realize the project?" The letter prompted a response from the then Norwegian ambassador Henrik Ofstad, in which he defended his decision to finance the project, and other similar investments at the ICTY and the International Commission for Missing Persons (ICMP). He emphasized that donor funding came with no instructions from the government and that Norway believed in independent research.[31] Another associate of the Institute accused Tokača of suffering from the Stockholm syndrome, during which a hostage begins to sympathize with his or her captor.[32] He was also frequently referred to as a traitor to his nation and/or a person on the payroll of foreign governments.

The letter writing campaign continued in the press, with other respected intellectuals affiliated with a Bosniak nationalist position weighing in. Nijaz Duraković, professor of political science at the University of Sarajevo, argued in *Oslobođenje*: "Tokača intentionally decreased the number of victims of the genocide which was committed in the Republic

---

29. "Bosanski Barometer: Smail Čekić; Grozan potez" (Bosnian Barometer: Smail Cekic; Terrible Move), *Dani*, January 20, 2006, 17.

30. Rasim Muratović, "Tako bi to uradili Norvežani" (There Are Hidden Agendas in Norwegian Donations), *Oslobođenje*, February 19, 2006. The author uses the initial title of the project "Population Losses in Bosnia and Herzegovina 1991–1995," which was later changed to "Human Losses."

31. Henrik Ofstad, "Nema skrivenih namjera u norveškim donacijama" (There Are No Hidden Agendas in Norwegian Donations), *Oslobođenje*, February 27, 2006.

32. Muhamed Mešić, John Craig, and Alvin B. Marchaird, "Žrvte genocida ili demografskog amaterizma" (Victims of Genocide or Demographic Amateurism), *Oslobođenje*, July 8, 2006.

of Bosnia and Herzegovina from 1992–1995."[33] His was yet another personal attack, and he argued further that the project folded all types of victims into the category of military victims.[34] Then he cited early studies by international experts conducted during the war (when that original number of 250,000 surfaced), asserting that actual figures were at least twice as high.

Project critics used the comments of different "experts" for political purposes. For example, around the anniversaries of the end of the war, or after the arrest of a major war criminal, members of the press would often call on individuals who were involved in Bosnia during the war, but did not remain actively engaged in developments. These experts were unaware of the ICTY and Sarajevo-based projects, and continued to claim 250,000 deaths. Critics would then use these quotes to discredit the newer findings, using the quotes of other "international" sources and experts. For example, commenting on the arrest and transfer of indicted war criminal Radovan Karadžić in July 2008, Dayton Peace Agreement architect Richard Holbrooke cited the figure of 300,000 dead, the figure he had used in his account of the peace negotiations.[35] The international quotes, unwittingly, seemed to present a challenge to this locally based documentation effort.

All of the attacks failed to mention a detailed study of the same issue produced by the ICTY, which arrived at a similar figure through an entirely different and independent effort. Taking a particular interest in this issue, the Norwegian government had earlier supported the establishment of the Demography Unit of the Office of the Prosecutor (OTP) of the ICTY. The Demography Unit, however, had different objectives than the RDC: being focused on producing analyses for ICTY trials, and ultimately contributing to the establishment of individual criminal liability.[36] The OTP study arrived at the figure of 102,622 deaths using a methodology in which it collected reports of the wartime death, which contained individual-level reporting on war-related deaths (both direct and indirect). The study found a slightly different mix of civilian (53 percent) and military casualties (46 percent) than the RDC. Published in the *European Journal of Population* in 2005, the findings, however, did not elicit a strong public reaction

33. Nijaz Duraković, "I škorpioni su 'fotografirali,'" (And the Scorpions Took Photographs), *Oslobođenje*, January 28, 2006.

34. The categorization of victims was a problem due to reporting errors, as will be discussed later.

35. See, for example, Richard Holbrooke, "The Face of Evil," *Washington Post*, July 23, 2008. In the memoir of his role in the negotiations that ended the war in Bosnia, he is more conservative. He states that close to 300,000 died in the former Yugoslavia between 1991 and 1995. See Richard C. Holbrooke, *To End a War* (New York: Random House, 1998).

36. See Tabeau and Bijak, "War-Related Deaths."

from elites, the way the RDC project did. ICTY demography experts said that in private, some in Bosnia were disappointed with the court's findings. In web discussions, as with the RDC's effort, Bosnian Serb nationalists enthusiastically received the new figures.[37]

Another study published after the presentation of RDC's initial results (which references the study), had a higher estimate. A report of the *British Medical Journal* analyzing thirteen postconflict states estimated that 167,000 people perished in the Bosnian war.[38] The report utilized world health surveys conducted before and after the war to estimate the numbers of killed in direct violence. The *British Medical Journal's* survey argued that there was systematic underreporting of conflict violence across cases. The source of this new estimate was a survey of 1,028 Bosnian households conducted by the World Health Organization. Some experts argue that documentation efforts based on written sources tend to be lower than survey-based estimates in which overreporting can be common.[39] This figure may confuse a public uneducated in the strengths and weakness of various methodologies used to document conflict deaths. Andrew Mack, Director of the Human Security Report Project at Simon Fraser University, argues:

> Different fatality estimation methodologies not only have different strengths and weaknesses, but also different uses. "The Bosnian study represents a gold standard in terms of the sort of precise documentation needed for prosecuting gross violations of human nights. But they take years to produce and for this reason can't be used for—say—humanitarian needs assessments—or the timely tracking of global trends in armed conflict."[40]

Other experts emphasized that survey-based efforts can often lead to overreporting because individuals are prone to exaggerate losses when asked.

Changes in postwar Bosnian society had much to do with the reaction. One astute Sarajevan observed in a letter to the editor that part of the reason the project caused such a furor in some circles was due to bruised egos. "With his project he insulted the vanity of academic elite whom he didn't ask [to participate], under whose supervision he didn't receive a degree, nor did he include the governing parties which wish to manipulate

---

37. Ewa Tabeau, Demography Unit, ICTY, author's e-mail correspondence, March 30, 2009.

38. Ziad Obermeyer, Christopher J. L. Murray, and Emmanuela Gakidou, "Fifty Years of Violent War Deaths from Vietnam to Bosnia: Analysis of Data from the World Health Survey Programme," *British Medical Journal*, 336 (2008): 1482–86.

39. Lara J. Nettelfield, "Documenting the Victims of Conflict," Institute of War and Peace Reporting, Tribunal Update, no. 558, July 4, 2008, http://www.iwpr.net/?p=tri&s=f&o=345570&apc_state=henptri.

40. Nettelfield, "Documenting the Victims..."

the data."[41] The reader recommended that Tokača, with his research documentation, get a degree at a neutral university somewhere in the world so that his jealous critics would not continue to broadcast their imagined theories and numbers of victims. This academic elite, a circle of university professors and intellectuals in a small town, were the keepers of the narrative of the war: that genocide happened, that 250,000 people were killed, that the Bosniak nation was the victim of both Serb aggressors and the international community. The separate parts of this narrative were so intertwined that when the project threatened one of its sacred pillars—the number of dead—the only response was a full-scale attack.

Because "Human Losses" was initiated by an independent organization outside of this circle, its existence threatened the very survival of these elites by proving that others outside of their circle could yield results. The prospect of liberal democracy threatened them and their monopoly on "truths." Although many were not party members during the communist era, they came of age intellectually in a system in which specific groups produced and created knowledge. Therefore, even though the countries of the former Yugoslavia excelled in all things technical and scientific, this project was a threat to the hierarchy and system of production of knowledge of a previous era. Junior scholars, supportive of the project and utilization of the latest methodologies, still faced dissertation defenses under the tutelage of members of the old hierarchy and consequently self-censored themselves, or ignored the debate.[42]

The fusion of the number with a particular narrative of the war and current political goals was illustrated in the public statements of the man credited with creating the 250,000 figure. Haris Silajdžić, elected as the Bosniak member of Bosnia's tripartite Presidency in October 2006, continued to publicly affirm his wartime estimate, interpreting the new data as largely unsupportive of his current political desires. His primary stated objective in office was to create a Bosnia without entities (a goal incidentally shared by many in Bosnia, including the RDC staff). The new figure apparently did not aid that effort, in his opinion. In one press report he claimed: "It looks as if there was a civil war here that we shouldn't have defended.... The reality is, unfortunately, 200,000 dead and with

41. Ismet Hatibović, "Zaštinici 'režimske' nauke" (Guardians of the Regime's Science), *Oslobođenje*, January 31, 2006.

42. Others, however, celebrated the effort. Bosnian filmmaker Jasmila Žbanić, winner of the prestigious Golden Bear Award at the Berlin Film Festival for her film *Grbavica*, Professors Zdravko Grebo (University of Sarajevo) and Dubravko Lovrenović (University of Sarajevo) congratulated Tokača for his efforts in a letter to the editor in the Sarajevo weekly *Dani* that was also signed by several others. See Dubravko Lovrenović et al., "Svaka Čast Tokači" (Congratulations Tokača), *Dani*, July 27, 2007.

their lives and with the killing of the citizens of Bosnia-Herzegovina the entity structure was created."[43] In another report he made a vague reference to the RDC's project, implicitly challenging the new figure, arguing: "Milošević's project left more than 100,000 dead."[44] The wartime narrative that included the number he created was seen as essential to the goal of creating a unified state. Silajdžić continued to publicly support the efforts of Čekić's Institute and invited members of the press to meet there.

The shortsightedness of a *political* decision to continue to support a number without scientific merit had concrete consequences. The initial results of the project were manipulated by the Serbian defense team in Bosnia's case against Serbia and Montenegro at the ICJ. The court reached its final decision in February 2007, finding that although genocide had occurred in Srebrenica, Serbia was not legally responsible for it.[45] Testifying for Serbia, a French demographer pointed to "Human Losses" figures as evidence that the applicants' claims were spurious, resulting in a letter to the president of the court from Tokača, who stated that he was shocked by Belgrade's use of the numbers out of context.[46] The local response was predictable. Amor Mašović, head of the Federal Commission for Missing Persons and representative of the Bosniak nationalist Party of Democratic Action (SDA) said in an interview: "Unfortunately, it looks like the biggest use of the research of Mr. Tokača will in fact be those who are responsible for the deaths of hundreds of thousands of people, for example, the country which organized and conducted aggression and genocide, Serbia."[47] One Sarajevo-based academic argued that it was a *medvjeđa usluga* (literally translated "bear favor"), a disservice—a project that came about at the wrong time. In an interview in Croatia's *Nacional* and many similar publications, Tokača continued to frame the debate in rational terms about the real implications of the findings: "The character of the war is not changed if we state the real number: 100,000 is an enormous and gruesome number."[48] The Bosnian legal team in the

43. Edina Sarač, "Rešenje koje name se nudi vodi ka getoizaciji države" (The Solutions Offered to Us Will Lead Us to the Ghettoization of the Country), *Oslobođenje*, March 13, 2006.

44. L. S., "U BiH je iza Miloševića ostalo više od 100,000 mrtvih" (In Bosnia, Milosevic Left More Than 100,000 Dead) *Dnevni Avaz*, March 12, 2006.

45. International Court of Justice, "Case Concerning the Application of the Convention on the Prevention and Punishment of the Crime of Genocide," February 26, 2007, http://www.icj-cij.org/docket/files/91/13685.pdf#view=FitH&pagemode=none&search=%22Bosnia-Herzegovina%201993%22.

46. Letter dated March 13, 2006.

47. "NO Comment" weekly column, reporting Mašovic's comments for Bošnjaci.net, *SAFF*, March 17, 2006.

48. "U Bosni je ubijeno pet tisuća Hrvata" (In Bosnia, Five Thousand Croats Were Killed), *Nacional*, November 29, 2006.

ICJ decision failed to make use of the project findings, instead utilizing only foreign experts as witnesses, overlooking how their legal case would have been bolstered by the project. Still, the timing was unfortunate given the fact that the legal team for Bosnia failed to proactively make use of the findings and anticipate manipulation by Serbia's lawyers.

The public reaction all over the country was difficult to gauge especially in the absence of more systematic data. In the blog chatter, there was both support and heated discussion about the project with nationalist sites taking predictable positions. For example, one commentator in the Bosnian blogosphere argued that it was the most detailed and exact estimate to date, but was dismayed that such an effort had to be conducted by an independent nongovernmental organization.[49] Overall, the project's documentation challenged both the Serb and Bosniak nationalist perspectives in different ways, and the response was largely unsurprising. The RDC's failure to engage elite groups as stakeholders in the project early on also contributed to the strong reaction.

Presentation, Project Findings, and Expert Reports

The findings of the project were presented in an auditorium located in Sarajevo's largest office building, the UNITIC Towers, on June 21, 2007. Representatives from various parties were in the audience, including the former Bosniak member of the Presidency, Suleiman Tihić, whose presence signified that the attack initiated by some members of the Bosniak nationalist elite was by no means representative of the opinions of all. Members of family associations came in from around the country, but notably absent were members of the groups that represented Srebrenica's killed and missing. Some local organizations, such as the Federation Commission for Missing Persons, also did not send representatives. The auditorium, with 150 attendees, was not even filled to half capacity. It was difficult to assess whether nonattendance was an indication of a lack of support, or simply other commitments.

Mirsad Tokača opened the presentation by reminding the crowd, "This isn't a story of numbers, it is one of human fates."[50] Some members of the press had incorrectly characterized the effort as about the numbers and not the people behind them. He proceeded to present slides, which outlined the details, purpose, and findings of the project. The project had thus far documented 97,207 unique deaths and, although not complete, called into

49. See the comments of M. on the "Bosanska Knjiga Mrtvih" (Bosnian Book of the Dead) blog, http://www.blogger.ba/komentari/4442/999996.

50. Dženana Karup Druško, "Bosanska knijga mrtvih" (Bosnian Book of the Dead), *Dani*, June 29, 2007.

question some dominant narratives about the Bosnian war. This number represented the number of deaths resulting from direct military violence. This narrow definition excluded indirect victims of the war, for example, soldiers who died as a result of poisoning from wild mushrooms on the front line, or babies who died from dehydration.[51] In addition, the RDC is analyzing long-term human losses and demographic consequences of the war, such as impact on postwar birth rates and the population distribution in Bosnia.

Several other findings of the project contrasted with beliefs held about the war, notably the ratio of civilian to military deaths. Conventional wisdom in general, about wars in the 1990s, was that nine out of ten violent deaths were civilian, in marked contrast to wars of previous eras.[52] The Bosnian war, when viewed through this lens and through that of the media was a war against civilians, primarily Bosniaks. The proportion of military versus civilian deaths added information to that dominant narrative. The project documented 57,523 military deaths and 39,684 civilian deaths, 59 and 41 percent of the totals respectively (figure 7.2).

The project also unwittingly uncovered a problem in the classification of civilian and military victims in some 1,000 plus cases—one that would pose a quandary for the nascent Bosnian state, if not the overall statistical breakdown of the casualties. Some victims registered as military were in fact civilian casualties. There was an incentive to be the family of a military victim as the benefits from the state are greater for veterans' families than for civilian families. The RDC argued that this was an issue for the state to work through in further investigations. The breakdown raised the difficult task facing such documentation efforts in postconflict countries.

In terms of civilian victims, the data would largely confirm that Bosniak civilians suffered by far the most casualties of the war. Of all civilian deaths reported, Bosniaks constituted 83 percent, Serbs 10 percent, and Croats 5 percent, indicating that Bosniak civilians were in fact targeted during the war. Additional analysis would illustrate that patterns of death over specific time periods could be used in court to illustrate intent to cause suffering. For example, at the beginning of the war, deaths in three municipalities in eastern Bosnia showed that the number of killed and missing spiked at precisely the same points in time across a vast geographic distance, indicating systematic intent.

---

51. Ibid. The RDC estimates this group of individuals to number between 2,000 and 3,000.

52. See *Final Report: Preventing Deadly Conflict* (Washington, DC: Carnegie Commission on Preventing Deadly Conflict, 1997), http://www.wilsoncenter.org/subsites/ccpdc/pubs/rept97/finfr.htm. Recent studies have placed this figure between 30 percent and 60 percent. See the Uppsala Conflict Data Program at http://www.pcr.uu.se/research/UCDP/index.htm; and Human Security Center, *Human Security Report 2005* (Oxford: Oxford University Press, 2005), 75.

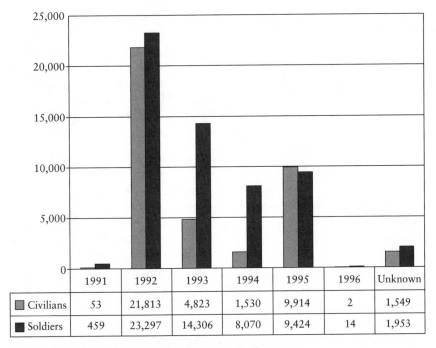

	1991	1992	1993	1994	1995	1996	Unknown
Civilians	53	21,813	4,823	1,530	9,914	2	1,549
Soldiers	459	23,297	14,306	8,070	9,424	14	1,953

Figure 7.2. Killed and missing persons by year and military status
Source: Research and Documentation Center, 2007

Furthermore, the war brought to the forefront the role of women in wartime, and the use of rape as a tool of war. This led to international legal precedents, including the first judgment that rape was a war crime, in the so-called Foča trial at the ICTY. The RDC project revealed, however, that men were overwhelmingly the largest group of war victims at 87,451 versus 9,756 females, a fact also deserving of further analysis. Much foreign scholarship and media attention on the war addresses the consequences of crimes committed against women.

The data also brought into question the dominant lens of the war, which was focused on the massacre in Srebrenica in July 1995.[53] Though Srebrenica was the single most horrifying crime of the war, project results illustrated that half of the war's casualties occurred during the first year of the conflict. Tokača argued "Srebrenica was a [culmination] of the crimes

53. On Srebrenica, see also H. Brunborg, T. H. Lyngstad, and H. Urdal, "Accounting for Genocide: How Many were Killed in Srebrenica?" *European Journal of Population* 19 (2003): 229–48. In this article, the number of persons on both Physicians for Human Rights and the International Committee of the Red Cross' lists was 7,490, from which individuals found to be still alive were subtracted using post-war voter registration lists and other sources.

that occurred during the rest of the war."[54] Because individual citizens were listed by both municipality of residence and municipality of death, the findings also confirmed earlier studies that showed that many of the victims of the Srebrenica massacre were from other municipalities in eastern Bosnia. They had fled to the safe area in search of protection they assumed would be offered by the United Nations. The enormity of the crimes committed in Bosnia's eastern enclave in 1995 are chilling even in impersonal graphical representation (figure 7.4).

Expert Assessment

The "Human Losses" presentation moved on to the expert assessment of the report. The expert committee was comprised of some of the world's leading experts in the small but growing field of human rights data analysis. These included, Ewa Tabeau, ICTY chief demographer; Patrick Ball, a University of Michigan trained sociologist and chief scientist at the Human Rights Data Analysis Group of the Benetech Initiative; and Philip Verwimp, director of the Households in Conflict project. Very few people in the world had the skills to assess the RDC's project. The experts divided various aspects of the database for evaluation among themselves, commenting in several joint papers.[55] The ambassadors of Norway and Switzerland, and Mirsad Tokača himself, extended the invitation to form an expert team to assess the database along several lines. Some questions loomed large: How complete was the database? How accurately did it capture the sources it utilized? What was it good for? The committee added international credibility to common claims inside Bosnia about the results being biased, incomplete, inaccurate, or politically derived. The use of foreign experts to assess the database was meant to provide an assessment of the project's results, in order to bolster their claims of objectivity and completeness. Far from being an exercise in which international experts implemented a foreign methodology in a less developed country, as was often the case with do-good technical advisers, here the experts found that the database and data collection efforts upheld the international standards.

Patrick Ball claimed that the database was ready for "descriptive statistics," a relatively cautious assessment. Ball's evaluation concluded that the

---

54. Mirsad Tokača, president of the Research and Documentation Center, author interview, Sarajevo, July 31, 2007.
55. Their reports included an assessment project, report, and an executive summary. The reports evaluate the database as of July 2006, though work continued on it after this point. Patrick Ball, Ewa Tabeau, and Philip Verwimp, "The Bosnian Book of the Dead: Assessment of the Database," Project Documentation, dated June 14, 2007. Published as the *HiCN Research Design Note 5*, June 17, 2007, http://www.hicn.org.

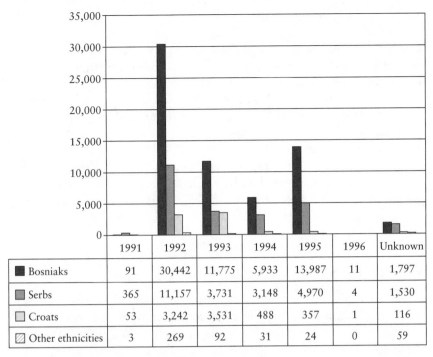

	1991	1992	1993	1994	1995	1996	Unknown
■ Bosniaks	91	30,442	11,775	5,933	13,987	11	1,797
▨ Serbs	365	11,157	3,731	3,148	4,970	4	1,530
☐ Croats	53	3,242	3,531	488	357	1	116
▨ Other ethnicities	3	269	92	31	24	0	59

Figure 7.3. Killed and missing persons by ethnicity and year
Source: Research and Documentation Center, 2007

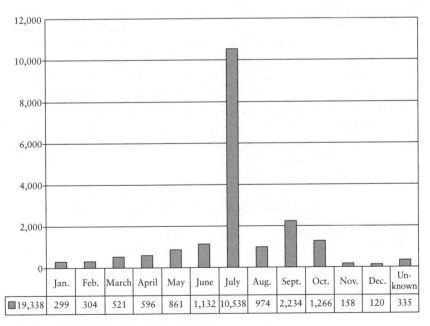

	Jan.	Feb.	March	April	May	June	July	Aug.	Sept.	Oct.	Nov.	Dec.	Un-known
■19,338	299	304	521	596	861	1,132	10,538	974	2,234	1,266	158	120	335

Figure 7.4. Killed and missing persons, 1995
Source: Research and Documentation Center, 2007

database included between 1,000 and 5,000 duplicates, a finding that was not detrimental to the project overall. He did not expect the total number of estimated deaths to rise by more than 10,000 when the project was completed.[56] Tabeau looked at the quality and completeness of data reporting in the database, the loss of information related to deficiencies and hidden biases in data, and assessed coding errors. She found that "the level of incompleteness and deficiency in the BBD database is low and fairly acceptable."[57] Philip Verwimp addressed, among other things, how well the source data was captured in the database. To do so, he took a random sample of fifty cases, comparing twenty-one variables with the underlying documentation in the database, finding that 85 percent of active records were relatively complete.

Forthcoming: A Final Death Toll

The RDC planned to have Patrick Ball derive a final calculation of the number of deaths in the war. Though not a primary goal of the "Human Losses" project, the estimate would put the stamp of scientific accuracy on debates over numbers. The methodology used to estimate the total number of deaths is called Multiple Systems Estimation (MSE), or capture-recapture. It is "a technique that uses two separately collected but incomplete lists of a population to estimate the total population size."[58] It essentially uses overlapping records to enable researchers to estimate how many records *are not* in the database. The technique is "known to date back to at least the late nineteenth century as a technique for counting fish populations."[59] A *New York Times* reporter used an animal kingdom analogy—the problem of counting rattlesnakes experienced by Skidmore College biology professor, William Brown.[60] Brown knew how many rattlesnakes he had counted because he identified and recorded them, what he wanted to know was how many had he not counted.[61] In projects like "Human Losses," each death is likely to be reported multiple times, in multiple sources. Some deaths are not reported at all.

56. "Research Shows Estimates of Bosnian War Death Toll Were Inflated," *International Herald Tribune*, June 21, 2007.

57. Ewa Tabeau, presentation of expert assessment of project, Sarajevo, June 21, 2007.

58. Human Rights Data Analysis Group, Benetech Initiative, 2007, http://www.hrdag.org/resources/mult_systems_est.shtml.

59. Ibid.

60. Jim Giles, "The Forensic Humanitarian," *New York Times*, February 17, 2008.

61. Ibid. On Ball, see also Jina Moore, "A Human Rights Statistician Finds Truth in Numbers," *Christian Science Monitor*, February 7, 2008.

Multiple Systems Estimation is bolstered when as many sources as possible are recorded for each individual death. Each of these records is put in the database, with numeric representations of the type of source, and where it was found.[62]

For over a decade, Patrick Ball has applied this methodology to human rights problems, utilizing it for projects all over the world—truth commissions, tribunals, and NGOs. Ball traveled to Sarajevo in September 2004 on a pro bono basis to evaluate the Center's database. Upon assessing it, he claimed that the RDC's project was "probably one of the largest human rights databases in the world."[63]

Ball had done similar estimates in different projects in places as varied as Peru and East Timor. In Peru, his research team "observe[d] that total estimated number of victims (69,280) differs considerably from the figures commonly advanced before the creation of the [Peruvian Truth and Reconciliation Commission]."[64] Earlier estimates had placed the number of deaths in Peru at 24,000.[65] This finding was in contrast to Bosnia, where overreporting occurred, but in East Timor this same inflationary phenomenon had occurred. In Ball's work there, his research team found that despite a death toll originally reported to be around 400,000, around 18,000 people had died from military action and another 80,000–85,000 died of starvation and hunger.[66] In each of these cases, the figures were used in similar ways to support various political positions.[67] The planned use of this technique for a final estimate made an understanding of how scientific findings are interpreted by the public even more important.

---

62. It should be noted that MSE is not the only way to make a mortality estimate. Household surveys also help estimate mortality rates within a given population and time period. Although each methodology has its problems, obtaining a representative sample size is always a problem for survey researchers, as current debates about deaths in Iraq show.

63. Patrick Ball, author interview, Sarajevo, June 23, 2007.

64. Patrick Ball et al., "How Many Peruvians Have Died? An Estimate of the Total Number of Victims Killed or Disappeared in the Armed Internal Conflict between 1980 and 2000," American Association for the Advancement of Science, August 28, 2003, http://shr.aaas.org/peru/aaas_peru_5.pdf.

65. Ibid.

66. Patrick Ball, author interview, Sarajevo, June 23, 2007.

67. The Yad Vashem Museum in Jerusalem undertook a comparable project to capture the identities of as many Holocaust victims as possible. Six million deaths was always a sacred number in discussions of the Holocaust and derived by "comparing prewar censuses with lists of survivors compiled by the Red Cross and other relief organizations" (Joseph Berger, "At Holocaust Museum, Turning a Number into a Name." *New York Times,* Nov. 21, 2004). The project has a searchable database, which takes into account various ways of spelling names. Like the RDC's project, survivors can submit and correct information. This project has generated over three million names and continues. The database is available at http://www.yadvashem.org/wps/portal/IY_HON_Welcome.

Understanding the Response

Although the RDC above all sought to preserve the memory of citizens who perished in the war, the decision to use quantification was an effort to alter the discussion inside Bosnia and place the issue in the realm of the empirical and scientific, where myths had once been dominant. Theodore Porter argues: "Quantification is a technology of distance.... [R]eliance on numbers and quantitative manipulation minimizes the need for intimate knowledge and personal trust" and is a form of communication that transcends boundaries of all types.[68] There was still distrust both among and within the country's ethnic communities, even if the project had a diverse group of supporters in Bosnia. The project was an effort to use the tools of science to bridge some of the country's looming divides. The objectivity promised in such a documentation effort created what Porter has called a "a set of strategies for dealing with distance and distrust."[69]

How should we understand the strong response by some elites? How did the public respond? The project received local and international media coverage in the days and weeks following the presentation but then largely slipped out of public view. Some commented that perhaps there was a deliberate attempt to ignore the project altogether, hoping the results would just fade away. The most notable immediate effect was use of the new figures by the press services with representatives in Bosnia, including the Associated Press, Agence France Press, and Reuters. The revised total—100,000—had now become the standard in their reporting. At the time of the presentation, some journalists fought with their editors to use the new estimate as it implicitly raised the question of why they had adopted the initial number without question. Changing its decade-old policy, the Associated Press, for example, started to use the new number, citing the project's findings as justification. Scholars discovered the project and started to utilize the new figures, and talk about the RDC. Tokača was asked to join an international experts group that seeks to improve methods for documenting casualties in conflict, validation that locally derived knowledge—continually undervalued by foreign overseers—was important on the international stage as well.[70]

---

68. Theodore M. Porter, *Trust in Numbers: The Pursuit of Objectivity in Science and Public Life* (Princeton: Princeton University Press, 1995), ix.

69. Ibid.

70. See the Recording Casualties in Armed Conflict Project of the Oxford Research Group, http://www.oxfordresearchgroup.org.uk/work/global_security/casualties.php. On the importance of local knowledge see, for example, James C. Scott, *Seeing Like a State: How Certain Schemes to Improve the Human Condition Have Failed* (New Haven: Yale University Press, 1999).

The response to the project is more palatable, predictable even, when placed within the context of current research about attitudes toward science and the acceptance of scientific knowledge more generally. Psychologists have long sought to understand what factors influence the reception of scientific findings, especially when the methodologies used to glean that knowledge are foreign to the public or are deemed difficult to explain or understand. Yale University psychologists Paul Bloom and Deena Weisberg argue that resistance to scientific ideas is reflected in biases that start in childhood and clash with common sense understandings of the world.[71] The credibility of sources also influences how technical findings are received. They find: "Resistance to science, then, is particularly exaggerated in societies where nonscientific ideologies have the advantages of being both grounded in common sense and transmitted by trustworthy sources."[72] In a study of attitudes toward evolution, for example, Eastern European countries are near the bottom of a list of thirty-four surveyed, just above attitudes in the United States, which is second to last only to Turkey.[73] Myths had long dominated discussions about the war in Bosnia, and propaganda was used extensively, so that this transmission phenomenon was one of the project's obstacles.

Furthermore, in such an environment, the role of elites is crucial. Another study by Yale University psychologist Geoffrey Cohen, shows that when people do not understand the findings or a methodology, they assess the source.[74] In a series of experiments, he found that when asked to assess a particular social welfare policy, even though subjects thought they were assessing the policy on objective criteria, the main determinant of whether or not a participant supported it was if his/her political party endorsed it. In other words, in the absence of a personal understanding of the methods of science, people turn to elites whom they trust. Two factors "facilitate the effect of in-group judgments on attitude change behavior (i.e., the choice to take action for or against the policy)."[75] The first factor is the "ambiguity in the attitude object" or the perceived benefits of the event in question. For this project, this would mean largely how, for example, Bosniaks would interpret the decrease in the number of deaths in moral terms. "To the extent that the merits or deficiencies

71. P. Bloom and D. S. Weisberg, "Childhood Origins of Adult Resistance to Science," *Science*, May 18, 2007.

72. Ibid., 996.

73. Paul Bloom and Deena Skolnick Weisberg, "Why Do Some People Resist Science," *Edge*, http://www.edge.org/3rd_culture/bloom07/bloom07_index.html.

74. Geoffrey L. Cohen, "Party over Policy: The Dominating Impact of Group Influence on Political Beliefs," *Journal of Personality and Social Psychology* 85 (2003): 808–22.

75. Ibid., 809.

of the object are unambiguous, and its moral connotations established (as with abortion and capital punishment), neither its factual qualities nor its moral qualities will be amenable to alternative interpretation and attitude change will thus be limited."[76] Given that attitudes toward science in Eastern European countries and in the United States are similar, this study can inform our understanding of the "Human Losses" project in Bosnia. Above all, these findings illustrate the tremendous task facing the project's architects. Any threat to the moral "correctness" of the narrative of the war will be extremely difficult to introduce to groups that have an "unambiguous" view of the new information. The second condition Cohen identified is "issue relevance to the group."[77] If the group's view is not critical to the particular issue under consideration, it will not have a decisive affect on attitude change. Both of the main factors that lead to the acceptance of new scientific findings were unfavorable to the "Human Losses" project.[78] Thus, the project has faced and will continue to confront significant challenges for the reception of the RDC's findings. In addition, the role of "anchoring effects" discussed in this volume—the tendency of people to fixate on numbers they have heard even if they are inaccurate—can also inform our understanding of the project's reception in Bosnia.[79]

Attitudes are fluid, however, and will change over time. Furthermore, these studies have real implications for how the outreach for similar future projects is conducted, and how the RDC continues its efforts in the region regarding ongoing analyses of its database. These findings imply that elite-focused outreach may be just as important as similar efforts within the public at large. The strategy the RDC has used in Bosnia, casting itself as the lone crusader, far removed from politics or any other compromising influences, has certain limits when viewed in light of this research. These are precisely the individuals to whom they should reach out. If the reception of new social scientific information is imbedded in social networks, project coordinators should also conduct informational sessions within elite circles to explain the findings and the value of scientific methodologies. Furthermore, it is important that elites understand the benefits (both short- and long-term) of accurate representation and reporting about human rights violations, as discussed below, as their perspectives will affect public opinion at large.

76. Ibid.
77. Ibid.
78. It would be interesting, however, to understand attitudes toward this project along generational lines, as most elites and opinion shapers are usually middle aged and older.
79. See the introductory chapter to this volume for a discussion of anchoring effects.

Importance of Documentation Efforts

Does it ultimately matter whether 100,000 or 200,000 perished in Bosnia's brutal war in which genocide, mass rape, and the expulsion of more than half of Bosnia's prewar population occurred? For researchers interested in war, documentation, and demographic losses, not to mention the public at large, the answer is a resounding yes. The field of human rights data analysis is in the early phases of development but projects are sure to expand as abilities to document violations increase. There are several reasons why accurate documentation is important. First, projects like "Human Losses" enable demographic estimates of the war's real impact. The human loss sustained in conflict will have effects on the countries in question for decades to come. The more precise the data, the more accurate the forecast on important questions such as the overall demographic impact of the conflicts in question. Evolving norms of accountability may cause these forecasts to be used in courts of law to hold perpetrators responsible for more than their immediate crimes. Second, the public has a right to know. In Bosnia, victims of the Srebrenica massacre of July 1995 used a lack of knowledge about their missing relatives as a basis for a complaint that was filed in the country's now defunct Human Rights Chamber, arguing that their rights outlined in the European Convention on Human Rights were being violated, an argument accepted by the Chamber. Third, documentation projects can establish patterns of atrocities. The "Human Losses" project can now plot casualties according to time and place of death. An example from Central America can inform our understanding of future uses of the database. In El Salvador, using the data from over 9,000 detailed testimonies from the war, Patrick Ball coded information about human rights violations, placed them in a database, and matched that information with the military officers in each region of the country. In doing so, he generated a dossier of the human rights violations likely committed or overseen by each officer in the military. When members of an NGO placed posters of those dossiers all over El Salvador's capital they were taken to court for libel. After reading Ball's expert reports generated from his meticulous data collection, and realizing the strength of the data, the judges dismissed the case. After that, the Ad Hoc Commission used the data in combination with another, similar study by a group called El Rescate and purged the officers in question from the military.[80] Studies like this one and the "Human Losses" project have the potential to initiate substantial changes. Their conclusions will also contain important suggestions for the prevention of

---

80. Patrick Ball, author interview, Sarajevo, June 23, 2007.

conflict. Furthermore, inflated numbers cause publics to be desensitized to mass atrocities, subconsciously requiring high numbers before action can seem justified. Inflated estimates make parties to a conflict seem like dishonest brokers and inhibit the effective delivery and allocation of aid. Finally, documentation efforts relying on multiple sources of information can combat climates of denial in postconflict countries. Over time, scrupulously collected documentation makes it difficult to deny human rights violations.

Conclusion

Conventional wisdom holds that 250,000 people died in the Bosnian war. The "Human Losses" project found that the true figure was around 100,000. This finding caused uproar in some Bosniak nationalist circles, forcing the project director, Mirsad Tokača, to defend both himself and the project's methodology from numerous attacks. In the short term, the intense response obscured the fact that the project succeeded in creating one of the largest human rights databases in the world, amassing thousands of pages of documentation in the process.

The RDC anticipated many of the objections to the findings. They also anticipated that some of the features and communication strategies of the old regime would characterize the reaction. They, however, had ulterior motives. Beyond the stated project goals of the documentation effort, they also had a larger purpose: to change the caliber and locus of dialogue about human rights issues in the country. They hoped to banish the use of mythology that characterized the discussion of this and related issues both in the socialist period and after the war. It was an attempt to develop some of the desirable features of liberal democracies. Research in psychology, however, has shown that elites are key to understanding how scientific findings are interpreted, even in liberal democracies. Thus, for the "Human Losses" team, as it moves forward, the opinions of elite groups will be key to influencing how the project continues to reverberate through Bosnian society. Elites should be educated in the value and accuracy of the findings, and the soundness of the methodology.

The implications of this case study reach far beyond Bosnia. As human rights data analysis increases in use around the world, citizens in conflict-ridden societies will be increasingly asked to understand the technical findings of demographers, epidemiologists, and statisticians who measure and document some of their most traumatic experiences. Although politicians will continue to spin data in their favor, ultimately sound technical knowledge and assessment is integral to helping societies in need, both during conflict and after the arms have been laid down. Scholars and activists who use these powerful tools of systematization and quantification must understand that the pursuit of objectivity will continue to be another kind of battlefield, at least initially, and they should wield their best weapons: facts and documentation.

8

The Ambiguous Genocide

THE U.S. STATE DEPARTMENT AND
THE DEATH TOLL IN DARFUR

John Hagan and Wenona Rymond-Richmond

Gérard Prunier has called Darfur "the ambiguous genocide."[1] A key source of this ambiguity has derived from the failure of U.S. government agencies to meaningfully hold the Sudanese government accountable for the death toll in Darfur. In fact, as this chapter argues, in a textbook example of the politics of numbers in action, the U.S. State Department has been a key source of low and uncertain estimates of the scale of mortality in Darfur. The chapter examines the origins and implications of this systematic undercounting and offers an alternative, more reliable approach to tallying the dead in Darfur.

Specifically, we contend that the State Department has vacillated in its public policies on Darfur. In doing so, it has inappropriately applied concepts and methods from a population health paradigm, while ignoring the (more suitable) crime victimization approach. It appears to have done so for plainly political reasons—to assure Sudan's cooperation in the global war on terror. Unfortunately for the victims of this genocide, the State Department's official underestimate has had the concomitant effect of reducing public certainty about mass atrocities in Darfur, which in turn decreased the public sense of urgency about stopping the genocide and holding its architects accountable.

Portions of this chapter were published by John Hagan and Wenona Rymond-Richmond in "The Disturbing Case of the British Advertising Standards Authority, the *New York Times*, and the State Department's Low Estimate of the Death Toll in Darfur," *Ohio State Journal of Criminal Law* 5 (2008).

1. Gérard Prunier, *Darfur: The Ambiguous Genocide* (Ithaca: Cornell University Press, 2005).

"Complex Humanitarian Emergencies" and the Population Health Paradigm

Since the early 1990s and the end of the cold war, the concept of a "complex humanitarian emergency" has often been used by population health researchers to refer to coerced circumstances of forced migration and mortality in many parts of the world.[2] These emergencies include situations in which efforts to drastically restructure a state, society, or social group have led to civil conflict or international war. This led to the violent death of large civilian populations and in their substantial displacement to detrimental living conditions—typically to overflowing and inadequately resourced camps—that in turn become breeding grounds for disease, dehydration, starvation, malnutrition, and other sources of excessive deaths.[3]

The identification of humanitarian emergencies as "complex" reflects from the outset the concerns of public health researchers about the political complications of initiating and sustaining humanitarian relief and assistance.[4] The first concern reflects the priority these researchers attach to the work of relief agencies in improving the chances that refugees can survive emergency conditions in the face of the "complex social, political, and economic issues" that confront them.[5] The second concern reflects the desire to neutrally if not euphemistically understand the contexts and arrangements that relief programs adapt to as "by nature complex."[6] The third concern is that relief agencies should not ignore "complex and political" arguments about providing equal medical services to communities where refugee camps are located.[7]

The hard and intrusive political realities of the complex humanitarian emergencies just described led health researchers to call on the post–cold war international community to adopt a policy that recognized and acted on the need to intervene at early stages in "the evolution of complex disasters involving civil war, human rights abuses, food shortages, and mass displacement."[8]

2. Ronald Waldman and Gerald Martone, "Public Health and Complex Emergencies: New Issues, New Conditions," *American Journal of Public Health* 89 (1999): 1483–85.

3. Charles Keely, Holly Reed, and Ronald Waldman, "Understanding Mortality Patterns in Complex Humanitarian Emergencies," in *Forced Migration and Mortality*, ed. Holly Reed and Charles Keely (Washington, DC: National Academy Press, 2001).

4. M. J. Toole and R. J. Waldman, "Prevention of Excess Mortality in Refugee and Displaced Populations in Developing Countries," *Journal of the American Medical Association* 263 (1990): 3296–302.

5. Ibid., 3300.

6. Ibid., 3301.

7. Ibid.

8. M. J. Toole and R. J. Waldman, "Refugees and Displaced Persons: War, Hunger, and Public Health," *Journal of the American Medical Association,* 270 (1993): 600–605.

A crucial element of Toole and Waldman's health-initiated agenda was their recognition that once health-oriented practitioners achieved access to a humanitarian emergency situation and began to prevent excess mortality, they could also begin to play a role in empirically documenting the unfolding course of the emergency as well as its distribution and magnitude.[9]

Mortality—which is of obvious interest to scholars who study criminal victimization, international criminal law, and the criminology of human rights and war crimes—is the most common dimension used to trace and assess the course of complex humanitarian emergencies. The related study of famines has identified a paradigmatic sequence of mortality and related problems marked by the onset of the crisis, followed by its rise to a peak, by the arrival of emergency assistance, and by a hopefully rapid if belated stabilization.[10] Crude mortality rates (CMRs) are calculated to assess the occurrence of deaths for the population affected by the emergency and its duration.

Crude mortality rates are usually calculated as deaths per 10,000-population per day to allow comparisons across settings and situations. These rates are classically expected to rise and fall across the stages noted above, tracing an inverted U-shaped curve of mortality that is negatively skewed by the slower pace of onset, followed by a peak and faster rate of decline in deaths. At least this is the expectation for "standard" rural famines. The forced migration and mortality at the end of the twentieth century in Kosovo, the southern most province in the Republic of Serbia, further exemplified this pattern.[11]

A CMR of 1.0 was identified by the U.S. State Department in the mid-1980s as a useful threshold of elevated mortality in complex humanitarian emergencies.[12] This is two to three times the level of mortality that is regarded as expected or normal in sub-Saharan Africa, and this criterion was adopted in 1992 for public health purposes by the Centers for Disease Control (CDC). At the same time, the CDC recommended a program of response in which a rapid health assessment would use sample survey methods to establish a baseline mortality rate in a setting, followed by the implementation of a health information system to collect ongoing

9. Ibid., 605.

10. B. T. Burkholder and M. J. Toole, "Evolution of Complex Disasters," *Lancet* 346 (1995): 1012–15.

11. P. B. Spiegel and P. Salama, "War and Mortality in Kosovo, 1998–1999: An Epidemiological Testimony," *Lancet* 355 (2000): 2204–9.

12. Bureau of Refugee Programs, *Assessment Manual for Refugee Emergencies* (Washington, DC: Department of State, 1985).

health data, including mortality.[13] These developments were spearheaded by epidemiological trained health researchers and have provided an increasingly important picture of the mortality and morbidity surrounding humanitarian emergencies. If criminologists had been involved in these developments, they might have focused more specific attention on identifying criminal sources and responsibility for mortality in these emergency situations. However, criminologists did not become involved in this work during the early post–cold war period.

The primary goal of the population health research on complex humanitarian emergencies has been support for the provision of relief (food, medicine, and shelter) for conflict-affected populations suffering elevated mortality levels. The goal of this research is more often to prospectively plan and provide relief than to retrospectively assign criminal responsibility. Organizations, such as the CDC, have been largely concerned with gathering data as a means to prevent further death, sometimes if not often neglecting the need to assess mortality resulting from state-led criminal violence and deaths of civilians that occur before they assume refugee status. Yet this epidemiologically and demographically guided research can provide insight into the patterning of politically instigated violence, which is characteristically revealed to be highly contingent on the people involved and the places where these humanitarian emergencies occur.[14]

Perhaps most important, this research reveals that internal and external politics, including the reaction (or lack thereof) by the international community, can radically alter the form and scale of humanitarian and human rights emergencies. For example, in the Democratic Republic of the Congo, mortality rates have not significantly improved from an average of 0.7 deaths per 10,000-population per day since 2002, and these rates are 75 percent higher in conflict-prone regions of this country.[15] Overall, less developed countries have higher CMRs and are more vulnerable to upward variations from baseline rates than developed countries, making their humanitarian and human rights emergencies quantitatively and qualitatively distinct. In Zaire in 1994, CMRs for Rwandan refugees reached levels as high as thirty-five deaths per 10,000 per day.[16]

13. Center for Disease Control, "Famine Affected, Refugee and Displaced Populations: Recommendations for Public Health Issues," *MMWR Recommendations Report* 41, RR-13 (July 24, 1992): 1–76.

14. Ian M. Timaeus and Momodou Jasseh, "Adult Mortality in sub-Saharan Africa: Evidence from Demographic and Health Surveys," *Demography* 41 (2004): 757–72.

15. International Rescue Committee, *Mortality in the Democratic Republic of the Congo: Results from a Nationwide Survey* (New York: International Rescue Committee, 2004).

16. Goma Epidemiological Group, "Public Health Impact of Rwandan Refugee Crisis: What Happened in Goma, Zaire in July 1994," *Lancet* 345 (1995): 339–44.

Although not specifically designed to do so, this body of research further reveals that the population most at risk varies with the nature of the specific roots of the conflict. In the Democratic Republic of Congo, infants and children under age five have had the most highly elevated mortality rates.[17] In contrast, the elderly were most at risk during the siege of Sarajevo.[18] In the Srebrenica massacre, military-age males were most at risk of death, while women tend to be most at risk of rape during politically instigated violence within and between nations.[19]

The health research literature on complex humanitarian emergencies is increasingly organized around interpersonal age-sex dimensions and the global North-South divide of development. These are clearly powerful contingencies that shape the form and scale of humanitarian emergencies. We still lack comprehensive data on the age-sex composition of elevated mortality in these emergencies, and this kind of data and analysis needs to be better connected to our understanding of the North-South dynamic of development that slowly but increasingly is the focus of thought and attention in the post–cold war world.[20]

Despite the social and political dimensions of human rights emergencies and war crimes, epidemiologically and demographically trained health researchers are inclined to focus mainly on health outcomes, whereas criminologists prioritize issues of political and ultimately legal responsibility. Criminology and law can bring further attention to the understanding of war and human rights crimes that a population health approach neglects. A common sequence in these emergencies involves the onset of violent attacks, the flight of the resulting victims, followed by ensuing health problems, all of which contribute to mortality. The key point is that "the root cause of most complex humanitarian emergencies is that governments and other combatants use violence and deprivation to seek solutions to political problems."[21]

The challenge is simultaneously to keep in mind the cumulative and multiplicative effects of violence, flight, and displacement to concentrated encampments, and the political state and nonstate origins of the disastrous consequences. From a criminological as well as methodological perspective,

17. International Rescue Committee, *Mortality in the Democratic Republic of the Congo*.

18. F. Watson, I. Kulenovic, and J. Vespa, "Nutritional Status and Food Security: Winter Nutrition Monitoring in Sarajevo, 1993–1994," *European Journal of Clinical Nutrition 49*, supplement 2 (1995): S23–32.

19. David Rohde, *Endgame: The Betrayal and Fall of Srebrenica, Europe's Worst Massacre since World War II* (New York: Farrar, Straus and Giroux, 1997).

20. Rosemarie Rogers and Emily Copeland, *Forced Migration: Policy Issues in the Post-Cold War World* (Medford: Tufts University Press, 1993).

21. Keely, Reed, and Waldman, "Understanding Mortality Patterns," 12.

it is insufficient to concentrate on health outcomes of these emergencies without simultaneously acknowledging their political and state origins. When the health and crime perspectives are juxtaposed, important socio-legal issues become apparent. For example, treatment of the "missing" and of "excess as distinct from normal and expected mortality" and, even more fundamentally, the substitution of the concept of "complex humanitarian emergency" for "war and human rights crimes" raise major questions about our understanding of this subject matter.

It is useful to begin with the treatment of the missing in the calculation of CMRs from population-based surveys, which was introduced as a central concept and method of the health approach. The calculation of CMRs involves dividing (a) the number of household members reported as deceased for a specified period by (b) the estimated size of the sampled population (with the number of respondents multiplied by average household size) and (c) multiplying the dividend by 10,000. The denominator in this calculation is designed to represent the population at risk of death.

The convention in the health literature on complex humanitarian emergencies is to include in this denominator the sum of the sampled population and half of the reported dead, missing, and absent from it, assuming that these dead, missing, and absent people on average were at risk of death for half of this survey period. Yet health surveys of these emergencies conventionally do not include consideration of the missing in the numerator of observed deaths, instead essentially treating these persons as missing data. Often, if not usually, the missing persons in these surveys have disappeared in the chaos of the emergency and are feared or presumed dead by family members and human rights groups. However, the focus in health studies is typically on deaths that can be directly identified as resulting from disease and nutritional or other specified causes, and the missing are therefore omitted from consideration.[22]

At times, those who study complex humanitarian emergencies add a further category for injuries and violence. However, the inclusion of injuries and violence often covers a restricted period of risk or the period while in displacement or refugee camps. Violence that results in deaths and disappearances that precedes flight to camps is often treated as of secondary importance or ignored and, like the missing, is often simply overlooked. Rather than focus on assigning criminal responsibility for deaths that precede flight to camps, the health focus is typically on saving the lives of those who survive long enough to get to the camps. Our point is that from

---

22. See, for example, World Health Organization, *Retrospective Mortality Survey Among the Internally Displaced Population, Greater Darfur, Sudan* (Geneva: World Health Organization, 2004).

a criminological perspective, acknowledging and analyzing those who die and become missing before, as well as while in displacement and refugee camps, is important for the purposes of assigning legal responsibility and understanding the root causes of underlying conflicts.

The concept of excess mortality raises a related set of concerns. Analyses of complex humanitarian emergencies often construct a baseline estimate of mortality by identifying an expected mortality rate for the population of interest and at risk, assuming the absence of the risk. The idea is to estimate those who would have been expected to die under normal circumstances. This can be difficult to do because circumstances in settings like sub-Saharan Africa are so seldom "normal." Thus, the task is to construct a "counterfactual" estimate of the "normal" mortality. This expected or normal mortality is then subtracted from the level of mortality observed during the period of the humanitarian emergency. The difference between the "expected" and "observed" mortality is deemed "excessive" and is used by health researchers as a means of determining the extent and duration of the emergency.

From a criminological perspective, this approach is problematic. Consider the following. An individual or group of individuals in actuarial terms may be expected to die for health reasons within a given period, but instead during this period dies as a result of a criminal human rights violation. Dying in one's normal place of residence or work is one thing, but dying in a refugee camp is quite another. This is no longer "expected" or "normal." The implication is that although designating such deaths as expected or normal may be quite useful for some analytic purposes—such as charting the timing and scale of a humanitarian emergency, it is misleading for other purposes—such as the legal documentation of the form and extent of human rights crimes and war crimes.

The problems considered for illustrative purposes here—the neglect of missing persons, the failure to consider predisplacement or refugee camp violence, and the treatment of excess mortality—anticipate a broader problem with the concept of complex humanitarian emergencies. This concept, though helpful in encouraging the creation of population and public health based methods for the study of these disasters, can also have the unhelpful effect of blunting and obscuring the meaning of much that is observed to be happening in such emergencies.

Often as a part of working with affected nations, within and alongside the United Nations, humanitarian organizations seek nonthreatening and unobtrusive methods for addressing human rights abuses. Even threatening nomenclature can result in being denied access to settings and people in dire need of humanitarian assistance. The problem, of course, is that the same states and groups that create these emergencies also restrict access to their victims. Insistence on a criminological perspective has the potential to serve as a counterweight to this problem, but first it is important to appreciate how great this problem can be.

The Humanitarian Strategic Embrace

The humanitarian dilemma posed by efforts to divert and co-opt research on human rights abuses is a challenging practical issue that is provocatively depicted in Alex de Waal's *Famine Crimes: Politics and the Disaster Relief Industry in Africa.*[23] De Waal argues that what he calls the "Humanitarian International"—the complex of NGOs and relief agencies that respond to humanitarian emergencies—often finds itself engaged in a compromised strategic embrace with states that commit the human rights abuses and war crimes whose consequences they seek to alleviate.[24] Accessing and treating the urgent and deadly consequences of these emergencies can obscure if not obstruct efforts to identify and hold their instigators responsible. This observation is particularly apt in Darfur, a setting that highlights differences in health and criminological perspectives.

The tension that the contradiction between health and crime priorities generates in the politics of the United Nations briefly broke into public view when the British House of Commons International Development Committee received testimony in early 2005 from the former UN resident and humanitarian coordinator for Sudan, Mukkesh Kapila.[25] Kapila was the highest in-country UN official dealing with the response to the unfolding violence against African villagers in the Darfur region of Sudan in February 2003. More than six months later, in October 2003, Kapila asked that the violence in Darfur be referred to the International Criminal Court. This did not take place until the United States finally agreed to abstain from voting in the UN Security Council, and allowed the referral to go forward in early 2005.

Kapila, who had previously served the United Nations in the Rwandan genocide, was determined that similar events would not be repeated in Darfur. Yet in March 2004 Kapila was removed from Darfur, with the killing still near its peak. The killing was still in progress in early 2005 when

---

23. Alex de Waal, *Famine Crimes: Politics and the Disaster Relief Industry in Africa* (Oxford, UK: Currey, 1997).

24. A backdrop to these arguments is set in Alex de Waal, *Famine that Kills: Darfur, Sudan* (London: Oxford University Press, 1985).

25. House of Commons International Development Committee, *Darfur, Sudan: The Responsibility to Protect*, Fifth Report of the Session 2004–2005, Vol. II, Oral and Written Evidence (London: Station Office Limited, 2005).

Kapila testified to the British parliamentary committee that the death toll was large and still rising because "fundamentally the issue was that the Sudan government refused to allow us access when we needed it most." Yet this summary comment only scratches the surface of Kapila's account, which goes on to painfully highlight the conflicted nature of the UN's work with the Sudanese government in response to the killing, and the resulting health problems in Darfur. When Kapila was asked how effectively the humanitarian and human rights—or health and crime—parts of the Sudan mission worked together in Darfur, he responded that these were actually competing efforts, that "we had a real struggle to overcome," that a "culture of distrust" existed, and that it was a challenge to "create one UN approach." He explained that political crises are typically categorized as "humanitarian problems" and that those in charge of aid operations are "burdened with the task of doing something about it and when they inevitably fail the blame is put on the humanitarians."[26]

The point here is that if the government instigates the attacks and killings that lead to displacement into camps where many more victims die of disease and malnutrition, the same government can then also conveniently claim that the fault lies with the humanitarian response rather than with the government. At the same time, the rush to meet the humanitarian need for health and nutritional assistance can compete with and produce compromised efforts to highlight the human rights abuses leading to these humanitarian needs. Kapila clearly saw the violence as ethnic cleansing, a form of genocide. Yet he reported that the response from the international community fit into the Sudan government's strategy of demanding that he and his staff work harder to find humanitarian solutions.

Kapila particularly emphasized another side of this dilemma that involved a competition for scarce resources, saying, "this happens in organizations that are funded in a way which is reliant on what sort of image you can present and so on. That means that we had $100 million available for food aid but we had only $1 million available for human rights." Still, his conclusion was that "even if twice the money came in from the world...the arguments would have been the same," and that the real problem was "the systematic obstruction by the Sudanese government of humanitarian access."[27] Kapila's testimony starkly highlights how difficult the relationship is between responding to health and crime issues in humanitarian emergencies. The U.S. State Department and the U.S. Government Accountability Office were implicated in this

26. Ibid., EV 50, 52, 50.
27. Ibid., EV 52, 50.

complicated relationship as they became involved in investigations of genocidal victimization in Darfur.

The Atrocities Documentation Survey

The State Department countered the "humanitarian embrace" by launching its own victimization survey with refugees from Darfur who received sanctuary across the border with UN assistance in Chad. In September 2004, it published an eight-page report, titled *Documenting Atrocities in Darfur*.[28] Its chillingly cogent tables, charts, maps, and pictures were based on survey interviews in 1,136 refugee households in Chad and is the empirical foundation for much of the further analysis presented herein. The so-called Atrocities Documentation Survey (ADS) on which the report was based enumerated more than 12,000 deaths and many more rapes and other atrocities that respondents personally had seen or heard about before fleeing attacks on their farms and villages.

Secretary of State Colin Powell made headlines when he summarized the survey results for the UN Security Council and the U.S. Congress as evidence of a racially targeted and militarily unjustified Sudanese-sponsored genocide in Darfur. Powell's testimony was quickly followed by a separate White House statement from President Bush that also used the ADS as its foundation:

> I sent Secretary of State Powell to Darfur and Khartoum to demand that the Sudanese Government act to end the violence....Secretary Powell later sent a team of investigators into the refugee camps to interview the victims of atrocities. As a result of these investigations and other information, we have concluded that genocide has taken place in Darfur. We urge the international community to work with us to prevent and suppress acts of genocide. We call on the United Nations to undertake a full investigation of the genocide and other crimes in Darfur.[29]

This was the first time a U.S. president had rebuked a sovereign nation by invoking the Genocide Convention, and certainly the first time that a crime victimization survey had played a support role in the formation of U.S. foreign policy. This victimization survey recorded a level of criminal

---

28. U.S. Department of State Bureau of Democracy, Human Rights, and Labor and Bureau of Intelligence and Research, *State Publication 11182: Documenting Atrocities in Darfur* (Washington, DC: State Department, September 2004).

29. U.S. White House Office of the Press Secretary, "Statement by the President: President's Statement on Violence in Darfur, Sudan," September 9, 2004, http://www.whitehouse.gov/news/releases/2004/09/20040909-10.html.

detail that no health survey could provide. The resulting report outlined the criminology of genocide.

Yet the U.S. declaration of genocide was accompanied by no more than a provisional request by Powell for more African Union troops to act as "monitors" and a qualified call by Bush for a UN investigation. These actions were a timid response to genocidal atrocities and signaled the Administration's fundamental ambivalence. Powell insisted in his Congressional testimony that "no new action is dictated by this determination," and this undercut the potential force of his genocide charge. In order to understand the confusing politics behind these events, it is important to understand the uniqueness of the ADS.

Surveying Hostile Circumstances

In the summer of 2004, Secretary Powell and the State Department were motivated by horrific news stories of attacks and killings in Darfur, and by the fact that Congress had already passed a unanimous condemnation of the genocide. The Administration wanted to reassert its leadership on this foreign policy issue by providing systematic evidence of the seriousness of the crimes that were reportedly taking place.

As a step toward this goal, in June 2004, former U.S. Agency for International Development administrator and later Special Envoy to Sudan, Andrew Natsios appeared at a donors' conference in Geneva and presented satellite images of the destruction of a village in Darfur. The images were described by David Springer, a State Department geospatial analyst, who pointed to a pair of pictures that recorded the fate of the village of Shattay before and after a militia attack. Springer offered a detailed explanation of changes in the surrounding vegetation and the further geophysical signs of the destruction of Shattay.

One purpose of this presentation was to place the Sudanese on notice that their activities were being observed and recorded. An official who described the event nonetheless cautioned "that the images are not hard evidence until they are corroborated by testimony of witnesses on the ground."[30] Under the increasing pressure to provide a reliable assessment of the situation, the State Department had sent an atrocities documentation team into the field to survey the refugees fleeing Darfur.

The ADS was conducted under the direction of Stephanie Frease of the Coalition for International Justice (CIJ) and Jonathan Howard, a research

---

30. Monica Amarelo, "Using Science to Gauge Sudan's Humanitarian Nightmare," *American Association for the Advancement of Science News Release,* October 26, 2004, http://www.aaas.org/news/releases/2004/1026sudan.shtml.

analyst with the State Department's Office of Research. Frease volunteered and was asked by the U.S. Ambassador on War Crimes and the State Department to complete the survey in just two months time.[31] This was an audacious demand, but Frease had already demonstrated her capacity to organize and complete challenging data-collection projects. (Years earlier, working inside what she had called "the Srebrenica ghost team," Frease located and successfully brought to court the "smoking gun" audio intercept evidence for the genocide trial of General Radislav Krstic at the International Criminal Tribunal for the Former Yugoslavia.)[32]

The current challenge was no less daunting. It included developing a survey instrument, recruiting interviewers and interpreters, planning the logistics of conducting surveys in nineteen locations in eastern Chad that were unreachable by roads, designing a sampling plan, moving the research team in and out of the survey locations, and organizing the coding and analysis of over 1,000 interviews. Several hundred of the interviews were conducted for Powell's use in his appearance before the UN Security Council in July, and the full survey of 1,136 households in Chad was completed with a preliminary analysis for the brief *Documenting Atrocities* report that accompanied Powell's Congressional testimony in early September. A protocol was developed for the survey that mixed the closed-ended format of a crime victimization survey with the semi-structured format of legal witness statements. The interviewers worked with interpreters in ten camps and nine settlements across the West Darfur border in Chad.

The sampling was systematic. Interviewers randomly selected a starting point in each camp or settlement and then from within this designated sector selected every tenth dwelling unit for interview. All the adults living in the unit were listed on the survey instrument and one adult from the household was randomly chosen for an interview, resulting in the final 1,136 sampled households.

Up to twenty incidents were coded for each household interview, with detailed information collected about the nature of the crimes. The legally oriented interviewers were intent on collecting responses to their survey questions with sufficient detail to support potential courtroom claims. The *Documenting Atrocities* report of the survey used univariate descriptive statistics and formed the background for Secretary of State Powell's testimony on September 9, 2004 to the U.S. Senate Foreign Relations Committee that genocide was occurring in Darfur.

31. Mark Goldberg, "Khartoum Characters," *American Prospect Online*, July 3, 2005, 14.

32. See John Hagan, *Justice in the Balkans: Prosecuting War Crimes in The Hague Tribunal* (Chicago: University of Chicago Press. 2003), ch. 5.

Important survey work has also been reported by the French human rights group, Médecins Sans Frontières (MSF). Although the MSF survey work was limited to a smaller number of camps in West Darfur, this initiative represents a unique attempt to combine attention to pre-camp and in-camp experiences, including attention to mortality in both settings.

Early Findings from the World Health Organization Surveys

Organizations such as the World Health Organization (WHO), the World Food Program, and the Centers for Disease Control and Prevention—especially in a setting such as Darfur—are understandably more preoccupied with the immediate and ongoing challenges of disease and malnutrition than they are with the past violence that leads displaced persons to flee camps. This is a key reason why the ADS was conducted.

At about the same time, the WHO was conducting its own surveys of mortality and other health and nutrition issues with the Sudanese Ministry of Health (WHO/SMH survey) across a large number of camps inside the three states of Darfur. This work produced estimates of CMRs. A WHO retrospective survey for two summer months of 2004 produced a CMR of 2.14 for the states of North and West Darfur (South Darfur was less fully surveyed). This level of mortality is four to seven times greater than what is normally expected in sub-Saharan Africa. It is a meaningful estimate of mortality following displacement, due to health problems in the camps, with some added deaths resulting from forays outside the camps during this period to collect firewood or other necessities. Few of the deaths included in the calculation could have been due to violent attacks prior to displacement. Unfortunately, the latter point was not well understood at the time and remains so today. Nevertheless, for criminological purposes, it is essential to have information on the violent deaths resulting from attacks prior to displacement.

The WHO survey also became the source of an influential seven-month estimate that 70,000 Darfurian refugees had died in just seven months of 2004, with the deaths resulting almost entirely from malnutrition and disease.[33] This estimate was announced by WHO spokesman David Nabarro.[34] Nabarro concluded that deaths were occurring in Darfur at the rate of approximately 5,000 to 10,000 persons per month. This estimate required going beyond the original retrospective survey by linking the CMRs

33. David Nabarro, "Mortality Projections for Darfur," *Media Briefing Notes*, UN Palais Press Corps, Geneva, October 15, 2004.

34. Donald McNeil, "The Worrier: At the UN: This Virus Has an Expert 'Quite Scared,'" *New York Times*, March 28, 2006.

with separate estimates of the larger population at risk in Darfur. The latter population was estimated from counts of displaced persons in the camps and reported in UN reports known as "Humanitarian Profiles." This count of the population at risk can be used along with the CMR, expressed as the number-of-deaths per 10,000-population per day, to estimate a monthly death toll. Both the CMR and the internal displaced camp population varies from month to month. However, in the 2004 summer months covered by the WHO survey, the death toll was probably near its peak, and the emphasis was on trying to gauge this emergency level of mortality.

On March 10, 2005, when UN emergency relief coordinator Jan Egeland returned from a fact-finding trip to Darfur, he was pressed by the UN press corps to provide an updated estimate of the death toll. At first he enigmatically responded that it was impossible to estimate because "it is where we are not that there are attacks." Then when he was asked to comment on the outdated estimate of 70,000, he responded by saying, "Is it three times that? Is it five times that? I don't know but it is several times the number of 70,000 that have died altogether."[35]

Several days later, Egeland obviously had concluded that the imprecision of his earlier answer was unsatisfactory. In a new response, he extrapolated from the WHO survey by multiplying Nabarro's 10,000 per month figure by eighteen months instead of seven. The official UN estimate thus jumped to 180,000.[36] Although it was based on no additional data collection or analysis, Egeland's estimate began to consolidate an early media appraisal of the scale of the genocide in Darfur. Although it is doubtful that deaths remained at a constant peak level of 10,000 per month in Darfur for eighteen months, there were reasons to think the peak monthly death toll was actually higher than 10,000.

A Gathering Consensus

The projection of 180,000 deaths from the WHO survey was at the lower end of a collection of estimates receiving attention in the media. In February 2005, Jan Coebergh, a British physician, noted the absence of violent deaths from the WHO survey and, drawing some simple inferences from the ADS, estimated that the true death toll was nearer 300,000.[37] The scale of this estimate echoed the U.S. activist-scholar Eric Reeves of

---

35. Evelyn Leopold, "UN Envoy Says Deaths in Darfur Underestimated," Reuters, March 10, 2005.

36. Evelyn Leopold, "Over 180,000 Darfur Deaths in 18 Months—UN Envoy," Reuters, March 15, 2005.

37. Jan Coebergh, "Sudan: Genocide Has Killed More Than Tsunami," *Parliamentary Brief*, February 2005, 5–6.

Smith College, who had been posting on the Internet similarly large estimates based on parallel assumptions.[38] Reeves soon updated his work in a *Boston Globe* op-ed piece, projecting a death toll of 400,000.[39] The importance of Coebergh and Reeves's estimates is that they made explicit that their higher projections involved adding deaths resulting from violence recorded in the ADS work to the deaths mainly following from disease and malnutrition in the WHO survey. These estimates were attempts to bridge the crime and health paradigms.

At almost the same time, in conjunction with the CIJ, we issued a press release detailing an estimate based on a combination of the WHO and ADS surveys. The estimate involved going back through each of the 1,136 ADS surveys and retracing all of the steps necessary to make this projection clearly and completely transparent. We concluded that as many as 350,000 persons might have died, and that nearly 400,000 persons were likely either missing or dead in Darfur.[40] The *New York Times* and the *Washington Post* now began reporting with some frequency an estimate of 300,000 deaths. UN Secretary-General Kofi Annan seemingly endorsed the higher assessment when he indicated in a *New York Times* op-ed article that 300,000 "or more" Darfurians were thought to have died.[41] In April 2005, Marc Lacey cited our nearly 400,000 dead and missing figure for the first time in the *New York Times*.[42] A consensus was emerging that hundreds of thousands had died, with the estimates now ranging from 180,000 to 400,000 deaths.

The Consensus Breaks

In the early spring of 2005, Assistant Secretary of State Robert Zoellick—deputy to the new Secretary of State Condoleezza Rice—paid a personal visit to Darfur. The *New York Times* described Zoellick as "a diplomatic lone ranger with 3 × 5 cards." Much of his previous government service involved negotiating trade agreements, and he saw himself as bringing the "comparative advantage" of economic thinking to his State Department diplomacy.[43] Rice spoke to the press before Zoellick's departure to

---

38. Eric Reeves, "Darfur Mortality Update: June 30, 2005," *Sudan Tribune*, July 1, 2005.
39. Eric Reeves, "Humanitarian Intervention in Darfur?" *Boston Globe*, April 17, 2005.
40. John Hagan, Wenona Rymond-Richmond, and Patricia Parker, "Press Release," Coalition for International Justice, April 21, 2005.
41. Kofi Annan, "Billions of Promises to Keep," *New York Times*, April 13, 2005.
42. Marc Lacey, "Nobody Danced. No Drugs. Just Fear. Some Holiday!" *New York Times*, April 22, 2005.
43. Joel Brinkley, "A Diplomatic Lone Ranger with 3 × 5 Cards," *New York Times*, April 17, 2005.

emphasize the importance she attached to the trip. So the press was attentive when Zoellick's visit produced a revised and highly unexpected, upbeat assessment of events in Darfur.

In a press conference held in Khartoum with the first vice president of Sudan, Ali Uthman Muhammad Taha, Zoellick startled reporters by declining to reaffirm Powell's earlier determination that genocide had occurred. When asked about the characterization of the conflict in Darfur as genocide, he answered that he did not want to "debate terminology."[44] He went on to dispute the then-prevailing consensus estimates of the number of deaths. Zoellick instead reported a new State Department estimate that as few as 60,000 and at most 146,000 "excess" deaths had occurred. The State Department subsequently posted a new report on its website, stating that "violent deaths were widespread in the early stages of this conflict, but a successful, albeit delayed, humanitarian response and a moderate 2004 rainy season combined to suppress mortality rates by curtailing infectious disease outbreaks and substantial disruption of aid deliveries."[45]

The reference to "excess" deaths was a sign that the new estimate was now tilting toward the public health side of a disciplinary divide, while simultaneously stepping away from its own victimization methodology. The more explicit sign of this shift was that the State Department had now chosen to exclude the results from its own ADS in its new estimate. This was a unique indication of the extent to which the new estimate was framed in the health paradigm of "complex humanitarian emergencies" rather than the war crimes context of genocide. The new estimate was based on the troubling assumption that the kind of survey work done by the WHO comprehensively measured the scale of mortality in Darfur.

Yet it was already clear from public statements by Nabarro that the WHO survey only represented a partial picture of the death toll, because it did not take into account those killed in the attacks on the villages that had provoked flight to the camps. Moreover, Zoellick's visit came just a week after the UN had given the names of fifty-one persons identified by its Commission of Inquiry on Darfur to the International Criminal Court (ICC) for possible prosecution.[46] The list of suspects included high-ranking Sudanese government officials, perhaps even Zoellick's vice presidential host and Sudanese President Omar al Bashir.

44. Robert B. Zoellick, "Press Briefing," United States Department of State, April 14, 2005, http://www.state.gov/s/d/former/zoellick/rem/44656.htm.

45. U.S. State Department Bureau of Intelligence and Research, *Fact Sheet Sudan: Death Toll in Darfur*, March 25, 2005, http://www.state.gov/s/inr/rls/fs/2005/45105.htm.

46. Warren Hoge, "International War-Crimes Prosecutor Gets List of 51 Sudan Suspects," *New York Times*, April 6, 2005.

The immediate response to Zoellick's announcement of the new estimate was shock. The *American Prospect*'s Mark Goldberg called the visit
"Zoellick's Appeasement Tour."[47] John Prendergast, speaking for the International Crisis Group, summarized the feelings of much of the NGO
community, saying "for Zoellick to float 60,000 as a low end number
is criminally negligent."[48] He added, "it's a deliberate effort by the Bush
administration to downplay the severity of the crisis in order to reduce the
urgency of an additional response. I find that to be disingenuous and perhaps murderous."[49] Prendergast, who served as a National Security Council official in the Clinton administration, also indicated a motivation for
the low estimate, saying "[w]e have not taken adequate measures given the
enormity of the crimes because we don't want to directly confront Sudan
when it is cooperating on terrorism."[50]

Nonetheless, State Department's new estimate had its apparently intended effect on major media news outlets. Whereas these sources were
previously regularly reporting *hundreds of thousands* of deaths in Darfur, boilerplate articles reporting of the death toll now shrunk to *tens of
thousands.*[51] Major mainstream news services—including Reuters, United
Press International, and the British Broadcasting Company—now included
the tens of thousands framing of the conflict as a stock phrase in their
news stories, a practice that would continue for more than a year. A picture soon began to emerge of why the State Department's Robert Zoellick
had shifted its framing of the conflict in Darfur. In short, as Prendergast
suggested, it supported earlier speculation about the Bush Administration's
war on terrorism.

The Osama bin Laden Connection

Within a week of Zoellick's return to the United States, the *Los Angeles
Times* reported that just prior to the announcement of the new mortality
assessment, the CIA had provided a jet to bring the Sudanese government
intelligence chief Major General Salah Abdallah Gosh to Washington.[52]

---

47. Mark Goldberg, "Zoellick's Appeasement Tour," *American Prospect Online*, April 29,
2005, http://www.prospect.org/cs/articles?articleId=9622.
48. Sue Pleming, "Aid Group Criticizes U.S. Policy on Sudan," Reuters, April 26, 2005.
49. Ibid.
50. Ken Silverstein, "Official Pariah Sudan Valuable to American War on Terror," *Los
Angeles Times*, April 29, 2005.
51. John Hagan and Wenona Rymond-Richmond, *Darfur and the Crime of Genocide*
(New York: Cambridge University Press, 2009), figure 4.2.
52. Ken Silverstein, "Sudanese Visitor Split U.S. Officials," *Los Angeles Times*, June 17,
2005.

The purpose of the visit was apparently to elicit information in the war on terrorism. The *Los Angeles Times* quoted State Department sources as attesting to the importance of Sudanese cooperation, following Sudan's role in the early 1990s in providing sanctuary to Osama bin Laden and a base for Al Qaeda operations. General Gosh now was quoted as saying "we have a strong partnership with the CIA."[53]

The *New York Times* reported that the CIA flew Gosh from Khartoum to Baltimore-Washington International Airport on April 17, returning him to Khartoum on April 22, making Gosh's trip coincide with Zoellick's stay in Sudan.[54] The *Los Angeles Times* reported Gosh met with CIA officials in Washington on April 21 and 22.[55] Zoellick arrived in Sudan on April 14 and his estimate was reported in the *Washington Post* on April 24.[56]

As chief of Sudan's intelligence and security service, observers have frequently charged that Gosh directed or at least knew of the role of the Sudanese military in the attacks in Darfur. A follow-up *Los Angeles Times* story indicated that the Justice and State departments were at odds over Gosh's Washington visit, with some in Justice Department suggesting that the trip would have been an opportunity to detain a suspected war criminal.[57] Instead, Gosh met with Porter Goss, the Bush administration CIA chief who later resigned under a cloud of allegations of bribery and government contract irregularities.

The suggestion that Gosh is a suspected war criminal is not new, and responsibility for his protective treatment extends beyond the United States. Alex de Waal writes: "the real power in Khartoum is not President Bashir, who is a pious, tough soldier, but a cabal of security officers who have run both the Sudanese Islamist movement and the Sudanese state as a private but collegial enterprise for the last 15 years.... And the members of this cabal are serial war criminals."[58] Congress also cited Gosh as having played a key role in orchestrating the genocide.[59]

Yet the Bush administration saw Gosh as potentially useful in its war on terrorism, and in May 2004, it had removed Sudan from its list of countries

---

53. Gosh had been an official "minder" of bin Laden during his time in Darfur. Silverstein, "Official Pariah."

54. Scott Shane, "C.I.A. Role in Visit of Sudan Intelligence Chief Causes Dispute within Administration," *New York Times*, June 18, 2005.

55. Silverstein, "Sudanese Visitor Split."

56. Editorial, "Darfur's Real Death Toll," *Washington Post*, April 24, 2005.

57. Silverstein, "Sudanese Visitor Split."

58. Alex de Waal, "Tragedy in Darfur," *Boston Review*, October/November 2004, http://www.bostonreview.net/BR29.5/dewaal.html. See also Julie Flint and Alex de Waal, *Darfur: A Short History of a Long War* (London: Zed Books, 2005).

59. Marisa Katz, "A Very Long Engagement: Bush Channels Neville Chamberlain," *New Republic*, May 15, 2006.

not cooperating with its counterterrorism agenda. The trip seemed intended to reward his past cooperation in providing information and to encourage the possibility of future assistance. The *Los Angeles Times* has continued to report on the links between the CIA and Sudan's security service—the Mukhabarat, noting that "Gosh has not returned to Washington since, but a former official said that 'there are liaison visits every day' between the CIA and the Mukhabarat."[60] In 2006, the State Department issued a report calling Sudan a "strong partner in the war on terror."[61]

It appears that the reduced mortality estimate and the temporarily suspended references to genocide were part of a cooperative strategy. President Bush did not mention the genocide in Darfur for over four months in 2005. In May 2005, the columnist Nicholas Kristof wrote: "Today marks Day 141 of Mr. Bush's silence on the genocide, for he hasn't let the word Darfur slip past his lips publicly since January 10 (even that was a passing reference with no condemnation)."[62] The nonpartisan Congressional Research Service indicates that although Gosh and other Sudanese officials played "key roles in directing [...] attacks against civilians," the administration was "concerned that going after these individuals could disrupt cooperation on counter-terrorism."[63] This was actually a return to a recurring policy dating at least to George H. W. Bush's administration, when it was reported that: "Washington bureaucrats turned a blind eye towards the policy of the authorities in Khartoum, mainly in the hope of securing their support for American goals in the Middle East."[64]

Gosh's visit generated benefits both for Sudan and for himself. Sudan subsequently was allowed to enter into a $530,000 public relations contract with a Washington-based lobbying firm, C/L International, although it was in violation of Executive Order 13067—which prohibits U.S. companies and citizens from doing business with Sudan.[65] Congress forced an end to this deal in February 2006. Moreover, Sudanese foreign minister Mustafa Osman Ismail met with Secretary Rice in Washington and was promised a review of economic sanctions, while Deputy Secretary Zoellick attended Sudan's presidential inauguration.

60. Greg Miller and Josh Meyer, "U.S. Relies on Sudan Despite Condemning It," *Los Angeles Times,* June 11, 2007.

61. U.S. Department of State, "Country Reports on Terrorism 2006," http://www.state.gov/s/ct/rls/crt/2006/82736.htm, ch. 3.

62. Nicholas Kristof, "Day 141 of Bush's Silence," *New York Times,* May 31, 2005.

63. Silverstein, "Official Pariah."

64. John Burton, "Development and Cultural Genocide in the Sudan," *Journal of Modern African Studies* 29 (1991): 511–20.

65. See Ted Dagne, *"CRS Issue Brief for Congress: Sudan: Humanitarian Crisis, Peace Talks, Terrorism, and U.S. Policy,"* Congressional Research Service, April 12, 2006, http://www.fas.org/sgp/crs/row/IB98043.pdf, 11.

More important, however, was General Gosh's success in evading personal sanctions. Gosh is reportedly ranked number two on the widely leaked UN list of senior Sudanese officials blamed for allowing, if not directing, the ethnic cleansing in Darfur by the *janjaweed* militias he is accused of controlling. One year after Gosh's visit to Washington and Zoellick's low death toll estimate announcement in Khartoum, the UN belatedly imposed sanctions on four men for Darfurian war crimes, but the most highly ranked and only government official was a Sudanese Air Force officer.[66] A senior State Department official, Donald Steinberg, explained that U.S. interests "cut on the side of not offending the regime in Khartoum." In other words, the Bush administration pushed to keep Gosh off the list.[67]

State Department's New View of Death in Darfur

To alter its perspective and reframe the killing in Darfur, the State Department had to reorganize its survey research by shifting attention away from its Bureau of Democracy, Human Rights and Labor (DRL) and Bureau of Intelligence and Research (INR). These two bureaus had worked together to produce the State Department/CIJ ADS survey of Darfur refugees in Chad and the *Documenting Atrocities in Darfur Report*. The State Department shifted its focus by outsourcing a reanalysis to a research group in Brussels at the University of Louvain's Centre for Research on the Epidemiology of Disasters. Working with Mark Phelan, a new liaison in a different part of the State Department who has extensive research experience in public health and nutrition surveys, and using surveys done outside the Department, the Brussels group reported the background details of the new low estimate that Deputy Secretary Zoellick had announced in Khartoum. This report does not provide the full details on the primary source surveys it relied on. However, the report is otherwise detailed in "Darfur: Counting the Deaths" and was the foundation for the State Department's new calculations.[68]

On the Sunday following his Khartoum announcement, the *Washington Post* reproached Zoellick regarding the validity of his mortality estimate in an editorial, "Darfur's Real Death Toll." The *Post* insisted "the 60,000

66. Warren Hoge, "UN Council Imposes Sanctions on Four Men in Darfur War Crimes," *New York Times*, April 26, 2006.

67. Katz, "Very Long Engagement," 25.

68. Debarati Guha-Sapir and Olivier Degomme with Mark Phelan, "Darfur: Counting the Deaths: Mortality Estimates from Multiple Survey Data," Centre for Research on the Epidemiology of Disasters, University of Louvain, School of Public Health, Brussels, May 26, 2005, http://www.cred.be/docs/cedat/DarfurCountingTheDeaths-withClarifications.pdf.

number that Mr. Zoellick cited as low-but-possible is actually low-and-impossible" and concluded that "next time he should cite better numbers." The editorial cited the estimate we had posted on the CIJ website to make its point.[69] Zoellick took the unusual step of responding with a letter of protest, in which he defended his actions and referred by implication to parallel disputes involving charges that Administration officials invented and stretched intelligence—in this case scientific surveys—to support policy preferences.[70] The description of the population-based survey mortality estimates as "intelligence" was unusual, but perhaps understandable when viewed in conjunction with the Washington visit of the Sudanese security and intelligence minister, General Gosh. Zoellick protested in his letter that: "I did not invent intelligence or stretch it. I did not recommend that the analysts change their assessment. I did indicate that estimates varied widely and that many were higher. Our estimate was based on more than 30 health and mortality surveys by public health professionals, and it was corroborated by a World Health Organization research center."[71] To support Zoellick's claim, the State Department had previously posted on its website a brief report, *Sudan: Death Toll in Darfur.*[72]

The corroborative role of the WHO-affiliated research center is more fully revealed in the outsourced report from the Brussels group, but here WHO's own characterization of this and the later Brussels "multiple survey" analysis is notable. A late May 2005 protocol from WHO concluded that "even if, overall, the findings of these surveys are consistent in showing broad spatial and time trends, they cannot be directly compared or combined in a meta-analysis due to differences in the study populations or methods utilized." A follow-up *Washington Post* article quoted a "senior State Department official" as saying that the report was "less scientific than you'd think."[73]

Why was the State Department now relying on a review involving Phelan, a health and nutrition expert, and based on uncited sources that reported results substantively at odds with its earlier report issued under Colin Powell? What were these uncited sources and what could they tell us about death in Darfur during this continuing conflict? How could scientific studies of such a lethal and protracted conflict produce such different

69. Editorial, "Darfur's Real Death Toll," *Washington Post,* April 24, 2005.

70. Robert Zoellick, "On Darfur, A Call for the Wrong Action," Letter to the Editor, *Washington Post,* April 27, 2005.

71. Ibid.

72. U.S. State Department Bureau of Intelligence and Research, *Fact Sheet: Sudan: Death Toll.*

73. Glenn Kessler, "State Department Defends Estimate of Deaths in Darfur Conflict," *Washington Post,* April 27, 2005.

conclusions? What can this experience tell us about the place of criminology in science and diplomacy? The answers to these questions may not definitively tell us whether outsourced scientific research in this episode was, to use Zoellick's words, "invented or stretched intelligence," but the answers do help to reveal the ways in which scientific research can flip-flop in response to demands of diplomacy, in this case involving a denial of the deaths of many Darfurians.

The answers again involve the health and crime perspectives applied in surveying the events in Darfur. The tension between these approaches is apparent from the outset of the outsourced Brussels report. In a broadside against the State Department's ADS work from the previous summer (i.e., the survey that was the foundation of Colin Powell's testimony about genocide to the UN and U.S. Congress), the Brussels report complains that "these interviews...were not designed in any way to function as a mortality survey nor was there an overall systematic sampling methodology used that could make it representative of the roughly 200,000 refugees that fled to eastern Chad, much less of the entire 2.4 million people affected of Darfur."[74] Yet the ADS applied a probability sampling methodology described above, and that is explicitly described in the State Department's *Documenting Atrocities in Darfur*.[75] Why would the Brussels report suggest otherwise?

The answer at least partly involves the criminal-victimization approach as contrasted with the public health approach followed in the earlier State Department/CIJ work. Despite the common social and political causes of the health and crime dimensions of such humanitarian emergencies, epidemiologists and demographers are inclined to focus mainly on health outcomes in order to support the provision of relief (food, medicine, and shelter) for conflict-affected populations suffering elevated mortality levels, whereas criminologists prioritize issues of legal responsibility.[76] As has been noted, a common sequence in these emergencies involves the onset of violent attacks, the flight of the resulting victims, and ensuing health problems that all contribute to mortality. The challenge is to simultaneously keep in mind the cumulative and multiplicative effects of violence, flight, and displacement to concentrated encampments, and the political state and nonstate origins of these disastrous consequences.[77]

74. Guha-Sapir and Degomme, *Darfur: Counting the Deaths*, 7.

75. U.S. Department of State Bureau of Democracy, Human Rights, and Labor and Bureau of Intelligence and Research, "Documenting Atrocities in Darfur," State Publication 11182, September 9, 2004, 5–7.

76. John Hagan and Scott Greer, "Making War Criminal," *Criminology* 40 (2002): 231–64.

77. John Hagan, Heather Schoenfeld, and Alberto Palloni, "The Science of Human Rights, War Crimes, and Humanitarian Emergencies," *Annual Review of Sociology* 32 (August 2006): 329–49.

A New and Alternative Approach

Because the estimation of the death toll has been such a source of controversy and is widely believed to be central to a genocide charge, we developed an alternative approach to this estimation that did not rely on the ADS and instead took advantage of a unique study that bridged the concerns of the crime and health perspectives. The study was led by MSF[78] and published in the *Lancet* in October 2004.[79] The study was conducted in four displacement camps in West Darfur between April and June 2004, with recall periods from one to six months between October and June 2004, probably the most violent period. In retrospect, the limitation of sites is easy to understand: the Sudanese government would not authorize the scale of sampling required across many sites to representatively study the wide-ranging violence in Darfur.

As the larger WHO study, MSF found within-camp violence to account for only 6 to 21 percent of the deaths across several camps. But the MSF study also asked about the period leading to flight to three of the four camps, with nearly 90 percent of these deaths resulting from violence. In these camps, the village and flight CMRs (5.9–9.5) were much higher than the camp CMRs (1.2–1.3). Heavy rains and worsening camp conditions subsequently increased the camp mortality rates in the WHO study, and another camp studied by MSF already had a mortality rate heading into this period of 5.6. Overall, the average mortality rate across the four MSF camps—with pre-camp violence included in three of the camps—was 3.2. Note that this combined rate is approximately the same level of mortality we estimated above with the joined State Department/CIJ and WHO/SMH studies.

We concluded that it would be more persuasive to develop a new and alternative estimate that adopted the second State Department's approach of estimating mortality in Darfur on a month-by-month basis and that took advantage of the different time periods included in the MSF camp surveys. The latter use essentially the same sampling design as the WHO survey, although the former are limited to five camps in the state of West Darfur, while WHO surveyed camps in North and South Darfur as well. Both the MSF and WHO surveys report age-specific CMRs and some information on violence, although we have emphasized that the MSF surveys systematically included pre-camp as well as in-camp mortality. The

---

78. For a fascinating account of MSF and other French NGOs, see Johanna Siméant, "What Is Going Global? The Internationalization of French NGOs 'Without Borders,'" *Review of International Political Economy* 12 (2005): 851–83.

79. Evelyn Depoortere et al., "Violence and Mortality in West Darfur, Sudan (2003–4): Epidemiological Evidence from Four Surveys," *Lancet* 364 (2004): 1315–20.

strongest feature of the WHO surveys is the number of camps included, while the strongest feature of the MSF surveys is the coverage of pre-camp and in-camp mortality. We draw on the strengths of both sets of reports in our new estimate. We initially narrow the focus to the survey-estimated CMRs for nineteen months of the conflict and the state of West Darfur, and then draw broader conclusions. The risk population for corresponding months is taken from the UN humanitarian profiles of people counted in the internal displacement camps and people surrounding the camps who together constitute what the UN calls "conflict-affected persons." We include UN refugee camp counts in Chad to complete the estimate of the population at risk.

Our new estimate involves calculations of direct and indirect monthly estimates of CMRs to better take into account sources of over- and under-reporting of deaths. The premise is that if we have two estimations with contrasting upward and downward biases, then we can look for a more realistic estimate of the actual death toll in-between these upper and lower bound projections.

The direct estimation method is based on CMRs that are calculated for all age groups in the surveys. Our concern with regard to the ADS work in Chad is that respondents could use extended definitions of their families to include grandparents, uncles, aunts, cousins, and even more distant relatives in their reports of deaths. Put differently, these directly reported CMRs for family members of all ages likely are upwardly biased by reports of deaths of extended, as well as nuclear, family members, because kinship boundaries often expand and become more inclusive in response to war.

The indirect estimation method we use is alternatively based on CMRs that are calculated for only family members under age five. We expected that these reports are less likely to include extended family members because respondents are focused in a more narrow way when they are asked about their own children. (There is a different source of survivor bias involved in underreporting for this age group. These reports are likely downwardly biased by uncounted children whose entire unrepresented families have died.) Life tables for sub-Saharan Africa are used to estimate the full age distribution of mortality in peacetime, and violence is then reincorporated into the estimate based on the proportion of violence reported in the surveys.[80]

We found that the overall rise and decline in estimated deaths in West Darfur is consistent with a classically described pattern of complex

---

80. The results of this new alternative estimation approach are presented in an article by John Hagan and Alberto Palloni, "Death in Darfur," *Science* 313 (2006): 1578–79.

humanitarian emergencies. The peak mid-point monthly level of deaths estimated for West Darfur is about 4,000. There is reason to believe that deaths are distributed evenly across the three Darfur states. If this is so, the estimate is that the death toll in Darfur peaked in early 2004 at about 12,000 per month. Note that this figure is between the WHO estimate of 10,000 and our earlier estimate of 15,000, which combined the findings of the WHO and ADS. This 12,000-peak monthly death estimate does not include missing persons and is intended to provide a cautious baseline figure.

We can also now say something more specifically about the nineteen months that are most thoroughly surveyed in West Darfur in 2003–4, and then suggest some broader conclusions. When the mid-points between the high and low monthly death estimates are summed over nineteen months, the number of deaths is 49,288. When the right tail of this distribution is extended to May 2006 using additional data from a subsequent WHO survey, the death toll is 65,296 in West Darfur alone. This estimate covers thirty-one months of the conflict that has now been underway for more than four years. If further months of conflict were well estimated, and/or if all or most missing or disappeared persons were presumed dead, the death estimate would be much higher.

Largely as a result of the violence, more than one million individuals are now displaced or affected in West Darfur. About one million people are similarly displaced in each of the adjoining states of North and South Darfur. If the same ratio of death to displacement applies across states, this implies that close to 200,000 deaths have occurred over thirty-one months in Greater Darfur. This calculation divides the difference between the potential upward and downward biases of the direct and indirect methods. If the high direct and low indirect bands of estimates are extended across the three states for thirty-one months, the range is between 170,000 and 255,000 deaths. Thus, it is likely that the number of deaths for this conflict in Greater Darfur is higher than 200,000 individuals. If extended for another thirty-three months of the conflict to bring the mortality figures up to date, and include the dead and missing, the number of deaths is likely to be in the range of well over 400,000.[81] This estimate is particularly conservative given that the initial twelve months of conflict is not included. Since the government of Sudan has sharply curtailed survey work in Darfur, it is not possible to be more precise than this.

---

81. In a recent conference at Yale University, Luis Moreno Ocampo claimed, "as of today, 5,000 people are dying each month in Darfur." See Julie Flint and Alex de Waal, "Case Closed: A Prosecutor without Borders," *World Affairs: A Journal of Ideas and Debate* (Spring 2009), http://www.worldaffairsjournal.org/2009%20-%20Spring/full-DeWaalFlint.html.

Crime and Health Diplomacy

Although number of deaths is certainly not the only measure of genocide, scale is one inescapable aspect of the public understanding of this crime. We have demonstrated a tendency for health-oriented research to underreport violent deaths in what are characterized in this field as complex humanitarian emergencies. The U.S. State Department in April 2005 shifted its focus away from its ADS study of criminal violence and victimization in Darfur. It featured in its place a collection of studies that emphasized health-oriented surveys of disease and malnutrition in producing a low estimate of mortality in Darfur. In the period immediately following the State Department's low estimate, major news organizations joined in a pattern of reporting tens of thousands rather than hundreds of thousands of deaths. During this same period, the State Department stopped describing the Darfur conflict as genocide. Although former president Bush and the State Department have since then sometimes reasserted the genocide charge, there is also credible evidence that policy on this issue has been counterbalanced by an effort to nurture an alliance with the Sudanese government in the war on terrorism.

This article underlines the difference between crime- and health-oriented research and the political as well as humanitarian purposes in violence-driven disasters. It is not difficult to understand the cautious approach taken in health-oriented research. Two events in the spring and summer of 2005 highlighted the problems of sustaining important working relationships in countries like Sudan where the humanitarian needs are staggering.

The first event was the arrest of two senior MSF officials in Sudan after their NGO published a study reporting hundreds of rapes in Darfur. The second event was a meeting convened by the MacArthur Foundation of ICC representatives with NGOs doing aid work in Darfur. One representative at this meeting observed that "[n]obody wants to do anything that will compromise the security of workers on the ground or their ability to do their job." Another representative remarked that "gathering information for war crimes investigations is not part of our mission"; still another one said that "security for our staff and beneficiaries is totally dependent on how we are perceived in the area."[82] These are the problems that restricted MSF's mortality study to a handful of camps, that limited the WHO/SMH mortality survey to deaths occurring in the camps and not those that

---

82. Carol Giacomo, "Aid Groups to Meet War Crimes Prosecutor on Darfur," *Sudan Tribune,* June 17, 2005.

preceded flight to camp, and that led the State Department/CIJ to undertake its initial survey in the neighboring Chad refugee camps.

When the respective findings of such studies are not understood in terms of their limitations as well as possibilities, the results can be misleading and lend themselves to flip-flopping interpretations. The problem is not the underlying science. The problem is more likely the diplomatic purposes to which the science is put, with knowledge of the dimensions of the first genocide of the twenty-first century hanging in the balance. The conclusion reported in more than 100 newspaper articles worldwide—that hundreds of thousands rather than tens of thousands have died as a result of the conflict in Darfur—resulted in the State Department's politically motivated estimate being displaced from the public's mind.

9

Accounting for Absence

THE COLOMBIAN PARAMILITARIES
IN U.S. POLICY DEBATES

Winifred Tate

When describing his "million" trips to Bogotá as the coordinator of the Plan Colombia Interagency Task Force in the final months of 1999, Ambassador James Mack recalled the chilly meeting rooms in the colonial office buildings, and spoke at length and with pride on his role in promoting aerial fumigation. Yet when asked about paramilitary massacres in the region targeted for U.S. assistance, he replied, "What massacres? We knew the AUC [paramilitary umbrella group] carried out massacres in other areas of the country, in the north. There were massacres in Putumayo?...I can't remember any massacres in Putumayo."[1] Right-wing paramilitaries linked to local army outposts had moved into the Putumayo region, long a guerrilla stronghold, beginning with the massacre of more than twenty-six people on January 9, 1999 in the small hamlet of El Tigre and continuing throughout the area over the next several years. At the same time, the United States made the southern province of Putumayo, then the production site of the majority of the world's coca, the centerpiece of the billion-dollar aid package known as Plan Colombia. In the subsequent years of debate over the more than six and half billion dollars

This chapter is part of a larger project that examines U.S.-Colombian relations, the origin of Plan Colombia, and its implications in Putumayo, through fieldwork in Washington, D.C., and Putumayo, Colombia. This research consists of a combination of oral history interviews with policymakers and archival research with declassified and public government documents conducted while a visiting research fellow at the National Security Archive. I thank Michael Evans at the Archive for his invaluable assistance. I also draw on my experience as a policy analyst at the Washington Office on Latin America from 1998 to 2001, a progressive advocacy organization focusing on changing U.S. foreign policy toward Latin America.
   1. Author interview, January 17, 2008, Washington, D.C.

in U.S. assistance to Colombia, the majority destined for the Colombia military and police forces, paramilitary forces played a minimal role.[2] The absence of paramilitaries as a policy issue in these debates can only be explained by considering the ways in which particular narratives are deployed to explain violence statistics and drug production in the debates over U.S. foreign policy toward Colombia. This chapter contributes to discussions of how foreign policy issues are framed and the ways in which specific causal narratives are attached to statistics in order to naturalize certain policy options as "common sense" and erase others from serious discussion. What objects, people, and events count and get counted, and what remains unseen and uncounted, are critical for understanding these issues.

There is a long-standing and growing literature examining the limitations of statistical analysis in policymaking. Policy scholars, primarily political scientists, have developed an extensive literature exploring these issues.[3] Anthropologists as well have begun considering these issues, many in terms of larger questions of how governance is enforced and maintained over populations. Anthropologists "explore the cultural and philosophical underpinnings of policy—its enabling discourses, mobilizing metaphors, and underlying ideologies and uses."[4] Rather than simply evaluate policy in terms of their stated objectives, anthropologists explore governance as a problematizing sphere of activity that frames experiences as problems to be resolved in order to manage, regulate, and shape both individual behavior and social life.[5] Much of the new anthropological scholarship on policy has taken up James Scott's admonition to "see like the state," in which he posits "legibility as a central problem of statecraft."[6] In this work and others, scholars consider the process of governance as analyzing the administrative procedures and reporting that categorizes, and problematizes, the population into actionable policy issues.

Absence—that which is not counted—is just as central to this critical inquiry as understanding the process of producing statistics. Brazilian legal

2. This figure includes aid from 2000 until 2009 (estimated). See http://justf.org/Country? country=Colombia&year1=2000&year2=2009&funding=All+Programs&x=89&y=6.

3. See the introductory chapter to this volume for a more complete exploration of this literature.

4. Janine R. Wedel, Cris Shore, Gregory Feldman, and Stacy Lathrop, "Toward an Anthropology of Public Policy," *Annals of the American Academy of Political and Social Science* 600 (2005): 20–51, 34.

5. See Jonathon Xavier Inda, ed., *Anthropologies of Modernity: Foucault, Governmentality and Life Politics* (Malden, MA: Blackwell, 2005). For other ethnographic examinations of how the development and interpretation of statistics constitute a central part of governance, see Susan Greenhalgh, *Just One Child: Science and Policy in Deng's China* (Berkeley: University of California Press, 2008); and John Comaroff and Jean Comaroff, "Fighting Crime: Quanitfacts and the Production of the Un/real," *Public Culture* 18 (2006): 209–46.

6. James C. Scott, *Seeing Like a State* (New Haven: Yale University Press, 1998), 2.

theorist Boaventura da Sousa Santos has developed the idea of a "sociology of absences" to explore why alternative critiques and policies fail to thrive as part of his work on the World Social Forum and other alternative globalization social movements. He describes such a sociology as:

> An inquiry that aims to explain that what does not exist is, in fact, actively produced as non-existent, that is, as a non-credible alternative to what exists. The objective of the sociology of absences is to transform impossible into possible objects, absent into present objects.... Nonexistence is produced whenever a certain entity is disqualified and rendered invisible, unintelligible, or irreversibly discardable.[7]

The sociology of absences is a critical notion in the ethnography of policy. The absence of specific social actors in policy debates, and the failure to consider some phenomena as a social problem worthy of policy solutions, are produced through material and cultural processes, and not the natural or inevitable result of inherent qualities of social issues. Such an approach entails not simply mapping the existing policy discourses but also a focus on the institutions and individuals and the kinds of knowledge and policy action they produce. Because numbers and statistics often play a central role in policy debates, exploring the context of these debates to determine what is not counted that could contribute to alternative frameworks is an important part of such efforts.

This chapter focuses on the role of "framing" as central in policymaking, and the availability of certain narratives to explain problems and position specific policies as inevitable and reasonable. Theories of frame alignment, which examine how the representations of events and issues mobilize support for specific kinds of policies, have been important analytical tools for understanding the work of social movement organizations.[8] This theory was developed as a bridge between social psychological and resource mobilization views, based on Erving Goffman's "frame," which functions to organize experience and guide action. Scholars considering foreign policy have also begun to put these theories to use in order to examine the role of narratives produced by the media, policymakers, and pundits in shaping

---

7. Boaventura da Sousa Santos, "A Critique of Lazy Reason," Centro de Estudos Sociais, http://www.ces.uc.pt/bss/documentos/A%20critique%20of%20lazy%20reason.pdf, 14.

8. For more on frame alignment theory, see David Snow, E. Burke Rochford, Jr., Steven K. Worden, and Robert D. Benford, "Frame Alignment Processes, Micromobilization, and Movement Participation," *American Sociological Review* 51 (1986): 464–81; and David Snow and Robert Benford, "Framing Processes and Social Movements: An Overview and Assessment," *Annual Review of Sociology* 26 (2000): 611–39. For an example of a case study of frames used to articulate specific foreign policy alternatives, see Christian Smith, *Resisting Reagan: The U.S. Central America Peace Movement* (Chicago: University of Chicago Press, 1996), 231–79.

policymaking.[9] In many cases, numbers and statistics play a central role in such narratives. The apparent transparency of numbers and the centrality of what anthropologists have called "audit culture" (with a focus on measurable benchmarks for assessment) have placed more amorphous elements that are more difficult to measure—such as political culture, attitudes and affinities, forms of social coercion and identities—outside the realm of serious policy discussion, despite their central role in policy outcomes.[10] The limitations of numbers and reporting are particularly clear in the case of illicit economies, as many scholars have pointed out, given the lack of credible indicators, and because such behavior is by definition hidden.

Human rights groups, journalists, United Nations officials, and government prosecutors produced evidence of paramilitary ties to Colombia security forces and ongoing participation in drug trafficking. They were successful in convincing critics among Democratic congressional staffers and nongovernmental activists to argue against the policy; however State and Defense department officials and the majority of members of Congress continued to view paramilitary groups as only a marginal issue. In their view, lower rates of direct abuses attributed to the military forces were the result of reform, not collusion with the paramilitary forces that became responsible for the majority of political violence as the rates of military responsibility declined. In subsequent years, these policymakers interpreted the reduction in paramilitary violence, particularly of the spectacularly brutal massacres that characterized paramilitary territorial expansion in the first years of the twenty-first century, as a sign of their waning strength rather than as evidence of their consolidated power. Efforts to evaluate U.S. assistance programs have focused on competing statistics of hectares of coca grown and eradicated, rather than more nuanced attention to shifts within drug trafficking organizations. As these examples show, learning the lessons that numbers tell us is complicated and requires close attention to the intimate dynamics of complicated conflicts.

A Brief History of Colombian Paramilitary Organizations

Over the past decade paramilitary forces under the umbrella of the United Self-Defense Forces of Colombia (AUC) transformed themselves

9. Robert Entman, *Projections of Power: Framing News, Public Opinion and U.S. Foreign Policy* (Chicago: University of Chicago Press, 2004).

10. For a discussion of audit culture and its implications in higher education, see Marilyn Strathern, ed., *Audit Cultures: Accountability, Ethics and the Academy* (New York: Routledge, 2000).

from regional renegades to political operators respected in many quarters as valid interlocutors worthy of sitting at the negotiating table with the government. This metamorphosis involved changes in paramilitary tactics as well as a substantial public relations campaign aimed at changing public perceptions at home and abroad. These groups began new and wider military operations in the late 1990s, when they dramatically expanded their troop numbers and embarked on offensive military campaigns to conquer new territory. Paramilitary leaders carried out a public relations campaign employing a range of strategies to engender public acceptance of their role as political spokesmen for the government. Paramilitary groups were central in transforming the electoral map of Colombia, with significant links to a growing number of congressional and local politicians.[11]

Paramilitaries historically have acted in concert with and been supported by the state military apparatus, rather than in opposition to the state (an important exception to this is the paramilitary violent repression of state judicial efforts to investigate paramilitary crimes, particularly in relationship to the drug trade). Paramilitary groups have periodically been legally incorporated into counterinsurgency efforts, and the links between legal and illegal paramilitaries have historically been pervasive. The legal basis for state sponsorship of paramilitary organizations was Law 48, approved by the Colombian congress in 1968, allowing the government to "mobilize the population in activities and tasks" to restore public order.[12] International pressure and additional attacks against government officials led President Virgilio Barco to declare the creation of paramilitary groups illegal in 1989. The expansion of paramilitary groups in the 1990s coincided with the organization of legal rural defense forces, known as the "Convivir." Officially launched in 1995, the Convivir were enthusiastically supported by Alvaro Uribe during his tenure as governor of Antioquia (1995–98). Following numerous complaints of participation in human rights abuses, the Supreme Court of Colombia maintained the legal status of the Convivir in 1997, but prohibited it from collecting intelligence for the security forces and from receiving military-issued weapons.[13]

According to human rights groups and government investigators, during the first phase of paramilitary activity, there was considerable overlap between the civilians legally trained by local military forces in the 1970s and

11. See Leon Valencia and Mauricio Romero, "Informe Especial: Paramilitares y Politicos," *Lanzamiento Revista Arcanos* 13 (2007).

12. Michael McClintock, *Instruments of Statecraft: U.S. Guerrilla Warfare, Counterinsurgency and Counter Terrorism, 1940–1990* (New York: Pantheon Books, 1992), 222–23.

13. See Human Rights Watch, *Colombia's Killer Networks* (New York: Human Rights Watch, 1995); and Washington Office on Latin America, *Losing Ground: Colombian Human Rights Defenders Under Attack* (Washington, DC: WOLA, 1997).

illegal paramilitary death squads such as the American Anti-Communist Alliance (AAA), active in the Magdalena region. The first qualitative shift in Colombian paramilitary groups came in the 1980s, when money from the drug trade allowed such forces to grow from small groups linked to local military commanders to private armies. Unlike the death squad operations in other Latin American countries, the paramilitaries benefited from the spectacular resources provided by Colombia's most lucrative industry: drug trafficking.[14] During this second phase, the fusion of counterinsurgency ideology and illegal narcotics revenue produced one of the most lethal fighting forces in Latin America. As the owners of vast haciendas (the result of money laundering and efforts to buy their way into the landed gentry, known as the "reverse agrarian reform"), drug traffickers needed protection from the guerrillas, whose primary fundraising techniques involved *boleteo* (extortion), *vacunas* ("vaccination" against guerrilla attack), and increasingly, kidnapping of the rural elite. Paramilitary groups linked to drug cartels (particularly the Medellín Cartel) worked closely with Colombian military officers to eliminate suspected guerrilla sympathizers, while at the same time they attacked Colombian authorities who tried to investigate drug trafficking. Paramilitary groups were particularly vicious in targeting activists from the leftist parties, who enjoyed considerable support following the 1987 reforms allowing popular election of mayors and other local officials previously appointed to their posts.[15]

The third phase of expansion was marked by the creation of a national coordinating body of paramilitary groups, AUC.[16] Paramilitary leaders that had emerged from the cartel structure (including "Don Berna," the Castaño brothers, and Manuel Isaza) began to work with a new generation of regional drug traffickers and warlords, such as Salvatore Mancuso and "Jorge 40." Many of these leaders have been indicted by the

14. For more on this history, see Carlos Medina, *Autodefensas, Paramilitares y Narcotráfico en Colombia: Origen, Esarrollo y Consolidación: el Caso "Puerto Boyacá"* (Bogotá: Editorial Documentos Periodísticos, 1990); Alejandro Reyes and Ana Lucía Gómez, "Compra de Tierras por Narcotraficantes," in *Drogas Ilícitas en Colombia: Su Impacto Económico, Político y Social* (Bogotá: PNUD/ DNE/ Ariel Ciencia Política, 1997); and Mauricio Romero, *Paramilitares y Autodefensas, 1982–2003* (Bogotá: IEPRI, 2003).

15. Romero, *Paramilitares y Autodefensas;* and Steven Dudley, *Walking Ghosts: Murder and Guerrilla Politics in Colombia* (New York: Routledge, 2004).

16. For more on this history, see Francisco Cubides, "Los Paramilitares y su Estrategia," in *Reconocer la Guerra para Construir la Paz*, ed. Malcolm Deas and Maria Victoria Llorente (Bogotá: Grupo Editorial Norma, 1999); Mauricio Romero, ed., *Parapolitica: La Ruta de Expansion Paramilitar y los Acuerdos Politicos* (Bogotá: Corporacion Nuevo Arco Iris, Cerec, Asi, 2007); Francisco Gutierrez Sanin and Mauricio Baron, "Re-Stating the State: Paramilitary Territorial Control and Political Order in Colombia," London School of Economics Working Paper no. 66, September 2005; and Robin Kirk, *More Terrible Than Death: Massacres, Drugs and America's War in Colombia* (New York: Public Affairs, 2003).

U.S. government for drug trafficking. Following a summit in July 1997, the AUC issued a statement announcing an offensive military campaign into new regions of the country "according to the operational capacity of each regional group." Newly created 'mobile squads'—elite training and combat units—carried out these operations, which included numerous massacres targeting the civilian population in these areas. The July 1997 massacre in Mapiripán, Meta was the first step in implementing this new plan. Between July 15 and July 20, 1997, gunmen from the AUC took control of Mapiripán, killing at least forty people, and threatening others. The exact death toll could not be established, as many of the bodies were dismembered and thrown into a nearby river. Following a lengthy investigation, a military court sentenced General Jaime Uscategui to forty months in jail by a military court for dereliction of duty because he failed to respond to repeated requests for action by local authorities and his own subordinates.[17] AUC fighters carried out similar massacres throughout the country.[18]

Beginning in 2002, Uribe began to promote a "peace process" with the AUC leadership. Under the auspices of the Catholic Church, the first formal agreement between the government and five of the major AUC leaders was signed on July 15, 2003.[19] The first collective demobilization of paramilitary fighters occurred in November 2003; by the end of 2006, more than 32,000 people had participated in collective demobilization programs. A special jurisprudence, known as the Peace and Justice Law, was passed, granting legal privileges to demobilized paramilitaries who confessed their crimes. Testimony from demobilized paramilitary leaders and investigations by journalists and academics revealed extensive links among politicians, business leaders, and military officers since the early 1990s. These revelations became collectively known as the *parapolitica* scandal, with government prosecutors opening cases against more than 150 officials, causing the resignation of the foreign minister and the head of the national intelligence service, as well as members of congress, governors, mayors, and local officials. Investigations are ongoing as of this

17. One of the military officers who requested assistance, Colonel Lino Sanchez, was himself investigated for misconduct as a result of his public testimony in the case.

18. Among the many paramilitary massacres: May 16, 1998, in Barrancabermeja, Santander, 11 killed and 25 disappeared; January 9, 1999, in El Tigre, Putumayo, 26 killed and 14 disappeared; February 18, 2000, El Salado, Bolívar, more than 70 killed and disappeared; October 15, 2001, in Buga, Valle del Cauca, 24 killed; April 12, 2001, in Alto Naya, Cauca, 120 killed; January 17, 2001, in Chengue, Sucre, 36 killed. The total death tolls may be higher, as in many cases bodies were dismembered and scattered.

19. International Crisis Group, *Demobilizing the Paramilitaries in Colombia: An Achievable Goal?* (Brussels: ICG, August 2004).

writing.[20] Many analysts also criticized the demobilization process as contributing to impunity in Colombia by not fully investigating paramilitary crimes, and pointed to evidence of reorganized paramilitary forces, called "newly emerging groups" by government spokesmen, as evidence of the larger failure of the process to diminish paramilitary power.[21]

U.S. Policy: Counting Coca

Since the 1980s, despite Colombia's long running civil war, U.S.-Colombian relations have focused on counternarcotics issues. The U.S. sponsored few general development and poverty alleviation programs because Colombia is considered a middle income country and did not experience financial crises of other Latin American countries. Colombia was also not a priority for U.S. military assistance; despite the special relationship between the U.S. and Colombian security forces that began during the Korean War, the United States focused instead its on military efforts on Vietnam in the 1970s and Central America in the 1980s. In the late 1990s, however, the escalation of the armed conflict, increased coca cultivation within Colombia, and a severe economic crisis generated significant concern within Washington. The Plan Colombia package, passed in 2000 with an initial funding of $1.2 billion, built on existing policy initiatives but marked a significant shift in scale. Rather than primarily devote resources to supporting Colombian National Police counternarcotics programs, Plan Colombia made the Colombian military the central partner in U.S. anti-drug efforts and the beneficiary of the majority of aid. Instead of targeting traffickers through interdiction efforts, the United States now concentrated on coca eradication as the central counternarcotics strategy. In both arenas, numbers played a central role in controversy over military reforms and the rate of coca cultivation. These priorities also facilitated the marginalization of paramilitary groups in the debates.

Throughout the early 1990s, U.S. counternarcotics efforts in the Andean region had focused on interdiction, interrupting drug trafficking routes of coca paste from Bolivia and Peru to Colombia through the air bridge denial program and of cocaine from Colombia to the United States by the

20. John Otis, "Court Tell-Alls Tie the Elite to Paramilitary Killings," *Houston Chronicle*, May 20, 2007; Romero, ed., *Parapolitica*; and the website *Verdad Abierta* (The Open Truth), established by Colombian investigative journalists with international funding to compile information about the process, http://www.verdadabierta.com/web3/.

21. International Crisis Group, "Colombia's New Armed Groups," Latin America Report no. 20, May 10, 2007; Human Rights Watch, *Letting Paramilitaries Off the Hook* (New York: HRW, January 2005); "Preocupante Aumento de Bandas Armadas en Colombia," *Semana*, November 26, 2008.

Cali and Medellín Cartels.[22] The Drug Enforcement Administration and other U.S. agencies played a central role in pursuing and killing Pablo Escobar, the famed head of the Medellín Cartel, and dismantling the Cali Cartel.[23] During this period, almost all U.S. assistance was funneled to the Colombian National Police, led by the much praised General Serrano, who developed critical allies among Republican congressional staff. Debates over U.S. policy toward Colombia were devoted almost exclusively to examining the number and kind of military hardware destined for the Colombian National Police and their success in combating major cartel operations.

Many scholars of the drug trade argue that this focus on the demise of the cartels is misleading. Some, including Francisco Thoumi and Michael Kenney, argue that classifying trafficking operations as cartels is inherently misleading, describing these black market enterprises as only loosely integrated.[24] They and others have traced the ways in which the disintegration of the Medellín and Cali "cartels" did not lead to a reduction in trafficking, but rather a reorganization of their operations. Following the well-publicized death and arrest of the major leadership of the cartels, many of their associates continued trafficking in new forms, including reconfiguring their hitmen squads as paramilitary armies. The Northern Valle cartel was the largest and best known of these organizations, incorporating many of the remnants of the Medellín Cartel including several paramilitary leaders. Many drug traffickers linked to the Medellín Cartel, among them the Castaño brothers Diego Murillo (alias Don Berna) and Salvatore Mancuso, established independent trafficking operations that financed in part their leadership of expanding paramilitary armies. As of March 2009, seventeen high-ranking paramilitary leaders have been extradited to the United States to face drug trafficking charges.

Yet coca production became the largest funded and most visible focus of U.S. counternarcotics operations. Beginning in the mid-1990s and in part because of the success of counternarcotics policies elsewhere, Colombia became the world's primary source of coca, grown by small farmers throughout the expansive southern flood plains and jungles. U.S.-sponsored

---

22. For more on U.S. drug policy and relations with Colombia, see Russell Crandall, *Driven by Drugs: U.S. Policy Towards Colombia* (Boulder: Lynne Rienner, 2008).

23. Mark Bowden, *Killing Pablo* (New York: Penguin Books, 2001).

24. Francisco Thoumi, "The Numbers Game: Let's All Guess the Size of the Illegal Drug Industry!" *Journal of Drug Issues* 35 (2005): 185–200; and Francisco Thoumi, *Illegal Drugs, Economy and Society in the Andes* (Baltimore: Woodrow Wilson Center/Johns Hopkins University Press, 2003). Michael Kenny, *From Pablo to Osama: Trafficking and Terrorist Networks, Government Bureaucracies, and Competitive Adaptation* (University Park: Pennsylvania State University Press, 2008).

counternarcotics programs in Colombia targeting coca production for eradication employed fumigation—massive aerial spraying of chemical herbicides. Fumigation programs were first carried out in southern Colombia in 1996, and were dramatically expanded through Plan Colombia.[25] Manual eradication programs, used in Peru and Bolivia proved impossible in the region because of security concerns, primarily fear of guerrilla attacks. Although the United States began to offer support for alternative development programs in the region with Plan Colombia funding, security concerns severely hampered these efforts as well.

Within the United States, much of the debate was devoted to assessing the number of hectares sprayed and ongoing total coca production. The Central Intelligence Agency, the State Department, the United Nations, and the Colombian government each produced competing and often widely divergent coca production and eradication statistics, which were then used by supporters and critics of the policy to argue their case.[26] Critics argued that fumigation simply displaced coca production into new areas, and that drift of chemicals on wind current prevented accurate assessment, while State Department officials argued that GPS systems used on the spray planes allowed precise tracking. Ambassador James Mack, the coordinator of the Inter-Agency Task Force that designed Plan Colombia and now an official with the Organization of American States counter-narcotics program, recalled that there was a "titanic debate with the CIA over what [coca] had been killed or not."[27] He described the CIA as using "old Cold war technology, using cameras that relied on intelligence information to focus on specific areas in small areas," which were then used to estimate the average production in a given region. The Narcotics Affairs Section of the State Department produced its own numbers, using color photography from overflights, also based on intelligence but producing, Mack argued, "more comprehensive surveys." State Department officials argued that the CIA classified existing but uncounted coca as new production, making the program appear a failure. The United Nations employed satellite

25. Latin America Working Group, "Blunt Instrument: The United States' Punitive Fumigation Program in Colombia," Washington, D.C., 2002; Betsy Marsh, "Going to Extremes: The Aerial Spraying Program in Colombia" (Washington: Latin America Working Group, 2004).

26. Central Intelligence Crime and Narcotics Center, "Latin American Narcotics Cultivation and Production, Estimates 2001," Washington, D.C., 2002; General Accounting Office, "Drug Control: Coca Cultivation and Eradication Estimates in Colombia," Washington, D.C., January 2003; Latin America Working Group, "The Numbers Game: Coca Cultivation in Colombia," Washington, D.C., April 2003; United Nations' Drug Control Program, "Colombia: Annual Coca Cultivation Survey 2001," Bogotá: March 2002; John Wash, "Reality Check: Latest U.S. Coca Cultivation Estimates," Washington Office on Latin America, 2007.

27. Author interview, January 17, 2008, Washington, D.C.

photography to produce their numbers, which according to Mack have less resolution and do not include anything less than a hectare. Other interagency disputes over coca figures included what counted as dead coca that had been eradicated, and what was simply overgrown land. Numerous NGO reports focused on these issues, as critics argued that the overall production of coca in the Andean region remained constant and cocaine, the final product and ostensible target of these programs, remained cheap and plentiful on U.S. streets.[28]

There were no similar systems focusing on tracking the numbers of tons of cocaine, nor were the newly reorganized trafficking structures subject to similar scrutiny in public debates.[29] In part this reflected the difficulty of obtaining such statistics. Coca was grown in the relative open, and coca farmers were peasants with few resources. Cocaine refining and transit was hidden and protected by powerful, wealthy traffickers, including paramilitary warlords. Paramilitary strongholds along the Urabá gulf, Atlantic Coast, and Magdalena Valley were drug trafficking routes but coca cultivation remained concentrated in the southern lowland jungle regions, where the Colombian guerrillas had historically been strong.[30] These factors, and the focus on coca eradication rather than interdiction, contributed to the marginalization of paramilitaries in U.S. debates.

Coca eradication programs in southern Colombia did dovetail neatly with growing U.S. concern about the Colombia guerrillas, particularly the Revolutionary Armed Forces of Colombia (FARC). In large part financed by taxation and increasing involvement in coca production in their traditional southern strongholds, the FARC had expanded significantly throughout the 1990s, although the exact profits derived from the drug trade and other forms of income are disputed.[31] This growing

28. Adam Isacson, "Colombia Coca Cultivation in 2005," Center for International Policy, Washington, D.C., April 15, 2006; Latin America Working Group, "The Numbers Game: Coca Cultivation in Colombia," Washington, D.C., April 2003); John Wash, "Reality Check: Latest U.S. Coca Cultivation Estimates," Washington Office on Latin America, June 11, 2007; United Nations' Drug Control Program, "Colombia: Annual Coca Cultivation Survey 2001," General Accounting Office, "Drug Control: Coca Cultivation and Eradication Estimates in Colombia," Washington, D.C., January 2003.

29. For a more detailed discussion of the issues in the production of the statistics detailing narcotics production and trafficking, see Peter Andreas's chapter in this volume.

30. By the mid-2000s, this was no longer true; over the course of the implementation of Plan Colombia coca cultivation has spread throughout the country including paramilitary-controlled enclaves in the north.

31. See Marc Chernick, "Economic Resources and Internal Armed Conflicts: Lessons from the Colombian Case," in *Rethinking the Economics of War: The Intersection of Need, Creed, and Greed,* ed. Cynthia J. Arnson and I. William Zartman (Washington, DC: Woodrow Wilson Center and Johns Hopkins University Press, 2005).

military power allowed the guerrillas to employ the methods of a standing army, attacking army barracks in small towns throughout 1997 and 1998, eventually taking more than 800 soldiers and policemen hostage, some of whom remain in their control more than a decade later. The United States had long been a vocal critic of what U.S. policymakers perceive to be pervasive links between the guerrillas, particularly the FARC, and drug traffickers. U.S. ambassador to Colombia Lewis Tambs coined the phrase "narco-guerrilla" in the mid-1980s. Many official statements have repeated this preoccupation, despite limited evidence to support these claims throughout the 1990s, and abundant evidence that drug traffickers were deeply involved in supporting paramilitary forces targeting guerrillas in many areas.

According to senior Defense Department and U.S. Southern Command officials, Defense Intelligence Agency personnel were monitoring FARC behavior closely during the 1990s, and noted with alarm their increasing activity and weapons capability by the end of the decade.[32] Within Washington, the guerrillas were widely described as controlling 40 percent of the country's territory, and could be considered a serious threat to the government, a figure that most scholars agreed grossly exaggerated FARC presence in many rural areas of the country. Plan Colombia supporter Tom Marks has suggested that the figures were a distortion of a 1997 army report that stated 13 percent of the country's mayors had direct links to the guerrillas, with another 44 percent describing some degree of collaboration.[33] Although the Colombian military had been historically resistant to accepting a counternarcotics mission, by the late 1990s, U.S. counternarcotics assistance proved to be a persuasive carrot. The military leadership began to link the guerrillas and the international narcotics trade, in an effort to gain access to U.S. assistance that continued to be limited by law to counternarcotics operations. A growing number of U.S. policymakers, including General Barry McCaffrey (first as head of the U.S. Southern Command and then as drug czar), declared counternarcotics operations and counterinsurgency operations were one and the same.

The Paramilitary Challenge to U.S. Assistance

Although the Plan Colombia aid package offered a dizzying array of programs designed "for democracy and the strengthening of the state" (as the presentation documents attest), the vast majority of the aid was destined

---

32. Author interviews, January–March 2008, Washington, D.C.

33. Thomas Marks, *Colombian Army Adaptation to FARC Insurgency* (Carlisle: Strategic Studies Center of the U.S. Army War College, 2002), 23.

for fumigation efforts and military assistance. The extensive military hardware and training made the Colombian army the primary U.S. operational partner, the biggest single shift in U.S. policy, which had long favored the Colombian National Police, and made understanding the nature of paramilitary violence and the human rights record of the Colombian military critical issues for justifying the package as it was designed.

The principle debate was over the significance of the decline in military abuses. During the 1990s, political violence in Colombia increased, but both critics and supporters of the Colombian military agreed that direct military participation in human rights abuses declined. According to the Colombian Commission of Jurists (CCJ), on average, ten people were killed daily in political violence in 1990; by 2000 that figure had risen to almost twenty a day.[34] Prior to the mid-1990s, the Colombian security forces were generally considered to be the worst perpetrator of abuses, with approximately 55–60 percent of abuses catalogued by NGOs attributed to the military and the police; by the end of the 1990s the percentage had fallen to less than 4 percent.[35] Beginning in the late 1990s, paramilitary groups were responsible for the majority of human rights abuses, according to the statistics presented by human rights groups. Military supporters, including within the U.S. military and the Clinton administration, claimed that the reduction in direct attribution of abuses was the result of genuine reform within the military. Critics pointed to the escalation of paramilitary abuses, and the evidence of collaboration between military and paramilitary forces, to argue that the military had not reformed but had replaced direct action with collusion.

This policy debate took on particular urgency because Plan Colombia made the Colombian military the major U.S. partner in counternarcotics, and later counterinsurgency, operations. At stake were the material resources offered by the United States to Colombian military and police

34. Comisión Colombiana de Juristas, *El Deber de la Memoria: Informe Sobre el Año 2004* (Bogotá: Comisión Colombiana de Juristas, 2005), 4.

35. Colombian homicide rates had peaked in the early 1990s, at more than 28,000 violent deaths a year (a rate of 86 per 100,000 inhabitants). Since then, the death rate has declined but remains extremely high; during my research in 2002, the homicide rate was 66 per 100,000 inhabitants, almost eleven times that of the United States. Guerrilla abuses, including a dramatic escalation in kidnapping, also increased during this period. Colombian NGOs generally catalogued these abuses as violations of international humanitarian law, and considered them as a separate category of political violence. Government statistics generally reported guerrillas as the major source of political violence during this period. A comprehensive discussion of violence statistics can be found in Gonzalo Sanchez's introduction to the edited volume, *Violence in Colombia, 1990–2000* (Wilmington: Scholarly Resources Books, Inc., 2001). The 2002 figures were found on the U.S. Department of State website (http://travel.state.gov/travel/colombia.html) and are based on figures provided by the Colombian government.

forces, approximately $5.2 billion dollars from 2000 to 2009.[36] Human rights conditions written into legislation during the 1990s, and included in Plan Colombia, established standards the Colombians had to meet to legally receive U.S. assistance. According to the Leahy Amendment, first passed in 1997 and now permanent law, the State Department is required to certify that U.S. counternarcotics funds are not being delivered to foreign military units facing credible allegations of human rights abuses unless corrective steps were taken. Complying with this provision required the State Department to negotiate a formal end-use monitoring agreement with the Colombian defense ministry, and vet the military units to which aid and training was provided. Congress also wrote human rights conditions into the Plan Colombia aid package. These require the State Department to certify yearly that members of the security forces credibly alleged to be involved with abuses were suspended and cooperating with investigations, and that the government was bringing members and leaders of paramilitary forces and the military officers supporting them to trial within the civilian court system. If these conditions were not met, Congress could freeze assistance and training scheduled to be provided to Colombia. Because of human rights concerns, some portions of U.S. assistance have been periodically frozen, travel visas to the United States for certain military officers have been canceled, and some individuals have been denied training opportunities.

With growing coverage of military links to paramilitary groups by human rights groups and journalists, concern about the Colombian military's ability to meet these requirements clearly affected U.S. policy in the region. The scale of U.S. military assistance, and the choice of the Colombian military as the major partner for U.S. operations, was not changed, but military strategy and aid delivery was designed to minimize human rights concerns. Rather than attempt to work with existing military units, the United States sponsored the creation of new counternarcotics battalions for operations in southern Colombia. These battalions were first developed in the late 1990s, then expanded through the Plan Colombia package. According to declassified U.S. embassy cables, during the initial discussions, both U.S. and Colombian officials raised the issue that in order to meet the Leahy Amendment requirements, new units would have to be created from scratch.[37] As Ambassador Mack recalled in a 2008 interview, "The

---

36. For a detailed breakdown of U.S. assistance, see http://www.justf.org.

37. Consider two examples from 1998. State Department Embassy Cable 11602, "Colombian Army Counter-Narcotics Battalion Proposed for USG Assistance" (October 15, 1998, Confidential), reports that in order to meet all the human rights objectives, the embassy intends to pursue with the Ministry of Defense the "possibility of standing up 'clean' new

first vetting was done on the unit that was created out of scratch, because we knew that some of the Colombian units had been involved allegedly in human rights violations, and the vetting was required by U.S. legislation. I think the vetting was probably one of the reasons that we decided to start all over again, from scratch, with a new unit."

Alternative Narratives

Human rights and progressive policy advocates attempted to convince policymakers that paramilitary violence required a complete revision of U.S. policy toward Colombia. In many cases, they drew on assumptions developed during opposition to U.S. policy in Central America, arguing that continued assistance to the Colombian military while they maintained ties with paramilitary groups replicated the failures of U.S. policy toward El Salvador in the 1980s. One congressional staffer who was a vocal opponent of the aid package's military component—who had also been an activist opposing U.S. military assistance to Central America—summarized the argument that the Colombian military was not reformed. "Looking at the human rights statistics, [in the early 1990s,] 80% were attributed to the armed forces. The next period, half a decade later, 80% attributed to the paramilitaries, because they were contracting out the wet work to the paramilitaries," she said. "The shift wasn't 50–50, it flipped, the flip was too dramatic. So, we conclude they outsourced the 'wet work'—it's a dirty mafia term," she grimaced and laughed. "But it is appropriate. That is when the links to *paras* became an issue. The lowering of the attributable human rights violations made it look like the Colombian military was being rehabilitated."[38] The argument that the Colombian military was essentially privatizing political violence was documented in Human Rights Watch's 2001 report, "The Sixth Division: Colombia's Military-Paramilitary

---

units comprised of pre-screened troops," concluding that "in the context of a major boost in designated assistance (e.g., counternarcotics battalion) the [Colombian military] might be willing to consider such a move." And State Department Embassy Cable 011674, "Ambassador and Minister Lloreda on Leahy Amendment" (October 16, 1998, Confidential), reported that in order to facilitate supplying aid, the Ambassador "raised the possibility of standing up new, clean units." In these discussions, both the Colombian minister of defense and the U.S. ambassador acknowledged that the existing Colombian legal institutions were unable to provide "effective measures" to address human rights violations as required by the Leahy Amendment. The cable reports that the Colombian defense minister "was not optimistic that Colombia could readily meet the Leahy amendments standard (i.e., effective criminal prosecutions in civil courts) for taking 'effective measures' to bring hr abusers to justice any time soon. He noted that a culture of impunity prevails in Colombia, and opined that civilian courts would not be much more effective than military courts, if at all, in bringing human rights abusers to justice."

38. Author interview, August 13, 2007.

Strategy." The title refers to the fact that the Colombian military has five official divisions, and argues that paramilitary groups in many regions function as an unacknowledged "sixth division" of the military.

The argument that the Colombian military had not reformed and was colluding with paramilitary forces was one of the central arguments put forth by opponents of Plan Colombia, led by Representatives James McGovern (D-MA) and Jan Schakowsky (D-IL) and by the nongovernmental organizations gathered as the Colombia Steering Committee. Much of the evidence for this position was based on research by human rights groups such as Human Rights Watch and Amnesty International. In addition to their congressional testimony, annual reports and lobbying efforts arguing ongoing military-paramilitary ties, Human Rights Watch released three reports focusing on military-paramilitary connections, "Colombia's Killer Networks" (1997), "Ties That Bind" (2000), and "The Sixth Division" (2001). The last of these concluded:

> HRW has compiled abundant, detailed and consistent information that most Colombian Army brigades, some Navy units and police detachments in prominent areas continued to promote, work with, support and tolerate paramilitary groups. At most, this means active coordination in the field with paramilitary units; permanent communication via radios, cellular telephones, and beepers; the sharing of intelligence, including the names of suspected guerrilla collaborators; the sharing of fighters, including active-duty soldiers serving in paramilitary units and paramilitary commanders lodging on military bases; the sharing of vehicles, including army trucks used to transport paramilitary fighters; coordination of army roadblocks, which are suspended to let paramilitary fighters pass; and payments made from paramilitaries to military officers for their support.[39]

Through policy briefs, lobbying, and speaking tours by Colombian activists, advocates attempted to build a constituency opposing military assistance on human rights grounds.

The other central argument for revising Plan Colombia focused on drug policy, and the claim that source-country interdiction and eradication programs were less effective in reducing the amount of drug abuse than domestic treatment programs. This argument has been well documented by drug policy reform institutions such as the Drug Policy Alliance, as well as libertarian and conservative think tanks including the Cato Institute and the Rand Corporation. Even those arguing against Plan Colombia in drug policy terms focused on the general ineffectiveness of source country

---

39. Human Rights Watch, *The Sixth Division* (Washington, DC: HRW, 2001), 2.

policies rather than highlighting the role of paramilitary groups in drug trafficking. However, arguments for redirecting U.S. drug policy gained little or no political traction in the Plan Colombia debates. Representative Nancy Pelosi (D-CA) argued during the initial discussions that money should be moved from the Colombia package to drug treatment programs in the United States, but this proposal was not adopted or even seriously debated. As many scholars have documented, building constituencies advocating reform to drug policies is notoriously difficult, and drug policy is traditionally viewed as a "third rail" issue in Washington.[40]

Information Politics: Minimizing Paramilitary Groups

These efforts were unsuccessful in shifting the dominant policy narrative, which minimized paramilitary groups and portrayed the Colombian conflict as the guerrillas against the government, linking the growth of the guerrillas to the narcotics trade and high levels of generalized violence. If mentioned, paramilitary groups were described as a localized reaction of the middle class to guerrilla violence in the absence of the state. As Ambassador Mack said, "Our view was that they emerged from the vacuum of power, the government had no capacity to fill their own territory. So first, there was the FARC and other smaller guerrilla groups. Then the AUC rises up to satisfy the felt need for security."[41] Policymakers often dismissed human rights concerns by saying paramilitary groups were the same as the guerrillas in that they were both responses to local grievances with no relationship to the state beyond minor local alliances in remote regions. This version of paramilitary history erases the two central factors that were critical in paramilitary expansion in the 1990s: their connection to the drug trade, particularly through a generation of leaders schooled in the Medellín Cartel, and the historic role of the state, particularly the military, in establishing and supporting paramilitary groups. This narrative also erased the paramilitaries as a significant policy issue, by positing that the paramilitaries would simply fade away once the guerrillas were defeated (or, presumably, negotiated with), and state authority reinstated.

40. See Eva Bertram, Morris Blachman, Kenneth Sharpe, and Peter Andreas, *Drug War Politics: The Price of Denial* (Berkeley: University of California Press, 1996); Michael Massing, *The Fix* (New York: Simon & Schuster, October 1998); Ted Galen Carpenter, *Bad Neighbor Policy: Washington's Futile War on Drugs in Latin America* (New York: Palgrave Macmillan, 2003); Jonathan Caulkins, Peter Reuter, Martin Iguchi, and James Chiesa, *How Goes the "War on Drugs"? An Assessment of U.S. Drug Problems and Policy* (Washington, DC: Rand Corporation, 2005).
41. Author interview, January 17, 2008.

Many analysts also went on to note that in as much as paramilitary forces were fighting the guerrillas, they could be considered allies of the state forces ("the enemy of my enemy is my friend"), and given the realities of guerrilla warfare, resources should be devoted to dealing with the state's central threat, the guerrillas. "You see that in Colombia, a lot of the attitude was that the AUC was a counterweight to the FARC, they were providing security in areas where the military can't," according to a former senior United States Southern Command (SOUTHCOM) official active in Plan Colombia. "That is the rationale that people use, that kind of attitude, of rationale, swirls around very much in these kinds of issues."[42]

Military analysts like David Spencer played an important role in articulating a narrative of paramilitary history that portrayed them as independent of state support and as sympathetic opponents of the guerrillas. Like many critics of U.S. policy, he had been schooled in policy debates in Central America in the 1980s, in his case supporting military assistance and working as a consultant for the Salvadoran department of defense. Currently a professor of national security studies at the National Defense University, during the initial Plan Colombia debates and design (1999–2001) he worked for the Center for Naval Analyses on studies including analyses of the Colombian counternarcotics brigades and the Marine Corps. Until 2003, as an independent contractor for U.S. agencies including the CIA, Department of Justice and SOUTHCOM, he worked on policy analysis, design, and implementation. In 2001, he authored a study—*Colombian Paramilitaries: Criminals or Political Force?*—published by the Center for Strategic Studies of the U.S. Army War College. In it, he focused on the emerging political claims of the paramilitaries, while minimizing the history of legal paramilitary incorporation in counterinsurgency doctrine and operations as well as their pervasive, illegal links with military officials. In the report, he described the paramilitaries as simply the logical result of guerrilla violence:

> The core of their intense violence is the pent-up anger and frustration of important sectors of the rural population at guerrillas who have terrorized the countryside for 30-plus years. This has been exacerbated by a state that has been unable to provide more than fleeting relief from insurgent violence. The atrocities of the paramilitaries are not acts of abnormal men, but rather the acts of normal men subjected to and victimized by unremitting violence, who see the disappearance of the guerrillas as the only sure solution to their plight.[43]

42. Author interview, April 30, 2008, Washington, D.C.
43. David Spencer, *Colombian Paramilitaries: Criminals or Political Force?* (Carlisle, PA: Center for Strategic Studies of the U.S. Army War College, 2001), 2.

Spencer uncritically accepts Colombian military statistics, for example using Colombian officers' inability to recall any counternarcotics operations against paramilitaries as evidence that "the guerillas seem to be more heavily involved in drug trafficking."[44] He consistently minimizes paramilitary attacks by erasing their high civilian death toll. He describes the Mapiripán massacre as a "bold strike at the heart of FARC-controlled territory. The people killed were not chosen randomly, but were deliberately targeted for their involvement with the FARC."[45] Although the area was, according to paramilitary pronouncements, chosen for its strategic importance to the FARC, the attack was carried out on unarmed civilians, and did not involve combat with the FARC. Spencer also does not mention the desperate efforts of the local judge to call military forces to protect the town, the dismemberment of living victims in the town's slaughterhouse over the course of a week, and the widespread allegations that military commanders in the region assisted in the paramilitary logistics.[46]

Of the "mainstream" think tanks, paramilitary groups were only a marginal concern. Groups like the InterAmerican Dialogue and the Council on Foreign Relations, prominent supporters of U.S. military assistance to Colombia, rarely featured paramilitary groups in their policy briefs and lobbying efforts. The Council on Foreign Relations' website entries on Colombia are typical. The Council's Americas program played a central role in producing widely circulated reports on Colombia policy, the result of a task force convened in 1999. Yet in their backgrounder titled: "FARC, ELN, AUC," the page devotes only two sentences to the AUC, with the remainder of the document explaining the history, development, and "terrorist attacks" committed by the FARC and the National Liberation Army (ELN).[47]

Senior State and Defense department officials report that the United States devoted few intelligence resources to following these groups. Then under secretary of state Thomas Pickering, who was charged by President Clinton with chairing the interagency task force that developed Plan Colombia, admitted that it was more difficult to obtain significant intelligence

44. Ibid., 11.

45. Ibid., 14.

46. For an alternative accounting of the massacre, see "Mapiripan: A Shortcut to Hell," by award-winning Colombian journalist María Cristina Caballero, first published in *Cambio16*, in the July 28 and November 3, 1997 issues and translated and published in the *Colombian Labor Monitor*, August 29, 1999, http://www.hartford-hwp.com/archives/42/074.html.

47. Council on Foreign Relations, "Backgrounder: FARC, ELN, AUC," http://www.cfr. org/publications/colombia. The website has since been updated with more extensive background publications that offer separate documents on the guerrillas and the paramilitary demobilization and *parapolitica* scandal.

on the paramilitaries than the guerrillas. In part this was because of intelligence sharing: the United States could benefit from Colombian intelligence gathered against the guerrillas, but did not offer information about paramilitary forces. Given the extensive evidence of widespread military collusion with paramilitary forces, that they did not provide intelligence to their U.S. allies on these groups is not surprising. According to Pickering, the "bulk of our technological collection was focused on the guerrillas for historical reasons, maybe political reasons."

Similarly, counternarcotics and counterinsurgency intelligence officials reported focusing on the guerrillas, while they waited for convincing evidence of paramilitary abuses and links with official sources from nongovernmental groups. Brian Sheridan was a former CIA agent who rose through the ranks as a Clinton appointee to the position of assistant secretary of defense for Special Operations and Low Intensity Warfare. He was one of the active architects of Plan Colombia, and deeply involved with the Colombia debates. As he reports, however, a focus on the guerrillas, and little active intelligence gathering on the paramilitaries, drove the policy debates. He recalled:

> What drove Colombia policy was that the situation kept getting worse, not the drug side but the guerrilla side....we had a completely different crowd, the intel guys, DIA [Defense Intelligence Agency], focused on counterinsurgency. They were even in a different office in DIA. They track every attack, every movement, all the weapons, everything. And they are seeing all this stuff, moving new weapons, 10,000 new rifles, etc.[48]

During the early 1990s, the primary focus was on the Pablo Escobar and the Medellín Cartel. Following Escobar's death in 1993, the FARC became their primary target. When I asked Sheridan about DIA reporting on the paramilitaries, he responded that they relied on NGOs to provide them with evidence of paramilitary activity. "When human rights groups would come to me, WOLA, Human Rights Watch, I would say, show me some evidence, something that I can sink my teeth into. Apart from that, I am inclined to adopt a more conventional view and see them as isolated cases." Although he had earlier said that they were "concerned" about paramilitary activity, he concluded with the oft-repeated military point that the paramilitaries were not attacking the Colombian military, and understandably were not a primary concern for the state. "When you talk to the Colombian military guys out in the middle of nowhere, they say, well, this guy is trying to kill me—the guerrilla—and this guy isn't, so guess which guy

48. Author interview, October 12, 2007, Washington, D.C.

I am going after. And you can't fault that logic. So my position was, absent the evidence, I am not going to go contrary to the national interest."[49]

State Department reporting on the number of paramilitaries also minimized their true strength. The AUC was added to the State Department list of designated terrorists on September 10, 2001, and beginning in 2002 was included in the State Department's annual "Patterns of Global Terrorism" report.[50] Despite the fact that breaking existing links between military officials and paramilitary groups was a stated objective of U.S. policy, the paramilitaries were consistently described as "supported by economic elites, drug traffickers, and local communities lacking effective government security," erasing their ties with the Colombian military acknowledged in other venues by State Department officials. The 2002 and 2003 reports described the growth of paramilitary groups, including their expansion into areas targeted by U.S.-sponsored operations. Beginning in 2004, the report focused on demobilization efforts.

The numbers of paramilitary members reported in the State Department's yearly accounting for terrorist activity is particularly striking. In the reports covering 2001 and 2002, the total number of members of the AUC was listed as "between 6,000 and 8,150."[51] In the report covering 2003, however, the numbers were revised upward, to an "estimated 8,000 to 11,000 and an unknown number of active supporters"; the report further noted that 1,000 paramilitaries had reportedly demobilized.[52] The report covering 2004 described the demobilization of 3,600 paramilitaries, with "about 8,000–11,000 remaining active paramilitary members with an unknown number of active supporters."[53] The report covering 2005 described 23,000 paramilitaries as demobilized, with "about 10,000 remaining active paramilitary members and unarmed support network members."[54] The report covering 2006 states that more than 31,000 paramilitaries have demobilized, that according to the Colombian government the AUC no longer exists, and that approximately 3,000 former members have

49. Ibid.
50. This section draws on the Office of the Coordinator for Counterterrorism, U.S. Department of State "Country Reports on Global Terrorism" (2004, 2005, 2006) and the "Global Patterns of Terrorism" (2001, 2002, 2003), http://www.state.gov/s/ct/rls/crt/index.htm.
51. These figures were included in Appendix B: "Background on Designated Foreign Terrorist Organizations," page 111 in the report covering 2001 and page 124 in the report covering 2002.
52. These figures were included in Appendix B: "Background on Designated Foreign Terrorist Organizations," page 137 in the report covering 2003.
53. These figures come from chapter 6: "Terrorist Groups," http://www.state.gov/s/ct/rls/crt/45394.htm.
54. From chapter 8: "Foreign Terrorist Organizations," http://www.state.gov/s/ct/rls/crt/2005/65275.htm.

"re-engaged with criminal activity."[55] Thus, from the report covering 2003 to that covering 2005, the paramilitaries went from a total high estimate of 12,000 members to 23,000 demobilized with 10,000 remaining—three times the previous total estimate of paramilitary forces. Yet this discrepancy was not debated during the assessments of ongoing U.S. assistance to Colombia.

Accounting for Massacres

Human rights reporting by the State Department and the United Nations High Commissioner for Human Rights Office in Colombia offers an opportunity to trace the ways in which accounting for paramilitary violence, and perceptions of their institutional positioning, have changed. A close reading of the 2002 State Department Colombia Country Human Rights report, using the 2001 report and the UN report for comparison, reveals consistent minimizing of paramilitary strength and activities.[56] These reports cover the Uribe administration's first year in office, as he was strongly lobbying for international support for paramilitary demobilization efforts. This period also marked a major shift in paramilitary tactics, from large-scale massacres employed to facilitate the take-over of new territory to consolidation of political control through intimidation, extortion, and selective assassinations. In covering the human rights situation of a close ally and partner, the 2002 State Department report emphasizes government pledges to reform while meticulously avoiding language ascribing military institutional collusion or support to paramilitary forces. The report avoids drawing conclusions about the pervasiveness of close relations between the regular armed forces and paramilitary forces, referring only to individual ties, while stressing progress in eliminating this relationship. Any criticism is presented alongside praise, with the emphasis on high-level rhetorical commitments to rights-respecting policies rather than examining ongoing paramilitary violence.

For time-pressed policymakers, the language of the report's summary is particularly important as few will read the report in full. A close reading of the summary of the report reveals significantly less detail on paramilitary

55. From chapter 6: "Terrorist Organizations," http://www.state.gov/s/ct/rls/crt/2006/82738.htm.

56. Department of Democracy, Human Rights and Labor, U.S. Department of State, "Country Reports on Human Rights Practices: Colombia" (2001 and 2002), http://www.state.gov/g/drl/rls/hrrpt/2001/wha/8326.htm; http://www.state.gov/g/drl/rls/hrrpt/2002/18325.htm. The Office of the High Commissioner for Human Rights Office in Colombia, "Report of the High Commissioner for Human Rights on the Situation of Human Rights in Colombia," E/CN.4/2002/17, February 28, 2002.

activity than guerrilla actions. Existing links with "some" members of security forces are mentioned only once in the summary, in the section on human rights. The paragraph focusing on the AUC does not mention any ties between the security forces and paramilitaries, unlike the 2001 report, which stated that "paramilitary forces still find support among the military and police." The proportion of killings committed by paramilitary groups is not mentioned in the summary (the previous year's report said that NGOs reported the majority were committed by paramilitary groups). Paramilitaries are not described as disrupting elections; guerrillas are.[57]

The required paragraph on the security forces does not refer to paramilitary structures. This contrasts with the same section of the 2001 report, which stated that: "Many observers maintain that government action to combat paramilitarism has been inadequate, and in the past security forces regularly failed to confront paramilitary groups." The 2002 report's paragraph on the security system concludes with a summary statement highlighting progress, even while acknowledging continuing abuses by individuals: "Over the years, the public security forces have taken important steps to improve their human rights record; however, some members of the armed forces and the police continued to commit serious of human rights abuses." A subsequent paragraph on paramilitary forces does not reference any official ties—unlike the same section in the 2001 report, in which evidence of such ties was the principal theme. Similarly, in the section on the arbitrary deprivation of the right to life, the military's commitment to break with abusive paramilitary forces is headlined.

The report states as fact that state security forces "doubled operations against paramilitaries during the year and quadrupled the number of paramilitaries captured since 2000," drawing uncritically on Colombian Ministry of Defense statistics. The United Nations Human Rights Report for 2002, in contrast, observes that in assessing Ministry of Defense statistics on paramilitaries captured or killed: "It should be borne in mind that such statistics are not easy to evaluate, since there is no means of knowing how many are really members of illegal armed groups and how many are civilians released after capture."[58]

The country report also suggests that the overall level of violence attributed to paramilitary forces was diminishing, without stating this directly.

57. In the section on elections, they include reports of intimidation by paramilitaries in favor of certain candidates, but dismiss this by saying that those candidates did not win. The UN report includes a paragraph describing paramilitary pressure over local authorities, control of local municipal budgets, and interference in local elections.

58. The Office of the High Commissioner for Human Rights Office in Colombia, "Report of the High Commissioner for Human Rights on the Situation of Human Rights in Colombia," E/CN.4/2002/17, February 28, 2002, 3.

The 2001 report said that NGOs had attributed the majority of political killings to paramilitary groups (in contrast to killings by opposition guerrilla groups and the regular security forces). In 2002 paramilitary forces are reported as having committed "numerous" abuses, considerably fewer such cases are detailed, and no indication of scale is given, although statistics on killings by guerrilla groups are included.

Descriptions of progress in reining in the paramilitaries contrast dramatically with the findings of the annual report on the same period prepared by the United Nations human rights office in Colombia. The UN report highlights government inaction in the face of evidence of paramilitary operations, describes the ubiquity of abusive paramilitary groups, and the evidence that the military persistently provides a shield for them. The United Nations report also cites reports in which the regular security forces went into areas in advance of paramilitary forces, and cases "where local inhabitants recognized members of the military forces among paramilitary contingents."

The State Department report describes only three specific instances of paramilitary crimes for 2002. In every case, the point of the description is to show that the military has taken steps to pursue those responsible. None of the cases in which military involvement was widely reported (including a massacre in El Limón, Guajira, August 31, one of numerous massacres described in the UN report) received attention. The collapse of high-level support for the former Attorney General's investigations of military involvement in massacres attributed to paramilitaries is not reported and the lack of progress in most ongoing prosecutions is not adequately covered. The report acknowledges that impunity remains "at the core of the country's human rights problems" but does not link this directly to the armed forces' continued resistance to prosecutions for paramilitary human rights crimes.

Accounting for the decline in paramilitary massacres is one of the central issues in the report, and in debates over the nature of Colombian political violence. Massacres have long been one of many contentious issues in human rights reporting in Colombia. In the general consensus for Colombian human rights reporting, a massacre involves three (although some sources use four) individuals killed at the same place during a single incident. Human rights advocates and critics of U.S. policy allege that the reduction was the result of changing paramilitary tactics, not a decline in their strength, as well as the difficulty in obtaining accurate information from many remote areas under paramilitary control. Once the AUC had established territorial control through massacres and selective assassinations, they employed different methods to consolidate political control. Paramilitary groups had also begun employing different tactics in order to evade human rights reporting, killing groups of people over several days, or scattering their bodies in different locations in order to not be counted as massacres.

The State Department 2002 report states in two different sections a "significant" and "dramatic" reduction in large-scale paramilitary massacres following AUC spokesman Carlos Castaño's public statement promising their reduction. The report attributes the reduction in paramilitary massacres to an improvement in the conduct of paramilitary forces, based on their public statements that they intend to respect international law. In contrast, the UN report explicitly attributes the decline in massacres to paramilitary public relations concerns rather than reform or reduction in strength. "In their search for legitimacy, and in order to lessen the impact of practices such as massacres, the paramilitary groups opted for selective killings and death threats, issuing specific instructions to this effect within their ranks."

In addressing the shift of paramilitary tactics from widespread violence to territorial control, the report mentions only one very well-known case of "social control" in Barrancabermeja, repeated from the previous year's report with some detail removed. The difference with the UN report is dramatic. The UN report concludes that the expansion of paramilitary activities into new areas of the country, and new arenas of political life, mark a fundamental shift in their strategy. "Such activities go beyond purely military aspects and include extortion and tighter control over the civilian population, plus control over access routes, State institutions and illegal trafficking (coca crops and contraband gasoline) and even agricultural, stockbreeding and commercial activities. In this way, paramilitarism has succeeded in permeating the social fabric by dominating its public and private sectors."

The UN report discusses the exercise of state functions by paramilitaries in many regions of the country, and the "persistence of links" between such groups and public servants:

> The expansion and consolidation of paramilitary forces in several areas under their control have enabled them to infiltrate the State system as part of their strategy, going so far in several regions as to set up a kind of parallel State, at great implicit risk to the continued enforcement of the rule of law. Perhaps the most blatant public sign of this de facto assumption of State functions, though by no means the only one, is the way they have imposed codes of conduct on the whole population. The Office in Colombia has received complaints of municipal or departmental decisions having to be approved by paramilitary chiefs, and of pressure being brought to bear on the choice of recipients of funds, with indications of where and how funds should be invested, or requiring public resources to be channeled through organizations under the paramilitaries' control.[59]

59. Ibid., 20.

Paramilitary Expansion and Public Relations

This shifting use of violence occurred as part of the paramilitary leadership's broader strategy to gain political recognition. Since their formal incorporation, the AUC has been engaged in a major public relations campaign to improve its image and represent itself as a legitimate political force. Their first communiqués copied the style of the guerrillas, issued with a dateline "from the mountains of Colombia" (previously, the guerrillas were the only armed actors inhabiting *el monte*), with a color logo in the letterhead of a peasant man silhouetted against a map of Colombia. In marked contrast to other forms of communication from paramilitary groups, such as the death threats intended to strike fear in the recipients (often sent in creative forms such as funeral invitations), these communiqués showcased the political nature of the organization. In addition to written communiqués, the paramilitaries began to use the Internet with a series of sophisticated web pages that reflected their preoccupation with public relations, launching Colombialibre.org in 1999. By 2005, the website was home to links to articles featuring paramilitary commanders and activities, as well as links to the home pages of the regional blocs making up the AUC, which featured their own communiqués and command structure diagrams.[60]

The AUC leadership under the command of Carlos Castaño also launched a media outreach offensive. After major interviews with the Colombian newsweekly *Cambio 16* in 1997 and 1998, widespread and apparently systematic interviews with the press began until 2000, including a prime-time television special in March of that year. Moreover, Castaño was featured on the cover of the international edition of *Time* magazine on November 27, 2000, and profiled in the *Washington Post* (under the headline, "King of the Jungle") on March 12, 2001. That same year, Castaño approved the release of *My Confession,* a fawning biography resulting from a series of interviews with a Colombian journalist; the book became a Colombian bestseller.[61] Regional paramilitary leaders also began appearing frequently in the Colombian press during this period. Following Castaño's disappearance on April 16, 2004, Northern Bloc commander Salvatore Mancuso was often featured in the press, and his biography (*Salvatore Mancuso: Life Enough for One Hundred Years*) was published in late 2004; in

60. As of June 2007, a reduced version of the "Colombialibre.org" website was dedicated to the "National Movement of Demobilized Self-Defense Forces," with empty pages and no links to regional groups.

61. Mauricio Molina, *Mi Confesión: Carlos Castaño revela sus secretos* (Bogotá: Oveja Negra, 2001).

May 2005 he launched his own website highlighting his analysis and speeches.[62] In his first press interview, Castaño's brother Vicente Castaño Gil was featured on the cover of Colombian news magazine *Semana* in June 2005. In the interview, he clearly attempted to position himself as a longstanding power behind Carlos's public face, and stressed the political evolution and focus of the paramilitaries under his command.

Paramilitary leaders also attempted to transform perceptions of their organizational structure and behavior through the publication of command diagrams and internal regulations, and the emphasis on their acceptance of human rights and international humanitarian law standards (in marked contrast to the guerrillas, who publicly rejected such norms). According to the Constitutional Statutes and Disciplinary Regime, adopted at the AUC's second national conference in May 1998, the organization developed a highly regimented military command structure incorporating regional groups. Part of their military discipline included instructing new recruits to obey international humanitarian law, also known as the rules of war, and to refrain from violating human rights.

In part, this was the result of active consultation with well-educated advisers. In his biography, Carlos Castaño claims to have worked extensively with Jesuit-trained intellectuals to develop the AUC's political strategy. International organizations, foremost among them the International Committee of the Red Cross (ICRC), also played a role. In 1997, the ICRC negotiated a new memorandum of agreement with the Colombian government allowing its representatives to have direct contacts with illegal armed groups. As a result of that agreement, the then head of the ICRC Pierre Gassman was one of the first international officials to meet with Castaño, and the ICRC began offering international humanitarian law training to paramilitary commanders and their groups.

This knowledge of international humanitarian and human rights law standards was incorporated into AUC military strategy. Mayors in three conflictive regions reported during author interviews in 2002 that paramilitary commanders told them paramilitary forces would continue to terrorize local populations who resisted their control, but would do that so their actions would not attract the attention of human rights activists, avoiding press-worthy massacres in favor of selective assassinations. Human rights groups developed a new category known as "multiple homicides," defined as the killing of four or more individuals in a single incident and at the same location and measured as a separate and particularly important

---

62. As of July 2007, the website was dismantled. After offering relatively extensive testimony to Colombian government prosecutors Mancuso was extradited to the United States to face drug trafficking charges.

human rights category. People in multiple homicides were killed over a period of several days and their bodies scattered, evidently in order to avoid
the designation of a massacre. Similarly, human rights and refugee groups
began reporting the "confinement" of populations, in which rural people
are prevented from traveling as a means of territorial control, rather than
forced displacement. The humanitarian issues caused by displacement
often attract international and governmental attention, including investigative commissions and humanitarian interventions. Confinement permits
paramilitary control in a region without attracting such scrutiny.[63]

Paramilitary leaders freely admitted that efforts to increase social control in the areas where they maintain a permanent presence were part of
their new strategy to expand their authority. Community and religious
leaders from areas where paramilitary groups have consolidated military
control including parts of southern Colombia, the Magdalena Medio region, and the northern coast have reported that paramilitary commanders
have begun to take over state regulatory functions—including mediating
domestic disputes, establishing codes of conduct and dress, and meting
out harsh punishments for community members who do not comply with
these codes. According to Comandante Andrés, a senior member of the
Norte Block, "We became the police in the region. If a woman says, 'my
husband hit me,' we have to solve their problems. We solve money disputes, and the issue of inheritances."[64] Despite the decline in homicides
in regions of consolidated paramilitary control, violence and intimidation
are still employed to enforce compliance. Religious leaders in southern
Colombia reported that young men who fail to obey the rules of conduct
in their communities were punished, first by having their heads shaven,
then with beatings, amputation of fingers, and even death. Paramilitary
commanders also freely admit that they are closely involved with official
structures of local governance in the areas they control. "We advise the authorities so they take advantage of the best opportunities for their communities," Comandante Andrés said. Both Jorge 40 and Salvatore Mancuso
made similar pronouncements during interviews.[65] The Bogotá Office of
the United Nations High Commissioner for Human Rights and the International Crisis Group have reported alleged links between paramilitary
groups and local government agencies including the Administrators of
the Subsidized (Health) Regime (ARS) and a Barranquilla-based government contracted tax collection service. They also reported links among

63. For more on the issue of confinement in Colombia, see U.S. Office on Colombia,
"Tools of the Colombian Conflict: Civilian Confinement and Displacement," January, 2005.
64. Author interview, January 14, 2005, Ralito, Colombia.
65. Author interviews, January 14, 2005, Ralito, Colombia.

paramilitary groups, political leaders, and the Administrative Department for Security (DAS, a specialized branch of the police), the Attorney General's Office in the department of Norte de Santander.[66]

Conclusion

The decline in the number of paramilitary massacres, and the large-scale participation of paramilitary fighters in government demobilization efforts, have been consistently offered by Colombian and U.S. officials as evidence of the paramilitary's declining strength, the reform of the Colombian military and the strengthening of the Colombian democratic state. "This critical ally of America has done all of the right things to try to bring stability, democracy, and prosperity to its own citizens," Secretary of State Condoleezza Rice said in a statement supporting further U.S. assistance for Colombia.[67] Here, I argue that alternative readings of these statistics based on a closer examination of the shifts in political violence demonstrates that the decline in the number of paramilitary massacres was the result of the consolidation of their political, economic, and military power, not their weakness. The public demobilization of their forces coincided with evidence of pervasive penetration of the Colombian political system by paramilitary leaders; the reorganization of paramilitary forces following their public demobilization demonstrate the ongoing weakness of Colombia democracy. As former High Commissioner for Peace Daniel García-Peña wrote in a 2009 editorial:

> The truth is that the mass demobilization did not mean the dismantlement of paramilitarism, but instead formed part of its consolidation. Such a large number of armed men was no longer needed. They had already killed the political and social leaders who had to be eliminated, and chopped up and displaced all the *campesinos* who had land that needed to be stolen. Mission accomplished. In addition, to maintain an army of mercenaries, at 500,000 pesos per month (about US$200) times 32,000 heads, requires a respectable amount of money. As a result, the business was an all-around success: the "reinserted" passed into the care of the public treasury and the paramilitary leaders remain with all the treasure they accumulated as a fruit of their terror, keeping only the strictly necessary number of armed men.[68]

66. The Office of the High Commissioner for Human Rights Office in Colombia, "Report of the High Commissioner for Human Rights on the Situation of Human Rights in Colombia," E/CN.4/2006/9, January 20, 2006; International Crisis Group, "Colombia: Towards Peace and Justice?" Latin America Report 16, March 14, 2006.

67. "Statement by Secretary of State Condoleezza Rice: Colombia Free Trade Agreement," March 10, 2008, http://bogota.usembassy.gov/sp_003_10042008.html.

68. Daniel García-Peña, "Poorly Named 'Emerging Groups,'" *El Espectador*, March 10, 2009, translation by the Center for International Policy, http://www.cipcol.org/?p=759.

These examples illuminate the limitations of numbers, in this case the numbers of paramilitaries and the numbers of massacres, in attempting to understand the underlying causal factors and dynamics of political violence. This issue should be of critical importance to policymakers, because myopic focus on these numbers without a more sophisticated and grounded analysis of their meaning ultimately undermines efforts to develop effective policies to address violence and build stability.

It is likely that the full extent of paramilitary crimes will never be known. The revelations of the *parapolitica* scandal offer evidence of paramilitary groups' institutional power, links to politicians, role in electoral politics, and ties to state resources. However, the Justice and Peace process, established to investigate demobilized paramilitary forces, is pitifully understaffed and underresourced.[69] As of March 2009, Uribe had extradited seventeen of the highest ranking paramilitary commanders to the United States on drug trafficking charges, in a move *Time* magazine reported as "widely interpreted as a move to halt the embarrassing revelations," as testimony implicated high ranking politicians, military officers who were also political allies of the president. "The mass extraditions have stymied Colombian prosecutors looking into paramilitary massacres and land grabs and hamstrung their efforts to compensate the victims of these crimes. True, the extradited all face lengthy prison terms in the U.S. But because they only have to answer for their drug crimes, the warlord defendants now have little motive for elaborating on their human rights atrocities back in their homeland."[70]

According to the chief prosecutor of Justice and Peace cases, more than 4,000 unmarked graves have yet to be located and exhumed. One important case is that of Heberth Veloza, a paramilitary leader who admitted to personally killing more than 100 people, and said that paramilitaries under his command were responsible for multiple massacres and the deaths of more than 480 people. Colombian prosecutors estimate these to represent about half of the crimes for which he is responsible. Veloza was extradited to the United States in early March 2009, in a move that Colombian prosecutors and human rights activists said would hamper their investigations and prevent finding the location of many of his victims.[71]

---

69. Adam Isacson, "The 'Justice and Peace' Process Takes a Grotesque Turn," June 24, 2007, Center for International Policy, http://www.cipcol.org/?p=431#more-431; Human Rights Watch Report, "Letting Paramilitaries Off the Hook," New York, 2005; Otis, "Court Tell-Alls."

70. John Otis, "Colombia's Drug Extraditions: Are They Worth It?" *Time*, February 25, 2009.

71. Frank Bajak, "Colombia Extradites Cooperative Warlord," Associated Press, March 6, 2009.

Similarly, it is impossible to know policymakers' full knowledge of Colombian paramilitary groups. Much of the relevant government reporting remains fully classified, and those documents that were released have been heavily redacted.[72] The relevant policymakers have yet to make full statements on the record. Whether or not the U.S. position was the result of ignorance or denial, however, the public minimizing of paramilitary groups was clearly the result of strategic denial. Strategic in that publicly acknowledged intelligence systematically minimized the threat of paramilitary forces, despite abundant open source evidence. This denial was also required by U.S. strategy in the region, which made Colombian military forces working with paramilitary groups in many parts of the country its major partners and aid recipients.

U.S. efforts in the region have failed to reduce cocaine production and trafficking, while Colombian demobilization programs have failed to dismantle the underlying power structures of paramilitary groups, replacing the leadership and members, but not the dynamic of privatized violence employed by elites and military officers to ensure economic and political control of specific regions. The Corporación Nuevo Arco Iris reported in *Semana* the emergence of more than 100 new militias, many with ties to older paramilitary groups. These groups are active in 246 of Colombia's 1,100 municipalities, and total an estimated 10,000 members.[73] According to the former director of the Jesuit think tank the Center for Popular Research and Education:

> They have not taken on the same forms of organizing and perpetrating violence, but they are all paramilitaries. Once they take over public posts, thanks to the terror they manage to inspire, the illegal bands re-establish extortion, in the clientelistic manner of traditional politics, but strengthened by the fear that massacres leave floating in the short memory of public opinion. It is a metamorphosis of armed violence into economic and social violence.[74]

The failure to understand the origins, history, causes, and nature of paramilitary groups in Colombia contributes to the ongoing failure to comprehend the current dynamics of political violence, evolving structures of illicit narcotics production and trafficking, and ongoing challenges to Colombian democracy. The revelations of the *parapolitica* scandal have

---

72. For a summary of available sources, see the National Security Archives Colombia Project, http://www.gwu.edu/~nsarchiv/colombia/index.htm.

73. "Preocupante Aumento de Bandas Armadas en Colombia," *Semana*, November 26, 2008.

74. Alejandro Angulo, "The Rearrangement," *Centro de Investigación y Educación Popular*, March 2009, http://www.cinep.org.co.

put into evidence what many critics of U.S. military assistance to Colombia have long argued: that the decline in direct military attribution of abuses did not reflect reform. Likewise, the reduction in the number of reported massacres did not signify withering of paramilitary forces. Rather, these numbers indicated changes in political and military strategy, with profound implications for U.S. assistance and the long-term development of the Colombian state. This case demonstrates that what counts as a significant policy issue, and how statistics are deployed to make the case for particular policy options, are not transparent or self-evident. Understanding policymaking, and policy outcomes, requires attention to the meaning assigned to statistics and the narratives that make such policies the norm.

10

(Mis)Measuring Success in Countering the Financing of Terrorism

Sue E. Eckert and Thomas J. Biersteker

One of the most oft-cited and highly touted success stories of the U.S. global effort to counter terrorism concerns the Bush administration's efforts to stem the flow of money to terrorists. In fact, the first official act of the Administration's campaign to counter terrorism after the attacks of September 11 took place on September 24, 2001—weeks before military action commenced in Afghanistan. In a well-orchestrated Rose Garden ceremony, President Bush launched "a strike on the financial foundation of the global terror network" by freezing the assets of eleven individuals, thirteen groups, and three charities suspected of funding Al Qaeda.[1] With the rhetorical flourish of "starving the terrorists of money," a process of regular presidential announcements commenced, demonstrating to the world that the United States was serious about pursuing financial targets.[2] Public designations of terrorists and blocking of bank accounts became the first indicators of progress in the effort to counter terrorism.

The commitment of acts of terrorism requires resources—the recruitment of human resources, training of those individuals, material for munitions, the dissemination of information (both before and after attacks),

1. "President Freezes Terrorist Assets," Remarks of the President, Secretary of the Treasury O'Neill, and Secretary of State Powell on Executive Order, The White House, September 24, 2001, http://georgewbush-whitehouse.archives.gov/news/releases/2001/09/20010924-4.html.

2. John Roth, Douglas Greenberg, and Serena Willie, "Monograph on Terrorist Financing" (Staff Report to the Commission), National Commission on Terrorist Attacks upon the United States (Staff Monograph), 2004, http://www.9-11commission.gov/staff_statements/911_TerrFin_Monograph.pdf.

and finance. It is for this reason that one of the central components of efforts to combat terrorism logically consists of attempts to cut off its financing. As such, there are four principal reasons for countering the financing of terrorism:

- Prevention—to prevent acts of terrorism or disrupt and reduce the impact of acts of terrorism that cannot be prevented;
- Deterrence—to educate people about the potential diversion of resources from legitimate purposes (charitable giving, for example) and provide them with an incentive to ensure their funds are properly utilized;
- Intelligence—to gather financial intelligence, which is among the most reliable tools in reconstructing networks after an attack (and potentially provides a basis for disrupting and preventing future attacks);
- Political utility—to garner public attention to counterterrorism efforts, demonstrate government resolve, and portray action/progress against terrorism.

This fourth and final point, political utility, is the reason why the politics of numbers matters so much in terrorist financing, as well as why the numbers and surrounding rhetoric are often politicized.

This chapter analyzes the politics of numbers in the terrorist financing realm by addressing the metrics of designations/frozen assets, political considerations underlying claims of success, obstacles to accurate measurement of progress, the discursive placement of qualitative and quantitative indicators in policymakers' statements, and alternative considerations regarding the effectiveness of policies to counter terrorist financing.

Political Context of Terrorist Financing

Prior to the attacks of September 11, 2001, terrorist financing was not an international or even U.S. priority, and there was little sense of urgency regarding the need for a strategy to combat terrorist financing.[3] The domain of a handful of government experts, financial sanctions were generally considered technical and arcane. Within two weeks of the attacks, however, President Bush harnessed the little known and understood tools of terrorist designations and assets freezes to launch the highly touted and much vaunted first front in the administration's global effort against terrorism. As President Bush announced on September 24, 2001,

---

3. Staff Monograph, 4–34.

This morning a major thrust of our war on terrorism began with a stroke of a pen. Today, we have launched a strike on the financial foundation of the global terror network...We will starve the terrorists of funding, turn them against each other, rout them out of their safe hiding places and bring them to justice....Money is the lifeblood of terrorist operations. Today, we're asking the world to stop payment.[4]

In what became known as the "Rose Garden Strategy," the President commenced a series of regular announcements concerning the freezing of assets of terrorist-related organizations. In doing so, an extraordinary process ensued, one that departed from traditional procedures to compile and verify evidentiary information about those listed. The rush to designate came primarily from the National Security Council staff, leaving the technical experts scrambling to deliver up targets. According to the then secretary of the treasury Paul O'Neill, a premium was placed on quickly seizing assets: "We just listed out as many of the usual suspects as we could and said, let's go freeze some of their assets."[5]

Much of the first phase of the effort to counter terrorist financing was dominated by two types of action, which together became the primary metrics associated with terrorist financing. Such measures were regularly cited by U.S. officials and widely reported in the media as early indicators of progress in the overall counterterrorism effort.

Terrorist Financing Metrics

The most commonly cited metrics associated with terrorist financing efforts are the number of individuals and entities designated on the lists of terrorists, and the amount of assets frozen or blocked.

Designations

One of the first quantitative indicators related to terrorist financing was the number of individuals and entities publicly designated through UN, regional (EU), and national (U.S.) listings. As of February 2009, the U.S. Treasury's Office of Foreign Assets Control (OFAC) had designated more than 500 individuals and entities as terrorists, including their financiers or facilitators since 9/11 (which also include U.S.-unilaterally listed terrorist groups such as Hamas and Hezbollah). The bulk of these designations occurred within the first year following the attacks, with the pace slowing in 2003. In subsequent years, the number increased only marginally—as of the

---

4. "President Freezes Terrorist Assets."
5. Ron Suskin, *The Price of Loyalty* (New York: Simon & Schuster, 2004), 193.

end of 2006, the number of Specially Designated Global Terrorists numbered 466, increasing only to 470 by September 2007. Of the 466 names, more than 340 individuals and entities designated by the U.S. government (USG) were also listed by the United Nations Security Council Committee, established pursuant to resolution 1267 (1999) concerning Al-Qaida and the Taliban and Associated Individuals and Entities ("1267 Committee").[6]

Assets Frozen

The total dollar amount of assets blocked is the other most frequently cited metric associated with terrorist financing. Within one month after the attacks, Treasury officials cited $4 million of assets frozen; within one year, $112 million had been frozen worldwide; by May 2003, the figure had climbed to $137 million. On the two-year anniversary of the 9/11 attacks, the *Progress in the War on Terrorist Financing* reported that the United States and its international partners had seized or frozen nearly $200 million in terrorist-related assets. This number appears to have been rounded upward, as the same document stated that $136.7 million in assets had been frozen worldwide (of which $36.6 million in the United States). Subsequent statements by USG officials raised the figure to $147 million in frozen assets as of January 2005.[7] No higher figure has since been found in government documents.

By the 100th day of the global campaign against terrorism, President Bush declared significant progress in attacking the terrorists' international financial network, in touting both of these metrics:

> Our attack on terrorist finances is progressing...The assets of more than 150 known terrorists, their organizations and their bankers have been frozen by the United States. One hundred forty-two countries have issued freezing orders of their own. The result: more than $33 million in terrorist assets have been blocked inside the United States; more than $33 million more have been blocked abroad by our partners in the international coalition.[8]

---

6. U.S. Department of the Treasury, Office of Foreign Assets Control, "Terrorist Assets Report, Fifteenth Annual Report to Congress on Assets in the United States of Terrorist Countries and International Terrorism Program Designees," 2006, http://www.ustreas.gov/offices/enforcement/ofac/reports/tar2006.pdf.

7. U.S. Department of Treasury, "Progress in the War on Terrorist Financing," September 11, 2003, http://www.treas.gov/press/releases/reports/js721.pdf. See also United Nations, "Security Council Committee Meets Senior U.S. Officials to Discuss Implementation of Sanctions Against Al-Qaida, Taliban," Press Release, November 1, 2005.

8. "The Global War on Terrorism: The First 100 Days," December 21, 2001, http://www.usembassy.at/en/download/pdf/globalwar.pdf. See also "President Blocks More Assets in Financial War on Terrorism," December 20, 2001, http://www.whitehouse.gov/news/releases/2001/12/20011220-11.html.

Problematic Nature of Indicators

Questions have been raised, however, about the reliability and significance of these figures. For example, the $147 million in frozen assets likely includes Taliban and Al Qaeda funds blocked prior to 9/11, pursuant to UNSCR 1267. The figure also appears to be cumulative and not a current total, because frozen Taliban funds subsequently were returned to the government of Afghanistan after the toppling of the Taliban regime.[9] Moreover, in comparing statements about frozen assets, considerable inconsistency is evident. Some USG statements cite $36 million of Al Qaeda funds frozen in the United States. However, the official annual report of the Treasury Department's Office of Foreign Assets Control claims that the United States retains $20.7 million of terrorist organizations as of the end of 2007, of which only $11.3 million was directly related to Al Qaeda (with an additional $8.7 million Hamas-related assets).[10] Indeed, the increasing amounts of funds frozen (and individuals listed) seem to have more to do with the addition of new groups and their affiliated front organizations than they do with the enhanced effectiveness of a global campaign against Al Qaeda finances. The increase in the USG totals come largely from the addition of new groups (organizations associated with Hamas and Hezbollah and the Liberation Tigers of Tamil Eelam) to the Office of Foreign Assets Control Specially Designated Terrorist list (OFAC SDT), not from the freezing of additional Al Qaeda-related accounts. The relative stasis of the total amounts frozen as noted in several 1267 Committee's monitoring team reports derives from the fact that there have been few new names added to the list.[11] As many international banks have concluded, virtually all of the funds related to Al Qaeda have already been frozen.

The total number listed also does not indicate the number of individuals and corporate entities under surveillance on the "gray" lists of the U.S. Treasury Department, that is, individuals under financial surveillance, but not publically listed. Given the highly classified nature of ongoing investigations, this would be impossible, for obvious reasons. Indeed, we do not

9. Approximately $261.5 million in Afghan assets were unblocked and turned over to the Afghan Interim Authority between February and April 2002 as the Authority established control over Afghanistan following the U.S.-led military campaign. U.S. Department of the Treasury, Office of Foreign Assets Control, "Terrorist Assets Report, Sixteenth Annual Report to Congress on Assets in the United States of Terrorist Countries and International Terrorism Program Designees," 2007, http://www.ustreas.gov/offices/enforcement/ofac/reports/tar2007.pdf.

10. "2007 Terrorist Assets Report."

11. See Eric Rosand's critique of the moribund nature of the Al Qaeda listing process in article by Colum Lynch, "UN-U.S. Actions Sometimes at Odds with Afghan Policy," *Washington Post*, July 5, 2007.

Box 10.1
Authoritative Sources: Skepticism Warranted

Even the most authoritative numbers concerning frozen assets, those from respected sources such as the 1267 Committee's monitoring team, raise questions on closer examination. Although the 1267 Committee reports are among the most authoritative cited and available, there is cause to question some of the estimates contained in its early reports.

For example, the current monitoring team acknowledged problems with the group's first report regarding the number of countries that have a legal basis for freezing assets. The report stated that "legal basis for freezing assets related to Al-Qaida, the Taliban and associated groups and entities now (25 August 2004) exists in all but three Member States." On closer scrutiny and questioning, a member of the monitoring team noted:

> I'm afraid the first report was wrong and in this respect not clearly worded. I think we revised our method of counting or of assessing what constituted a legal basis for freezing assets following our first report. Our latest published figures are in S/2005/761 Annex 1. In that we pointed out that 140 States had sent in a report under resolution 1455 (para 4) and that of these it appeared 117 had a "clearly identified" legal basis for freezing assets (para 20). I think what happened was that we reexamined what States claimed to be an adequate legal basis and found it wanting in several of them, despite their 1455 report. I am sorry to shake your faith in the accuracy of our reports, but it was the first one.[1]

---

1. E-mail correspondence between one of the authors and 1267 Committee monitoring team member, September 2007.

---

even know the scope of the ongoing surveillance activities. Our lack of knowledge about the gray lists renders the defenses of claims about the intelligence value of the countering the financing of terrorism (CFT) regime virtually impossible to evaluate.

In addition, there is conflicting information within the same organizations' reports. Previously the 1267 Committee's monitoring team cited a figure of $91.4 million in assets that remain frozen, but reduced it in the September 2007 report to $85 million, due to a mistaken identity by one state and the deduction of Taliban assets that were released to the Afghan government. The latter is based on reports from UN member states and does not include the cumulative figures reported by U.S. Treasury, hence its lower estimates. Such problems should make one skeptical about placing too much stock in even "official numbers."[12]

Moreover, discrepancies between figures used by the U.S. government and those provided by the 1267 Committee's monitoring team can be found, with the team consistently estimating lower amounts frozen worldwide. Notwithstanding these discrepancies and even acknowledging the limitations of these metrics, nearly every report between 2001 and 2008 by the monitoring team references the amount of assets frozen and/or number of designations as indicators in the fight against terrorist financing (see figure 10.1). Even so, according to the monitoring team, "Inevitably, the effect of the assets freeze is generally measured in terms of the amounts of assets frozen, but this overlooks the unquantifiable deterrent effect of the assets freeze on potential donors and its inhibiting effect on listed groups that have had to find alternative and perhaps more costly ways to move and store their money."[13]

Perhaps the clearest acknowledgement of problems associated with terrorist financing metrics comes from former USG officials who admit that neither the number of assets frozen nor terrorists designated are very reliable or particularly useful:

> [T]he metrics most often used to assess efforts against terrorism financing— the total amount of money seized and the overall number of designations— are both inadequate and misleading....It is impossible to "dry the swamp" of funds available for illicit purposes, but, by targeting key nodes in the financing network, we can constrict the operating environment to the point that terrorists will not be able to get funds where and when they need them. The number of overall designations is also misleading. It is not uncommon for a potential designation target to remain unnamed due to diplomatic or intelligence issues, policy considerations, or ongoing investigations. What we are left with are trends and anecdotes—most of them classified—that point to success.[14]

12. UNSC Committee established pursuant to resolution 1267 (1999) concerning Al-Qaida and the Taliban and associated individuals and entities, "Seventh Report of the Analytical Support and Sanctions Monitoring Team appointed pursuant to resolutions 1526 (2004) and 1617 (2005)," November 29, 2007, http://www.un.org/sc/committees/1267/monitoringteam.shtml, 18.

13. Ibid.

14. Matthew Levitt, comment as reported by Jake Lipton, "Follow the Money: Challenges and Opportunities in the Campaign to Combat Terrorism Financing," Washington Institute for Near East Policy, March 6, 2007, http://www.washingtoninstitute.org/templateC05. php?CID=2576; Matthew Levitt, "Finance as a Tool of National Security: Update on the

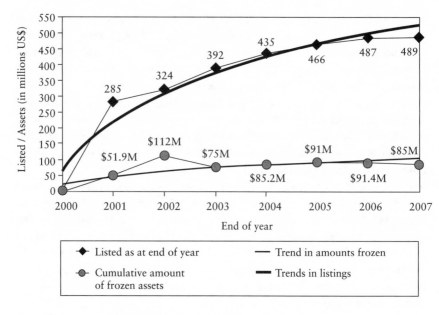

Figure 10.1. Impact of listings on the value of frozen assets
Source: Annex III, Seventh Report of the 1267 Monitoring Team (UN)

Shift from Metrics to Objectives

By 2002, it was clear that quantity of assets frozen as a metric was of diminishing political utility. The "low hanging fruit" had been secured, and the amount of additional assets to be frozen would necessarily decline. Acknowledging this, Deputy Secretary of the Treasury Kenneth Dam noted in June 2002 that the first phase of the financial front of the war on terrorism had been dominated by public designations of terrorists and attempts to freeze their accounts. "To be sure, this was—and remains—an important aspect of the fight against terrorist financing" but the effort had entered second phase, *one not able to be quantified,* and in which "public designations and blockings will not dominate."[15] Though it is unclear whether this shift away from numeric metrics was deliberate, or merely a change in the rhetorical characterization of terrorist finance, the early

---

Effort to Combat Terrorist Financing," Washington Institute for Near East Policy, November 29, 2007, http://www.washingtoninstitute.org/print.php?template=CO7&CID=385.

15. Kenneth Dam, "The Financial Front of the War on Terrorism: The Next Front," Speech to the Council on Foreign Relations, June 8, 2002, http://www.cfr.org/publication/4608/financial_front_of_the_war_on_terrorism_the_next_phase.html.

indicators came to be replaced with less quantifiable and more amorphous policy objectives.

This progression is most evident in the discursive discussion of terrorist financing in U.S. policymakers' statements. Since 2001, four primary rationales have been articulated regarding the objectives of terrorist financing measures.

The first concerns the importance of financial information as a critical investigative and intelligence tool. It was financial information that helped law enforcement establish the first links between the hijackers and other conspirators after 9/11. As noted by Treasury General Counsel David Aufhauser, "money is the Achilles' heel of a terrorist that leaves a signature which once discovered has proven to be the best single means of identification, prevention, and capture."[16]

The second objective articulated by the Bush administration was to degrade terrorists' capabilities by disrupting financial support. "Degradation of finances translates into a degradation in operational capability...without funds, terrorists cannot move around as easily or as quickly."[17]

Perhaps in part due to the difficulty of measuring the impact of terrorist financing policies, Bush administration officials began to focus on the isolation of terrorists and how terrorists view the measures: "Ultimately, the most revealing indicator will be how the target itself sees our measures. Although such information can be fragmentary and highly classified, we have seen high-ranking officials within terrorist or criminal organizations or regimes subject to our sanctions programs struggling to manage the effects of our measures and worrying about what may be coming next."[18]

Finally, one of the most oft-cited objectives of terrorist financing measures concerns deterring would-be supporters of terrorists.[19] Evidence exists that wealthy donors who previously supported charitable organizations with links to Al Qaeda have become more concerned about putting their financial

16. David D. Aufhauser, "Written Testimony before Senate Judiciary Committee on Terrorism, Technology and Homeland Security," June 26, 2003, http://www.kyl.senate.gov/legis_center/subdocs/sc062603_aufhaus.pdf.

17. Marshall Billingslea, Principal Deputy Assistant Secretary Of Defense For Special Operations/Low Intensity Conflict, Statement before the Subcommittee on Terrorism, Unconventional Threats and Capabilities, House Armed Services Committee, United States House of Representatives, April 2003, http://armedservices.house.gov/comdocs/openingstatementsandpressreleases/108thcongress/03-04-01billingslea.html.

18. Adam Szubin, Director, Office of Foreign Assets Control, Testimony before the House Committees on Foreign Affairs and Financial Services, April 18, 2007, http://financialservices.house.gov/hearing110/ht041807.shtml.

19. Matthew Levitt, comment as recorded by Drake Bennett, "Small Change: Why We Can't Fight Terrorist by Cutting Off Their Money," *Boston Globe,* January 20, 2008.

resources at risk and cut back on donations. The deterrent effect of terrorist financing policies continues to be one of the most powerful rationales.[20]

Thus, after an initial focus on the quantifiable indicators of frozen assets and designations, U.S. officials shifted their discursive treatment of terrorist financing policies from showcasing quantitative indicators to discussion of broad objectives which, however important, are essentially unquantifiable:

> But this is not a box score game. Only a small measure of success in the campaign is counted in the dollars of frozen accounts. The larger balance is found in the wariness, caution, and apprehension of donors; in the renunciation of any immunity for fiduciaries and financial intermediaries who seek refuge in notions of benign neglect and discretion, rather than vigilance; in pipelines that have gone dry; in the ability to focus our resources on those avenues of last resort; and in the gnawing awareness on the part of those who bank terror that the symmetry of borderless war means that there is no place to hide the capital that underwrites terror.[21]

(Mis)Perceptions of Success?

Despite many difficulties in verifying the accuracy of terrorist financing numbers, it is important to note how such measures have been broadly perceived as not only successful, but also among the *most* successful aspects of U.S. counterterrorism strategy. Administration officials' assertions of progress in terrorist financing have been taken largely at face value, with little questioning or critical scrutiny. Indeed, terrorist financing initiatives have enjoyed near universal support from across the political spectrum in the United States. Although the topic of terrorism is inherently political, it is not partisan. The only critique to be heard from the Congress concerns the need to do even more to sanction terrorists and proliferators such as Iran and North Korea, and to improve interagency coordination.

Such perceptions of success are particularly intriguing, given the fact that there has been no attempt to explain how the methodology behind the initial metrics (e.g., how the total amount of assets frozen was determined), or how conflicting numbers can be reconciled. The Bush administration neither volunteered such information on the public record (or in

20. The negative externalities associated with a reduction of charitable giving, however, should also be considered.

21. David D. Aufhauser, Written Testimony before the Senate Judiciary Committee Subcommittee on Terrorism, Technology and Homeland Security, June 26, 2003, http://www.au.af.mil/au/awc/awcgate/congress/terrorist_financing.htm.

classified form to the authors' knowledge), nor was it called by the Congress to account for claims of success. Such assertions remain unsubstantiated without the benefit of oversight and interrogation.

Moreover, authoritative sources such as the 9/11 Commission and its follow-up Public Discourse Project served to validate overall Administration claims. Without commenting on the effectiveness of terrorist financing initiatives, the 9/11 Commission recommended that tracking terrorist financing remain "front and center in U.S. counterterrorism efforts," while acknowledging that such efforts are not the primary weapon.[22] The *9/11 Commission Report* noted:

> While definitive intelligence is lacking, these efforts have had a significant impact on al Qaeda's ability to raise and move funds, on the willingness of donors to give money indiscriminately, and on the international community's understanding of and sensitivity to the issue. Moreover, the U.S. government has used the intelligence revealed through financial information to understand terrorist networks, search them out and disrupt their operations.
>
> While a perfect end state—the total elimination of money flowing to al Qaeda—is virtually impossible, current government efforts to raise the costs and risks of gathering and moving money are necessary to limit al Qaeda's ability to plan and mount significant mass casualty attacks. We should understand, however, that success in these efforts will not of itself immunize us from future terrorist attacks.[23]

The 9/11 Commission Public Discourse Project accorded its highest grade of A- for *"Vigorous effort against terrorist financing."*[24] Although there is no explanation as to the basis for the grade, it appears that the overall effort to convince other countries to combat terrorist financing, as well as the importance of financial information for intelligence purposes generally were important considerations.[25] Without specifically endorsing the Bush administration's claims of effectiveness, the grade implied success of the overall terrorist financing policy, which government officials routinely cited.[26]

22. National Commission on Terrorist Attacks Upon the United States, *9/11 Commission Report* (Washington: Government Printing Office: 2004), 382.

23. Staff Monograph, 16.

24. Thomas H. Kean et al., "Final Report on 9/11 Commission Recommendations," 9/11 Public Discourse Project, December 2005, http://www.9-11pdp.org/press/2005-12-05_report.pdf.

25. Ibid.

26. Stuart Levey, Under Secretary for Terrorism and Financial Intelligence, U.S. Department of the Treasury, Testimony before Senate Appropriations Subcommittee on Transportation, Treasury, the Judiciary Housing and Urban Development, and Related Agencies, April 6, 2006, http://www.treas.gov/press/releases/js4163.htm.

Beyond the validation provided by these groups, there is also considerable benefit-of-the-doubt accorded to any administration when it comes to security-related issues. There is a long tradition of deference to the Executive branch in security matters be it the U.S. courts, the Congress, or the public. This tendency to unquestionably accept statements and numbers from sources viewed as reliable has contributed to the lack of serious questioning or scrutiny of claims regarding success of terrorist financing policy. Given the unique position and overwhelming consideration accorded to security issues, there is reason to question if better information and more reliable quantitative metrics ultimately would make a decisive difference in these policy domains.[27]

Evaluating Policy Effectiveness

There are inherent difficulties in quantifying and assessing measures designed to counter terrorist financing. This is not an uncommon problem in the security realm, and well recognized in attempting to assess counterterrorism measures more broadly.[28] Most significant is the fact that much of the underlying information upon which such an evaluation could be made is classified. In fact, secrecy is frequently invoked in dealing with terrorism, some would claim to the point of being overprotected, as evinced by the June 2006 disclosure by the *New York Times* that the United States obtained financial information from the SWIFT messaging service.[29] If the information is not publicly available and cannot be discussed in a transparent manner, there can be no critical questioning of the policy or the characterizations of its effectiveness. We are left with assurances of "trust us," which former president Bush made clear would be the case in terrorist financing:

> I want to assure the American people that in taking this action and publishing this list, we're acting based on clear evidence, much of which is classified,

27. The circumstances surrounding terrorism and weapons of mass destruction are not unlike the cold war period, in which there was limited information about the true costs of export control policies. When efforts were made to understand and quantify the costs of regulatory policy, especially those borne by the private sector, ultimately such considerations were given little weight. No costs were compelling enough, when weighed against risks to national security. Perhaps this was due in part to the fact that the costs were essentially "free" for government, because industry bears the costs of regulatory policy.

28. Raphael Perl, "Combating Terrorism: The Challenge of Measuring Effectiveness," Congressional Research Service Issue Brief RL 33160, updated March 12, 2007, http://www.fas.org/sgp/crs/terror/RL33160.pdf.

29. Comments by Victor Comras, "Reports of U.S. Monitoring of SWIFT Transactions Are Not New: The Practice Has Been Known by Terrorism Financing Experts for Some Time," June 23, 2006, http://counterterrorismblog.org/2006/06/reports_of_us_monitoring_of_sw.php.

so it will not be disclosed. It's important as this war progresses that the American people understand we make decisions based upon classified information, and we will not jeopardize the sources; we will not make the war more difficult to win by publicly disclosing classified information.[30]

In particular, the staunchest advocates and supporters of U.S. terrorist financing initiatives tend to be former Treasury officials who have had access to classified information while in office, but cannot comment on specifics other than indicating that there are plenty of success stories. "Perhaps most important, prosecutions and designations should not be mistaken for the sum total of the counter-terror finance efforts, when in fact they are only the most visible."[31] We cannot assess what we do not know, leaving us with generic anecdotes of success, the veracity of which cannot be determined.

Even agreeing with former government officials that the total amount of money frozen or the number of people added to the list are inadequate measures of the effectiveness of efforts to counter the financing of terrorism, it remains extremely difficult to evaluate the degree of isolation and difficulty experienced by the targets. Exacerbating the problem of classified data is the more basic fact that there is simply no information available regarding the derivation of official numbers by the U.S. Treasury Department and even the 1267 Committee's monitoring team. There is a fundamental lack of concrete and verifiable data, making it impossible to measure success (or failure) on these criteria, impartially or objectively.

Assessing policy effectiveness also depends on how objectives are defined. If the criteria are so general as in the case of U.S. foreign policy export controls to "send signals," or so broad as to "make it more difficult for targets to use the international financial system," then claims of success cannot be disputed. Exactly what constitutes appropriate criteria to gauge effectiveness has not been debated. For example, according to Vice President Cheney the absence of terrorist attacks within the United States since 2001 is evidence of success, with the war in Iraq as "in part responsible" for the lack of further attacks.[32] Academic skeptics claim, however, that the end of terrorism, or at least a steep decline in acts of terror, should be an appropriate measure of success: "But in the parallel universe of the financial war, rules and processes have taken on a life of their own, and the measure of success is no longer a reduction in the number of acts of terror,

30. "President Freezes Terrorist Assets."

31. Matthew Levitt, "Are We Winning the Financial War on Terror?" January 25, 2008, http://blogs.law.harvard.edu/mesh/2008/01/financial_war_on_terrorism/.

32. Richard Cheney, "Interview of the Vice President by Sean Hannity," June 15, 2006, http://www.whitehouse.gov/news/releases/2006/06/20060615-13.html.

but rather the multiplication of rules and the hyperactivity of process. The much touted 'aggressiveness' of the global effort to counter the financing of terrorism was seen as synonymous with effectiveness."[33] Although a legitimate critique can be made that the Bush administration tended to conflate activity (be it the number of terrorist designations, amount of assets frozen, or suspicious activity reports filed by banks) with effectiveness, it is simply not credible to argue that success of counterterrorism measures should be defined by the end of terrorism. Neither of these extreme positions constitutes a reasonable criterion upon which to measure effectiveness of counterterrorist financing initiatives.

Are there more appropriate measures by which to gauge the effectiveness of terrorist financing policies? Perhaps we should begin by accepting that there are no definitive metrics by which success or effectiveness can be assessed, but rather a variety of information and indicators that can help paint an overall picture. For example, anecdotal information, including statements by terrorist groups, as well as the intelligence community's claims regarding sources of funding or difficulty terrorists have financing operations are important.[34] More public information regarding how financial intelligence has helped to disrupt terrorist plans would be helpful in supporting claims of success. Greater clarity regarding how the Treasury Department derived early statistics regarding frozen assets would be useful. Perhaps most important, an enhanced public dialogue, especially with the Congress and including greater oversight of classified initiatives, would go some distance in addressing the natural skepticism that comes with a lack of verifiable metrics. In short, serious efforts to generate and scrutinize more information concerning terrorist financing policies are necessary. More detailed analysis of terrorist financing prosecutions and convictions could help shed light on ways terrorists view government efforts and attempt to circumvent them. Even a better understanding of how terrorists have utilized the formal financial sector in past transactions could reveal useful information as to appropriate guidance for financial institutions in the future. Greater analysis of the numerous suspicious activity reports filed with governments may assist in determining if there are better indicators available to help counter the financing of terrorism.

33. Ibrahim Warde, *The Price of Fear: The Truth behind the Financial War on Terror* (Los Angeles: University of California Press, 2007).

34. There have been increasing references to the difficulty Al Qaeda has had in raising funds. See Matthew Levitt and Michael Jacobson, "The Money Trail: Finding, Following, and Freezing Terrorist Finances," Washington Institute for Near East Policy, November 2008, http://www.washingtoninstitute.org/templateC04.php?CID=302, 40–41.

Conclusion

We conclude with a self-reflective comment on the role of academics, even our own participation in knowledge production on this topic. We are not just consumers of these statistics and indicators, we are ourselves engaged in their use, their promulgation, and their production. In our previous research in this issue domain, we attempted to measure the implementation of counterterrorist financing policies with a qualitative assessment of the implementation of CFT policies in ten countries in the Islamic world for the Council on Foreign Relations Independent Task Force on Terrorist Financing.[35] We have also cooperated with the 1267 Committee's monitoring team in convening discussions about the challenges of implementation by global financial institutions. In addition, we have reviewed the relevant literature on terrorist financing, and either by including or omitting information in our own book, have engaged in an assessment of the credibility of such information.[36] Finally, our effort to illustrate changing financing patterns of Al Qaeda is an effort to interrogate the conventional wisdom about the wide variety of mechanisms available for the financing of terrorism and potentially to resist the political impulse to regulate everything associated with each new attack.

Our issue domain is relatively recent, its institutionalization globally is still very much in process (and capable of being reversed), and there are relatively few quantitative indicators and reliable sources of statistical information to analyze. It is important to try to devise additional metrics and to further investigate the discursive placement of these quantitative and qualitative indicators in speeches and texts of leading advocates, experts, and their critics; that is, to explore how leading policymakers, scholarly experts, and critics rhetorically place and use these indicators. An analysis of how the topic tends to be valorized linguistically and how numbers are utilized within public presentations might reveal further insights into the politics of numbers in the metaphorical "financial war on terrorism."

Ultimately, the metrics most commonly associated with terrorist financing initiatives—the total number of designations and the amount of money frozen—are inadequate and can be misleading. In our book, *Countering the Financing of Terrorism*, we recommended that a thorough analysis of the costs and benefits of the existing regime should be undertaken. As

35. Council on Foreign Relations Task Force on Terrorist Financing, "Update on the Global Campaign Against Terrorist Financing," June 2004, Appendix C: "A Comparative Assessment of Saudi Arabia with Other Countries of the Islamic World," prepared by the Watson Institute Project on Terrorist Financing, http://www.cfr.org/publication.html?id=7111.

36. Thomas J. Biersteker and Sue E. Eckert, *Countering the Financing of Terrorism* (New York: Routledge, 2007).

Box 10.2
Costs of Terrorists' Operations: Fact by Repetition?

As an example of the difficulty in determining the veracity of numbers, the following genealogy is provided as case in point as to the need for skepticism in relying on quantitative indicators. This is a good illustration of how little reliable information exists about the costs associated with terrorist attacks, as well as of how the relatively few seemingly authoritative estimates available can take on an unquestioned legitimacy.

In our *Countering the Financing of Terrorism,* we cited the Australian Commonwealth Director of Public Prosecutions, Damian Bugg, regarding the small percentage that operational costs of committing acts of terrorism represent compared to overall costs required to maintain a terrorist organization:

> The direct operational costs are only part of the costs of running a terrorist organization. It is estimated that Al Qaida spends about 10% of its income on operational costs. The other 90% goes to the cost of administering and maintaining the organization, including the cost of operating training camps and maintaining an international network of cells. So called "sleepers" must also cost significant sums to establish and maintain.[1]

It is unclear what the original source of his estimate is—the information may come from classified intelligence estimates or it may be the product of speculative judgments of those involved in the investigation and prosecution of terrorism cases. Though no specific reference was cited, it appeared an authoritative source that made intuitive sense and we included it in our introduction.

Upon further examination, however, we discovered that Bugg's statement appeared to rely on a report by Jean-Charles Brisard, titled "Terrorism Financing" Roots and Trends of Saudi Terrorism Financing" (December 19, 2002). Brisard (who refers to himself as "an international expert on terrorist financing," stated on the cover page of the document that it was a "Report prepared for the President of the Security Council, United Nations." Page 7 of the document contains

---

1. Damian Bugg, "The Reach of Terrorist Financing and Combating It: The Links between Terrorism and Ordinary Crime," Speech at the International Association of Prosecutors Conference, December 8, 2003.

the graphic, "Al-Qaida's financial needs: Infrastructure (communication, networks, training facilities, protections) 90% and Operational (day to day money, terrorist attacks planning & execution) <10%." No other data sourcing the information was found (and, in fact, the thirty-five-page "report" does not contain a single reference).

Subsequently, an article appeared, "French Investigator Tricked UN over Terror Report, says Al-Qadi Lawyers," that contains a denial by the United Nations of any link to the report.[2] In addition, it came to light that Brisard is the object of a defamation case and is considered by some to be an unreliable source. Notwithstanding his discredited "Report for the UN," a Congressional Research Service document heavily relies on the report's claims, and even a Financial Action Task Force (FATF) document seems to refer to this same source.[3]

---

2. Abdul Wahab Bashir, "French Investigator Tricked UN over Terror Report, says Al-Qadi Lawyers," *Arab News*, March 1, 2004, http://www.arabnews.com/?page=17& section=21&d=1&m=3&y=2004&mode=dynamic&sectionlist=no&pix=interact. jpg&category=Interact.

3. Alfred B. Prados and Christopher Blanchard, "Saudi Arabia: Terrorist Financing Issues," Congressional Research Service Issue Brief RL32499, December 8, 2004, http://www.fas.org/irp/crs/RL32499.pdf.

---

difficult as such an endeavor would be, it is important to attempt to assess the numbers associated with terrorist financing. The consequences of failing to do so are the promulgation of inappropriate and potentially ineffective policies to thwart acts of terrorism. Policymakers and academics alike must insist on better and more transparent sources of information in order to understand and assess more thoroughly the politics of numbers in the realm of terrorist financing. Notwithstanding years of experience since September 11, 2001, it is humbling to conclude with the admission of how little we still know about the financing of acts of terrorism. Terrorist financing remains a little understood and inadequately researched topic.

11

Conclusion

THE NUMBERS IN POLITICS

Peter Andreas and Kelly M. Greenhill

The statistics you don't compile never lie.

Stephen Colbert

Numbers, measures, and metrics profoundly influence our daily existence.[1] This includes the realm of politics, where they can distort and distract as much as inform and enlighten. The effort to quantify has long enjoyed a privileged status. As Sir William Thomson put it in 1889, "When you can measure what you are speaking about and express it in numbers you know something about it, but when you cannot express it in numbers, your knowledge is of a meager and unsatisfactory kind; it may be the beginning of knowledge, but you have scarcely in your thoughts, advanced to the state of *science*, whatever the matter may be."[2]

Yet it is precisely because numbers are equated with science that they provide such a tempting and powerful political tool. The legitimacy of quantification is based on lofty claims about "scientific measures" and "objective data," however dubious such claims may be. For the media and the broader public, this too often means accepting and regurgitating the claims rather than questioning and challenging them. Simply put, bad numbers masquerading as good science is pseudoscience. Thomson and others claim that we are scientifically blind without numbers, but we can also be blinded by numbers.

---

1. See Martha Lampland and Susan Leigh Star, eds., *Standards and Their Stories: How Quantifying, Classifying, and Formalizing Practices Shape Everyday Life* (Ithaca: Cornell University Press, 2009). For a more philosophical treatment, see Alain Badiou, *Number and Numbers* (Cambridge: Polity Press, 2008).

2. Quoted in Kevin D. Haggerty, *Making Crime Count* (Toronto: University of Toronto Press, 2001), 3.

The alternative to a naive trust in numbers is not knee-jerk cynical dismissal. Instead, we should treat numbers with much greater skepticism and scrutiny, always aware that they are human constructs. As Joel Best tells us, statistics are created by people, they are not simply discovered. They do not exist "out there" on their own.[3] Numbers should therefore prompt basic questions: Who produced them? Why? How? For whom? Numbers should provoke especially tough questions when the activity being measured is secretive, hidden, and clandestine. "How could they know that? How could they measure that?"[4] Often, "even a moment's thought can reveal that an apparently solid statistic must rely on some pretty squishy measurement decisions."[5] This observation is powerfully confirmed by the case studies in this volume, ranging from quantifying drug flows to refugee flows.

The contributions to this volume reveal patterns of overcounting, undercounting, and selective counting (or noncounting) in the realms of global crime and conflict, whether by state agencies, intergovernmental organizations (IGOs), or nongovernmental organizations (NGOs). This includes, for instance, inflating the death toll in the wars in Bosnia (Nettelfield and Greenhill chapters) and Kosovo (Greenhill chapter), deflating the death toll in Darfur (Hagan and Rymond-Richmond chapter), and understating the drug trafficking role and political significance of Colombian paramilitaries (Tate chapter). Although systematically underestimated numbers are sometimes deployed, inflated numbers appear to be a more common problem. This pattern is evaluated in detail in Greenhill's contribution on conflict-related statistics, where large numbers often help stimulate and increase funding flows to agencies and organizations whose mission is dealing with the negative externalities of conflict (such as humanitarian crises). Conversely, small numbers help to reinforce claims that particular issues do not demand more intervention and attention. They can also be used to suggest that what may in fact be a much bigger problem is actually quite manageable—consider, for instance, recurrent efforts to downplay the size of the insurgency in Iraq and of a resurgent Taliban in Afghanistan. In addition, statistics can serve a legitimating function, in that they can be used to muster both domestic and international support for warfighting or crime-fighting missions that might otherwise engender more tepid responses, as well as to bolster flagging support for missions already

---

3. Joel Best, *Damned Lies and Statistics: Untangling Numbers from the Media, Politicians, and Activists* (Berkeley: University of California Press, 2001), 160.

4. Joel Best, *Stat-spotting: A Field Guide to Identifying Dubious Data* (Berkeley: University of California Press, 2008), 51.

5. Ibid., 52.

undertaken. This has been evident across a range of issues explored in this book, from the war on drugs to the war on terrorist financing (Eckert and Biersteker chapter).

As many of the case studies in this volume illustrate, the producers of numbers in the policy realms of global crime and conflict face particularly extreme measurement obstacles. This is not only true for government and intergovernmental agencies but also NGOs, which are often the only source of information in highly fluid situations and difficult to access areas—becoming the "eyes and ears" of the international community on the ground. Indeed, NGOs are often the principal or sole source of information on local conditions and events. As one UN humanitarian officer has lamented, "simply by virtue of being the singular source of information in many areas, however spotty or soft the information, NGOs end up playing a significant role in shaping the ultimate policy decisions of donor governments and intergovernmental bodies."[6] Yet, as UNESCO's David Feingold emphasizes in his chapter, many NGOs that are relied on for numbers are overstretched, underfunded, and untrained in research—and indeed believe such training detracts from their primary mission of advocacy work. In many cases, there is little evidence to suggest that IOs or NGOs have sought to deliberately distort or politicize relevant statistics. Instead, the problem is often that highly imperfect IO and NGO information is seized upon by political actors to support their desired policy positions and by journalists eager for an eye-catching story.

As emphasized in the chapters by Tate and Warren, among others, researchers also need to go beyond the numbers to carefully unpack the relationship between numbers and narratives (and related images). Numbers do not float freely. Numbers alone are too abstract. They resonate most powerfully if there is an accompanying story and image. Consider, for example, the counting of U.S. soldiers killed in Iraq in the years following the invasion. The death toll mounted, but its resonance was muted by the Pentagon's policy during the Bush administration of not allowing the coffins to be photographed by the media—and the more out of sight, the more out of the public's mind. And just as numbers need narratives, narratives need numbers. The discursive treatment of numbers—the stories told about numbers and the use of numbers to tell stories—is emphasized in many of the case studies in this volume.

As demonstrated throughout this volume, the politics of numbers is also about the metrics and measures used to evaluate country performance and

---

6. Abby Stoddard, *Humanitarian Alert: NGO Information and Its Impact on U.S. Foreign Policy* (Sterling, VA: Kumarian Press, 2007), ix–x.

policy effectiveness. At the national level, this is evident in the official metrics used to assess the performance of government agencies responsible for missions such as drug enforcement (see Andreas's chapter). The standard quantitative indicators—such as numbers of arrests, deportations, seizures, confiscations, and so on—are built into the funding mechanism, creating powerful bureaucratic incentives to sustain them.

At the international level, the importance of metrics and measures is readily evident, for instance, in efforts to categorize and rank country efforts to counter terrorist financing, the illicit drug trade, and human trafficking (see especially the chapters by Eckert and Biersteker, Friman, and Warren).[7] It is also strikingly evident in other issue areas, perhaps most notably the proliferation of corruption indices since the mid-1990s, including rankings of countries based on perceived levels of corruption—starting with Transparency International's "Corruption Perception Index," followed by the "Bribe Payers Index" and "Global Corruption Barometer."[8] Ivan Krastev points to the defining role of the Transparency International index in constructing corruption as a global policy problem: "The impact of the corruption index was shattering. All major newspapers around the world published it and commented on it. Opposition parties started to refer to it. Governments began attacking it. But the most important effect was the public conviction that it was possible to compare levels in certain countries and to monitor the rise of corruption in any one individual country."[9] The corruption case, similar to the other illicit activities examined in this volume, powerfully illustrates how quantification can make previously invisible behavior at least seem visible—and thus more accessible for public debate and policy action.

Policy Pathologies

As underscored in the case studies in this volume, inflated, deflated, and misleading data related to global crime and conflict can be readily exploited and manipulated: by the media to stir up public opinion, by organizations

7. This is part of a much wider trend of proliferating rankings. On its broader social significance, see Wendy Nelson Espeland and Michael Sauder, "Rankings and Reactivity: How Public Measures Recreate Social Worlds," *American Journal of Sociology* 113 (2007): 1–40.

8. Hans Krause Hansen, "Bribery Risk Governance: The Politics of Measurement in International Anti-Corruption," paper presented at the International Studies Association Annual Convention, New York, February 15–18, 2009, 9. Also see Alan Doig, Stephanie McIvor, and Robin Theobald, "Numbers, Nuances and Moving Targets: Converging the Use of Corruption Indicators or Descriptors in Assessing State Development," *International Review of Administrative Sciences* 72 (2006): 239–52; and Marianne Camerer, "Measuring Public Integrity," *Journal of Democracy* 17 (January 2006): 152–65.

9. Quoted in Hansen, "Bribery Risk Governance," 8.

to further their missions and imperatives, by political entrepreneurs and by governments to justify the political objectives they embrace or avoid. As many of the volume's authors demonstrate, the politics of numbers can help to perpetuate failing and flawed policies, distort funding, generate and support misleading indicators of policy "progress" and "success," manipulate media coverage and cloud public debate, and fuel societal fear and anxiety. At the same time, it can also inhibit policy action (as Hagan and Rymond-Richmond show in the case of undercounting the atrocities in Darfur, and Greenhill shows in the case of undercounting refugees in Zaire) and distract attention away from key culprits (as Tate documents in the case of U.S. policy debates downplaying the importance of Colombian paramilitaries). Depending on the circumstances, the politics of numbers in the realms of transnational crime and conflict can lead to some combination of the following policy pathologies identified by the collective findings in this volume.

Misallocated resources

Whether they are fighting wars or crime, operations in which figures are inflated often receive disproportionate shares of resources that might be better spent elsewhere. This problem may be exacerbated by pecuniary incentives to distort numbers. For instance, during the Mozambican Civil War, local officials quickly learned that inflating numbers of "needy populations" could bring more food aid to their localities, which in turn offered an increased possibility of diverting a portion for public or private benefit. As a result, the figures sent to the government by provincial authorities "were highly inflated, at the same time as corruption was surfacing as a serious issue in the relief operations carried out by the government."[10] A related problem is that funds may go toward activities that generate the most impressive sounding numbers even if this is not necessarily the most effective use of resources. Drug enforcement agents, for example, may go after the easiest and most visible targets in the drug trade to boost arrest statistics and demonstrate anti-drug resolve, even though these "small fish" are the most expendable and replaceable. As Tate shows in her chapter on Colombia, the same is also true of relying on simple quantitative indicators of drug crop eradication while glossing over more qualitative shifts in the structure and organization of drug trafficking. Meanwhile, preventive measures often get short-changed because it is more difficult to

---

10. Sam Barnes, "Humanitarian Aid Coordination during War and Peace in Mozambique, 1985–1995," *Studies on Emergencies and Disaster Relief Report* 7 (Nordic Africa Institute, Uppsala, 1998), 13.

show immediate measurable results—they do not generate numbers that can be used to justify budgets and mobilize action.

Compromised and Distorted Implementation

As documented by Greenhill in her chapter, the politics of numbers can compromise the conduct and/or efficacy of operations on the ground, including undermining the ability to comprehend the magnitude and scope of a problem. Inaccurate or misleading statistics permit decision makers to believe they are making more headway on a problem than they really are. Examples abound. In the realm of military conflict, a particularly prominent recent case was the George W. Bush administration's stubborn resistance to acknowledge the scale and scope of the insurgency it was facing in Iraq following the 2003 occupation, which, to put it mildly, long undermined the prospects for success of the mission.[11] This problem was made still worse by concomitant and repeated U.S. overestimations of the number of Iraqi military units that had been successfully "stood up"—that is, trained, equipped, and capable of autonomous (and reliable) action.

By extension, politicization can also prolong wars, both by contaminating battlefield assessments and by misleading those who are destined to fight them. This problem goes back at least as far as the Crimean War, and has persisted ever since. As British prime minister Lloyd George put it during the dark days of World War I, "If people really knew [the real numbers of dead and the horrors that accompanied their demise], the war would be stopped tomorrow."[12]

The distorting effects of numbers on policy implementation can have other perverse and counterproductive consequences. Consider the recent sharp rise in raids by U.S. immigration officials, which has had more to do with bureaucratic incentives to reach a rising quota and generate more funding than with the stated policy objective. With catchy sounding names like "Operation Return to Sender," agents raided homes across the nation officially targeting dangerous immigrant fugitives. As the arrest numbers went up, so too did the funding—$9 million in 2003 to $218 million in the 2008

11. See, for instance, testimony by Deputy Secretary of State Richard Armitage to the Senate Armed Services Committee on the Transition in Iraq, June 25, 2004, http://www.defenselink.mil/speeches/speech.aspx?speechid=134; quotes by Secretary of Defense Donald Rumsfeld in Walter Pincus, "CIA Studies Provide Glimpse of Insurgents in Iraq," *Washington Post*, February 6, 2005; and Johanna Mcgeary, "Mission Still Not Accomplished," *TIME*, September 20, 2004.

12. Lloyd George, quoted in Phillip Knightley, *The First Casualty: The War Correspondent as Hero and Myth-Maker from the Crimea to Kosovo* (Baltimore: Johns Hopkins University Press, 2002), 116–17. On negative effects of casualty politicization in the Crimean War, see Helmut Gernsheim and Alison Gernsheim, *Roger Fenton: Photographer of the Crimean War: His Photographs and his Letters From The Crimea* (London: Secker and Warburg, 1954).

fiscal year. The problem was that to inflate arrest numbers, the rules were quietly changed to include arrests of immigrants with no criminal backgrounds or even deportation orders against them. As the arrest quotas were raised in 2006, the required focus on criminals was loosened—and soon only a small percentage of those arrested were actually fugitives. In this perverse numbers game, the focus was increasingly on "the easiest targets, not the most dangerous fugitives."[13] Enforcement agents kept generating high monthly arrest numbers to impress Congress and increase funding, even as this had less and less to do with the stated mission of the operation.

Muddled Evaluations

Many of the case studies in this volume also stress that the politicization of numbers can result in muddled evaluations of policy success and failure, which in turn can affect levels of support for current and future operations. Chronically inflated bomb damage assessments, for instance, have helped sustain support for the mythical supremacy of strategic bombing far beyond what objective evidence can support. In terms of refugees and casualties, "misremembered" assessments of what NATO bombing accomplished in Bosnia, for instance, made the Clinton administration overly sanguine about what "a few days of bombing" would do to change the mind of Slobodan Milosevic on the issue of Kosovo (see Greenhill's chapter for a detailed discussion).[14] Politically driven underestimation can also provide political cover to actors eager to avoid undesirable missions— as Hagan and Rymond-Richmond argue in their chapter on the undercounting of killings in Darfur, and Greenhill argues vis-à-vis peacekeeping in Zaire.

As shown especially in the case studies in this book on combating drugs, human trafficking, and terrorist financing, the politics of numbers can also muddle the evaluation process by turning numbers into ends in themselves rather than a means to an end. In other words, generating numbers can be confused with, and used as a substitute for, actually achieving the stated policy objective. Take, for example, the effort to curb money laundering. U.S. law requires banks to submit currency transaction reports for all deposits over $10,000. Although such reporting generates massive paperwork and provides a constant indicator of "activity" in fighting dirty

---

13. See Nina Bernstein, "Target of Immigration Raids Shifted," *New York Times,* February 4, 2009.

14. "Kosovo: The Untold Story; How the War Was Won," *Observer,* July 18, 1999; Kelly M. Greenhill, "The Use of Refugees as Political and Military Weapons in the Kosovo Conflict," in *Yugoslavia Unraveled: Sovereignty, Self-Determination, and Intervention,* ed. Raju G.C. Thomas (Lanham, MD: Lexington Books, 2003), 205–42.

money, it is not at all clear that it actually reduces the laundering of the proceeds of crime. Similarly, as Eckert and Biersteker show in their chapter, governments and financial institutions have scrambled to adopt reporting procedures and fill out the requisite paperwork to comply with new international counterterrorist financing measures, even though the utility of these activities in terms of actually curbing terrorism is highly questionable. As they put it, "activity" has too often been equated with "effectiveness." Similarly, as discussed in the chapters by Andreas and Friman, the most popular drug war statistics—crop eradication levels, arrest numbers, and so on—have also become ends in themselves, losing sight of the stated ultimate policy goal of reducing drug use.

Good Intentions Rationalizations

Some have argued that the ultimate veracity of the numbers is irrelevant if the underlying sentiment that motivates their adoption and promulgation is sound. Put another way, if the policy being bolstered by dubious data is ultimately a "good" or virtuous one, then the fact that the numbers might be inflated (or deflated) is deemed acceptable. From this perspective, good intentions justify bad numbers. For instance, in defending the U.S. government's apparently significantly inflated human trafficking figures, Bush's deputy White House press secretary Tony Fratto said that the issue is "not about the numbers. It's really about the crime and how horrific it is."[15] Moreover, as one prominent academic and advocate of intervention in Sudan has argued, "Sometimes it just isn't possible to get the 'right' number. So I just pick one that is large enough and shocking enough, as a way of assuring it gets attention."[16] And to be clear, if one's aim is to catalyze governments or international organizations to take action, it is useful to employ shocking numbers.

This sort of "intentions-based" position is similarly evident in the case of nuclear smuggling. When discussing the issue of nuclear leakage it has been argued that "the fact that a large number of the reported attempts to move nuclear materials across international borders are either failure or fiction is less important than the reality that even a tiny number of successes in transferring nuclear weapons or weapons quantities of fissile material could have disastrous consequences."[17] At its most extreme, the

---

15. Jerry Markon, "Human Trafficking Evokes Outrage, Little Evidence, U.S. Estimates Thousands of Victims, but Efforts to Find Them Fall Short," *Washington Post*, September 23, 2007.

16. Personal communication with Kelly M. Greenhill, February 2009.

17. Graham Allison et al., *Avoiding Nuclear Anarchy: Containing the Threat of Loose Russian Nuclear Weapons and Fissile Material* (Cambridge: MIT Press, 1996), 24.

intentions-based position has even been used to rationalize opposition to accurate counting. For example, "officials of a major donor organization are reported to have criticized efforts toward accurate enumeration [of displaced persons], and *urged that generous overestimates would suffice.*"[18]

Yet however much one may try to rationalize the political uses of bad data, a failure to at least strive for, if not achieve, statistical accuracy and honesty tends to be not only unhelpful, but can deepen public cynicism and distrust and erode credibility. Well-intended initiatives can also potentially be manipulated and abused through the politics of numbers in unforeseen ways. Take, for example, the recent efforts to promote the so-called Responsibility to Protect (R2P). The premise behind R2P is that states that prove unwilling or unable to protect the rights of their own citizens temporarily forfeit the moral claim to be treated as legitimate entities. Their sovereignty and their right to nonintervention in their internal affairs are suspended, and a residual responsibility necessitates vigorous action by outsiders to protect populations at risk. The threshold conditions for external action are "large-scale loss of life and ethnic cleansing, both actual and apprehended."[19] Some well-meaning R2P proponents have gone so far as to suggest that these threshold conditions be turned into concrete and measurable criteria that can be used to trigger outside intervention (and in cases where the international community is slow to respond, as in Darfur, these criteria can be used to shame recalcitrant states into action).

A workshop designed to identify such criteria was held at Harvard University in May 2008. When confronted with the possibility that such criteria could encourage systematic inflation of statistics by those who want intervention, and deflation by those who oppose it, the conference organizer rejoined that "well, the criteria need not be quantitative, they could be qualitative."[20] However, as the chapters in this volume have made clear, identification of such criteria, whether quantitative or qualitative, would not necessarily solve the problem, for the politics of numbers entails more than simple counting. In fact, when numbers alone prove insufficient, politicization may focus as well on issues of degree and intent. So for instance, the number of dead becomes less important than complexion of the dead—killing noncombatants is worse than killing soldiers, and killing

18. Peter Romanovsky and Rob Stephenson, *A Review of Refugee Enumeration: Proposals for the Development of a Unified System* (Geneva: UNHCR, September 1995), 3; quoted in Jeff Crisp, "Who Has Counted the Refugees? UNHCR and the Politics of Numbers," New Issues in Refugee Research Working Paper no. 12, UNHCR, Geneva, 1999 (emphasis added).

19. Peter Hoffman and Thomas G. Weiss, *Sword and Salve: Confronting New Wars and Humanitarian Crises* (Lanham, MD: Rowman & Littlefield, 2006), 110–11.

20. Robert Rotberg, in discussion with Kelly M. Greenhill, April 2008.

women and children is particularly egregious. But then how should one count a female child soldier? It depends on the agenda of those doing the counting. When does sporadic killing become massacre, and concentrated killing, genocide? Again, agendas matter and matter profoundly. Similarly, all human trafficking is viewed as "bad," but sex trafficking of children is particularly unconscionable. How then does one tally unaccompanied minor migrants who prefer paid independent sex work to indentured servitude in sweatshops or remaining in abusive homes? Several of the contributions to this volume have tackled this qualitative aspect of the politics of numbers (see especially the chapters on human trafficking by Feingold and Warren).

Blowback and Traps from Prior Numerical Commitments

The politicization of numbers can backfire, sabotaging the very objectives that politicizing figures (or failing to count at all) were designed to achieve in the first place. There is always the danger that the revelation that a number is fantastically overblown will prompt skepticism about the seriousness of the problem. For example, the German government's report of more than 700 cases of attempted illicit nuclear sales between 1991 and 1994 was soon viewed as preposterous—and thus the effort to sound the alarm bells about nuclear smuggling backfired.[21] This in turn can lead to a grossly insufficient allocation of resources to address real problems, which may happen to be smaller than the exaggerated figures suggest.[22]

A closely related problem is that policymakers can find themselves trapped by their own bad numbers. Sometimes, political commitment to a particular number (however flawed it may be) can be intensely emotional and even viewed as a test of one's patriotism—as evident in the hostile reaction in some political circles in Sarajevo to the downward reassessment of the number of people who died in the 1992–95 Bosnian War. As Lara Nettelfield shows in her chapter, publicly questioning the longstanding accepted number of 200,000–250,000 dead has been viewed in some

21. Cited in Allison et al., *Avoiding Nuclear Anarchy*, 23.

22. In this vein, it should be noted that even after evidence that Al Qaeda has attempted to acquire fissile material has surfaced, the International Atomic Energy Agency's Nuclear Trade and Technology Analysis unit—which collects and analyzes information on black market nuclear technology networks—remains understaffed, and has little money and still less authority. Matti Tarvainen, "Procurement Outreach in Revealing Proliferation Networks," in "Finding Innovative Ways to Detect and Thwart Illicit Nuclear Trade," Carnegie International Nonproliferation Conference, June 25, 2007, http://www.carnegieendowment.org/events/index.cfm?fa=eventDetail&id=1029; see also Matthew Bunn, "Corruption and the Proliferation of Nuclear, Chemical, and Biological Weapons," in *Corruption, Global Security and World Order*, ed. Robert Rotberg (Washington, DC: Brookings Institution Press, 2009).

quarters as heresy and a political ploy by opponents to diminish the gravity and seriousness of the country's wartime suffering.

There can also be powerful political disincentives to acknowledge previous use of "bad numbers," even if failing to do so means embracing and perpetuating costly and ultimately counterproductive policies. For instance, the Kennedy administration's admission that the much-vaunted, but ultimately illusory, missile gap that had been instrumental in Kennedy's electoral success resulted in the first embarrassing "flap" for his new administration. President Eisenhower found inflammatory claims of such a gap so galling that in his final message to Congress he said: "The bomber gap of several years ago was always a fiction, and the missile gap shows every sign of being the same."[23] We now know that Kennedy was aware—at least by the summer of 1960—that Eisenhower was correct.[24] However, even after acknowledging that the earlier numbers were wrong, he declared: "to the extent possible, I want to avoid the conflicting claims and confusions over dates and numbers. These largely involve difference of degree. I say only that the evidence is strong enough to indicate that we cannot be certain of our security in the future, any more than we can be certain of disaster…If we are to err in an age of uncertainty, I want us to err on the side of security."[25] Feeling trapped by his earlier assertions, the momentum of the fear pushed President Kennedy into substantial increases in the defense budget, including procuring many more intercontinental ballistic missiles (ICBMs) than he and his advisers actually deemed necessary.[26]

Oversimplification and Creation of Misleading Categories

The problem with politicized counting is not simply that the numbers may be inaccurate, but the fact that the very process of counting can create rigid and oversimplified categories. There is numerical discomfort with

---

23. "The Missile Gap Flap," *TIME,* February 17, 1961; see also Peter J. Roman, *Eisenhower and the Missile Gap* (Ithaca: Cornell University Press, 1995); Julien Mercille, "Mind the Gap: Security, 'Crises,' and the Geopolitics of Military Spending," *Geopolitics* 13 (2008): 54–72; Roy E. Licklider, "The Missile Gap Controversy," *Political Science Quarterly* 85 (1970): 600–615.

24. In July 1960, Kennedy was given an intelligence briefing about a broad array of subjects, including Soviet missile capabilities. Vice Presidential candidate Lyndon Johnson was given a similar briefing. See Central Intelligence Agency, "Memorandum for the President," Eisenhower Administration Presidential Decision File, Washington, DC, August 3, 1960.

25. "Missile Gap Flap."

26. Jane Kellett-Cramer, "Sounding the Tocsin Redux: Persistent Patterns of Threat Inflation," paper presented at the International Studies Association Annual Convention, March 2004, Montreal.

"gray areas." This is strikingly evident in efforts to measure human trafficking, as highlighted in the chapters by Feingold, Friman, and Warren. The very category itself creates a sharp distinction between "trafficked" (defined as coerced) and "smuggled" (considered voluntary and economically motivated). The categories and the counting process demand clear—even if highly misleading and oversimplified—distinctions between "innocent trafficked victims" and "illegal economic migrants." As Feingold emphasizes in his evaluation of the politics of human trafficking in Southeast Asia, moral ambiguity and complexity are not captured by the demand for clear categories and numbers in each category. Warren reinforces this conclusion in her tracing of the politics of numbers in sex trafficking between Colombia and Japan. Similar categorization hurdles are evident in the realm of conflict, as illustrated in intelligence efforts to compute aggregate levels of violence against civilians in Iraq. In attempting to differentiate and categorize attacks as "combat," "civilian," or "criminal," one intelligence analyst described the seemingly arbitrary counting methodology: "If a bullet went through the back of the head, it's sectarian," but "if it went through the front, it's criminal."[27] Forcing casualty numbers into these separate categories can be highly misleading, to say the least.

The problem with oversimplified and misleading categories is equally apparent in official efforts to rank, measure, and quantitatively evaluate country performance in combating various illicit cross-border flows. Take, for example, the U.S. State Department's practice of placing countries into three different "tiers" depending on their efforts to curb human trafficking, or the even more simplistic categorization of countries as either cooperative or noncooperative in fighting international drug trafficking. These categories, and the number games they provoke and sustain, are masterfully interrogated in the chapter contributions by Friman and Warren. In the case of assessing country performance in anti-drug efforts, Friman shows that the State Department categories and metrics are so vague that they invite political abuse and manipulation—as evident in the U.S. praising or bashing of foreign governments based more on geopolitical considerations than anti-drug performance. In the realm of human trafficking, Warren notes that reliable comparable data across states does not exist, making nonsense of State Department efforts to meaningfully rank and compare country performance with any accuracy. Equally important, as she shows, countries such as Colombia and Japan have quickly adapted to the ranking process and figured out how to game the system—producing the activities

<hr />

27. Quoted in Karen DeYoung, "Experts Doubt Drop in Violence in Iraq: Military Statistics Called into Question," *Washington Post*, September 6, 2007.

and numbers needed to pacify the State Department monitors and assure a "Tier 1" ranking in the face of continued high levels of trafficking. As Warren characterizes it, "counting becomes a performance designed to please auditors."

Final Thoughts

Given the centrality of numbers, metrics, and measures in the policy process and in public debates, it is surprising that the politicization of quantification is not placed more front and center in scholarly and policy analysis. Although reports of all stripes are replete with numbers and other quantitative indicators, remarkably few consumers—policymakers, journalists, scholars, the broader public—sufficiently question their source or challenge their accuracy. Doing so requires a greater focus on what Kevin Haggerty calls the "micro-politics of knowledge production."[28] Accessing this micro-politics necessarily requires careful tracing of policy discourse and deliberations, bureaucratic practices and routines, the activities and incentives of intergovernmental and nongovernmental organizations.

With this objective in mind, this volume extends and builds on a growing but still relatively small interdisciplinary literature on the social and political construction of measures, metrics, and numbers. For the most part, work in this area remains largely focused on domestic policy issues, ranging from wrangling over state budget figures to evaluating street crime statistics. This book has pushed to extend the analysis to the realm of international politics, focusing on murky measurement issues related to global crime and conflict. As the chapters in this volume demonstrate, issues such as sex trafficking, terrorist financing, drug smuggling, war fatalities, and refugee flows are especially susceptible to distortion and manipulation, given that they not only present particularly severe measurement challenges but are also highly emotive "hot button" issues that can inhibit critical sensibilities. The advantage of focusing on such extreme, "easy" cases is that the power and pathologies of politicized numbers are most starkly revealed. Though the politics of numbers may be subtler in other policy realms, this does not necessarily make it less influential and consequential. In this regard, the politics of numbers in the realms of global crime and conflict is distinct but not unique.

The case studies in this volume represent only a sampling of the kind of work possible in this area. For future research on the politics of numbers, there is clearly a great need for more systematic, comparative work across

---

28. Haggerty, *Making Crime Count.*

time, place, and issues. Many questions raised in this volume would benefit from further research: How and why does the politics of numbers vary across countries and issue areas? How and how much has the politics of numbers changed over time? Is the numbers fetish a particularly U.S. or Western phenomenon, or a more global one, irrespective of local setting and cultural context? Are some audiences more trusting of numbers than others? Who are the savviest, and who are the most naive, consumers of numbers?

Depending on the particular research question, a wide variety of methodological tools can potentially be utilized and even combined, ranging from controlled psychological experiments, to focus groups and survey research, to process tracing, ethnographies, and discourse analysis. Mixed methods and analytical eclecticism are called for in fully deciphering the politics of numbers.[29] For instance, quantitatively oriented scholars should be more attuned to the insights of more qualitative social constructivist approaches, and vice versa. To fully understand the social and political construction of numbers, for example, one could creatively combine both quantitative and ethnographic methods—an all-too-rare combination.

But it is not just scholars who should more carefully scrutinize and unpack the politics of numbers (including acknowledging their own role and complicity, as discussed in the Eckert and Biersteker chapter) but also the broader public. Journalists, in particular, have a special responsibility here in making the media more a part of the solution than the problem. Doing so requires that they relentlessly ask tough, demanding questions about numbers rather than simply going to press conferences and reporting on the announced official numbers, as is so often the case. And indeed, the production of the numbers should be a major topic of investigative journalism—as exemplified in the highly revealing reports by Carl Bialik in the *Wall Street Journal* and Jack Shafer in *Slate* (for more detail, see Andreas's chapter).

To some degree, the politics of numbers is inevitable and unavoidable. And to some degree, it is even desirable, as there can be many reasonable and legitimate differences in the collection, organization, and interpretation of data that should be thoroughly scrutinized, interrogated, and evaluated as part of public debate and the policymaking process. The point here is not to simply reject the politics of numbers and condemn quantification, but rather to promote more careful and more educated (and yes, more skeptical) discussion and consumption of the numbers. This should

---

29. On the merits of "analytical eclecticism," see Peter J. Katzenstein and Nobuo Okawara, "Japan, Asian-Pacific Security, and the Case for Analytical Eclecticism," *International Security* 26 (2001): 153–85.

include an honest and humble recognition that sometimes and in some cases, we simply cannot measure and quantify with any degree of statistical certainty. Acknowledging that we "don't know" is certainly progress over the all-too-common practice of pretending to know by generating, promoting, and consuming mythical numbers.

Index